The Life & Teachings of Jesus

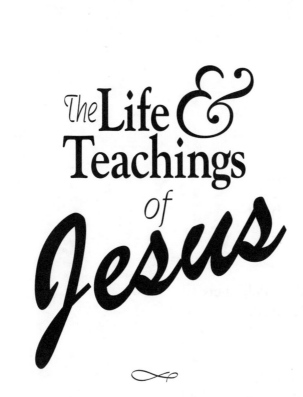

The Life & Teachings of Jesus

James Stalker

Studies on the
Person of Christ

Originally published by
Henry A. Sumner & Company, 1890,
and Fleming H. Revell Company, 1899.

ISBN 0-529-10450-4

Printed in the United States of America

Contents

Foreword

Studies on the Person of Christ is a compilation of three matchless works by James Stalker, the eminent Scottish minister of the late 1800s. Stalker's *The Life of Christ, Imago Christi: The Example of Christ*, and *The Teaching of Jesus Concerning Himself* are each presented here in their entirety and give readers unique insights into Christ's earthly ministry. Part one, *The Life of Christ*, describes the events during our Lord's thirty-three years on earth, while in part two, *Imago Christi*, Stalker shows how Christ lived as a model for us relationally and spiritually. Finally, in *The Teaching of Jesus Concerning Himself*, Stalker explicates the words of Christ regarding his Messiahship, and he works through some of the interpretive theories surrounding them.

In compiling these works, we at AMG Publishers have made a few minor changes to the original books to help make their content more clear to modern readers: We have updated spelling and some archaic terms in accordance with how our language has changed over the years; in some cases, unusual forms of punctuation have been simplified; and footnotes that were originally in German have been translated into English. We are grateful for the work of Ron Cates in translating these. Readers should also note that the points of current history mentioned by Stalker are from late nineteenth-century Scotland.

Our hope is that readers will be moved to seek Christ through His Word, and that this book will support them in their endeavors to know Him more fully.

The Life of Christ

Preface

SINCE the first publication of this *Life of Jesus Christ* many important additions have been made to the literature of the subject, such as the *Lives*, by Nicoll, Edersheim, Weiss, Beyschlag, Vallings and Didon. But no other book has, as far as the author is aware, been written on the plan of this one — to exhibit in the briefest possible space the main features and the general course of the Life, so as to cause the well-known details to flow together in the reader's mind and shape themselves into an easily comprehended whole. That, alongside of so many voluminous works, there is room for this little one has been amply proved by a large and steady demand for it up to the present time; and the author hopes that the changes introduced into this new editon, to bring the Notes up to date, may contribute to prolong its course of modest usefulness.

Chapter two of the former editions has been divided into two chapters.

J. S.

May, 1891.

1
The Birth, Infancy, and Youth of Jesus

The Nativity

Augustus was sitting on the throne of the Roman empire, and the touch of his finger could set the machinery of government in motion over well-nigh the whole of the civilized world. He was proud of his power and wealth, and it was one of his favorite occupations to compile a register of the populations and revenues of his vast dominions. So he issued an edict, as the Evangelist Luke says, "that all the world should be taxed," or to express accurately what the words probably mean, that a census, to serve as a basis for future taxation, should be taken of all his subjects. One of the countries affected by this decree was Palestine, whose king, Herod the Great, was a vassal of Augustus. It set the whole land in motion; for, in accordance with ancient Jewish custom, the census was taken, not at the places where the inhabitants were at the time residing, but at the places to which they belonged as members of the original twelve tribes.

Among those whom the edict of Augustus thus from afar drove forth to the highways were a humble pair in the Galilean village of Nazareth—Joseph, the carpenter of the village, and Mary, his espoused wife. They had to go a journey of nearly a hundred miles in order to inscribe themselves in the proper register; for, though peasants, they had the blood of kings in their veins, and belonged to the ancient and royal town of Bethlehem, in the far south of the country. Day by day the emperor's will, like an invisible hand, forced them southward along the weary road, till at last they climbed the rocky ascent that led to the gate of the town—he terrified with anxiety, and she well-nigh dead with fatigue. They reached the inn, but found it crowded with strangers, who, bent on the same errand as themselves, had arrived before them. No friendly house opened its door to receive them, and they were fain to clear for their lodging a corner of the inn yard, else occupied by the beasts of the numerous travelers. There, that very night, she brought forth her firstborn Son; and because there was neither womanly hand to assist her, nor couch to receive Him, she wrapped Him in swaddling clothes and laid Him in a manger.

Such was the manner of the birth of Jesus. I never felt the full pathos of the scene, till, standing one day in a room of an old inn in the market town of Eisleben, in Central Germany, I was told that on that very spot, four centuries ago, amidst the noise of a market day and the bustle of a public house, the wife of the poor miner, Hans Luther, who happened to be there on business, being surprised like Mary with sudden distress, brought forth in sorrow and poverty the child who was to become Martin Luther, the hero of the Reformation and the maker of modern Europe.

Next morning the noise and bustle broke out again in the inn and inn yard; the citizens of Bethlehem went about their work; the registration proceeded; and in the meantime the greatest event in the history of the world had taken place. We never know where a great beginning may be happening. Every arrival of a new soul in the world is a mystery and a shut casket of possibilities. Joseph and Mary alone knew the tremendous secret—that on her, the peasant maiden and carpenter's bride, had been conferred the honor of being the mother of Him who was the Messiah of her race, the Savior of the world, and the Son of God.

It had been foretold in ancient prophecy that He should be born on this very spot: "But thou, Bethlehem Ephratah, though thou be little among the thousands of Judah, yet out of thee shall He come forth unto me that is to be ruler in Israel." The proud emperor's decree drove southward the anxious couple. Yes, but another hand was leading them on—the hand of Him who overrules the purposes of emperors and kings, of statesmen and parliaments, for the accomplishment of His designs, though they know them not; who hardened the heart of Pharaoh, called Cyrus like a slave to His foot, made the mighty Nebuchadnezzar His servant, and in the same way could overrule for His own far-reaching purposes the pride and ambition of Augustus.

The Group around the Infant

Although Jesus made His entry on the stage of life so humbly and silently; although the citizens of Bethlehem dreamed not what had happened in their midst; although the emperor of Rome knew not that his decree had influenced the nativity of a king who was yet to bear rule, not only over the Roman world, but over many a land where Rome's eagles never flew; although the history of mankind went thundering forward next morning in the channels of its ordinary interests, quite unconscious of the event which had happened, yet it did not altogether escape notice. As the babe leaped in the womb of the aged Elizabeth when the mother of her Lord approached her, so, when He who brought the new world with Him appeared, there sprang up anticipations and forebodings of the truth in various representatives of the old world that was passing away. There went through sensitive and waiting souls, here and there, a dim and half-conscious thrill, which drew them round the Infant's cradle. Look at the group which gathered to gaze on Him! It represented in miniature the whole of His future history.

First came the Shepherds from the neighboring fields. That which was unnoticed by the kings and great ones of this world, was so absorbing a theme to the princes of heaven, that they burst the bonds of the invisibility in which they shroud themselves, in order to express their joy and explain the significance of the great event. And seeking the most worthy hearts to which they might communicate it, they found them in these simple shepherds, living the life of contemplation and prayer in the suggestive fields where Jacob had kept his flocks, where Boaz and Ruth had been wedded, and David, the great Old Testament type, had spent his youth, and there, by the study of the secrets and needs of their own hearts, learning far more of the nature of the Savior who was to come than the Pharisee amidst the religious pomp of the temple, or the scribe burrowing without the seeing eye among the prophecies of the Old Testament. The angel directed them where the Savior was, and they hastened to the town to find Him. They were the representatives of the peasant people, with the "honest and good heart," who afterwards formed the bulk of His disciples.

Next to them came Simeon and Anna, the representatives of the devout and intelligent students of the Scriptures, who at that time were expecting the appearance of the Messiah, and afterwards contributed some of His most faithful followers. On the eighth day after His birth, the Child was circumcised, thus being "made under the law," entering into the covenant, and inscribing His name in His own blood in the roll of the nation. Soon thereafter, when the days of Mary's purification were ended, they carried Him from Bethlehem to Jerusalem to present Him to the Lord in the temple. It was "the Lord of the temple entering the temple of the Lord," but few visitors to the spot could have been less noticed by the priests, for Mary, instead of offering the sacrifice usual in such cases, could only afford two turtle doves, the offering of the poor. Yet there were eyes looking on, undazzled by the shows and glitter of the world, from which His poverty could not conceal Him. Simeon, an aged saint, who in answer to many prayers had received a secret promise that he should not die till he had seen the Messiah, met the parents and the child, when suddenly it shot through him like a flash of lightning that this at last was He, and, taking Him up in his arms, he praised God for the advent of the Light to lighten the Gentiles and the Glory of His people Israel. While he was still speaking, another witness joined the group. It was Anna, a saintly widow, who literally dwelt in the courts of the Lord, and had purified the eye of her spirit with the euphrasy and rue of prayer and fasting till it could pierce with prophetic glance the veils of sense. She united her testimony to the old man's, praising God and confirming the mighty secret to the other expectant souls who were looking for redemption in Israel.

The shepherds and these aged saints were near the spot where the new force entered the world. But it thrilled susceptible souls at a much greater distance. It was probably after the presentation in the temple and after the parents had carried back their child to Bethlehem, where it was their intention to reside instead of returning to Nazareth, that He was visited by the Wise Men of the East. These were members of the learned class of the Magians, the repositories for science, philosophy, medical skill, and religious mysteries in the countries beyond the Euphrates. Tacitus, Suetonius, and Josephus tell us that in the regions from whence they came, there then prevailed an expectation that a great king was to arise in Judea. We know also from the calculations of the great astronomer Kepler, that at this very time there was visible in the heavens a brilliant temporary star. Now the Magi were ardent students of astrology, and believed that any unusual phenomenon in the heavens was the sign of some remarkable event on earth; and it is possible that, connecting this star, to which their attention would undoubtedly be eagerly directed, with the expectation mentioned by the ancient historians, they were led westward to see if it had been fulfilled. But there must also have been awakened in them a deeper want, to which God responded. If their search began in scientific curiosity and speculation, God led it on to the perfect truth. That is His way always. Instead of making tirades against the imperfect, He speaks to us in the language we understand, even if it express His meaning very imperfectly, and guides us thereby to the perfect truth. Just as He used astrology to lead the world to astronomy, and alchemy to conduct it to chemistry, and as the Revival of Learning preceded the Reformation, so He used the knowledge of these men, which was half falsehood and superstition, to lead them to the Light of the world. Their visit was a prophecy of how in the future the Gentile world would hail His doctrine and salvation, and bring its wealth and talents, its science and philosophy, to offer at His feet.

All these gathered round His cradle to worship the Holy Child—the shepherds with their simple wonder, Simeon and Anna with a reverence enriched by the treasured wisdom and piety of centuries, and the Magi with the lavish gifts of the Orient and the open brow of Gentile knowledge. But while these worthy worshipers were gazing down on Him, there came and looked over their shoulders a sinister and murderous face. It was the face of Herod. This prince then occupied the throne of the country—the throne of David and the Maccabees. But he was an alien and low-born usurper. His subjects hated him, and it was only by Roman favor that he was maintained in his seat. He was able, ambitious, and magnificent. Yet he had such a cruel, crafty, gloomy, and filthy mind as you must go among Oriental tyrants to meet with. He had been guilty of every crime. He had made his very palace swim in blood, having murdered his own favorite wife, three of his sons, and many others of his relatives. He was now old and tortured with disease, remorse, the sense of unpopularity, and a cruel terror of every possible aspirant to the throne which he had usurped. The Magi had naturally turned their steps to the capital, to inquire where He was to be born whose sign they had seen in the East. The suggestion touched Herod in his sorest place, but with diabolical hypocrisy he concealed his suspicions. Having learned from the priests that the Messiah was to be born in Bethlehem, he directed the strangers thither, but arranged that they should return and tell him the very house where the new King was. He hoped to cut Him off at a single blow. But he was foiled; for, being warned by God, they did not come back to tell him, but returned to their own country another way. Then his fury burst forth like a storm, and he sent his soldiers to murder every babe under two years of age in Bethlehem. As well might he have attempted to cut a mountain of adamant asunder as cut the chain of the divine purposes. "He thrust his sword into the nest, but the bird was flown." Joseph fled with the Child to Egypt, and remained there till Herod died, when he returned and dwelt at Nazareth; being warned from Bethlehem, because there he would have been in the kingdom of Archelaus, the like-minded son of his blood-thirsty father. Herod's murderous face, glaring down on the Infant, was a sad prophecy of how the powers of the world would persecute Him and cut off His life from the earth.

The Silent Years at Nazareth

The records which we possess up to this point are, as we have seen, comparatively full. But with the settlement at Nazareth, after the return from Egypt, our information comes to a sudden stop, and over the rest of the life of Jesus, till His public ministry begins, a thick covering is drawn, which is only lifted once. We should have wished the narrative to continue with the same fullness through the years of His boyhood and youth. In modern biographies there are few parts more interesting than the anecdotes which they furnish of the childhood of their subjects, for in these we can often see in miniature and in charming simplicity the character and the plan of the future life. What would we not give to know the habits, the friendships, the thoughts, the words, and the actions of Jesus during so many years? Only one flower of anecdote has been thrown over the wall of the hidden garden, and it is so exquisite as to fill us with intense longing to see the garden itself. But it has pleased God, whose silence is no less wonderful than His words, to keep it shut.

It was natural that, where God was silent and curiosity was strong, the fancy of man should attempt to fill up the blank. Accordingly, in the early Church there appeared Apocryphal Gospels, pretending to give full details where the inspired Gospels were silent. They are particularly full of the sayings and doings of the childhood of Jesus. But they only show how unequal the human imagination was to such a theme, and bring out by the contrast of glitter and caricature the solidity and truthfulness of the Scripture narrative. They make him a worker of frivolous and useless marvels, who molded birds of clay and made them fly, changed his playmates into kids, and so forth. In short, they are compilations of worthless and often blasphemous fables.

These grotesque failures warn us not to intrude with the suggestions of fancy into the hallowed enclosure. It is enough to know that He grew in wisdom and stature, and in favor with God and man. He was a real child and youth, and passed through all the stages of a natural development. Body and mind grew together, the one expanding to manly vigor, and the other acquiring more and more knowledge and power. His opening character exhibited a grace that made every one who saw it wonder and love its goodness and purity.

But though we are forbidden to let the fancy loose here, we are not prohibited, but, on the contrary, it is our duty, to make use of such authentic materials as are supplied by the manners and customs of the time, or by incidents of His later life which refer back to His earlier years, in order to connect the infancy with the period when the narrative of the Gospels again takes up the thread of biography. It is possible in this way to gain, at least in some degree, a true conception of what He was as a boy and a young man, and what were the influences amidst which His development proceeded through so many silent years.

We know amidst what kind of home influences He was brought up. His home was one of those which were the glory of His country, as they are of our own—the abodes of the godly and intelligent working class. Joseph, its head, was a man saintly and wise, but the fact that he is not mentioned in Christ's afterlife has generally been believed to indicate that he died during the youth of Jesus, perhaps leaving the care of the household on His shoulders. His mother probably exercised the most decisive of all external influences on His development. What she was may be inferred from the fact that she was chosen from all the women of the world to be crowned with the supreme honor of womanhood. The song which she poured forth on the subject of her own great destiny shows her to have been a woman religious, fervently poetical, and patriotic; a student of scripture, and especially of its great women, for it is saturated with Old Testament ideas, and molded on Hannah's song; a spirit exquisitely humble, yet capable of thoroughly appreciating the honor conferred upon her. She was no miraculous queen of heaven, as superstition has caricatured her, but a woman exquisitely pure, saintly, loving, and high-souled. This is aureole enough. Jesus grew up in her love and passionately returned it.

There were other inmates of the household. He had brothers and sisters. From two of them, James and Jude, we have epistles in Holy Scripture, in which we may read what their character was. Perhaps it is not irreverent to infer from the severe tone of their epistles, that, in their unbelieving state, they must have been somewhat harsh and unsympathetic men. At all events, they never believed on Him during His lifetime, and it is not likely that they were close companions to Him in Nazareth. He was probably much alone; and the pathos of His saying that a prophet is not without honor save in his own country and in his own house, probably reached back into the years before His ministry began.

He received His education at home, or from a scribe attached to the village synagogue. It was only, however, a poor man's education. As the scribes contemptuously said, He had never learned, or, as we should say, He was not college-bred. Not, but the love of knowledge was early awake within Him. He daily knew the joy of deep and happy thought; He had the best of all keys to knowledge—the open mind and the loving heart; and the three great books lay ever open before Him—the Bible, Man, and Nature.

It is easy to understand with what fervent enthusiasm He would devote Himself to the Old Testament; and His sayings, which are full of quotations from it, afford abundant proof of how constantly it formed the food of His mind and the comfort of His soul. His youthful study of it was the secret of the marvelous facility with which He made use of it afterwards in order to enrich His preaching and enforce His doctrine, to repel the assaults of opponents and overcome the temptations of the Evil One. His quotations also show that He read it in the original Hebrew, and not in the Greek translation, which was then in general use. The Hebrew was a dead language even in Palestine, just as Latin now is in Italy, but He would naturally long to read it in the very words in which it was written. Those who have not enjoyed a liberal education, but amidst many difficulties have mastered Greek in order to read their New Testament in the original, will perhaps best understand how, in a country village, He made Himself master of the ancient tongue, and with what delight He was wont, in the rolls of the synagogue, or in such manuscripts as He may have Himself possessed, to pore over the sacred page. The language in which He thought and spoke familiarly was Aramaic, a branch of the same stem to which the Hebrew belongs. We have fragments of it in some recorded sayings of His, such as "Talitha, cumi," and "Eloi, Eloi, lama sabachthani." He would have the same chance of learning Greek as a boy born in the Scottish Highlands has of learning English, "Galilee of the Gentiles" being then full of Greek-speaking inhabitants. Thus He was probably master of three languages—one of them the grand religious language of the world, in whose literature He was deeply versed; another, the most perfect means of expressing secular thought which has ever existed, although there is no evidence that He had any acquaintance with the masterpieces of Greek literature; and the third, the language of the common people, to whom His preaching was to be specially addressed.

There are few places where human nature can be better studied than in a country village; for there one sees the whole of each individual life and knows all one's neighbors thoroughly. In a city far more people are seen, but far fewer known; it is only the outside of life that is visible. In a village the view outwards is circumscribed, but the view downwards is deep, and the view upwards unimpeded. Nazareth was a notoriously wicked town, as we learn from the proverbial question, Can any good thing come out of Nazareth? Jesus had no acquaintance with sins in His own soul, but in the town He had a full exhibition of the awful problem with which it was to be His life-work to deal. He was still further brought into contact with human nature by His trade. That He worked as a carpenter in Joseph's shop there can be no doubt. Who could know better than His own townsmen, who asked, in their astonishment at His preaching, Is not this the carpenter? It would be difficult to exhaust the significance of the fact that God chose for His Son, when He dwelt among men, out of all the possible positions in which He might have placed Him, the lot of a working man. It stamped men's common toils with everlasting honor. It acquainted Jesus with the feelings of the multitude, and helped Him to know what was in man. It was afterwards said that He knew this so well that he needed not that any man should teach Him.

Travelers tell us that the spot where He grew up is one of the most beautiful on the face of the earth. Nazareth is situated in a secluded, cup-like valley amid the mountains of Zebulon, just where they dip down into the plain of Esraelon, with which it is connected by a steep and rocky path. Its white house with vines clinging to their walls, are embowered amidst gardens and groves of olive, fig, orange, and pomegranate trees. The fields are divided by hedges of cactus, and enameled with innumerable flowers of every hue. Behind the village rises a hill five hundred feet in height, from whose summit there is seen one of the most wonderful views in the world—the mountains of Galilee, with snowy Hermon towering above them, to the north; the ridge of Carmel, the coast to Tyre, and the sparkling waters of the Mediterranean, to the west; a few miles to the east, the wooded, cone-like bulk of Tabor; and to the south, the plain of Esaraelon, with the mountains of Ephraim beyond. The preaching of Jesus shows how deeply He had drunk into the essence of natural beauty and reveled in the changing aspects of the seasons. It was when wandering as a lad in these fields that He gathered the images of beauty which he poured out in His parables and addresses. It was on that hill that He acquired the habit of His afterlife of retreating to the mountain tops to spend the night in solitary prayer. The doctrines of His preaching were not thought out on the spur of the moment. They were poured out in a living stream when the occasion came, but the water had been gathered into the hidden well for many years before. In the fields and on the mountainside he had thought them out during the years of happy and undisturbed meditation and prayer.

There is still one important educational influence to be mentioned. Every year, after He was twelve years old, He went with His parents to the Passover at Jerusalem. Fortunately we have preserved to us an account of the first of these visits. It is the only occasion on which the veil is lifted during thirty years. Every one who can remember his own first journey from a village home to the capital of his country will understand the joy and excitement with which Jesus set out. He traveled over eighty miles of a country where nearly every mile teemed with historical and inspiring memories. He mingled with the constantly growing caravan of pilgrims, who were filled with the religious enthusiasm of the great ecclesiastical event of the year. His destination was a city which was loved by every Jewish heart with a strength of affection that has never been given to any other capital — a city full of objects and memories fitted to touch the deepest springs of interest and emotion in his breast. It was swarming at the Passover time with strangers from half-a-hundred countries, speaking as many languages and wearing as many different costumes. He went to take part for the first time in an ancient solemnity suggestive of countless patriotic and scared memories. It was no wonder that, when the day came to return home, He was so excited with the new objects of interest, that He failed to join His party at the appointed place and time. One spot above all fascinated His interest. It was the temple, and especially the school there in which the masters of wisdom taught. His mind was teeming with questions which these doctors might be asked to answer. His thirst for knowledge had an opportunity for the first time to drink its fill. So it was there His anxious parents, who, missing Him after a day's journey northward, returned in anxiety to seek him, found Him, listening with excited looks to the oracles of the wisdom of the day. His answer to the reproachful question of His mother lays bare His childhood's mind, and for a moment affords a wide glance over the thoughts which used to engross Him in the fields of Nazareth. It shows that already, though so young, He had risen above the great mass of men, who drift on through life without once inquiring what may be its meaning and its end. He was aware that he had a God-appointed life-work to do, which it was the one business of His existence to accomplish. It was the passionate thought of all His afterlife. It ought to be the first and last thought of every life. It recurred again and again in His later sayings, and pealed itself finally forth in the word with which He closed His career—It is finished!

It has often been asked whether Jesus knew all along that He was the Messiah, and, if not, when and how the knowledge dawned upon Him; whether it was suggested by hearing from His mother the story of his Birth, or announced to Him from within. Did it dawn upon Him all at once, or gradually? When did the plan of His career, which He carried out so unhesitatingly from the beginning of His ministry, shape itself in His mind? Was it the slow result of years of reflection, or did it come to Him at once? These questions have occupied the greatest Christian minds and received very various answers. I will not venture to answer them, and especially with His reply to His mother before me, I cannot trust myself even to think of a time when He did not know what His work in this world was to be.

His subsequent visits to Jerusalem must have greatly influenced the development of His mind. If He often went back to hear and question the rabbis in the temple schools, He must soon have discovered how shallow was their far-famed learnings. It was probably on these annual visits that He discovered the utter corruption of the religion of the day and the need of a radical reform of both doctrine and practice, and marked the practices and the persons that He was by and by to assail with the vehemence of His holy indignation.

Such were the external conditions amidst which the manhood of Jesus waxed towards maturity. It would be easy to exaggerate the influence which they may be supposed to have exerted on his development. The greater and more original a character is, the less dependent is it on the peculiarities of its environment. It is fed from deep wellsprings within itself, and in its germ there is a type enclosed which expands in obedience to its own laws and bids defiance to circumstances. In any other circumstances, Jesus would have grown to be in every important respect the very same person as He became in Nazareth.

2
The Nation and the Time

WE now approach the time when, after thirty years of silence and obscurity in Nazareth, Jesus was to step forth on the public stage. This is therefore the place at which to take a survey of the circumstances of the nation in whose midst His work was to be done, and also to form a clear conception of His character and aims. Every great biography is the record of the entrance into the world of a new force, bringing with it something different from all that was there before, and of the way in which it gradually gets itself incorporated with the old, so as to become a part of the future. Obviously, therefore, two things are needed by those who wish to understand it—first, a clear comprehension of the nature of the new force itself; and secondly, a view of the world with which it is to be incorporated. Without the latter the specific difference of the former cannot be understood, nor can the manner of its reception be appreciated—the welcome with which it is received, or the opposition with which it has to struggle. Jesus brought with Him into the world more that was original and destined to modify the future history of mankind than anyone else who has ever entered it. But we can neither understand Him nor the fortunes which He encountered in seeking to incorporate with history the gift He brought, without a clear view of the condition of the sphere within which His life was to be passed.

The Theater of His Life

When, having finished the last chapter of the Old Testament, we turn over the leaf and see the first chapter of the New, we are very apt to think that in Matthew we are still among the same people and the same state of things as we have left in Malachi. But no idea could be more erroneous. Four centuries elapsed between Malachi and Matthew, and wrought as total a change in Palestine as a period of the same length has almost ever wrought in any country. The very language of the people had been changed, and customs, ideas, parties, and institutions had come into existence which would almost have prevented Malachi, if he had risen from the dead, from recognizing his country.

Politically, the nation had passed through extraordinary vicissitudes. After the Exile, it had been organized as a kind of sacred State under its high priests, but conqueror after conqueror had since marched over it, changing everything; the old hereditary monarchy had been restored for a time by the brave Maccabees; the battle of freedom had many times been won and lost; a usurper had sat on the throne of David; and now at last the country was completely under the mighty Roman power, which had extended its sway over the whole civilized world. It was divided into several small portions, which the foreigner held under different tenures, as the English at present hold India. Galilee and Perea were ruled by petty kings, sons of that Herod under whom Jesus was born, who occupied a relation to the Roman emperor similar to that which the subject Indian kings hold to our Queen; and Judea was under the charge of a Roman official, a subordinate of the governor of the Roman province of Syria, who held a relation to that functionary similar to that which the Governor of Bombay holds to the Governor-General at Calcutta. Roman soldiers paraded the streets of Jerusalem; Roman standards waved over the fastnesses of the country; Roman tax gatherers sat at the gate of every town. To the Sanhedrin, the supreme Jewish organ of government, only a shadow of power was still conceded, its presidents, the high priests, being mere puppets of Rome, set up and put down with the utmost caprice. So low had the proud nation fallen whose ideal it had ever been to rule the world, and whose patriotism was religious and national passion as intense and unquenchable as ever burned in any country.

In religion the changes had been equally great, and the fall equally low. In external appearance, indeed, it might have seemed as if progress had been made instead of retrogression. The nation was far more orthodox than it had been at many earlier periods of its history. Once its chief danger had been idolatry, but the chastisement of the Exile had corrected that tendency forever, and thenceforward the Jews, wherever they might be living, were uncompromising monotheists. The priestly orders and offices had been thoroughly reorganized after the return from Babylon, and the temple services and annual feasts continued to be observed at Jerusalem with strict regularity. Besides, a new and most important religious institution had arisen, which almost threw the temple with its priesthood into the background. This was the synagogue with its rabbis. It does not seem to have existed in ancient times at all, but was called into existence after the Exile by reverence for the written Word. Synagogues were multiplied wherever Jews lived; every Sabbath they were filled with praying congregations; exhortations were delivered by the rabbis—a new order created by the need of expounders to translate from the Hebrew, which had become a dead language; and nearly the whole Old Testament was read over once a year in the hearing of the people. Schools of theology, similar to our divinity halls, had sprung up, in which the rabbis were trained and the sacred books interpreted.

But, in spite of all this religiosity, religion had sadly declined. The externals had been multiplied, but the inner spirit had disappeared. However rude and sinful the old nation had sometimes been, it was capable in its worst periods of producing majestic religious figures, who kept high the ideal of life and preserved the connection of the nation with Heaven; and the inspired voices of the prophets kept the stream of truth running fresh and clean. But during four hundred years no prophet's voice had been heard. The records of the old prophetic utterances were still preserved with almost idolatrous reverence, but there were not men with even the necessary amount of the Spirit's inspiration to understand what He had formerly written.

The representative religious men of the time were the Pharisees. As their name indicates, they originally arose as champions of the separateness of the Jews from other nations. This was a noble idea, so long as the distinction emphasized was holiness. But it is far more difficult to maintain this distinction than such external differences as peculiarities of dress, food, language, etc. These were in course of time substituted for it. The Pharisees were ardent patriots, ever willing to lay down their lives for the independence of their country, and hating the foreign yoke with impassioned bitterness. They despised and hated other races, and clung with undying faith to the hope of a glorious future for their nation. But they had so long harped on this idea, that they had come to believe themselves the special favorites of Heaven, simply because they were descendants of Abraham, and to lose sight of the importance of personal character. They multiplied their Jewish peculiarities, but substituted external observances, such as fasts, prayers, tithes, washings, sacrifices, and so forth, for the grand distinctions of love to God and love to man.

To the Pharisaic party belonged most of the scribes. They were so called because they were both the interpreters and copyists of the Scriptures and the lawyers of the people; for, the Jewish legal code being incorporated in the Holy Scriptures, jurisprudence became a branch of theology. They were the chief interpreters in the synagogues, although any male worshiper was permitted to speak if he chose. They professed unbounded reverence for the Scriptures, counting every word and letter in them. They had a splendid opportunity of diffusing the religious principles of the Old Testament among the people, exhibiting the glorious examples of its heroes and sowing abroad the words of the prophets; for the synagogue was one of the most potent engines of instruction ever devised by any people. But they entirely missed their opportunity. They became a dry ecclesiastical and scholastic class, using their position for selfish aggrandizement, and scorning those to whom they gave stones for bread as a vulgar and unlettered *canaille*. Whatever was most spiritual, living, human, and grand in the Scriptures they passed by. Generation after generation the commentaries of their famous men multiplied, and the pupils studied the commentaries instead of the text. Moreover, it was a rule with them that the correct interpretation of a passage was as authoritative as the text itself; and, the interpretations of the famous masters being as a matter of course believed to be correct, the mass of opinions which were held to be as precious as the Bible itself grew to enormous proportions. These were "the traditions of the elders." By degrees an arbitrary system of exegesis came into vogue, by which almost any opinion whatever could be thus connected with some text and stamped with divine authority. Every new invention of Pharisaic peculiarities was sanctioned in this way. These were multiplied until they regulated every detail of life, personal, domestic, social, and public. They became so numerous, that it required a lifetime to learn them all; and the learning of a scribe consisted in acquaintance with them, and with the dicta of the great rabbis and the forms of exegesis by which they were sanctioned. This was the chaff with which they fed the people in the synagogues. The conscience was burdened with innumerable details, every one of which was represented to be as divinely sanctioned as any of the ten commandments. This was the intolerable burden which Peter said neither he nor his fathers had been able to bear. This was the horrible nightmare which sat so long on Paul's conscience. But worse consequences flowed from it. It is a well-known principle in history, that, whenever the ceremonial is elevated to the same rank with the moral, the latter will soon be lost sight of. The scribes and Pharisees had learned how by arbitrary exegesis and casuistical discussion to explain away the weightiest moral obligations, and make up for the neglect of them by increasing their ritual observances. Thus men were able to flaunt in the pride of sanctity while indulging their selfishness and vile passions. Society was rotten with vice within, and veneered over with a self-deceptive religiosity without.

There was a party of protest. The Sadducees impugned the authority attached to the traditions of the fathers, demanding a return to the Bible and nothing but the Bible, and cried out for morality in place of ritual. But their protest was prompted merely by the spirit of denial, and not by a warm opposite principle of religion. They were skeptical, cold-hearted, worldly men. Though they praised morality, it was a morality unwarmed and unilluminated by any contact with that upper region of divine forces from which the inspiration of the highest morality must always come. They refused to burden their consciences with the painful punctilios of the Pharisees, but it was because they wished to live the life of comfort and self-indulgence. They ridiculed the Pharisaic exclusiveness, but had let go what was most peculiar in the character, the faith, and the hopes of the nation. They mingled freely with the Gentiles, affected Greek culture, enjoyed foreign amusements, and thought it useless to fight for the freedom of their country. An extreme section of them were the Herodians, who had given in to the usurpation of Herod, and with courtly flattery attached themselves to the favor of his sons.

The Sadducees belonged chiefly to the upper and wealthy classes. The Pharisees and scribes formed what we should call the middle class, although also deriving many members from the higher ranks of life. The lower classes and the country people were separated by a great gulf from their wealthy neighbors, but attached themselves by admiration to the Pharisees, as the uneducated always do to the party of warmth. Down below all these was a large class of those who had lost all connection with religion and well-ordered social life—the publicans, harlots, and sinners, for whose souls no man cared.

Such were the pitiable features of the society on which Jesus was about to discharge His influence—a nation enslaved; the upper classes devoting themselves to selfishness, courtiership, and skepticism; the teachers and chief professors of religion lost in mere shows of ceremonialism, and boasting themselves the favorites of God, while their souls were honeycombed with self-deception and vice; the body of the people misled by false ideals; and seething at the bottom of society, a neglected mass of unblushing and unrestrained sin.

And this was the people of God! Yes; in spite of their awful degradation, these were the children of Abraham, Isaac and Jacob, and the heirs of the covenant and the promises. Away back beyond the centuries of degradation towered the figures of the patriarchs, the kings after God's own heart, the psalmists, the prophets, the generations of faith and hope. Ay, and in front there was greatness too! The word of God, once sent forth from heaven and uttered by the mouths of His prophets, could not return to Him void. He had said that to this nation was to be given the perfect revelation of Himself, that in it was to appear the perfect ideal of manhood, and that from it was to issue forth the regeneration of all mankind. Therefore a wonderful future still belonged to it. The river of Jewish history was for the time choked and lost in the sands of the desert, but it was destined to reappear again and flow forward on its God-appointed course. The time of fulfillment was at hand, much as the signs of the times might seem to forbid the hope. Had not all the prophets from Moses onward spoken of a great One to come, who, appearing just when the darkness was blackest and the degradation deepest, was to bring back the lost glory of the past?

So not a few faithful souls asked themselves in the weary and degraded time. There are good men in the worst of periods. There were good men even in the selfish and corrupt Jewish parties. But especially does piety linger in such epochs in the lowly homes of the people; and, just as we are permitted to hope that in the Romish Church at the present time there may be those who, through all the ceremonies put between the soul and Christ, reach forth to Him, and by the selection of a spiritual instinct seize the truth and pass the falsehood by, so among the common people of Palestine there were those who, hearing the Scriptures read in the synagogues and reading them in their homes, instinctively neglected the cumbrous and endless comments of their teachers, and saw the glory of the past, of holiness and of God, which the scribes failed to see.

It was especially to the promises of a Deliverer that such spirits attached their interest. Feeling bitterly the shame of national slavery, the hollowness of the times, and the awful wickedness which rotted under the surface of society, they longed and prayed for the advent of the coming One and the restoration of the national character and glory.

The scribes also busied themselves with this element in the Scriptures; and the cherishing of Messianic hopes was one of the chief distinctions of the Pharisees. But they had caricatured the prophetic utterances on the subject by their arbitrary interpretations, and painted the future in colors borrowed from their own carnal imaginations. They spoke of the advent as the coming of the kingdom of God, and of the Messiah as the Son of God. But what they chiefly expected Him to do was, by the working of marvels and by irresistible force, to free the nation from servitude and raise it to the utmost worldly grandeur. They entertained no doubt that, simply because they were members of the chosen nation, they would be allotted high places in the kingdom, and never suspected that any change was needed in themselves to meet

Him. The spiritual elements of the better time, holiness and love, were lost in their minds behind the dazzling forms of material glory.*

Such was the aspect of Jewish history at the time when the hour of realizing the national destiny was about to strike. It imparted to the work which lay before the Messiah a peculiar complexity. It might have been expected that He would find a nation saturated with the ideas and inspired with the visions of His predecessors, the prophets, at whose head He might place Himself, and from which He might receive an enthusiastic and effective cooperation. But it was not so. He appeared at a time when the nation had lapsed from its ideals and caricatured their sublimest features. Instead of meeting a nation mature in holiness and consecrated to the heaven-ordained task of blessing all other people, which He might easily lead up to its own final development, and then lead forth to the spiritual conquest of the world, He found that the first work which lay before Him was to proclaim a reformation in His own country, and encounter the opposition of prejudices that had accumulated there through centuries of degradation.

---

* I have not thought it necessary to describe the state of the world beyond Palestine; for although the gifts Jesus brought were for all mankind, yet His own activity was confined almost entirely to the house of Israel within its original home. In a history of Early Christianity, or even a life of the Apostle Paul, it would be necessary to extend our view over the whole disc of civilization which surrounded the Mediterranean, and in which the world's center, which has since shifted to other latitudes, was then to be found; and to show how marvelously, by the dispersion of the Jews through all civilized countries, the elementary conceptions of God which were necessary for the reception of Christianity had been diffused beforehand far and wide; how the conquests of Alexander had, by making the Greek language universally understood, prepared a vehicle by which the gospel might be carried to all nations; how a pathway for it had been provided by the Roman power, whose military system had made all lands accessible; and, above all, how the decay of the ancient religions and philosophies, the wearing out everywhere of the old ideals of life, and the prevalence of heart-sickening sin, had made the world ready for Him who was the Desire of all nations.

3
The Final Stages
of His Preparation

MEANWHILE He, whom so many in their own ways were hoping for, was in the midst of them, though they suspected it not. Little could they think that He about whom they were speculating and praying was growing up in a carpenter's home away in despised Nazareth. Yet so it was. There He was preparing Himself for His career. His mind was busy grasping the vast proportions of the task before Him, as the prophecies of the past and the facts of the case determined it; His eyes were looking forth on the country and His heart smarting with the sense of its sin and shame. In Himself He felt moving the gigantic powers necessary to cope with the vast design; and the desire was gradually growing to an irresistible passion, to go forth and utter the thought within Him, and do the work which had been given Him to do.

Jesus had only three years to accomplish His lifework. If we remember how quickly three years in an ordinary life pass away, and how little at their close there usually is to show for them, we shall see what must have been the size and quality of that character, and what the unity and intensity of design in that life, which in so marvelously short a time made such a deep and ineffaceable impression on the world, and left to mankind such a heritage of truth and influence.

It is generally allowed that Jesus appeared as a public man with a mind whose ideas were completely developed and arranged, with a character sharpened over its whole surface into perfect definiteness, and with designs that marched forward to their ends without hesitation. No deflection took place during the three years from the lines on which at the beginning of them He was moving. The reason of this must have been, that during the thirty years before His public work began, His ideas, His character and designs went through all the stages of a thorough development. Unpretentious as the external aspects of His life at Nazareth were, it was, below the surface, a life of intensity, variety and grandeur. Beneath its silence and obscurity there went on all the processes of growth which issued in the magnificent flower and fruit to which all ages now look back with wonder. His preparation lasted long. For one with His powers at command, thirty years of complete reticence and reserve were a long time. Nothing was greater in Him afterwards than the majestic reserve in both speech and action which characterized Him. This, too, was learned in Nazareth. There He waited till the hour of the completion of His preparation struck. Nothing could tempt Him forth before the time — not the burning desire to interfere with indignant protest amidst the crying corruptions and mistakes of the age, not even the swellings of the passion to do His fellowmen good.

At last, however, He threw down the carpenter's tools, laid aside the workman's dress, and bade His home and the beloved valley of Nazareth farewell. Still, however, all was not ready. His manhood, though it had waxed in secret to such noble proportions, still required a peculiar endowment for the work He had to do; and His ideas and designs, mature as they were, required to be hardened in the fire of a momentous trial. The two final incidents of His preparation — the Baptism and the Temptation — had still to take place.

His Baptism

Jesus did not descend on the nation from the obscurity of Nazareth without note of warning. His work may be said to have been begun before He Himself put His hand to it.

Once more, before hearing the voice of its Messiah, the nation was to hear the long-silent voice of prophecy. The news went through all the country that in the desert of Judea a preacher had appeared, not like the numbers of dead men's ideas who spoke in the synagogues, or the courtier-like, smooth-tongued teachers of Jerusalem, but a rude, strong man, speaking from the heart to the heart, with the authority of one who was sure of his inspiration. He had been a Nazarite from the womb; he had lived for years in the desert, wandering, in communion with his own heart, beside the lonely shores of the Dead Sea; he was clad in the hair cloak and leather girdle of the old prophets; and his ascetic rigor sought no finer fare than locusts and the wild honey which he found in the wilderness. Yet he knew life well; he was acquainted with all the evils of the time, the hypocrisy of the religious parties, and the corruption of the masses: he had a wonderful power of searching the heart and shaking the conscience, and without fear laid bare the darling sins of every class. But that which most of all attracted attention to him and thrilled every Jewish heart from one end of the land to the other, was the message which he bore. It was nothing less than that the Messiah was just at hand, and about to set up the kingdom of God. All Jerusalem poured out to him; the Pharisees were eager to hear the Messianic news; and even the Sadducees were stirred for a moment from their lethargy. The provinces sent forth their thousands to his preaching, and the scattered and hidden ones who longed and prayed for the redemption of Israel flocked to welcome the heart-stirring promise. But along with it John had another message, which excited very different feelings in different minds. He had to tell his hearers that the nation as a whole was utterly unprepared for the Messiah; that the mere fact of their descent from Abraham would not be a sufficient token of admission to His kingdom; it was to be a kingdom of righteousness and holiness, and Christ's very first work would be to reject all who were not marked with these qualities, as the farmer winnows away the chaff with his fan, and the master of the vineyard hews down every tree that brings forth no fruit. Therefore he called the nation at large—every class and every individual—to repentance, so long as there still was time, as an indispensable preparation for enjoying the blessings of the new epoch; and, as an outward symbol of this inward change, he baptized in the Jordan all who received his message with faith. Many were stirred with fear and hope and submitted to the rite, but many more were irritated by the exposure of their sins and turned away in anger and unbelief. Among these were the Pharisees, upon whom he was specially severe, and who were deeply offended because he had treated so lightly their descent from Abraham, on which they laid so much stress.

One day there appeared among the Baptist's hearers One who particularly attracted his attention, and made his voice, which had never faltered when accusing in the most vigorous language of reproof even the highest teachers and priests of the nation, tremble with self-distrust. And when He presented Himself, after the discourse was done, among the candidates for baptism, John drew back, feeling that This was no subject for the bath of repentance, which without hesitation he had administered to all others, and that he himself had no right to baptize Him. There were in His face a majesty, a purity, and a peace which smote the man of rock with the sense of unworthiness and sin. It was Jesus, who had come straight hither from the workshop of Nazareth. John and Jesus appear never to have met before, though their families were related and the connection of their careers had been predicted before their birth. This may have been due to the distance of their homes in Galilee and Judea, and still more to the Baptist's peculiar habits. But when, in obedience to the injunction of Jesus, John proceeded to administer the rite, he learned the meaning of the overpowering impression which the Stranger had made on him; for the sign was given by which, as God had instructed him, he was to recognize the Messiah, whose forerunner he was. The Holy Ghost descended on Jesus, as He emerged from the water in the attitude of prayer, and the voice of God pronounced Him in thunder His beloved Son.

The impression made on John by the very look of Jesus reveals far better than many words could do His aspect when He was about to begin His work, and the qualities of the character which in Nazareth had been slowly ripening to full maturity.

The baptism itself had an important significance for Jesus. To the other candidates who underwent the rite it had a double meaning; it signified the abandonment of their old sins, and their entrance into the new Messianic era. To Jesus it could not have the former meaning, except insofar as He may have identified Himself with His nation, and taken this way of expressing His sense of its need of cleansing. But it meant that He too was now entering through this door into the new epoch, of which He was Himself to be the Author. It expressed His sense that the time had come to leave behind the employments of Nazareth and devote himself to His peculiar work.

But still more important was the descent upon Him of the Holy Ghost. This was neither a meaningless display nor merely a signal to the Baptist. It was the symbol of a special gift then given to qualify Him for His work, and crown the long development of His peculiar powers. It is a forgotten truth that the manhood of Jesus was from first to last dependent on the Holy Ghost. We are apt to imagine that its connection with His divine nature rendered this unnecessary. On the contrary, it made it far more necessary, for in order to be the organ of His divine nature, His human nature had both to be endowed with the highest gifts and constantly sustained in their exercise. We are in the habit of attributing the wisdom and grace of His words, His supernatural knowledge of even the thoughts of men, and the miracles He performed, to His divine nature. But in the Gospels they are constantly attributed to the Holy Ghost. This does not mean that they were independent of His divine nature, but that in them His human nature was enabled to be the organ of His divine nature by a peculiar gift of the Holy Ghost. This gift was given Him at His baptism. It was analogous to the possession of prophets, like Isaiah and Jeremiah, with the Spirit of inspiration on those occasions, of which they have left accounts, when they were called to begin their public life, and to the special outpouring of the same influence still sometimes given at their ordination to those who are about to begin the work of the ministry. But to Him it was given without measure, while to others it has always been given only in measure; and it comprised especially the gift of miraculous powers.

The Temptation

An immediate effect of this new endowment appears to have been one often experienced, in less degree, by others who, in their small measure, have received this same gift of the Spirit for work. His whole being was excited about His work, His desires to be engaged in it were raised to the highest pitch, and his thoughts were intensely occupied about the means of its accomplishment. Although His preparation for it had been going on for many years, although His whole heart had long been fixed on it, and His plan had been clearly settled, it was natural that, when the divine signal had been given that it was forthwith to commence, and He felt Himself suddenly put in possession of the supernatural powers necessary for carrying it out, His mind should be in a tumult of crowding thoughts and feelings, and He should seek a place of solitude to revolve once more the whole situation. Accordingly, He hastily retreated from the bank of the Jordan, driven, we are told, by the Spirit, which had just been given Him, into the wilderness, where, for forty days, He wandered among the sandy dunes and wild mountains, His mind being so highly strung with the emotions and ideas which crowded on Him, that he forgot even to eat.

But it is with surprise and awe we learn that His soul was, during those days, the scene of a frightful struggle. He was tempted of Satan, we are told. What could He be tempted with at a time so sacred? To understand this we must recall what has been said of the state of the Jewish nation, and especially the nature of the Messianic hopes which they were indulging. They expected a Messiah who would work dazzling wonders and establish a worldwide empire with Jerusalem as its center, and they had postponed the ideas of righteousness and holiness to these. They completely inverted the divine conception of the kingdom, which could not but give the spiritual and moral elements precedence of material and political considerations. Now what Jesus was tempted to do was, in carrying out the great work which His Father had committed to Him, to yield in some measure to these expectations. He must have foreseen that, unless He did so, the nation would be disappointed and probably turn away from Him in unbelief and anger. The different temptations were only various modifications of this one thought. The suggestion that He should turn stones into bread to satisfy His hunger was a temptation to use the power of working miracles, with which He had just been endowed, for a purpose inferior to those for which alone it had been given, and was the precurser of such temptations in His afterlife as the demand of the multitude to show them a sign, or that He should come down from the cross, that they might believe Him. The suggestion that He should leap from the pinnacle of the temple was probably also a temptation to gratify the vulgar desire for wonders, because it was a part of the popular belief that the Messiah should appear suddenly, and in some marvelous way; as, for instance, by a leap from the temple roof into the midst of the crowds assembled below. The third and greatest temptation, to win the empire of all the kingdoms of the world by an act of worship to the Evil One, was manifestly only a symbol of obedience to the universal Jewish conception of the coming kingdom as a vast structure of material force. It was a temptation which every worker for God, weary with the slow progress of goodness, must often feel, and to which even good and earnest men have sometimes given way—to begin at the outside instead of within, to get first a great shell of external conformity to religion, and afterwards fill it with the reality. It was the temptation to which Mahommed yielded when he used the sword to subdue those whom he was afterwards to make religious, and to which the Jesuits yielded when they baptized the heathen first and evangelized them afterwards.

It is with awe we think of these suggestions presenting themselves to the holy soul of Jesus. Could He be tempted to distrust God, and even to worship the Evil One? No doubt the temptations were flung from Him, as the impotent billows retire broken from the breast of the rock on which they have dashed themselves. But these temptations pressed in on Him, not only at this time, but often before in the valley of Nazareth, and often afterwards, in the heats and crises of His life. We must remember that it is no sin to be tempted, it is only sin to yield to temptation. And, indeed, the more absolutely pure a soul is, the more painful will be the point of the temptation, as it presses for admission into his breast.

Although the tempter only departed from Jesus for a season, this was a decisive struggle; he was thoroughly beaten back, and his power broken at its heart. Milton has indicated this by finishing his *Paradise Regained* at this point. Jesus merged from the wilderness with the plan of His life, which, no doubt, had been formed long before, hardened in the fire of trial. Nothing is more conspicuous in His afterlife than the resolution with which He carried it out. Other men, even those who have accomplished the greatest tasks, have sometimes had no definite plan, but only seen by degrees in the evolution of circumstances the path to pursue; their purposes have been modified by events and the advice of others. But Jesus started with His plan perfected, and never deviated from it by a hair's breadth. He resented the interference of His mother or His chief disciple with it as steadfastly as He bore it through the fiery opposition of open enemies. And His plan was to establish the kingdom of God in the hearts of individuals, and rely not on the weapons of political and material strength, but only on the power of love and the force of truth.

The Divisions of
His Public Ministry

THE public ministry of Jesus is generally reckoned to have lasted three years. Each of them had peculiar features of its own. The first may be called the Year of Obscurity, both because the records of it which we possess are very scanty, and because He seems during it to have been only slowly emerging into public notice. It was spent for the most part in Judea. The second was the Year of Public Favor, during which the country had become thoroughly aware of Him, His activity was incessant, and His fame rang through the length and breadth of the land. It was almost wholly passed in Galilee. The third was the Year of Opposition, when the public favor ebbed away, His enemies multiplied and assailed Him with more and more pertinacity, and at last He fell a victim to their hatred. The first six months of this final year were passed in Galilee, and the last six in other parts of the land.

Thus the life of the Savior in its external outline resembled that of many a reformer and benefactor of mankind. Such a life often begins with a period during which the public is gradually made aware of the new man in its midst, then passes into a period when his doctrine or reform is borne aloft on the shoulders of popularity, and ends with a reaction, when the old prejudices and interests which have been assailed by him rally from his attack, and, gaining to themselves the passions of the crowd, crush him in their rage.

4

The Year of Obscurity

THE records of this year which we possess are extremely meager, comprising only two or three incidents, which may be here enumerated, especially as they form a kind of program of His future work.

When He emerged from the wilderness after the forty days of temptation, with His grasp of His future plan tightened by that awful struggle and with the inspiration of His baptism still swelling His heart, He appeared once more on the bank of the Jordan, and John pointed Him out as the great Successor to himself of whom he had often spoken. He especially introduced Him to some of the choicest of His own disciples, who immediately became His followers. Probably the very first of these to whom He spoke was a man who was afterwards to be His favorite disciple, and to give to the world the divinest portrait of His character and life. John the Evangelist—for he it was—has left an account of this first meeting and the interview that followed it, which retains in all its freshness the impression which Christ's majesty and purity made on his receptive mind. The other young men who attached themselves to Him at the same time were Andrew, Peter, Philip, and Nathaniel. They had been prepared for their new Master by their intercourse with the Baptist, and although they did not at once give up their employments and follow Him in the same way as they did at a later period, they received impressions at their very first meeting which decided their whole after-career. The Baptist's disciples do not seem to have at once gone over in a body to Christ. But the best of them did so. Some mischief-makers endeavored to excite envy in his mind by pointing out how his influence was passing away to Another. But they little understood that great man, whose chief greatness was his humility. He answered them that it was his joy to decrease, while Christ increased, for it was Christ who as the Bridegroom was to lead home the bride, while he was only the Bridegroom's friend, whose happiness consisted in seeing the crown of festal joy placed on the head of another.

With His newly attached followers Jesus departed from the scene of John's ministry, and went north to Cana in Galilee, to attend a marriage to which He had been invited. Here He made the first display of the miraculous powers with which He had been recently endowed, by turning water into wine. It was a manifestation of His glory intended specially for his new disciples, who, we are told, thenceforward believed on Him, which means, no doubt, that they were fully convinced that He was the Messiah. It was intended also to strike the keynote of His ministry as altogether different from the Baptist's. John was an ascetic hermit who fled from the abodes of men and called his hearers out into the wilderness. But Jesus had glad tidings to bring to men's hearths; He was to mingle in their common life, and produce a happy revolution in their circumstances, which would be like the turning of the water of their life into wine.

Soon after this miracle He returned again to Judea to attend the Passover, and gave a still more striking proof of the joyful and enthusiastic mood in which He was then living, by purging the temple of the sellers of animals and the money changers, who had introduced their traffic into its courts. These persons were allowed to carry on their sacrilegious trade under the pretense of accommodating strangers who came to worship at Jerusalem, by selling them the victims which they could not bring from foreign countries, and supplying, in exchange for foreign money, the Jewish coins in which alone they could pay their temple dues. But what had been begun under the veil of a pious pretext had ended in gross disturbance of the worship, and in elbowing the Gentile proselytes from the place which God had allowed them in His house. Jesus had probably often witnessed the disgraceful scene with indignation during His visits to Jerusalem, and now, with the prophetic zeal of His baptism upon Him, He broke out against it. The same look of irresistible purity and majesty which had appalled John, when He sought baptism, prevented any resistance on the part of the ignoble crew, and made the onlookers recognize the lineaments of the prophets of ancient days, before whom kings and crowds alike were wont to quail. It was the beginning of His reformatory work against the religious abuses of the time.

He wrought other miracles during the feast, which must have excited much talk among the pilgrims from every land who crowded the city. One result of them was to bring to His lodging one night the venerable and anxious inquirer to whom He delivered the marvelous discourse on the nature of the new kingdom He had come to found, and the grounds of admission to it, which has been preserved to us in the third chapter of John. It seemed a hopeful sign that one of the heads of the nation should approach Him in a spirit so humble, but Nicodemus was the only one of them on whose mind the first display of the Messiah's power in the capital produced a deep and favorable impression.

Thus far we follow clearly the first steps of Jesus. But at this point our information in regard to the first year of His ministry, after commencing with such fullness, comes to a sudden stop, and for the next eight months we learn nothing more about Him but that He was baptizing in Judea—"though Jesus Himself baptized not, but his disciples"—and that He "made and baptized more disciples than John."

What can be the meaning of such a blank? It is to be noted too, that it is only in the Fourth Gospel that we receive even the details given above. The Synoptists omit the first year of the ministry altogether, beginning their narrative with the ministry in Galilee, and merely indicating in the most cursory way that there was a ministry in Judea before.

It is very difficult to explain all this. The most natural explanation would perhaps be, that the incidents of this year were imperfectly known at the time when the Gospels were composed. It would be quite natural that the details of the period when Jesus had not attracted much public attention should be much less accurately remembered than those of the period when He was by far the best known personage in the country. But, indeed, the Synoptists all through take little notice of what happened in Judea, till the close of His life draws nigh. It is to John we are indebted for the connected narrative of His various visits to the south.

But John, at least, could scarcely have been ignorant of the incidents of eight months. We shall perhaps be conducted to the explanation by attending to the little-noticed fact, which John communicates, that for a time Jesus took up the work of the Baptist. He baptized by the hands of his disciples, and drew even larger crowds than John. Must not this mean that He was convinced, by the small impression which His manifestation of Himself at the Passover had made, that the nation was utterly unprepared for receiving Him yet as the Messiah, and that what was needed was the extension of the preparatory work of repentance and baptism, and accordingly, keeping in the background His higher character, became for the time the colleague of John? This view is confirmed by the fact, that it was upon John's imprisonment at this year's end that he opened fully His Messianic career in Galilee.

A still deeper explanation of the silence of the Synoptists over this period, and their scant notice of Christ's subsequent visits to Jerusalem, has been suggested. Jesus came primarily to the Jewish nation, whose authoritative representatives were to be found at Jerusalem. He was the Messiah promised to their fathers, the Fulfiller of the nations' history. He had indeed a far wider mission to the whole world, but He was to begin with the Jews, and at Jerusalem. The nation, however, in its heads at Jerusalem, rejected Him, and so He was compelled to found His worldwide community from a different center. This having become evident by the time the Gospels were written, the Synoptists passed His activity at the headquarters of the nation, as a work with merely negative results, in great measure by, and concentrated attention on the period of His ministry when He was gathering the company of believing souls that was to form the nucleus of the Christian Church. However this may be, certainly at the close of the first year of the ministry of Jesus there fell already over Judea and Jerusalem the shadow of an awful coming event—the shadow of that most frightful of all national crimes which the world has ever witnessed, the rejection and crucifixion by the Jews of their Messiah.

5

The Year of Public Favor

AFTER the year spent in the south, Jesus shifted the sphere of His activity to the north of the country. In Galilee He would be able to address Himself to minds that were unsophisticated with the prejudices and supercilious pride of Judea, where the sacerdotal and learned classes had their headquarters; and He might hope that, if His doctrine and influence took a deep hold of one part of the country, even though it was remote from the center of authority, He might return to the south backed with an irresistible national acknowledgment, and carry by storm even the citadel of prejudice itself.

Galilee

The area of His activity for the next eighteen months was very limited. Even the whole of Palestine was a very limited country. Its length was a hundred miles less than that of Scotland, and its breadth considerably less than the average breadth of Scotland. It is important to remember this, because it renders intelligible the rapidity with which the movement of Jesus spread over the land, and all parts of the country flocked to His ministry; and it is interesting to remember it as an illustration of the fact that the nations which have contributed most to the civilization of the world have, during the period of their true greatness, been confined to very small territories. Rome was but a single city, and Greece a very small country.

Galilee was the most northerly of the four provinces into which Palestine was divided. It was sixty miles long by thirty broad; that is to say, it was less than some of our Scottish counties. It was about the size of Aberdeenshire. It consisted for the most part of an elevated plateau, whose surface was varied by irregular mountain masses. Near its eastern boundary it suddenly dropped down into a great gulf, through which flowed the Jordan, and in the midst of which, at a depth of five hundred feet below the Mediterranean, lay the lovely, harp-shaped Sea of Galilee. The whole province was very fertile, and its surface thickly covered with large villages and towns. The population was perhaps as dense as that of Lancashire or the West Riding of Yorkshire. But the center of activity was the basin of the lake, a sheet of water thirteen miles long by six broad. Above its eastern shore, round which ran a fringe of green a quarter of a mile broad, there towered high, bare hills, cloven with the channels of torrents. On the western side, the mountains were gently sloped and their sides richly cultivated, bearing splendid crops of every description; while at their feet the shore was verdant with luxuriant groves of olives, oranges, figs, and every product of an almost tropical climate. At the northern end of the lake the space between the water and the mountains was broadened by the delta of the river, and watered with many streams from the hills, so that it was a perfect paradise of fertility and beauty. It was called the plains of Gennesareth, and even at this day, when the whole basin of the lake is little better than a torrid solitude, is still covered with magnificent cornfields, wherever the hand of cultivation touches it; and where idleness leaves it untended, is overspread with thick jungles of thorn and oleander. In our Lord's time, it contained the chief cities on the lake, such as Capernaum, Bethsaida, and Chorazin. But the whole shore was studded with towns and villages, and formed a perfect beehive of swarming human life. The means of existence were abundant in the corps and fruits of every description which the fields yielded so richly; and the waters of the lake teemed with fish, affording employment to thousands of fishermen. Besides, the great highways from Egypt to Damascus, and from Phoenicia to the Euphrates, passed here, and made this a vast center of traffic. Thousands of boats for fishing, transport, and pleasure moved to and fro on the surface of the lake, so that the whole region was a focus of energy and prosperity.

The report of the miracles which Jesus had wrought at Jerusalem, eight months before, had been brought home to Galilee by the pilgrims who had been south at the feast, and doubtless also the news of

His preaching and baptism in Judea had created talk and excitement before He arrived. Accordingly, the Galileans were in some measure prepared to receive Him when He returned to their midst.

One of the first places He visited was Nazareth, the home of His childhood and youth. He appeared there one Sabbath in the synagogue, and, being now known as a preacher, was invited to read the Scriptures and address the congregation. He read a passage in Isaiah, in which a glowing description is given of the coming and work of the Messiah; "The Spirit of the Lord God is upon me, because He has anointed me to preach the gospel to the poor; He hath sent me to heal the brokenhearted, to preach deliverance to the captives, and recovering of sight to the blind, to set at liberty them that are bruised, to preach the acceptable year of the Lord." As He commented on this text, picturing the features of the Messianic time—the emancipation of the slave, the enriching of the poor, the healing of the diseased—their curiosity at hearing for the first time a young preacher who had been brought up among themselves passed into spellbound wonder, and they burst into the applause which used to be allowed in the Jewish synagogues. But soon the reaction came. They began to whisper: Was not this the carpenter who had worked among them? Had not His father and mother been their neighbors? Were not His sisters married in the town? Their envy was excited. And when He proceeded to tell them that the prophecy which He had read was fulfilled in Himself, they broke out into angry scorn. They demanded of Him a sign, such as it was reported He had given in Jerusalem; and when He informed them that He could perform no miracle among the unbelieving, they rushed on Him in a storm of jealousy and wrath, and hurrying Him out of the synagogue to a crag behind the town, would, if He had not miraculously taken Himself away from them, have flung Him over, and crowned their proverbial wickedness with a deed which would have robbed Jerusalem of her bad eminence of being the murderess of the Messiah.

From that day Nazareth was His home no more. Once again, indeed, in His yearning love for His old neighbors, He visited it, but with no better result. Henceforeward He made His home in Capernaum, on the northwestern shore of the Sea of Galilee. This town has completely vanished out of existence; its very site cannot now be discovered with any certainty. This may be one reason why it is not connected in the Christian mind with the life of Jesus in the same prominent way as Bethlehem, where He was born, Nazareth, where He was brought up, and Jerusalem, where He died. But we ought to fix it in our memories side by side with these, for it was His home for eighteen of the most important months of His life. It is called His own city, and He was asked for tribute in it as a citizen of the place. It was thoroughly well adapted to be the center of His labors in Galilee, for it was the focus of the busy life in the basin of the lake, and was conveniently situated for excursions to all parts of the province. Whatever happened there was quickly heard of in all the regions round about.

In Capernaum, then, He began His Galilean work; and for many months the method of His life was, to be frequently there as in His headquarters, and from this center to make tours in all directions, visiting the towns and villages of Galilee. Sometimes His journey would be inland, away to the west. At other times it would be a tour of the villages on the lake, or a visit to the country on its eastern side. He had a boat that waited on Him, for conveying Him wherever He might wish to go. He would come back to Capernaum, perhaps only for a day, perhaps for a week or two at a time.

In a few weeks the whole province was ringing with His name; He was the subject of conversation in every boat on the lake and every house in the whole region; men's minds were stirred with the profoundest excitement, and everyone desired to see Him. Crowds began to gather about Him. They grew larger and larger. They multiplied to thousands and tens of thousands. They followed Him wherever He went. The news spread far and wide beyond Galilee, and brought hosts from Jerusalem, Judea, and Perea, and even from Idumea in the far south, and Tyre and Sidon in the far north. Sometimes He could not stay in any town, because the crowds blocked up the streets and trod one on another. He had to take them out to the fields and deserts. The country was stirred from end to end, and Galilee was all on fire with excitement about Him.

How was it that He produced so great and widespread a movement? It was not by declaring Himself the Messiah. That would indeed have caused to pass through every Jewish breast the deepest thrill which it could experience. But although Jesus now and then, as at Nazareth, revealed Himself, in general He rather concealed His true character. No doubt the reason of this was, that among the excitable crowds of rude Galilee, with their grossly materialistic hopes, the declaration would have excited a revolutionary rising against the Roman Government, which would have withdrawn men's minds from His true aims and brought down on His head the Roman sword, just as in Judea it would have precipitated a murderous attack on His life by the Jewish authorities. To avert either kind of interruption, He kept the full revelation of Himself in reserve, endeavoring to prepare the public mind to receive it in its true inward and spiritual meaning, when the right moment for divulging it should come, and in the meantime leaving it to be inferred from His character and work who He was.

The two great means which Jesus used in His work, and which created such attention and enthusiasms, were His Miracles and His Preaching.

The Miracle Worker

Perhaps His miracles excited the widest attention. We are told how the news of the first one which He wrought in Capernaum spread like wildfire through the town, and brought crowds about the house where He was; and whenever He performed a new one of extraordinary character, the excitement grew intense and the rumor of it spread on every hand. When, for instance, He first cured leprosy, the most malignant form of bodily disease in Palestine, the amazement of the people knew no bounds. It was the same when He first overcame a case of possession; and when he raised to life the widow's son at Nain, there ensued a sort of stupor of fear, followed by delighted wonder and the talk of thousands of tongues. All Galilee was for a time in motion with the crowding of the diseased of every description who could walk or totter to be near Him, and with companies of anxious friends carrying on beds and couches those who could not come themselves. The streets of the villages and town were lined with the victims of disease as His benignant figure passed by. Sometimes He had so many to attend to that He could not find time even to eat; and at one period

He was so absorbed in His benevolent labors, and so carried along with the holy excitement which they caused, that His relatives, with indecorous rashness, endeavored to interfere, saying to each other that He was beside Himself.

The miracles of Jesus, taken altogether, were of two classes—those wrought on man, and those wrought in the sphere of external nature, such as the turning of water into wine, stilling the tempest, and multiplying the loaves. The former were by far the more numerous. They consisted chiefly of cures of diseases less or more malignant, such as lameness, blindness, deafness, palsy, leprosy, and so forth. He appears to have varied very much His mode of acting, for reasons which we can scarcely explain. Sometimes He used means, such as a touch, or the laying of moistened clay on the part, or ordering the patient to wash in water. At other times He healed without any means, and occasionally even at a distance. Besides these bodily cures, He dealt with the diseases of the mind. These seem to have been peculiarly prevalent in Palestine at the time, and to have excited the utmost terror. They were believed to be accompanied by the entrance of demons into the poor imbecile or raving victims, and this idea was only too true. The man whom Jesus cured among the tombs in the country of the Gadarenes was a frightful example of this class of disease; and the picture of him sitting at the feet of Jesus, clothed and in his right mind, shows what an effect His kind, soothing, and authoritative presence had on minds so distracted. But the most extraordinary of the miracles of Jesus upon man were the instances in which He raised the dead to life. They were not frequent, but naturally produced an overwhelming impression whenever they occurred. The miracles of the other class—those on external nature—were of the same inexplicable description. Some of His cures of mental disease, if standing by themselves, might be accounted for by the influence of a powerful nature on a troubled mind; and in the same way some of His bodily cures might be accounted for by His influencing the body through the mind. But such a miracle as walking on the tempestuous sea is utterly beyond the reach of natural explanation.

Why did Jesus employ this means of working? Several answers may be given to this question.

First, He wrought miracles because His Father gave Him these signs as proofs that He had sent Him. Many of the Old Testament prophets had received the same authentication of their mission, and although John, who revived the prophetic function, worked no miracles, as the Gospels inform us with the most simple veracity, it was to be expected that He who was a far greater prophet than the greatest who went before Him, should show even greater signs than any of them of His divine mission. It was a stupendous claim which He made on the faith of men when He announced Himself as the Messiah, and it would have been unreasonable to expect it to be conceded by a nation accustomed to miracles as the signs of a divine mission, if He had wrought none.

Secondly, the miracles of Christ were the natural outflow of the divine fullness which dwelt in Him. God was in Him, and His human nature was endowed with the Holy Ghost without measure. It was natural, when such a Being was in the world, that mighty works should manifest themselves in Him. He was Himself the great miracle, of which His particular miracles were merely sparks or emanations. He was the great interruption of the order of nature, or rather a new element which had entered into the order of nature to enrich and ennoble it, and His miracles entered with Him, not to disturb, but to repair its harmony. Therefore all His miracles bore the stamp of His character. They were not mere exhibitions of power, but also of holiness, wisdom, and love. The Jews often sought from Him mere gigantesque prodigies, to gratify their mania for marvels. But He always refused them, working only such miracles as were helps to faith. He demanded faith in all those whom He cured, and never responded either to curiosity or unbelieving challenges to exhibit marvels. This distinguishes His miracles from those fabled of ancient wonder-workers and medieval saints. They were marked by unvarying sobriety and benevolence, because they were the expressions of His character as a whole.

Thirdly, His miracles were symbols of His spiritual and saving work. You have only to consider them for a moment to see that they were, as a whole, triumphs over the misery of the world. Mankind is the prey of a thousand evils, and even the frame of external nature bears the mark of some past catastrophe: "The whole creation groaneth and travaileth in pain." This huge mass of physical evil in the lot of mankind is the effect of sin. Not that every disease and misfortune can be traced to special sin, although some of them can. The consequences of past sin are distributed in detail over the whole race. But yet the misery of the world is the shadow of its sin. Material and moral evil, being thus intimately related, mutually illustrate each other. When He healed bodily blindness, it was a type of the healing of the inner eye; when He raised the dead, He meant to suggest that He was the Resurrection and the Life in the spiritual world as well; when He cleansed the leper, His triumph spoke of another over the leprosy of sin; when He multiplied the loaves, He followed the miracle with a discourse on the bread of life; when He stilled the storm, it was an assurance that He could speak peace to the troubled conscience.

Thus His miracles were a natural and essential part of His messianic work. They were an excellent means of making Him known to the nation. They bound those whom He cured to Him with strong ties of gratitude; and without doubt, in many cases, the faith in Him as a miracle worker led on to a higher faith. So it was in the case of His devoted follower Mary Magdalene, out of whom He cast seven devils.

To Himself this work must have brought both great pain and great joy. To His tender and exquisitely sympathetic heart that never grew callous in the least degree, it must often have been harrowing to mingle with so much disease, and see the awful effects of sin. But He was in the right place; it suited His great love to be where help was needed. And what a joy it must have been to Him to distribute blessings on every hand and erase the traces of sin; to see health returning beneath his touch; to meet the joyous and grateful glances of the opening eyes; to hear the blessings of mothers and sisters, as He restored their loved ones to their arms; and to see the light of love and welcome in the faces of the poor, as He entered their towns and villages. He drank deeply of the well at which He would have his followers to be ever drinking—the bliss of doing good.

The Teacher

The other great instrument with which Jesus did His work was His teaching. It was by far the more important of the two. His miracles were only the bell tolled to bring the people to hear His words. They impressed those who might not yet be susceptible to the subtler influence, and brought them within its range.

The miracles probably made most noise, but His preaching also spread His fame far and wide. There is no power whose attraction is more unfailing than that of the eloquent word. Barbarians, listening to their bards and storytellers; Greeks, listening to the restrained passion of their orators, and matter-of-fact nations like the Roman, have alike acknowledged its power to be irresistible. The Jews prized it above almost every other attraction, and among the figures of their mighty dead revered none more highly than the prophets—those eloquent utterers of the truth, whom Heaven had sent them from age to age. Though the Baptist did not miracles, multitudes flocked to Him, because in his accents they recognized the thunder of this power, which for so many generations no Jewish ear had listened to. Jesus also was recognized as a prophet, and accordingly, His preaching created widespread excitement. "He spake in their synagogues, being glorified of all." His words were heard with wonder and amazement. Sometimes the multitude on the beach of the lake so pressed upon Him to hear, that He had to enter into a ship and address them from the deck, as they spread themselves out in a semicircle on the ascending shore. His enemies themselves bore witness that "never man spake like this man"; and meager as are the remains of his preaching which we possess, they are amply sufficient to make us echo the sentiment and understand the impression which He produced. All His words together which have been preserved to us would not occupy more space in print than half-a-dozen ordinary sermons; yet it is not too much to say, that they are the most precious literary heritage of the human race. His words, like His miracles, were expressions of Himself, and every one of them has in it something of the grandeur of His character.

The form of the preaching of Jesus was essentially Jewish. The Oriental mind does not work in the same way as the mind of the West.

Our thinking and speaking, when at their best, are fluent, expansive, closely reasoned. The kind of discourse which we admire is one which takes up an important subject, divides it out into different branches, treats it fully under each of the heads, closely articulates part to part, and closes with a moving appeal to the feelings, so as to sway the will to some practical result.

The Oriental mind, on the contrary, loves to brood long on a single point, to turn it round and round, to gather up all the truth about it in a focus, and pour it forth in a few pointed and memorable words. It is concise, epigrammatic, oracular. A Western speakers' discourse is a systematic structure, or like a chain in which link is firmly knit to link; an Oriental's is like the sky at night, full of innumerable burning points shining forth from a dark background.

Such was the form of the teachings of Jesus. It consisted of numerous sayings, every one of which contained the greatest possible amount of truth in the smallest possible compass, and was expressed in language so concise and pointed as to stick in the memory like an arrow. Read them, and you will find that every one of them, as you ponder it, sucks the mind in and in like a whirlpool, till it is lost in the depths. You will find, too, that there are very few of them which you do not know by heart. They have found their way into the memory of Christendom as no other words have done. Even before the meaning has been apprehended, the perfect, proverb-like expression lodges itself fast in the mind.

But there was another characteristic of the form of Jesus' teaching. It was full of figures of speech. He thought in images. He had ever been a loving and accurate observer of nature around Him—of the colors of the flowers, the ways of the birds, the growth of the trees, the vicissitudes of the seasons—and an equally keen observer of the ways of men in all parts of life—in religion, in business, in the home. The result was that He could neither think nor speak without His thought running into the mold of some natural image. His preaching was alive with such references, and therefore full of color, movement, and changing forms. There were no abstract statements in it; they were all changed into pictures. Thus, in His sayings, we can still see the aspects of the country and the life of the time as in a panorama—the lilies, whose gorgeous beauty His eyes feasted on, waving in the fields; the sheep following the shepherd; the broad and narrow city gates; the virgins with their lamps awaiting in the darkness the bridal processions; the Pharisee with his broad phylacteries and the publican with bent head at prayer together in the temple; the rich man seated in his palace at a feast, and the beggar lying at his gate with the dogs licking his sores; and a hundred other pictures that lay bare the inner and minute life of the time, over which history in general sweeps heedlessly with majestic stride.

But the most characteristic form of speech He made use of was the parable. It was a combination of the two qualities already mentioned—concise, memorable expression, and figurative style. It used an incident, taken from common life and rounded into a gem-like picture, to set forth some corresponding truth in the higher and spiritual region. It was a favorite Jewish mode of putting truth, but Jesus imparted to it by far the richest and most perfect development. About one-third of all His sayings which have been preserved to us consists of parables. This shows how they stuck in the memory. In the same way the hearers of the sermons of any preacher will probably, after a few years, remember the illustrations they have contained far better than anything else in them. How these parables have remained in the memory of all generations since! The Prodigal Son, the Sower, the Ten Virgins, the Good Samaritan—these and many others are pictures hung up in millions of minds. What passages in the greatest master of expression—in Homer, in Virgil, in Dante, in Shakespeare—have secured for themselves so universal a hold on men, or been felt to be so fadelessly fresh and true? He never went far for His illustrations. As a master of painting will make you, with a morsel of chalk or a brunt stick, a face at which you must laugh, or weep, or wonder, so Jesus took the commonest objects and incidents around Him—the sewing of a piece of cloth on an old garment, the bursting of an old bottle, the children playing in the marketplace at weddings and funerals, or the tumbling of a hut in a storm—to change them into perfect pictures and to make them the vehicles for conveying to the world immortal truth. No wonder the crowds followed Him! Even the simplest could delight in such pictures and carry away as a lifelong possession the expression at least of His ideas, though it might require the thought of centuries to pierce their crystalline depths. There never was speaking so simple yet so profound, so pictorial yet so absolutely true.

Such were the qualities of His style. The qualities of the preacher Himself have been preserved to us in the criticism of His hearers, and are manifest in the remains of His addresses which the Gospels contain.

The most prominent of them seems to have been Authority: "The people were astonished at His doctrine, for He taught them as one having authority, and not as the scribes." The first thing His hearers were struck with was the contrast between His words and the preaching which they were wont to hear from the scribes in the synagogues. These were the exponents of the deadest and direst system of theology that has ever passed in any age for religion. Instead of expounding the Scriptures, which were in their hands, and would have lent living power to their words, they retailed the opinions of commentators, and were afraid to advance any statement, unless it was backed by the authority of some master. Instead of dwelling on the great themes of justice and mercy, love and God, they tortured the sacred text into a ceremonial manual, and preached on the proper breadth of phylacteries, the proper postures for prayer, the proper length of fasts, the distance which might be walked on the Sabbath, and so forth; for in these things the religion of the time consisted. In order to see anything in modern times at all like the preaching which then prevailed, we must go back to the Reformation period, when, as the historian of Knox tells us, the harangues delivered by the monks were empty, ridiculous, and wretched in the extreme. "Legendary tales concerning the founder of some religious order, the miracles he performed, his combats with the devil, his watchings, fastings, flagellations; the virtues of holy water, chrism, crossing, and exorcism; the horrors of purgatory, and the numbers released from it by the intercessions of some powerful saint—these, with low jests, table talk, and fireside scandal, formed the favorite topics of the preachers, and were served up to the people instead of the pure, salutary, and sublime doctrines of the Bible." Perhaps the contrast which the Scottish people three and half centuries ago felt between such harangues and the noble words of Wishart and Knox, may convey to our mind as good an idea as can be got of the effect of the preaching of Jesus on His contemporaries. He knew nothing of the authority of masters and schools of interpretation, but spoke as One whose own eyes had gazed on the objects of the eternal world. He needed none to tell Him of God or of man, for He knew both perfectly. He was possessed with the sense of a mission, which drove Him on and imparted earnestness to every word and gesture. He knew Himself sent from God, and the words He spoke to be not His own, but God's. He did not hesitate to tell those who neglected His words that in the judgment they would be condemned by the Ninevites and the Queen of Sheba, who had listened to Jonah and Solomon, for they were hearing One greater than any prophet or king of the olden time. He warned them that on their acceptance or rejection of the message He bore would depend their future weal or woe. This was the tone of earnestness, of majesty and authority that smote His hearers with awe.

Another quality which the people remarked in Him was Boldness: "Lo, He speaketh boldly." This appeared the more wonderful because He was an unlettered man, who had not passed through the schools of Jerusalem or received the imprimatur of any earthly authority. But this quality came from the same source as His authoritativeness. Timidity usually springs from self-consciousness. The preacher who is afraid of his audience, and respects the persons of the learned and the great, is thinking of himself and of what will be said of his performance. But he who feels himself driven on by a divine mission forgets himself. All audiences are alike to him, be they gentle or simple; he is thinking only of the message he has to deliver. Jesus was ever looking the spiritual and eternal realities in the face; the spell of their greatness held Him, and all human distinctions disappeared in their presence; men of every class were only men to Him. He was borne along on the torrent of His mission, and what might happen to Himself could not make Him stop to question or quail. He discovered His boldness chiefly in attacking the abuses and ideals of the time. It would be a complete mistake to think of Him as all mildness and meekness. There is scarcely any element more conspicuous in His words than a strain of fierce indignation. It was an age of shams above almost any that have ever been. They occupied all high places. They paraded themselves in social life, occupied the chairs of learning, and above all debased every part of religion. Hypocrisy had become so universal that it had ceased even to doubt itself. The ideals of the people were utterly mean and mistaken. One can feel throbbing through His words, from first to last, an indignation against all this, which had begun with His earliest observation in Nazareth and ripened with His increasing knowledge of the times. The things which were highly esteemed among men, He broadly asserted, were abomination in the sight of God. There never was in the history of speech a polemic so scathing, so annihilating, as His against the figures to which the reverence of the multitude had been paid before His withering words fell on them—the scribe, the Pharisees, the priest, and the Levite.

A third quality which His hearers remarked was Power: "His word was with power." This was the result of that unction of the Holy One, without which even the most solemn truths fall on the ear without effect. He was filled with the Spirit without measure. Therefore the truth possessed Him. It burned and swelled in His own bosom, and He spoke it forth from heart to heart. He had the Spirit not only in such degree as to fill Himself, but so as to be able to impart it to others. It overflowed with His words and seized the souls of His hearers, filling with enthusiasm the mind and the heart.

A fourth quality which was observed in His preaching, and was surely a very prominent one, was Graciousness: "They wondered at the gracious words which proceeded out of His mouth." In spite of His tone of authority and His fearless and scathing attacks on the times, there was diffused over all He said a glow of grace and love. Here especially His character spoke. How could He who was the incarnation of love help letting the glow and warmth of the heavenly fire that dwelt in Him spread over His words? The scribes of the time were hard, proud, and loveless. They flattered the rich and honored the learned, but of the great mass of their hearers they said, "This people, which knoweth not the law, is cursed." But to Jesus every soul was infinitely precious. It mattered not under what humble dress or social deformity the pearl was hidden; it mattered not even beneath what rubbish and filth of sin it was buried; He never missed it for a moment. Therefore He spoke to His hearers of every grade with the same respect. Surely it was the divine love itself, uttering itself from the innermost recess of the divine being, that spoke in the parables of the fifteenth of Luke.

Such were some of the qualities of the Preacher. And one more may be mentioned, which may be said to embrace all the rest, and is perhaps the highest quality of public speech. He addressed men as men, not as members of any class or possessors of any peculiar culture. The differences which divide men, such as wealth, rank, and education, are on the surface. The elements in which they are all alike—the broad sense of the understanding, the great passions of the heart, the primary instincts of the conscience—are profound. Not that these are the same in all men. In some they are deeper, in others shallower, but in all they are far deeper than aught else. He who addresses them appeals to the deepest thing in His hearers. He will be equally intelligible to all. Every hearer will receive his own portion from Him; the small and shallow mind will get as much as it can take, and the largest and deepest will get its fill at the same feast. This is why the words of Jesus are perennial in their freshness. They are for all generations, and equally for all. They appeal to the deepest elements in human nature today in England or China as much as they did in Palestine when they were spoken.

When we come to inquire what the matter of Jesus' preaching consisted of, we perhaps naturally expect to find Him expounding the system of doctrine which we are ourselves acquainted with, in the forms, say, of the Catechism or the Confession of Faith. But what we find is very different. He did not make use of any system of doctrine. We can scarcely doubt, indeed, that all the numerous and varied ideas of His preaching, as well as those which He never expressed, coexisted in His mind as one world of rounded truth. But they did not so coexist in His teaching. He did not use theological phraseology, speaking of the Trinity, of predestination, of effectual calling, although the ideas which these terms cover underlay His words, and it is the undoubted task of science to bring them forth. But He spoke in the language of life, and concentrated His preaching on a few burning points, that touched the heart, the conscience and the time.

The central idea and the commonest phrase of His preaching was "the kingdom of God." It will be remembered how many of His parables begin with "The kingdom of Heaven is like," so and so. He said, "I must preach the kingdom of God to other cities also," thereby characterizing the matter of His preaching, and in the same way He is said to have sent forth the apostles "to preach the kingdom of God." He did not invent the phrase. It was a historical one handed down from the past, and was common in the mouths of His contemporaries. The Baptist had made large use of it, the burden of his message being, "The kingdom of God is at hand."

What did it signify? It meant the new era, which the prophets had predicted and the saints had looked for. Jesus announced that it had come, and that He had brought it. The time of waiting was fulfilled. Many prophets and righteous men, He told His contemporaries, had desired to see the things which they saw, but had not seen them. He declared that so great were the privileges and glories of the new time, that the least partaker of them was greater than the Baptist, though he had been the greatest representative of the old time.

All this was no more than His contemporaries would have expected to hear, if they had recognized that the kingdom of God was really come. But they looked around, and asked where the new era was which Jesus said He had brought. Here He and they were at complete variance. They emphasized the first part of the phrase, "the kingdom," He the second, "of God." They expected the new era to appear in magnificent material forms—in a kingdom of which God indeed was to be the ruler, but which was to show itself in worldly splendor, in force of arms, in a universal empire. Jesus saw the new era in an empire of God over the loving heart and the obedient will. They looked for it outside. He said, "It is within you." They looked for a period of external glory and happiness. He placed the glory and blessedness of the new time in character. So He began His Sermon on the Mount, that great manifesto of the new era, with a series of "Blesseds." But the blessedness was entirely that of character. And it was a character totally different from that which was then looked up to as imparting glory and happiness to its possessor—that of the proud Pharisee, the wealthy Sadducee, or the learned scribe. Blessed, said He, are the poor in spirit, they that mourn, the meek, they which do hunger and thirst after right-eousness, the merciful, the pure in heart, the peacemakers, they which are persecuted for righteousness' sake.

The main drift of His preaching was to set forth this conception of the kingdom of God, the character of its members, their blessedness in the love and communion of their Father in heaven, and their prospects in the glory of the future world. He exhibited the contrast be-tween it and the formal religion of the time, with its lack of spirituality and its substitution of ceremonial observances for character. He invited all classes into the kingdom—the rich by showing, as in the parable of the Rich Man and Lazarus, the vanity and danger of seeking their blessedness in wealth; and the poor by penetrating them with the sense of their dignity, persuading them with the most overflowing af-fection and winning words that the only true wealth was in character, and assuring them that, if they sought first the kingdom of God, their heavenly Father, who fed the ravens and clothed the lilies, would not suffer them to want.

But the center and soul of His preaching was Himself. He con-tained within Himself the new era. He not only announced it, but cre-ated it. The new character which made men subjects of the kingdom and sharers of its privileges was to be got from Him alone. Therefore the practical issue of every address of Christ was the command to come to Him, to learn of Him, to follow Him. "Come unto me, all ye that labor and are heavy laden," was the keynote, the deepest and final word of all His discourses.

It is impossible to read the discourses of Jesus without remarking that, wonderful as they are, yet some of the most characteristic doctrines of Christianity, as it is set forth in the epistles of Paul and now cherished in the minds of the most devoted and enlightened Christians, hold a very inconsiderable place in them. Especially is this the case in regard to the great doctrines of the gospel as to how a sinner is reconciled to God, and how, in a pardoned soul, the character is gradually pro-duced which makes it like Christ and pleasing to the Father. The lack of reference to such doctrines may indeed be much exagger-ated, the fact being that there is not one prominent doctrine of the great apostle the germs of which are not to be found in the teaching of Christ

Himself. Yet the contrast is marked enough to have given some color for denying that the distinctive doctrines of Paul are genuine elements of Christianity. But the true explanation of the phenomenon is very different. Jesus was not a mere teacher. His character was greater than His words, and so was His work. The chief part of that work was to atone for the sins of the world by His death on the cross. But His nearest followers never would believe that he was to die, and, until His death happened, it was impossible to explain its far-reaching significance. Paul's most distinctive doctrines are merely expositions of the meaning of two great facts—the death of Christ, and the mission of the Spirit by the glorified Redeemer. It is obvious that these facts could not be fully explained in the words of Jesus Himself, when they had not yet taken place, but to suppress the inspired explanation of them would be to extinguish the light of the gospel and rob Christ of His crowning glory.

The audience of Jesus varied exceedingly both in size and character on different occasions. Very frequently it was the great multitude. He addressed them everywhere—on the mountain, on the seashore, on the highway, in the synagogues, in the temple courts. But He was quite as willing to speak with a single individual, however humble. He seized every opportunity of doing so. Although He was worn out with fatigue, He talked to the woman at the well; He received Nicodemus alone; He taught Mary in her home. There are said to be nineteen such private interviews mentioned in the Gospels. They leave to His followers a memorable example. This is perhaps the most effective of all forms of instruction, as it is certainly the best test of earnestness. A man who preaches to thousands with enthusiasm may be a mere orator, but the man who seeks the opportunity of speaking closely of the welfare of their souls to individuals must have a real fire from heaven burning in his heart.

Often His audience consisted of the circle of His disciples. His preaching divided His hearers. He has Himself, in such parables as the Sower, the Tares and the Wheat, the Wedding Feast, and so forth, described with unequaled vividness its effects on different classes. Some it utterly repelled; others heard it with wonder, without being touched in the heart; others were affected for a time, but soon returned to their old interests. It is terrible to think how few there were, even when the son of God was preaching, who heard unto salvation. Those who did so, gradually formed around Him a body of disciples. They followed Him about hearing all his discourses, and often He spoke to them alone. Such were the five hundred to whom He appeared in Galilee after His resurrection. Some of them were women, such as Mary Magdalene, Susanna, and Joanna the wife of Herod's steward, who, being wealthy, gladly supplied His few simple wants. To these disciples He gave a more thorough instruction than to the crowd. He explained to them in private whatever was obscure in His public teaching. More than once He made the strange statement that He spoke in parables to the multitudes in order that, though hearing, they might not understand. This could only mean, that those who had no real interest in the truth were sent away with the mere beautiful shell but that the obscurity was intended to provoke to further inquiry, as a veil half drawn over a beautiful face intensifies the desire to see it; and to those who had a spiritual craving for more, He gladly communicated the hidden secret. These, when the nation as a whole declared itself unworthy of being the medium of the Messiah's worldwide influence, became the nucleus of that spiritual society, elevated above all local limitations and distinctions of rank and nationality, in which the spirit and doctrine of Christ were to be spread and perpetuated in the world.

The Apostolate

Perhaps the formation of the Apostolate ought to be placed side by side with miracles and preaching as a third means by which He did His work. The men who became the twelve apostles were at first only ordinary disciples like many others. This, at least, was the position of such of them as were already His followers during the first year of His ministry. At the opening of His Galilean activity, their attachment to Him entered on a second stage; He called them to give up their ordinary employments and be with Him constantly. And probably not many weeks afterwards, He promoted them to the third and final stage of nearness to Himself, by ordaining them to be apostles.

It was when His work grew so extensive and pressing that it was quite impossible for Him to overtake it all, that He multiplied Himself, so to speak, by appointing them his assistants. He commissioned them to teach the simpler elements of His doctrine, and conferred on them miraculous powers similar to His own. In this way many towns were evangelized which He had not time to visit, and many persons cured who could not have been brought into contact with Himself. But, as future events proved, His aims in their appointment were much more far-reaching. His work was for all time and for the whole world. It could not be accomplished in a single lifetime. He foresaw this, and made provision for it by the early choice of agents who might take up His plans after He was gone, and in whom He might still extend His influence over mankind. He Himself wrote nothing. It may be thought that writing would have been the best way of perpetuating His influence, and giving the world a perfect image of Himself; and we cannot help imagining with a glow of strong desire what a volume penned by His hand would have been. But for wise reasons He abstained from this kind of work and resolved to live after death in the lives of chosen men.

It is surprising to see what sort of persons He selected for so grand a destiny. They did not belong to the influential and learned classes. No doubt the heads and leaders of the nation ought to have been the organs of their Messiah, but they proved themselves totally unworthy of the great vocation. He was able to do without them; He needed not the influence of carnal power and wisdom. Ever wont to work with the elements of character that are not bound to any station of life or grade of culture, He did not scruple to commit His cause to twelve simple men, destitute of learning and belonging to the common people. He made the selection after a night spent in prayer, and doubtless after many days of deliberation. The event showed with what insight into character He had acted. They turned out to be instruments thoroughly fitted for the great design; two at least, John and Peter, were men of supreme gifts; and, though one turned out a traitor, and the choice of him will probably, after all explanations, ever remain a very partially explained mystery, yet the selection of agents who were at first so unlikely, but in the end proved so successful, will always be one of the chief monuments of the incomparable originality of Jesus.

It would, however, be a very inadequate account of His relation to the Twelve merely to point out the insight with which He discerned in them the germs of fitness for their grand future. They became very great men, and in the founding of the Christian Church achieved a work of immeasurable importance. They may be said, in a sense they little dreamed of, to sit on thrones ruling the modern world. They stand like a row of noble pillars towering far across the flats of time. But the sunlight that shines on them, and makes them visible, comes entirely from Him. He gave them all their greatness; and theirs is one of the most striking evidences of His. What must He have been whose influence imparted to them such magnitude of characters, and made them fit for so gigantic a task! At first they were rude and carnal in the extreme. What hope was there that they would ever be able to appreciate the designs of a mind like His, to inherit His work, to possess in any degree a spirit so exquisite, and transmit to future generations a faithful image of His character? But He educated them with the most affectionate patience, bearing with their vulgar hopes and their clumsy misunderstandings of His meaning. Never forgetting for a moment the part they were to play in the future, He made their training His most constant work. They were much more constantly in His company than even the general body of his disciples, seeing all He did in public and hearing all He said. They were often His only audience, and then he unveiled to them the glories and mysteries of His doctrine, sowing in their minds the seeds of truth, which time and experience were by and by to fructify. But the most important part of their training was one which was perhaps at the time little noticed, though it was producing splendid results—the silent and constant influence of His character on theirs. He drew them to Himself and stamped His own image on them. It was this which made them the men they became. For this, more than all else, the generations of those who love Him look back to them with envy. We admire and adore at a distance the qualities of His character, but what must it have been to see them in the unity of life, and for years to feel their molding pressure! Can we recall with any fullness the features of this character whose glory they beheld and under whose power they lived?

The Human Character of Jesus

Perhaps the most obvious feature which they would remark in Him was Purposefulness. This certainly is the ground tone which sounds in all His sayings which have been preserved to us, and the pulse which we feel beating in all His recorded actions. He was possessed with a purpose which guided and drove Him on. Most lives aim at nothing in particular, but drift along, under the influence of varying moods and instincts or on the currents of society, and achieve nothing. But Jesus evidently had a definite object before Him, which absorbed His thoughts and drew out His energies. He would often give as a reason for not doing something, "Mine hour is not yet come," as if His design absorbed every moment, and every hour had its own allotted part of the task. This imparted an earnestness and rapidity of execution to His life which most lives altogether lack. It saved Him, too, from that dispersion of energy on details, and carefulness about little things, on which those who obey no definite call throw themselves away, and made His life, various as were its activities, an unbroken unity.

Very closely connected with this quality was another prominent one, which may be called Faith, and by which is meant His astonishing confidence in the accomplishment of His purpose, and apparent disregard both of means and opposition. If it be considered in the most general way how vast His aim was—to reform His nation and begin an everlasting and worldwide religious movement; if the opposition which He encountered, and foresaw His cause would have to meet at every stage of its progress, be considered; and if it be remembered what, as a man, He was—an unlettered Galilean peasant—His quiet and unwavering confidence in His success will appear only less remarkable than His success itself. After reading the Gospels through, one asks in wonder what he did to produce so mighty an impression on the world. He constructed no elaborate machinery to ensure the effect, He did not lay hold of the centers of influence—learning, wealth, government, etc. It is true He instituted the Church. But He left no detailed explanations of its nature or rules for its constitution. This was the simplicity of faith, which does not contrive and prepare, but simply goes onward and does the work. It was the quality which He said could remove mountains, and which He chiefly desiderated in His followers. This was the foolishness of the gospel, of which Paul boasted, as it was going forth, in the recklessness of power, but with laughable meagerness of equipment, to overcome the Greek and Roman world.

A third prominent feature of His character was Originality. Most lives are easily explained. They are mere products of circumstances, and copies of thousands like them which surround or have preceded them. The habits and customs of the country to which we belong, the fashion and tastes of our generation, the traditions of our education, the prejudices of our class, the opinions of our school or sect—these form us. We do work determined for us by a fortuitous concourse of circumstances; our convictions are fixed on us by authority from without, instead of waxing naturally from within; our opinions are blown to us in fragments on every wind. But what circumstances made the Man Christ Jesus? There never was an age more dry and barren than that in which He was born. He was like a tall, fresh palm springing out of a desert. What was there in the petty life of Nazareth to produce so gigantic a character? How could the notoriously wicked village send forth such breathing purity? It may have been that a scribe taught Him the vocables and grammar of knowledge, but His doctrine was a complete contradiction of all that the scribes taught. The fashions of the sects never laid hold of his free spirit. How clearly, amidst the sounds which filled the ears of His time, He heard the neglected voice of truth, which was quite different from them! How clearly, behind all the pretentious and accepted forms of piety, He saw the lovely and neglected figure of real godliness! He cannot be explained by anything which was in the world and might have produced Him. He grew from within. He directed His eyes straight on the facts of nature and life and believed what He saw, instead of allowing His vision to be tutored by what others had said they saw. He was equally loyal to the truth in His words. He went forth and spoke out without hesitation what He believed, though it shook to their foundations the institutions, the creeds, and customs of His country, and loosened the opinions of the populace in a hundred points in which they had been educated. It may, indeed, be said that, though the Jewish nation of His own time was an utterly dry ground, out of which no green and great thing could be expected to grow, He reverted to the earlier history of His nation and nourished His mind on the ideas of Moses and the prophets. There is some truth in this. But affectionate and constant as was His familiarity with them, He handled them with a free and fearless hand. He redeemed them from themselves and exhibited in perfection the ideas which they taught only in germ. What a contrast between the covenant God of Israel and the Father in heaven whom He revealed; between the temple, with its priests and bloody sacrifices, and the worship in spirit and in truth; between the national and ceremonial morality of the Law and the morality of the conscience and the heart! Even in comparison with the figures of Moses, Elijah, and Isaiah, He towers aloft in lonely originality.

A fourth and very glorious feature of His character was Love to Men. It has been already said that He was possessed with an over-mastering purpose. But beneath a great life-purpose there must be a great passion, which shapes and sustains it. Love to men was the passion which directed and inspired Him. How it sprang up and grew in the seclusion of Nazareth, and on what materials it fed, we have not been informed with any detail. We only know that, when He appeared in public, it was a master-passion, which completely swallowed up self-love, filled Him with boundless pity for human misery, and enabled Him to go forward without once looking back in the undertaking to which He devoted Himself. We know only in general that it drew its support from the conception He had of the infinite value of the human soul. It overleapt all the limits which other men have put to their benevolence. Differences of class and nationality usually cool men's interest in each other; in nearly all countries it has been considered a virtue to hate enemies; and it is generally agreed to loathe and avoid those who have outraged the laws of respectability. But He paid no heed to these conventions; the overpowering sense of the preciousness which He perceived in enemy, foreigner, and outcast alike, forbade Him. This marvelous love shaped the purpose of His life. It gave Him the most tender and intense sympathy with every form of pain and misery. It was His deepest reason for adopting the calling of a healer. Wherever help was most needed, thither His merciful heart drew Him. But it was especially to save the soul that His love impelled

Him. He knew this was the real jewel, which everything should be done to rescue, and that its miseries and perils were the most dangerous of all. There has sometimes been love to others without this vital aim. But His love was directed by wisdom to the truest weal of those He loved. He knew He was doing His very best for them when He was saving them from their sins.

But the crowning attribute of His human character was Love to God. It is the supreme honor and attainment of man to be one with God in feeling, thought, and purpose. Jesus had this in perfection. To us it is very difficult to realize God. The mass of men scarcely think about Him at all; and even the godliest confess that it costs them severe effort to discipline their minds into the habit of constantly realizing Him. When we do think of Him, it is with a painful sense of a disharmony between what is in us and what is in Him. We cannot remain, even for a few minutes, in His presence without the sense in greater or less degree, that His thoughts are not our thoughts, nor His ways our ways. With Jesus it was not so. He realized God always. He never spent an hour, He never did an action, without direct reference to Him. God was about Him like the atmosphere He breathed, or the sunlight in which He walked. His thoughts were God's thoughts; His desires were never in the least different from God's; His purpose, He was perfectly sure, was God's purpose for Him. How did He attain this absolute harmony with God? To a large extent it must be attributed to the perfect harmony of His nature within itself, yet in some measure He got it by the same means by which we laboriously seek it—by the study of God's thoughts and purposes in His Word, which, from His childhood, was His constant delight; by cultivating all His life long the habit of prayer, for which He found time even when He had not time to eat; and by patiently resisting temptations to entertain thoughts and purposes of His own different from God's. This it was given which gave Him such faith and fearlessness in His work; He knew that the call to do it had come from God, and that He was immortal till it was done. This was what made Him, with all His self-consciousness and originality, the pattern of meekness and submission; for He was forever bringing every thought and wish into obedience to His Father's will. This was the secret of the peace and majestic calmness which imparted such a grandeur to His demeanor in the most trying hours of life. He knew that the worst that could happen to Him was His Father's will for Him; and this was enough. He had ever at hand a retreat of perfect rest, silence, and sunshine, into which He could retire from the clamor and confusion around Him. This was the great secret He bequeathed to His followers, when He said to them at parting, "Peace I leave with you; *My* peace I give unto you."

The Sinlessness of Jesus has been often dwelt on as the crowning attribute of His character. The Scriptures, which so frankly record the errors of their very greatest heroes, such as Abraham and Moses, have no sins of His to record. There is no more prominent characteristic of the saints of antiquity than their penitence: the more supremely saintly they were, the more abundant and bitter were their tears and lamentations over their sinfulness. But although it is acknowledged by all that Jesus was the supreme religious figure of history, He never exhibited this characteristic of saintliness; He confessed no sin. Must it not have been because He had no sin to confess? Yet the idea of sinlessness is too negative to express the perfection of his character. He was sinless, but He was so because He was absolutely full of love. Sin against God is merely the expression of lack of love to God, and sin against man of lack of love to man. A being quite full of love to both God and man cannot possibly sin against either. This fullness of love to His Father and His fellowmen, ruling every expression of His being, constituted the perfection of His character.

To the impression produced on them by their long-continued contact with their Master, the Twelve owed all they became. We cannot trace with any fullness at what time they began to realize the central truth of the Christianity they were afterwards to publish to the world, that behind the tenderness and majesty of this human character there was in Him something still more august, or by what stages their impressions ripened to the full conviction that in Him perfect manhood was in union with perfect Deity. This was the goal of all the revelations of Himself which He made to them. But the breakdown of their faith at His death shows how immature up till that time must have been their convictions in regard to His personality, however worthily they were able, in certain happy hours, to express their faith in Him.

It was the experience of the Resurrection and Ascension which gave to the fluid impressions, which had long been accumulating in their minds, the touch by which they were made to crystallize into the immovable conviction, that in Him with whom it had been vouchsafed to them to associate so intimately, God was manifest in the flesh.

6

The Year of Opposition

FOR a whole year Jesus pursued His work in Galilee with incessant energy, moving among the pitiable crowds that solicited His miraculous help, and seizing every opportunity of pouring His words of grace and truth into the ears of the multitude or of the solitary anxious inquirer. In hundreds of homes, to whose inmates He had restored health and joy, His name must have become a household word; in thousands of minds, whose depths His preaching had stirred, He must have been cherished with gratitude and love. Wider and wider rang the echoes of His fame. For a time it seemed as if all Galilee were to become His disciples, and as if the movement so set agoing might easily roll southward, overbearing all opposition, and enveloping the whole land in an enthusiasm of love for the Healer and of obedience to the Teacher.

But the twelve months had scarcely passed when it became sadly evident that this was not to be. The Galilean mind turned out to be stony ground, where the seed of the kingdom rushed quickly up, but just as quickly withered away. The change was sudden and complete, and at once altered all the features of the life of Jesus. He lingered in Galilee for six months longer, but these months were very unlike the first twelve. The voices that rose around Him were no longer the ringing shouts of gratitude and applause, but voices of opposition, bitter and blasphemous. He was no longer to be seen moving from one populous place to another in the heart of the country, welcomed everywhere by those who waited to experience or to see His miracles, and followed by thousands eager not to lose a word of His discourses. He was a fugitive, seeking the most distant and outlandish places, and accompanied only by a handful of followers. At the six months' end He left Galilee forever, but not, as might at one time have been anticipated, borne aloft on the wave of public acknowledgment, to make an easy conquest of the hearts of the southern part of the country, and take victorious possession of a Jerusalem unable to resist the unanimous voice of the people. He did indeed labor for six months more in the southern part of the land—in Judea and Perea; nor were they wanting, where His miracles were seen for the first time, the same signs of public enthusiasm as had greeted Him in the first months of joy in Galilee; but the most which He effected was to add a few to the company of His faithful disciples. He did indeed, from the day He left Galilee, set His face steadfastly towards Jerusalem; and the six months He spent in Perea and Judea may be regarded as occupied with a slow journey thither; but the journey was begun in the full assurance, which He openly expressed to the disciples, that in the capital He was to receive no triumph over enthusiastic hearts and minds convinced, but meet with a final national rejection, and be killed instead of crowned.

We must trace the cause and the progress of this change in the sentiment of the Galileans, and this sad turn in the career of Jesus.

From the very first the learned and influential classes had taken up an attitude of opposition to Him. The more worldly sections of them, indeed—the Sadducees and Herodians—for a long time paid little attention to Him. They had their own affairs to mind—their wealth, their court influence, their amusements. They cared little for a religious movement going on among the lower orders. The public rumor that one professing to be the Messiah had appeared did not excite their interest, for they did not share the popular expectations on the subject. They said to each other that this was only one more of the pretenders whom the peculiar ideas of the populace were sure to raise up from time to time. It was only when the movement seemed to them to be threatening to lead to a political revolt, which would bring down the iron hand of the Roman masters on the country, afford the Procurator an excuse for new extortions, and imperil their property and comforts, that they roused themselves to pay any attention to Him.

Very different was it, however, with the more religious sections of the upper class—the Pharisees and scribes. They took the deepest interest in all ecclesiastical and religious phenomena. A movement of a religious kind among the populace excited their eager attention, for they themselves aimed at popular influence. A new voice with the ring of prophecy in it, or the promulgation of any new doctrine or tenet, caught their ear at once. But, above all, anyone putting himself forward as the Messiah produced the utmost ferment among them; for they ardently cherished Messianic hopes, and were at the time smarting keenly under the foreign domination. In relation to the rest of the community, they corresponded to our clergy and leading religious laymen, and probably formed about the same proportion of the population, and exercised at least as great an influence as these do among us. It has been estimated that they may have numbered about six thousand. They passed for the best persons in the country, the conservators of respectability and orthodoxy; and the masses looked up to them as those who had the right to judge and determine in all religious matters.

They cannot be accused of having neglected Jesus. They turned their earnest attention to Him from the first. They followed Him step by step. They discussed His doctrines and His claims, and made up their minds. Their decision was adverse, and they followed it up with acts, never becoming remiss in their activity for an hour.

This is perhaps the most solemn and appalling circumstance in the whole tragedy of the life of Christ, that the men who rejected, hunted down, and murdered Him, were those reputed the best in the nation, its teachers and examples, the zealous conservators of the Bible and the traditions of the past—men who were eagerly waiting for the Messiah, who judged Jesus, as they believed, according to the Scriptures and thought they were obeying the dictates of conscience and doing God service when they treated Him as they did. There cannot fail sometimes to sweep across the mind of a reader of the Gospels a strong feeling of pity for them, and a kind of sympathy with them. Jesus was so unlike the Messiah whom they were looking for and their fathers had taught them to expect! He so completely traversed their prejudices and maxims, and dishonored so many things which they had been taught to regard as sacred! They may surely be pitied; there never was a crime like their crime, and there was never punishment like their punishment. There is the same sadness about the fate of those who are thrown upon any great crisis of the world's history, and, not understanding the signs of the times, make fatal mistakes; as those did, for example, who at the Reformation were unable to go forth and join the march of Providence.

Yet, at bottom, what was their case? It was just this, that they were so blinded with sin that they could not discern the light. Their views of the Messiah had been distorted by centuries of worldliness and unspirituality, of which they were the like-minded heirs. They thought Jesus a sinner, because He did not conform to ordinances which they and their fathers had profanely added to those of God's Word, and because their conception of a good man, to whom He did not answer, was utterly false. Jesus supplied them with evidence enough, but He could not give them eyes to see it. There is a something at the bottom of hearts that are honest and true, which, however long and deeply it may have been buried under prejudice and sin, leaps up with joy and desire to embrace what is true, what is reverend, what is pure and great, when it draws near. But nothing of the kind was found in them; their hearts were scared, hardened, and dead. They brought their stock rules and arbitrary standards to judge Him by, and were never shaken by His greatness from the fatal attitude of criticism. He brought truth near them, but they had not the truth-loving ear to recognize the enchanting sound. He brought the whitest purity, such as archangels would have veiled their faces at, near them, but they were not overawed. He brought near them the very face of mercy and heavenly love, but their dim eyes made no response. We may indeed pity the conduct of such men as an appalling misfortune, but it is better to fear and tremble at it as appalling guilt. The more utterly wicked men become, the more inevitable it is that they should sin; the vaster the mass of a nation's sin becomes, as it rolls down through the centuries, the more inevitable does some awful national crime become. But when the inevitable takes place, it is an object not for pity only, but also for holy and jealous wrath.

One thing about Jesus which from the first excited their opposition to Him was the humbleness of His origin. Their eyes were dazzled with the ordinary prejudices of the rich and the learned, and could not discern the grandeur of the soul apart from the accidents of position and culture. He was a son of the people; He had been a carpenter; they believed He had been born in rude and wicked Galilee; He had not passed through the schools of Jerusalem or drunk at the acknowledged wells of wisdom there. They thought that a prophet, and above all the Messiah, should have been born in Judea, reared at Jerusalem in the center of culture and religion, and allied with all that was distinguished and influential in the nation.

For the same reason they were offended with the followers He chose and the company He kept. His chosen organs were not selected from among themselves, the wise and high-born, but were uneducated laymen, poor fishermen. Nay, one of them was a publican. Nothing that Jesus did, perhaps, gave greater offense than the choice of Matthew, the tax gatherer, to be an apostle. The tax gatherers, as servants of the alien power, were hated by all who were patriotic and respectable, at once for their trade, their extortions, and their character. How could Jesus hope that respectable and learned men should enter a circle such as that which He had formed about Himself? Besides, He mingled freely with the lowest class of the population—with publicans, harlots, and sinners. In Christian times we have learned to love Him for this more than anything else. We easily see that, if He really was the Savior from sin, He could not have been found in more suitable company than among those who needed salvation most. We know now how He could believe that many of the lost were more the victims of circumstances than sinners by choice, and that, if He drew the magnet across the top of the rubbish, it would attract to itself many a piece of precious metal. The purest minded and highest born have since learned to follow His footsteps down into the purlieus of squalor and vice to seek and save the lost. But no such sentiment had up till His time been born into the world. The mass of sinners outside the pale of respectability were despised and hated as the enemies of society, and no efforts were made to save them. On the contrary, all who aimed at religious distinction avoided their very touch as a defilement. Simon the Pharisee, when he was entertaining Jesus, never doubted that, if He had been a prophet and known who the woman was who was touching Him, He would have driven her off. Such was the sentiment of the time. Yet when Jesus brought into the world the new sentiment, and showed them the divine face of mercy, they ought to have recognized it. If their hearts had not been utterly hard and cruel, they would have leaped up to welcome this revelation of a diviner humanity. The sight of sinners forsaking their evil ways, of wicked women sobbing for their lost lives, and extortioners like Zaccheus becoming earnest and generous, ought to have delighted them. But it did not, and they only hated Jesus for His compassion, calling Him a friend of publicans and sinners.

A third and very serious ground of their opposition was, that He did not Himself practice, nor encourage His disciples to practice, many ritual observances, such as fasts, punctilious washing of the hands before meals, and so forth, which were then considered the marks of a saintly man. It had been already explained how these practices arose. They had been invented in an earnest but mechanical age in order to emphasize the peculiarities of Jewish character, and keep up the separation of the Jews from other nations. The original intention was good, but the result was deplorable. It was soon forgotten that they were merely human inventions; they were supposed to be binding by divine action; and they were multiplied, till they regulated every hour of the day and every action of life. They were made the substitutes for real piety and morality by the majority; and to tender consciences they were an intolerable burden, for it was scarcely possible to move a step or lift a finger without the danger of sinning against one or other of them. But no one doubted their authority, and the careful observance of them was reputed the badge of a godly life. Jesus regarded them as the great evil of the time. He therefore neglected them, and encouraged others to do so; not, however, without at the same time leading them back to the great principles of judgment, mercy, and faith, and making them feel the majesty of the conscience and the depth and spirituality of the law. But the result was, that He was looked upon as both an ungodly man Himself, and a deceiver of the people.

It was especially in regard to the Sabbath that this difference between Him and the religious teachers came out. In this field their inventions of restrictions and arbitrary rules had run into the most portentous extravagance, till they had changed the day of rest, joy, and blessing into an intolerable burden. He was in the habit of performing His cures on the Sabbath. They thought such work a breach of the command. He exposed the wrongness of their objections again and again, by explaining the nature of the institution itself as "made for man," by reference to the practice of ancient saints, and even by the analogy of some of their own practices on the holy day. But they were not convinced; and, as He continued His practice in spite of their objections, this remained a standing and bitter ground of their hatred.

It will be easily understood that, having arrived at these conclusions on such low grounds, they were utterly disinclined to listen to Him when He put forward His higher claims—when He announced Himself as the Messiah, professed to forgive sins, and threw out intimations of His high relation to God. Having concluded that He was an impostor and deceiver, they regarded such assertions as hideous blasphemies, and could not help wishing to stop the mouth which uttered them.

It "may cause surprise," that they were not convinced by His miracles. If He really performed the numerous and stupendous miracles which are recorded of Him, how could they resist such evidence of his divine mission? The debate held with the authorities by the tough reasoner whom Jesus cured of blindness, and whose case is recorded in the ninth chapter of John, shows how sorely they may sometimes have been pressed with such reasoning. But they had satisfied themselves with an audacious reply to it. It is to be remembered that among the Jews miracles had never been looked upon as conclusive proofs of a divine mission. They might be wrought by false as well as true prophets. They might be traceable to diabolical instead of divine agency. Whether they were so or not, was to be determined on other grounds. On these other grounds they had come to the conclusion that He had not been sent from God; and so they attributed His miracles to an alliance with the powers of darkness. Jesus met this blasphemous construction with the utmost force of holy indignation and conclusive argument, but it is easy to see that it was a position in which minds like those of His opponents might entrench themselves with the sense of much security.

Very early they had formed their adverse judgment of Him, and they never changed it. Even during His first year in Judea they had pretty well decided against Him. When the news of His success in

Galilee spread, it filled them with consternation, and they sent deputations from Jerusalem to act in concert with their local adherents in opposing Him. Even during His year of joy He clashed with them again and again. At first He treated them with consideration and appealed to their reason and heart. But He soon saw that this was hopeless and accepted their opposition as inevitable. He exposed the hollowness of their pretensions to His audiences and warned His disciples against them. Meanwhile they did everything to poison the public mind against Him. They succeeded only too well. When at the year's end, the tide of His popularity began to recede, they pressed their advantage, assailing Him more and more boldly.

They even succeeded thus early in arousing the cold minds of the Sadducees and Herodians against Him, no doubt by persuading them that he was fomenting a popular revolt, which would endanger the throne of their master Herod, who reigned over Galilee. That mean and characterless prince himself also became His persecutor. He had other reasons to dread Him besides those suggested by his courtiers. About this very time he had murdered John the Baptist. It was one of the meanest and foulest crimes recorded in history, an awful instance of the way in which sin leads to sin, and of the malicious perseverance with which a wicked woman will compass her revenge. Soon after it was committed, his courtiers came to tell him of the supposed political designs of Jesus. But when he heard of the new prophet, an awful thought thrilled through his guilty conscience. "It is John the Baptist," he cried, "whom I beheaded; he is risen from the dead." Yet he desired to see Him, his curiosity getting the better of his terror. It was the desire of the lion to see the lamb. Jesus never responded to his invitation. But just on that account Herod may have been the more willing to listen to the suggestions of his courtiers that he should arrest Him as a dangerous person. It was not long before he was seeking to kill Him. Jesus had to keep out of his way, and no doubt this helped along with more important things to change the character of His life in Galilee during the last six months of His stay there.

It had seemed for a time as if His hold on the mind and the heart of the common people might become so strong as to carry irresistibly a national recognition. Many a movement, frowned upon at first by authorities and dignitaries, has, by committing itself to the lower classes and securing their enthusiastic acknowledgment, risen to take possession of the upper classes and carry the centers of influence. There is a certain point of national consent at which any movement which reaches it becomes like a flood, which no amount of prejudice or official dislike can successfully oppose. Jesus gave Himself to the common people of Galilee, and they gave Him in return their love and admiration. Instead of hating Him like the Pharisees and scribes, and calling Him a glutton and a wine-bibber, they believed Him a prophet; they compared Him with the very greatest figures of the past, and many, according as they were more struck with the sublime or with the melting side of His teaching, said He was Isaiah or Jeremiah risen from the dead. It was a common idea of the time that the coming of the Messiah was to be preceded by the rising again of some prophet. The one most commonly thought of was Elijah. Accordingly some took Jesus for Elijah. But it was only a precursor of the Messiah they supposed Him to be, not the Messiah Himself. He was not at all like their conception of the coming Deliverer, which was of the most grossly material kind. Now and then, indeed, after He had wrought some unusually striking miracle, there might be raised a single voice or a few voices, suggesting, Is this not He? But, wonderful as were His deeds and His words, yet the whole aspect of His life was so unlike their preconceptions, that the truth failed to suggest itself forcibly and universally to their minds.

At last, however, the decisive hour seemed to have arrived. It was just at that great turning point to which allusion has frequently been made—the end of the twelve months in Galilee. Jesus had heard of the Baptist's death, and immediately hurried away into a desert place with His disciples, to brood and talk over the tragic event. He sailed to the eastern side of the lake, and, landing on the grassy plain of Bethsaida, went up to a hill with the Twelve. But soon at its feet there gathered an immense multitude to hear and see Him. They found out where He was, and gathered to Him from every quarter. Ever ready to sacrifice Himself for others, He descended to address and heal them. The evening came on, as His discourse prolonged itself, when, moved with a great access of compassion for the helpless multitude, He wrought the stupendous miracle of feeding the five thousand. Its effect was overwhelming. They became instantaneously convinced that This was none other than the Messiah, and, having only one conception of what this meant, they endeavored to take Him by force and make Him a king; that is, to force Him to become the leader of a Messianic revolt, by which they might wrest the throne from Caesar and the princelings he had set up over the different provinces.

It seemed the crowning hour of success. But to Jesus Himself it was an hour of sad and bitter shame. This was all that His year's work had come to! This was the conception they yet had of Him! And they were to determine the course of His future action, instead of humbly asking what He would have them to do! He accepted it as the decisive indication of the effect of His work in Galilee. He saw how shallow were its results. Galilee had judged itself unworthy of being the center from which His kingdom might extend itself to the rest of the land. He fled from their carnal desires, and the very next day, meeting them again at Capernaum, He told them how much they had been mistaken in Him; they were looking for a Bread-king, who would give them idleness and plenty, mountains of loaves, rivers of milk, every comfort without labor. What He had to give was the bread of eternal life.

His discourse was like a stream of cold water directed upon the fiery enthusiasm of the crowd. From that hour His cause in Galilee was doomed; "many of His disciples went back and walked no more with Him." It was what He intended. It was Himself who struck the fatal blow at His popularity. He resolved to devote Himself thenceforward to the few who really understood Him and were capable of being the adherents of a spiritual enterprise.

The Changed Aspect of His Ministry

Yet, although the people of Galilee at large had shown themselves unworthy of Him, there was a considerable remnant that proved true. At the center of it were the apostles, but there were also others, to the number probably of several hundreds. These now became the objects of His special care. He had saved them as brands plucked from the burning, when Galilee as a whole deserted Him. For them it must have been a time of crucial trial. Their views were to a large extent those of the populace. They also expected a Messiah of worldly splendor. They had indeed learned to include deeper and more spiritual elements in their conception, but, along with these, it still contained the traditional and material ones. It must have been a painful mystery to them that Jesus should so long delay the assumption of the crown. So painful had this been to the Baptist in his lonely prison, that he began to doubt whether the vision he had seen on the bank of the Jordan and the great convictions of his life had not been delusions, and sent to ask Jesus if He really was the Christ. The Baptist's death must have been an awful shock to them. If Jesus was the Mighty One they thought Him, how could He allow His friend to come to such an end? Still they held on to Him. They showed what it was which kept them by their answer to Him, when, after the dispersion which followed the discourse at Capernaum, He put to them the sad question, "Will ye also go away?" They replied, "Lord, to whom shall we go? Thou hast the words of eternal life." Their opinions were not clear; they were in a mist of perplexities, but they knew that from Him they were getting eternal life. This held them close to Him, and made them willing to wait till He should make things clear.

During the last six months He spent in Galilee, He abandoned to a large extent His old work of preaching and miracle-working, and devoted Himself to the instruction of those adherents. He made long circuits with them in the most distant parts of the province, avoiding publicity as much as possible. Thus we find Him at Tyre and Sidon, far to the northwest; at Caesarea-Philippi, on the far northeast: and in Decapolis, to the south and east of the lake. These journeys, or rather flights, were due partly to the bitter opposition of the Pharisees, partly to fear of Herod, but chiefly to the desire to be alone with His disciples. The precious result of them was seen in an incident which happened at Caesarea-Philippi. Jesus began to ask His disciples what were the popular views about Himself and they told Him the various conjectures which were flying about, that He was a prophet, that He was Elias, that He was John the Baptist, and so on. "But whom say ye that I am?" He asked; and Peter answered for them all, "Thou art the Christ, the Son of the living God." This was the deliberate and decisive conviction by which they were determined to abide, whatever might come.

Jesus received the confession with great joy, and at once recognized in those who had made it the nucleus of the future Church, which was to be built on the truth to which they had given expression.

But this attainment only prepared them for a new trial of faith. From that time, we are told, He began to inform them of His approaching sufferings and death. These now stood out clearly before His own mind as the only issue of His career to be looked for. He had hinted as much to them before, but, with that delicate and loving consideration which always graduated His teaching to their capacity, He did not refer to it often. But now they were in some degree able to bear it; and, as it was inevitable and near at hand, He kept insisting on it constantly. But they themselves tell us they did not in the least understand Him. In common with all their countrymen, they expected a Messiah who should sit on the throne of David, and of whose reign there should be no end. They believed Jesus was this Messiah; and it was to them utterly incomprehensible that, instead of reigning, He should be killed on His arrival in Jerusalem. They listened to Him, they discussed His words among themselves, but they regarded their apparent meaning as a wild impossibility. They thought He was only using one of the parabolic sayings of which He was so fond, His real meaning being that the present lowly form of His work was to die and disappear, and His cause rise, as it were, out of the grave in a glorious and triumphant shape. He endeavored to undeceive them, going more and more minutely into the details of His approaching sufferings. But their minds could not take the truth in. How completely even the best of them failed to do so is shown by the frequent wranglings among them at this period as to which of them should in the approaching kingdom be the greatest, and by the request of Salome for her sons, that they should sit the one on the right and the other on the left hand in His kingdom. When they left Galilee and went up towards Jerusalem, it was with the conviction that "the kingdom of God should immediately appear," that is, that Jesus, on arriving in the capital, would throw off the guise of humiliation He had hitherto worn, and, overcoming all opposition by some forthputting of His concealed glory, take His place on the throne of His fathers.

What were the thoughts and feelings of Jesus Himself during this year? To Him also it was a year of sore trial. Now for the first time the deep lines of care and pain were traced upon His face. During the twelve months of successful work in Galilee, He was borne up with the joy of sustained achievement. But now He became, in the truest sense, the Man of Sorrows. Behind Him was His rejection by Galilee. The sorrow which He felt at seeing the ground on which He had bestowed so much labor turning out barren, is to be measured only by the greatness of His love to the souls He sought to save, and the depth of His devotion to His work. In front of Him was His rejection at Jerusalem. That was now certain; it rose up and stood out constantly and unmistakably, meeting His eyes as often as He turned them to the future. It absorbed His thoughts. It was a terrible prospect; and now that it drew nigh, it sometimes shook His soul with a conflict of feelings which we scarcely dare to picture to ourselves.

He was very much in prayer. This had all along been His delight and resource. In His busiest period, when He was often so tired with the labors of the day that at the approach of evening He was ready to fling Himself down in utter fatigue, He would nevertheless escape away from the crowds and His disciples to the mountaintop, and spend the whole night in lonely communion with His Father. He never took any important step without such a night. But now He was far oftener alone than ever before, setting forth His case to His God with strong crying and tears.

His prayers received a splendid answer in the Transfiguration. That glorious scene took place in the middle of the year of opposition, just before He quitted Galilee and set forth on the journey of doom. It was intended partly for the sake of the three disciples who accompanied Him to the mountaintop, to strengthen their faith and make them fit to strengthen their brethren. But it was chiefly intended for Himself. It was a great gift of His Father, an acknowledgment of His faithfulness up to this point, and a preparation for what lay before Him. It was about the decease He was to accomplish at Jerusalem He conversed with His great predecessors, Moses and Elias, who could thoroughly sympathize with Him, and whose work His death was to fulfill.

Immediately after this event He left Galilee and went south. He spent six months on His way to Jerusalem. It was part of His mission to preach the kingdom over the whole land, and He did so. He sent seventy of His disciples on before Him to prepare the villages and towns to receive Him. Again in this new field the same manifestations as Galilee had witnessed during the first months of His labors there showed themselves, the multitudes following Him, the wonderful cures, and so forth. We have no records of this period sufficient to enable us to follow Him step by step. We find Him on the borders of Samaria, in Perea, on the banks of the Jordan, in Bethany, in the village of Ephraim. But Jerusalem was His goal. His face was set like a flint for it. Sometimes He was so absorbed in the anticipation of what was to befall Him there, that His disciples, following His swift, mute figure along the highway, were amazed and afraid. Now and then, indeed, He would relax for a little, as when He was blessing the little children or visiting the home of His friends at Bethany. But His mood at this period was more stern, absorbed, and highly strung than ever before. His contests with His enemies were sharper, the conditions which He imposed on those who offered to be His disciples more stringent. Everything denoted that the end was drawing near. He was in the grip of His grand purpose of atoning for the sins of the world, and His soul was straitened till it should be accomplished.

The catastrophe drew nigh apace. He paid two brief visits to Jerusalem, before the final one, during His last six months. On both occasions the opposition of the authorities assumed the most menacing form. They endeavored to arrest Him on the first occasion, and took up stones to stone Him on the second. They had already issued a decree that anyone acknowledging Him to be the Messiah should be excommunicated. But it was the excitement produced in the popular mind by the raising of Lazarus at the very gates of the ecclesiastical citadel which finally convinced the authorities that they could not satisfy themselves with anything short of His death. So they resolved in council. This took place only a month or two before the end came, and it drove Him for the time from the neighborhood of Jerusalem. But He retired only until the hour which His Father had appointed Him should strike.

7
The End

AT length the third year of His ministry verged towards its close, and the revolving seasons brought round the great annual feast of the Passover. It is said that as many as two or three millions of strangers were gathered in Jerusalem on such an occasion. They not only flocked from every part of Palestine, but came over sea and land from all the countries in which the seed of Abraham were dispersed, in order to celebrate the event in which their national history began. They were brought together by very various motives. Some came with the solemn thoughts and deep religious joy of minds responsive to the memories of the venerable occasion. Some looked forward chiefly to reunion with relatives and friends who had been long parted from them by residence in distant places. Not a few of the baser sort brought with them the darling passions of their race, and were chiefly intent on achieving in so great a concourse some important stroke of business. But this year the minds of tens of thousands were full of an unusual excitement, and they came up to the capital expecting to see something more remarkable than they had ever witnessed there before. They hoped to see Jesus at the feast, and entertained many vague forebodings as to what might happen in connection with Him. His name was the word oftenest passing from mouth to mouth among the pilgrim bands that crowded along the highways and among the Jewish groups that talked together on the decks of the ships coming from Asia Minor and Egypt. Nearly all His own disciples no doubt were there, and were ardently cherishing the hope that at last in this concourse of the nation He would throw off the guise of humility which concealed His glory, and in some irresistible way demonstrate His Messiahship. There must have been thousands from the southern portions of the country, in which He had recently been spending His time, who came full of the same enthusiastic views about Him as were entertained in Galilee at the close of His first year there; and no doubt there were multitudes of the Galileans themselves who were favorably disposed towards Him and ready to take the deepest interest in any new development of His affairs. Tens of thousands from more distant parts, who had heard of Him, but never seen Him, arrived in the capital in the hope that He might be there, and that they might enjoy the opportunity of seeing a miracle or listening to the words of the new prophet. The authorities in Jerusalem, too, awaited His coming with very mingled feelings. They hoped that some turn of events might give them the chance of at last suppressing Him, but they could not help fearing that He might appear at the head of a provincial following which would place them at His mercy.

The Final Breach With the Nation

Six days before the Passover began, He arrived in Bethany, the village of His friends Martha, Mary, and Lazarus, which lay half-an-hour from the city on the other side of the summit of the Mount of Olives. It was a convenient place to lodge during the feast, and He took up His quarters with His friends. The solemnities were to begin on a Thursday, so that it was the previous Friday He arrived there. He had been accompanied the last twenty miles of His journey by an immense multitude of the pilgrims, to whom He was the center of interest. They had seen Him healing blind Bartimaeus at Jericho, and the miracle had produced among them extraordinary excitement. When they reached Bethany, the village was ringing with the recent resurrection of Lazarus, and they carried on the news to the crowds who had already arrived from all quarters in Jerusalem, that Jesus had come.

Accordingly, when, after resting over the Sabbath in Bethany, He came forth on the Sunday morning to proceed to the city, He found the streets of the village and the neighboring roads thronged with a vast crowd, consisting partly of those who had accompanied Him on the Friday, partly of other companies who had come up behind Him from Jericho and heard of the miracles as they came along, and partly of those who, having heard that he was at hand, had flocked out from Jerusalem to see Him. They welcomed Him with enthusiasm, and began to shout "Hosanna to the Son of David! Blessed is He that cometh in the name of the Lord! Hosanna in the highest!" It was a Messianic demonstration such as He had formerly avoided. But now He yielded to it. Probably He was satisfied with the sincerity of the homage paid to Him; and the hour had come when no considerations could permit Him any longer to conceal from the nation the character in which He presented Himself and the claim He made on its faith. But, in yielding to the desires of the multitude that He should assume the style of a king, He made it unmistakable in what sense He accepted the honor. He sent for an ass-colt, and, His disciples having spread their garments on it, rode at the head of the crowd. Not armed to the teeth or bestriding a war horse did He come, but as the King of simplicity and peace. The procession swept over the brow of Olivet and down the mountainside; it crossed the Kedron, and, mounting the slope which led to the gate of the city, passed on through the streets to the temple. It swelled as it went, great numbers hurrying from every quarter to join it; the shouts rang louder and more loud; the processionists broke off twigs from the palms and olives, as they passed, and waved them in triumph. The citizens of Jerusalem ran to their doors and bent over their balconies to look, and asked, "Who is this?" to which the processionists replied with provincial pride, "This is Jesus, the prophet of Nazareth." It was, in fact an entirely provincial demonstration. The Jerusalemites took no part in it, but held coldly aloof. The authorities knew only too well what it meant, and beheld it with rage and dread. They came to Jesus, and ordered Him to bid His followers hold their peace, hinting no doubt that, if He did not do so, the Roman garrison, which was stationed in the immediate vicinity, would pounce on Him and them, and punish the city for an act of treason to Caesar.

There is no point in the life of Jesus at which we are more urged to ask, What would have happened if His claim had been conceded— if the citizens of Jerusalem had been carried away with the enthusiasm of the provincials, and the prejudices of priests and scribes had been borne down before the torrent of public approval? Would Jesus have put Himself at the head of the nation and inaugurated an era of the world's history totally different from that which followed? These questions very soon carry us beyond our depth, yet no intelligent reader of the Gospels can help asking them.

Jesus had formally made offer of Himself to the capital and the authorities of the nation, but met with no response. The provincial recognition of His claims was insufficient to carry a national assent. He accepted the decision as final. The multitude expected a signal from Him, and in their excited mood would have obeyed it, whatever it might have been. But He gave them none, and, after looking round about Him for a little in the temple, left them and returned to Bethany.

Doubtless the disappointment of the multitude was extreme, and an opportunity was offered to the authorities which they did not fail to make use of. The Pharisees needed no stimulus, but even the Sadducees, those cold and haughty friends of order, espied danger to the public peace in the sate of the popular mind, and leagued themselves with their bitter enemies in the resolution to suppress Him.

On Monday and Tuesday He appeared again in the city and engaged in His old work of healing and teaching. But on the second of these days the authorities interposed. Pharisees, Sadducees, and Herodians, high priests, priests, and scribes were for once combined in a common cause. They came to Him, as He taught in the temple, and demanded by what authority He did such things. In all the pomp of official costume, of social pride and popular renown, they set themselves against the simple Galilean, while the multitudes looked on. They entered into a keen and prolonged controversy with Him on points selected beforehand, putting forward their champions of debate to entangle Him with the audience or to elicit something from His lips in the heat of argument which might form a ground of accusation against Him before the civil authority. Thus, for example, they asked Him if it was lawful to give tribute to Caesar. If He answered Yes, they knew that His popularity would perish on the instant, for it would be a complete contradiction of the popular Messianic ideas. If, on the contrary, He answered No, they would accuse Him of treason before the Roman governor. But Jesus was far more than a match for them. Hour by hour He steadfastly met the attack. His straightforwardness put their duplicity to shame, and His skill in argument turned every spear which they directed at Him round to their own breasts. At last He carried the war into their own territory, and convicted them of such ignorance or lack of candor as completely put them to shame before the onlookers. Then, when He had silenced them, He let loose the storm of His indignation, and delivered against them the philippic which is recorded in the twenty-third chapter of Matthew. Giving unrestrained expression to the pent-up criticism of a lifetime, He exposed their hypocritical practices in sentences that fell like strokes of lightning and made them a scorn and laughingstock, not only to the hearers then, but to all the world since.

It was the final breach between Him and them. They had been utterly humiliated before the whole people, over whom they were set in authority and honor. They felt it to be intolerable, and resolved not to lose an hour in seeking their revenge. That very evening the Sanhedrin met in passionate mood to devise a plan for making away with Him. Nicodemus and Joseph of Arimathea may have raised a solitary protest against their precipitate proceedings, but they indignantly silenced them, and were unanimously of opinion that He should forthwith be put to death. But circumstances checked their cruel haste. At least the forms of justice would have to be gone through; and besides, Jesus evidently enjoyed an immense popularity among the strangers who filled the city. What might not the idle crowd do if He were arrested before their eyes? It was necessary to wait till the mass of the pilgrims had left the city. They had just, with great reluctance, arrived at this conclusion, when they received a most unexpected and gratifying surprise. One of His own disciples appeared, and offered to betray Him for a price.

Judas Iscariot is the byword of the human race. In his *Vision of Hell*, Dante has placed him in the lowest of the circles of the damned, as the sole sharer with Satan himself of the very uttermost punishment; and the poet's verdict is that of mankind. Yet he was not such a monster of iniquity as to be utterly beyond comprehension or even sympathy. The history of his base and appalling lapse is perfectly intelligible. He had joined the discipleship of Jesus, as the other apostles did, in the hope of taking part in a political revolution and occupying a distinguished place in an earthly kingdom. It is inconceivable that Jesus would have made him an apostle if there had not at one time been some noble enthusiasm in him, and some attachment to Himself. That he was a man of superior energy and administrative ability may be inferred from the fact that he was made the purse bearer of the apostolic company. But there was a canker at the root of his character, which gradually absorbed all that was excellent in him, and became a tyrannical passion. It was the love of money. He fed it by the petty speculations which he practiced on the small sums which Jesus received from His friends for the necessities of His company and for distribution among the poor with whom He was daily mingling. He hoped to give it unrestrained gratification when He became chancellor of the exchequer in the new kingdom. The views of the other apostles were perhaps as worldly to begin with as his. But the history of their intercourse with their Master was totally different. They became ever more spiritual, he ever more worldly. They never, indeed, as long as Jesus lived, rose to the idea of a spiritual kingdom apart from an earthly one, but the spiritual elements which their Master had taught them to add to their material conception grew more and more prominent, till the earthly heart was eaten out of it, and merely the empty shell was left, to be in due time crushed and blown away. But Judas' earthly views became more and more engrossing, and were more and more divested of every spiritual adjunct. He grew impatient for their realization. Preaching and healing seemed to him waste of time; the purity and unworldliness of Jesus irritated him; why did He not bring on the kingdom at once, and then preach as much as He chose afterwards! At last he began to suspect that there was to be no kingdom such as he had hoped for at all. He felt that he had been deceived, and began not only to despise but even hate his Master. The failure of Jesus to take advantage of the disposition of the people on Palm Sunday finally convinced him that it was useless to hold on to the cause any longer. He saw that the ship was sinking and resolved to get out of it. He carried out his resolution in such a way as both to gratify his master passion and secure the favor of the authorities. His offer came to them just at the right moment. They closed with it greedily, and, having arranged the price with the miserable man, sent him away to find a convenient opportunity for the betrayal. He found it sooner than they expected—on the next night but one after the dastardly bargain had been concluded.

Jesus in the Prospect of Death

Christianity has no more precious possession than the memory of Jesus during the week when He stood face to face with death. Unspeakably great as He always was, it may be reverently said that He was never so great as during those days of direst calamity. All that was grandest and all that was most tender, the most human and the most divine aspects of His character, were brought out as they had never been before.

He came to Jerusalem well aware that He was about to die. For a whole year the fact had been staring Him constantly in the face, and the long-looked-for had come at last. He knew it was His Father's will, and, when the hour arrived, He bent His steps with sublime fortitude to the fatal spot. It was not, however, without a terrible conflict of feelings; the ebb and flow of the most diverse emotions—anguish and ecstasy, the most prolonged and crushing depression, the most triumphant joy and the most majestic peace—swayed hither and thither within Him like the moods of a vast ocean.

Some have hesitated to attribute to Him aught of that shrinking from death which is natural to man, but surely without good reason. It is an instinct perfectly innocent; and perhaps the very fact that His bodily organism was pure and perfect may have made it stronger in Him than it is in us. Remember how young He was—only thirty-three; the currents of life were powerful in Him; He was full of the instincts of action. To have these strong currents rolled back and the light and warmth of life quenched in the cold waters of death must have been utterly repugnant to Him. An incident which happened on the Monday caused Him a great shock of this instinctive pain. Some Greeks who had come to the feast expressed through two of the apostles their desire for an interview with Him. There were many heathens in different parts of the Greek-speaking world who at this period had found refuge from the atheism and disgusting immorality of the times in the religion of the Jews settled in their midst, and had accordingly become proselytes of the worship of Jehovah. To this class these inquirers belonged. But their application shook Him with thoughts which they little dreamed of. Only two or three times in the course of His ministry does He seem to have been brought into contact with representatives of the world lying outside the limits of His own people, His mission being exclusively to the lost sheep of the house of Israel. But on every such occasion He met with a faith, a courtesy and nobility, which He Himself contrasted with the unbelief, rudeness, and pettiness of the Jews. How could He help longing to pass beyond the narrow bounds of Palestine and visit nations of such simple and generous disposition? He must often have seen visions of a career like that afterwards achieved by Paul, when He bore the glad tidings from land to land, and evangelized Athens, Rome, and the other great centers of the West. What joy such a career would have been to Jesus, who felt within Himself the energy and overflowing benevolence which it would have exactly suited! But death was at hand to extinguish all. The visit of the Greeks caused a great wave of such thoughts to break over Him. Instead of responding to their request, He became abstracted, His face darkened, and His frame was shaken with the tremor of an inward conflict. But He soon recovered Himself, and gave expression to the thoughts on which in those days He was steadying up His soul: "Except a corn of wheat fall into the ground and die, it abideth alone; but if it die, it bringeth forth much fruit." "And I, if I be lifted up from the earth, will draw all men unto Me." He could see beyond death, terrible and absorbing as the prospect of it was, and assure Himself that the effect of His self-sacrifice would be infinitely grander and more extensive than that of a personal mission to the heathen world could ever have been. Besides, death was what his Father had appointed for Him. This was the last and deepest consolation with which He soothed His humble and trustful soul on this as on every similar occasion: "Now is my soul troubled; and what shall I say? Father, save me from this hour: but for this cause came I unto this hour. Father, glory Thyself."

Death approached Him with every terrible accompaniment. He was to fall a victim to the treachery of a follower of His own, whom He had chosen and loved. His life was to be taken by the hands of His own nation, in the city of His heart. He had come to exalt His nation to

heaven, and had loved her with a devotion nourished by the most intelligent and sympathetic acquaintance with her past history and
with the great men who had loved her before Him, as well as by the
sense of all which He Himself was able to do for her. But His death
would bring down the blight of a thousand curses on Palestine and
Jerusalem. How clearly He foresaw what was coming was shown by the
memorable prophetic discourse of the twenty-fourth chapter of
Matthew, which He spoke on Tuesday afternoon to His disciples, sitting on the side of Mount Olivet, with the doomed city at His feet.
How bitter was the anguish it caused Him was shown on the Sunday,
when, even in His hour of triumph, as the joyful multitude bore
Him down the mountain road, He stopped at the point where the city
burst upon the view, and with tears and lamentations predicted its fate.
It ought to have been the fair city's bridal day, when she should have
been married to the Son of God, but the pallor of death was on her
face. He who would have taken her to His heart, as the hen gathers her
chickens under her wings, saw the eagles already in the air, flying fast
to rend her in pieces.

In the evenings of this week He went out to Bethany, but in all
probability He spent most of the nights alone in the open air. He
wandered about in the solitude of the hilltop and among the olive
groves and gardens with which the sides of the mount were covered.
Many a time, perhaps, he went along the same road down which
the procession had passed, and, as He looked across the valley, from
the point where He had stopped before, at the city sleeping in the
moonlight, he startled the night with cries more bitter than the lamen-
tation which overawed the multitude; many a time he repeated to His
lonely heart the great truths he had uttered in the presence of the
Greeks.

He was terribly alone. The whole world was against Him—
Jerusalem panting for His life with passionate hate, the tens of thousands from the provinces turned from Him in disappointment. Not one
even of His apostles, not even John, was in the least aware of the real
situation, or able to be the confidant of His thoughts. This was one of
the bitterest drops in His cup. He felt, as no other person has ever felt,
the necessity of living on in the world after death. The cause He had

inaugurated must not die. It was for the whole world, and was to endure through all generations and visit every part of the globe. But after
His departure it would be left in the hands of His apostles, who were
now showing themselves so weak, unsympathetic, and ignorant. Were
they fit for the task? Had not one of them turned out a traitor? Would
not the cause, when He was gone—so perhaps the tempter whispered—go to wreck, and all His far-reaching plans for the regeneration
of the world vanish like the baseless fabric of a vision?

Yet He was not alone. Among the deep shadows of the gardens and
upon the summits of Olivet, He sought the unfailing resource of
other and less troubled days, and found it still in His dire need. His Father was with Him; and, pouring out supplications with strong crying
and tears, He was heard in that He feared. He hushed His spirit with
the sense that His Father's perfect love and wisdom were appointing
all that was happening to Him, and that He was glorifying His Father
and fulfilling the work given Him to do. This could banish every
fear, and fill Him with a joy unspeakable and full of glory.

At last the end drew very near. The Thursday evening arrived,
when in every house in Jerusalem the Passover was eaten. Jesus also with
the Twelve sat down to eat it. He knew that it was His last night on earth,
and that this was His farewell meeting with His own. Happily there has
been preserved to us a full account of it, with which every Christian
mind is familiar. It was the greatest evening in His life. His soul overflowed in indescribable tenderness and grandeur. Some shadows indeed
fell across His spirit in the earlier hours of the evening. But they soon
passed; and throughout the scenes of the washing of the disciples'
feet, the eating of the Passover, the institution of the Lord's Supper, the
farewell address, and the great high-priestly prayer, the whole glory of
His character shone out. He completely resigned Himself to the genial
impulses of friendship, His love to His own flowing forth without
limit; and, as if He had forgotten all their imperfections, He rejoiced
in the anticipation of their future successes and the triumph of His
cause. Not a shadow intercepted His view of the face of His Father or
dimmed the satisfaction with which He looked on His own work just
about to be completed. It was as if the passion were already past, and
the glory of His Exaltation were already breaking around Him.

But the reaction came very soon. Rising from the table at midnight, they passed through the streets and out of the town by the eastern gate of the city, and, crossing the Kedron, reached a well-known haunt of His at the foot of Olivet, the garden of Gethsemane. Here ensued the awful and memorable Agony. It was the final access of the mood of depression which had been struggling all the week with the mood of joy and trust whose culmination had been reached at the supper table. It was the final onset of temptation, from which His life had never been free. But we fear to analyze the elements of the scene. We know that any conception of ours must be utterly unable to exhaust its meaning. How, above all, can we estimate in the faintest degree the chief element in it—the crushing, scorching pressure of the sin of the world, which He was then expiating?

But the struggle ended in a complete victory. While the poor disciples were sleeping away the hours of preparation for the crisis which was at hand, He had thoroughly equipped Himself for it; He had fought down the last remnants of temptation; the bitterness of death was past; and He was able to go through the scenes which followed with a calmness which nothing could ruffle, and a majesty which converted His trial and crucifixion into the pride and glory of humanity.

The Trial

He had just overcome in this struggle when through the branches of the olives He saw, moving in the moonlight down the opposite slope, the mass of His enemies coming to arrest Him. The traitor was at their head. He was well acquainted with his Master's haunt and probably hoped to find Him there asleep. For this reason he had chosen the midnight hour for his dark deed. It suited his employers well too, for they were afraid to lay hands on Jesus in the daytime, dreading the temper of the Galilean strangers who filled the city. But they knew how it would overawe His friends, if, getting His trial over during the night, they could show Him in the morning, when the populace awoke, already a condemned criminal in the hands of the executors of the law. They had brought lanterns and torches with them, thinking they might find their victim crouching in some cave, or that they might have to pursue Him through the wood. But He came forth to meet them at the entrance to the garden, and they quailed like cravens before His majestic looks and withering words. He freely surrendered Himself into their hands, and they led Him back to the city. It was probably about midnight; and the remaining hours of the night and the early hours of the morning were occupied with the legal proceedings which had to be gone through, before they could gratify their thirst for His life.

There were two trials, an ecclesiastical one and a civil one, in each of which there were three stages. The former took place, first before Annas, then before Caiaphas and an informal committee of the Sanhedrin, and, lastly, before a regular meeting of this court; the latter took place, first before Pilate, then before Herod, and, lastly, before Pilate again.

The reason of this double legal process was the political situation of the country. Judea, as has been already explained, was directly subject to the Roman empire, forming a part of the province of Syria, and being governed by a Roman officer, who resided at Caesarea. But it was not the practice of Rome to strip those countries which she had subdued of all the forms of native government. Though she ruled with an iron hand, collecting her taxes with severity, suppressing every sign of rebellion with promptitude, and asserting her paramount authority on great occasions, yet she conceded to the conquered as many of the insignia as possible of their ancient power. She was especially tolerant in matters of religion. Thus the Sanhedrin, the supreme ecclesiastical court of the Jews, was still permitted to try all religious causes. Only, if the sentence passed was a capital one, its execution could not take place without the case being tried over again before the governor. So that, when a prisoner was convicted by the Jewish ecclesiastical tribunal of a capital crime, he had to be sent down to Caesarea and prosecuted before the civil court, unless the governor happened to be at the time in Jerusalem. The crime of which Jesus was accused was one which naturally came before the ecclesiastical court. This court passed on Him a death sentence. But it had not the power to carry it out. It had to hand Him on to the tribunal of the governor, who happened at the time to be in the capital, which he generally visited at the Passover.

Jesus was conducted first to the palace of Annas. He was an old man of seventy, who had been high priest a score of years before, and still retained the title, as did also five of his sons who had succeeded him, though his son-in-law Caiaphas was the actual high priest. His age, ability, and family influence gave him immense social weight, and he was the virtual, though not formal, head of the Sanhedrin. He did not try Jesus, but merely wished to see Him and ask a few questions; so that He was very soon led away from the palace of Annas to that of Caiaphas, which probably formed part of the same group of official buildings.

Caiaphas, as ruling high priest, was president of the Sanhedrin, before which Jesus was tried. A legal meeting of this court could not be held before sunrise, perhaps about six o'clock. But there were many of its members already on the spot, who had been drawn together by their interest in the case. They were eager to get to work, both to gratify their own dislike to Him and to prevent the interference of the populace with their proceedings. Accordingly they resolved to hold an informal meeting at once, at which the accusation, evidence and so forth might be put into shape, so that, when the legal hour for opening their doors arrived, there might be nothing to do but to repeat the necessary formalities and carry Him off to the governor. This was done; and, while Jerusalem slept, these eager judges hurried forward their dark designs.

They did not begin, as might have been expected, with a clear statement of the crime with which He was charged. Indeed, it would have been difficult for them to do so, for they were divided among themselves. Many things in His life which the Pharisees regarded as criminal were treated by the Sadducees with indifference; and other acts of His, like the cleansing of the temple, which had enraged the Sadducees, afforded gratification to the Pharisees.

The high priest began with questioning Him as to His disciples and doctrine, evidently with the view of discovering whether He had taught any revolutionary tenets, which might form a ground of accusation before the governor. But Jesus repelled the insinuation, indignantly asserting that He had ever spoken openly before the world, and demanded a statement and proof of any evil He had done. This unusual reply induced one of the minions of the court to smite Him on the mouth with His fist—an act which the court apparently did not rebuke, and which showed what amount of justice He had to expect at the hands of His judges. An attempt was then made to bring proof against Him, a number of witnesses repeating various statements they had heard Him make, out of which it was hoped an accusation might be constructed. But it turned out a total failure. The witnesses could not agree among themselves; and when at last two were got to unite in a distorted report of a saying of His early ministry, which appeared to have some color of criminality, it turned out to be a thing so paltry that it would have been absurd to appear with it before the governor as the ground of a serious charge.

They were resolved on His death, but the prey seemed slipping out of their hands. Jesus looked on in absolute silence, while contradictory testimonies of the witnesses demolished each other. He quietly took His natural position far above His judges. They felt it; and at last the president, in a transport of rage and irritation, started up and commanded Him to speak. Why was He so loud and shrill? The humiliating spectacle going on in the witness box and the silent dignity of Jesus were beginning to trouble even these consciences assembled in the dead of night.

The case had completely broken down when Caiaphas rose from his seat, and, with theatrical solemnity, asked the question: "I adjure Thee by the living God, that Thou tell us whether Thou be the Christ the Son of God." It was a question asked merely in order to induce Jesus to incriminate Himself. Yet He who had kept silence when He might have spoken now spoke when He might have been silent. With great solemnity He answered in the affirmative, that He was the Messiah and the Son of God. Nothing more was needed by His judges. They unanimously pronounced Him guilty of blasphemy and worthy of death.

The whole trial had been conducted with precipitancy and total disregard of the formalities proper to a court of law. Everything was dictated by the desire to arrive at guilt, not justice. The same persons were both prosecutors and judges. No witnesses for the defense were thought of. Though the judges were doubtless perfectly conscientious in their sentence, it was the decision of minds long ago shut against the truth and possessed with the most bitter and revengeful passions.

The trial was now looked upon as past, the legal proceedings after sunrise being a mere formality, which would be got over in a few minutes. Accordingly, Jesus was given up as a condemned man to the cruelty of the jailers and the mob. Then ensued a scene over which one would gladly draw a veil. There broke forth on Him an Oriental brutality of abuse which makes the blood run cold. Apparently the Sanhedrists themselves took part in it. This Man, who had baffled them, impaired their authority and exposed their hypocrisy, was very hateful to them. Sadducean coldness could boil up into heat enough when it was really roused. Pharisaic fanaticism was inventive in its cruelty. They smote Him with their fists, they spat on Him, they blindfolded Him, and, in derision of his prophetic claims, bade Him prophesy who struck Him, as they took their turn of smiting Him. But we will not dwell on a scene so disgraceful to human nature.

It was probably between six and seven in the morning when they conducted Jesus, bound with chains, to the residence of the governor. What a spectacle that was! The priests, teachers, and judges of the Jewish nation leading their Messiah to ask the Gentile to put Him to death! It was the hour of the nation's suicide. This was all that had come of God's choosing them, bearing them on eagles' wings and carrying them all the days of old, sending them His prophets and deliverers, redeeming them from Egypt and Babylon, and causing His glory for so many centuries to pass before their eyes! Surely it was the very mockery of Providence. Yet God was not mocked. His designs march down through history with resistless tread, waiting not on the will of man; and even this tragic hour, when the Jewish nation was turning His dealings into derision, was destined to demonstrate the depths of His wisdom and love.

The man before whose judgment seat Jesus was about to appear was Pontius Pilate, who had been governor of Judea for six years. He was a typical Roman, not of the antique, simple stamp, but of the imperial period; a man not without some remains of the ancient Roman justice in his soul, yet pleasure-loving, imperious, and corrupt. He hated the Jews whom he ruled, and, in times of irritation, freely shed their blood. They returned his hatred with cordiality, and accused him of every crime, maladministration, cruelty, and robbery. He visited Jerusalem as seldom as possible; for, indeed, to one accustomed to the pleasures of Rome, with its theaters, baths, games, and gay society, Jerusalem, with its religiousness and ever-smoldering revolt, was a dreary residence. When he did visit it, he stayed in the magnificent palace of Herod the Great; it being common for the officers sent by Rome into conquered countries to occupy the palaces of the displaced sovereigns.

Up the broad avenue, which led through a fine park, laid out with walks, ponds, and trees of various kinds, to the front of the building, the Sanhedrists and the crowd which had joined the processions, as it moved on through the streets, conducted Jesus. The court was held in the open air, on a mosaic pavement in front of that portion of the palace which united its two colossal wings.

The Jewish authorities had hoped that Pilate would accept their decision as his own, and without going into the merits of the case, pass the sentence they desired. This was frequently done by provincial governors, especially in matters of religion, which, as foreigners, they could not be expected to understand. Accordingly, when he asked what the crime of Jesus was, they replied, "If He were not a malefactor, we would not have delivered Him up unto thee." But he was not in the mood of concession, and told them that, if he was not to try the culprit, they must be content with such a punishment as the law permitted them to inflict. He seems to have known something of Jesus. "He knew that for envy they had delivered Him." The triumphal procession of Sunday was sure to be reported to him; and the neglect of Jesus to make use of that demonstration for any political end may have convinced him that He was politically harmless. His wife's dream may imply that He had been the subject of conversation in the palace; and perhaps the polite man of the world and his lady had felt the ennui of their visit to Jerusalem relieved by the story of the young peasant enthusiast who was bearding the fanatic priests.

Forced against their hopes to bring forward formal charges, the Jewish authorities poured out a volley of accusations, out of which these three clearly emerged—that He had perverted the nation, that He forbade to pay the Roman tribute, and that He set Himself up as a king. In the Sanhedrin they had condemned Him for blasphemy, but such a charge would have been treated by Pilate, as they well knew, in the same way as it was afterwards treated by the Roman governor Gallio, when preferred against Paul by the Jews of Corinth. They had therefore to invent new charges, which might represent Jesus as formidable to the government. It is humiliating to think that, in doing so, they resorted not only to gross hypocrisy, but even to deliberate falsehood; for how else can we characterize the second charge, when we remember the answer He gave to their question on the same subject on the previous Tuesday?

Pilate understood their pretended zeal for the Roman authority. He knew the value of this vehement anxiety that Rome's tribute should be paid. Rising from his seat to escape the fanatical cries of the mob, he took Jesus inside the palace to examine Him. It was a solemn moment for himself, though he knew it not. What a terrible fate it was which brought him to this spot at this time! There were hundreds of Roman officials scattered over the empire, conducting their lives on the same principles as his was guided by; why did it fall to him to bring them to bear on this case? He had no idea of the issues he was deciding. The culprit may have seemed to him a little more interesting and perplexing than others, but He was only one of hundreds constantly passing through his hands. It could not occur to him that, though he appeared to be the judge, yet both he and the system he represented were on their trial before One whose perfection judged and exposed every man and every system which approached Him. He questioned Him in regard to the accusations brought against Him, asking especially if He pretended to be a king. Jesus replied that He made no such claim in the political sense, but only in a spiritual sense, as King of the Truth. This reply would have arrested any of the nobler spirits of heathendom, who spent their lives in the search for truth, and was perhaps framed in order to find out whether there was any response in Pilate's mind to such a suggestion. But he had no such cravings and dismissed it with a laugh. However, he was convinced that, as he had supposed, there lurked nothing of the demagogue or Messianic revolutionist behind this pure, peaceful, and melancholy face; and, returning to the tribunal, he announced to His accusers that he had acquitted Him.

The announcement was received with shrieks of disappointed rage and the loud reiteration of the charges against Him. It was a thoroughly Jewish spectacle. Many a time had this fanatical mob overcome the wishes and decisions of their foreign masters by the sheer force of clamor and pertinacity. Pilate ought at once to have released and protected Him. But he was a true son of the system in which he had been brought up—the statecraft of compromise and maneuver. Amidst the cries with which they assailed his ears he was glad to hear one which offered him an excuse for getting rid of the whole business. They were shouting that Jesus had excited the populace "throughout all Jewry, beginning from Galilee unto this place." It occurred to him that Herod, the ruler of Galilee, was in town, and that he might get rid of the troublesome affair by handing it over to him; for it was a common procedure in Roman law to transfer a culprit from the tribunal of the territory in which he was arrested to that of the territory in which he was domiciled. Accordingly, he sent Him away in the hands of his bodyguard, and accompanied by His indefatigable accusers, to the palace of Herod.

They found this princeling, who had come to Jerusalem to attend the feast, in the midst of his petty court of flatterers and boon companions, and surrounded by the bodyguard which he maintained in imitation of his foreign masters, He was delighted to see Jesus, whose fame had so long been ringing through the territory over which he ruled. He was a typical Oriental prince, who had only one thought in life—his own pleasure and amusement. He came up to the Passover merely for the sake of the excitement. The appearance of Jesus seemed to promise a new sensation, of which he and his court were often sorely in want for he hoped to see Him work a miracle. He was a man utterly incapable of taking a serious view of anything, and even overlooked the business about which the Jews were so eager, for he began to pour out a flood of rambling questions and remarks, without pausing for any reply. At last, however, he exhausted himself, and waited for the response of Jesus. But he waited in vain, for Jesus did not vouchsafe him one word of any kind. Herod had forgotten the murder of the Baptist, every impression being written as if on water in his characterless mind, but Jesus had not forgotten it. He felt that Herod should have been ashamed to look the Baptist's friend in the face; He would not stoop even to speak to a man who could treat Him as a mere wonder-worker, who might purchase his judge's favor by exhibiting his skill; He looked with sad shame on one who had abused himself till there was no conscience or manliness left in him. But Herod was utterly incapable of feeling the annihilating force of such silent disdain. He and his men of war set Jesus at naught, and, throwing over His shoulders a white robe, in imitation of that worn at Rome by candidates who were canvassing for office, to indicate that He was a candidate for the Jewish throne, but one so ridiculous that it would be useless to treat Him with anything but contempt, sent Him back to Pilate. In this guise He retraced His weary steps to the tribunal of the Roman.

Then ensued a course of procedure on the part of Pilate by which he made himself an image of the time-server, to be exhibited to the centuries in the light falling on him from Christ. It was evidently his duty, when Jesus returned from Herod, to pronounce at once the sentence of acquittal. But, instead of doing so, he resorted to expediency, and, being hurried on from one false step to another, was finally hurled down the slope of complete treachery to principle. He proposed to the Jews that, as both he and Herod had found Him innocent, he should scourge and then release Him; the scourging being a sop to their rage, and the release a tribute to justice.

The carrying out of this monstrous proposal was, however, interrupted by an incident which seemed to offer to Pilate once more a way of escape from his difficulty. It was the custom of the Roman governor on Passover morning to release to the people any single prisoner they might desire. It was a privilege highly prized by the populace of Jerusalem, for there were always in jail plenty of prisoners who, by rebellion against the detested foreign yoke, had made themselves the heroes of the multitude. At this stage of the trial of Jesus, the mob of the city, pouring from street and alley in the excited Oriental fashion, came streaming up the avenue to the front of the palace, shouting for this annual gift. The cry was for once welcome to Pilate, for he saw in it a loophole of escape from his disagreeable position. It turned out, however, to be a noose through which he was slipping his neck. He offered the life of Jesus to the mob. For a moment they hesitated. But they had a favorite of their own, a noted leader of revolt against the Roman domination; and besides, voices instantly began to whisper busily in their ears, putting every art of persuasion into exercise in order to induce them not to accept Jesus. The Sanhedrists, in spite of the zeal they had manifested the hour before for law and order, did not scruple thus to take the side of the champion of sedition; and they succeeded only too well in poisoning the minds of the populace, who began to shout for their own hero, Barabbas. "What, then, shall I do with Jesus?" asked Pilate, expecting them to answer, "Give us Him too." But he was mistaken; the authorities had done their work successfully; the cry came from ten thousand throats, "Let Him be crucified!" Like priests, like people; it was the ratification by the nation of the decision of its heads. Pilate, completely baffled, angrily asked, "Why, what evil hath He done?" But he had put the decision into their power; they were now thoroughly fantasized, and yelled forth, "Away with Him; crucify Him, crucify Him!"

Pilate did not yet mean to sacrifice justice utterly. He had still a move in reserve, but in the meantime He sent away Jesus to be scourged—the usual preliminary to crucifixion. The soldiers took Him to a room in their barracks, and feasted their cruel instincts on His sufferings. We will not describe the shame and pain of this revolting punishment. What must it have been to Him, with His honor and love for human nature, to be handled by those coarse men, and to look so closely at human nature's uttermost brutality! The soldiers enjoyed their work and heaped insult upon cruelty. When the scourging was over, they set Him down on a seat, and, fetching an old cast-off cloak, flung it, in derisive imitation of the royal purple, on His shoulders; they thrust a reed into His hands for a scepter; they stripped some thorn twigs from a neighboring bush, and, twining them into the rough semblance of a crown, crushed down their rending spikes upon His brow. Then, passing in front of Him, each of them in turn bent the knee, while, at the same time, he spat in His face, and plucking the reed from His hand, smote Him with it over the head and face.

At last, having glutted their cruelty, they led Him back to the tribunal, wearing the crown of thrones and the purple robe. The crowds
raised shouts of mad laughter at the soldier's joke; and, with a sneer on
his face, Pilate thrust Him forward, so as to meet the gaze of all, and
cried, "Behold the man!" He meant that surely there was no use of
doing any more to Him; He was not worth their while; could one so
broken and wretched do any harm? How little he understood his
own words! That "Ecce Homo" of his sounds over the world and
draws the eyes of all generations to that marred visage. And lo, as we
look, the shame is gone; it has lifted off Him and fallen on Pilate himself, on the soldiery, the priests, and the mob. His outflashing glory has
scorched away every speck of disgrace, and tipped the crown of thorns
with a hundred points of flaming brightness. But just as little did Pilate understand the temper of the people he ruled when he supposed
that the sight of the misery and helplessness of Jesus would satisfy their
thirst for vengeance. Their objection to Him all along had been that
one so poor and unambitious should claim to be their Messiah; and
the sight of Him now, scourged and scorned by the alien soldiery, yet
still claiming to be their King, raised their hate to madness, so that they
cried louder than ever, "Crucify Him, crucify Him."

Now at last, too, they gave vent to the real charge against Him,
which had all along been burning at the bottom of their hearts, and
which they could no longer suppress: "We have a law," they cried, "and
by that law He ought to die, because He made Himself the Son of
God." But these words struck a chord in Pilate's mind which they had
not thought of. In the ancient traditions of his native land there were
many legends of sons of the gods, who in the days of old had walked
the earth in humble guise, so that they were indistinguishable from
common men. It was dangerous to meet them, for an injury done
them might bring down on the offender the wrath of the gods, their
sires. Faith in these antique myths had long died out, because no
men were seen on earth so different from their neighbors as to require
such an explanation. But in Jesus Pilate had discerned an inexplicable something which affected him with a vague terror. And now the
words of the mob, "He made Himself the Son of God," came like a

flash of lightning. They brought back out of the recesses of his memory the old, forgotten stories of his childhood, and revived the heathen terror, which forms the theme of some of the greatest Greek drams, of committing unawares a crime which might evoke the dire vengeance of Heaven. Might not Jesus be the Son of the Hebrew Jehovah—so his heathen mind reasoned—as Castor and Pollux were the sons of Jupiter? He hastily took Him inside the palace again, and, looking at Him with new awe and curiosity, asked, "Whence art Thou?" But Jesus answered him not one word. Pilate had not listened to Him when He wished to explain every thing to him; he had outraged his own sense of justice by scourging Him; and if a man turns his back on Christ when He speaks, the hour will come when he will ask and receive no answer. The proud governor was both surprised and irritated, and demanded, "Speakest Thou not to me? Knowest Thou not that I have power to crucify Thee, and have power to release Thee?" to which Jesus answered with the indescribable dignity of which the brutal shame of His torture had in no way robbed Him, "Thou couldst have no power at all against Me, except it were given thee from above."

Pilate had boasted of his power to do what he chose with the prisoner, but he was in reality very weak. He came forth from his private interview determined at once to release Him. The Jews saw it in His face; and it made them bring out their last weapon, which they had all along been keeping in reserve: they threatened to complain against him to the emperor. This was the meaning of the cry with which they interrupted his first words, "If thou let this man go, thou art not Caesar's friend." This had been in both their minds and his all through the trial. It was this which made him so irresolute. There was nothing a Roman governor dreaded as much as a complaint against him sent by his subjects to the emperor. At this time it was specially perilous; for the imperial throne was occupied by a morbid and suspicious tyrant, who delighted in disgracing his own servants, and would kindle in a moment at the whisper of any of his subordinates favoring a pretender to royal power. Pilate knew too well that his administration could not bear inspection, for it had been cruel and corrupt in the extreme. Nothing is able so peremptorily to forbid a man to do the good he would do as the evil of his past life. This was the blast of temptation which finally swept Pilate off his feet, just when he had made up his mind to obey his conscience. He was no hero, who would obey his convictions at any cost. He was a thorough man of the world, and saw at once that he must surrender Jesus to their will.

However, he was full not only of rage at being so completely foiled, but also of an overpowering religious dread. Calling for water, he washed his hands in the presence of the multitude, and cried, "I am innocent of the blood of this just Person." He washed his hands when he should have exerted them. Blood is not so easily washed off. But the mob, now completely triumphant, derided his scruples, rending the air with the cry, "His blood be upon us and on our children!"

Pilate felt the insult keenly, and, turning on them in his anger, determined that he, too, should have his triumph. Thrusting Jesus forward more prominently into view, he began to mock them by pretending to regard Him as really their king, and asking, "Shall I crucify your king?" It was now their turn to feel the sting of mockery; and they cried out, "We have no king but Caesar." What a confession from Jewish lips! It was the surrender of the freedom and the history of the nation. Pilate took them at their word, and forthwith handed Jesus over to be crucified.

The Crucifixion

They had succeeded in wresting their victim from Pilate's unwilling hands, "and they took Jesus and led Him away." At length they were able to gratify their hatred to the uttermost, and they hurried Him off to the place of execution with every demonstration of inhuman triumph. The actual executioners were the soldiers of the governor's guard, but in moral significance the deed belonged entirely to the Jewish authorities. They could not leave it in charge of the minions of the law to whom it belonged, but with undignified eagerness headed the procession themselves, in order to feast their vindictiveness on the sight of His sufferings.

It must by this time have been about ten o'clock in the morning. The crowd at the place had been gradually swelling. As the fatal procession, headed by the Sanhedrists, passed on through the streets, it attracted great multitudes. It happened to be a Passover holiday, so that there were thousands of idlers prepared for any excitement. All those especially who had been inoculated with the fanaticism of the authorities poured forth to witness the execution. It was therefore through the midst of myriads of cruel and unsympathizing onlookers that Jesus went to His death.

The spot where He suffered cannot now be identified. It was outside the gates of the city, and was doubtless the common place of execution. It is usually called Mount Calvary, but there is nothing in the Gospels to justify such a name, nor does there seem to be any hill in the neighborhood on which it could have taken place. The name Golgotha, "place of a skull," may signify a skull-like knoll, but more probably refers to the ghastly relics of the tragedies happening there that might be lying about. It was probably a wide, open space, in which a multitude of spectators might assemble; and it appears to have been on the side of a much frequented thoroughfare, for, besides the stationary spectators, there were others passing to and fro who joined in mocking the Sufferer.

Crucifixion was an unspeakably horrible death. As Cicero, who was well acquainted with it, says, it was the most cruel and shameful of all punishments. "Let it never," he adds, "come near the body of a Roman citizen; nay, not even near his thoughts, or eyes, or ears." It was reserved for slaves and revolutionaries whose end was meant to be marked with special infamy. Nothing could be more unnatural and revolting than to suspend a living man in such a position. The idea of it seems to have been suggested by the practice of nailing up vermin in a kind of revengeful merriment on some exposed place. Had the end come with the first strokes in the wounds, it would still have been an awful death. But the victim usually lingered two or three days, with the burning pain of the nails in his hands and feet, the torture of overcharged veins, and worst of all, his intolerable thirst, constantly increasing. It was impossible to help moving the body so as to get relief from each new attitude of pain; yet every movement brought new and excruciating agony.

But we gladly turn away from the awful sight to think how by His strength of soul, His resignation, and His love, Jesus triumphed over the shame, the cruelty, and horror of it; and how, as the sunset with its crimson glory makes even the putrid pool burn like a shield of gold and drenches with brilliance the vilest object held up against its beams, He converted the symbol of slavery and wickedness into a symbol for whatever is most pure and glorious in the world. The head hung free in crucifixion, so that He was able not only to see what was going on beneath Him, but also to speak. He uttered seven sentences at intervals, which have been preserved to us. They are seven windows by which we can still look into His very mind and heart and learn the impressions made on Him by what was happening. They show that He retained unimpaired the serenity and majesty which had characterized Him throughout His trial, and exhibited in their fullest exercise all the qualities which had already made His character illustrious. He triumphed over His sufferings not by the cold severity of a Stoic, but by self-forgetting love. When He was fainting beneath the burden of the cross in the Via Dolorosa, He forgot His fatigue in His anxiety for the daughters of Jerusalem and their children. When they were nailing Him to the tree, He was absorbed in a prayer for His murderers. He quenched the pain of the first hours of crucifixion by His interest in the penitent thief and His care to provide a new home for His mother. He never was more completely Himself—the absolutely unselfish Worker for others.

It was, indeed, only through His love that he could be deeply wounded. His physical sufferings, though intense and prolonged, were not greater than have been borne by many other sufferers, unless the exquisiteness of His bodily organism may have heightened them to a degree which to other men is inconceivable. He did not linger more than five hours—a space of time so much briefer than usual, that the soldiers, who were about to break His legs, were surprised to find Him already dead. His worst sufferings were those of the mind. He whose very life was love, who thirsted for love as the hart pants for the water-brooks, was encircled with a sea of hatred and of dark, bitter, hellish passion, that surged round Him and flung up its waves about His cross. His soul was spotlessly pure; holiness was its very life, but sin pressed itself against it, endeavoring to force upon it its loathsome contact, from which it shrank through every fiber. The members of the

Sanhedrin took the lead in venting on Him every possible expression of contempt and malicious hate, and the populace faithfully followed their example. These were the men He had loved and still loved with an unquenchable passion; and they insulted, crushed, and trampled on His love. Through their lips the Evil One reiterated again and again the temptation by which He had been all His life assaulted, to save Himself and win the faith of the nation by some display of supernatural power made for His own advantage. That seething mass of human beings, whose faces, distorted with passion, glared upon Him, was an epitome of the wickedness of the human race. His eyes had to look down on it, and its coarseness, its sadness, its dishonor of God, its exhibition of the shame of human nature were like a sheaf of spears gathered in His breast.

There was a still more mysterious woe. Not only did the world's sin thus press itself on His loving and holy soul in those near Him; it came from afar—from the past, the distant, and the future—and met on Him. He was bearing the sin of the world; and the consuming fire of God's nature, which is the reverse side of the light of His holiness and love, flamed forth against Him, to scorch it away. So it pleased the Lord to put Him to grief, when He who knew no sin was made sin for us.

These were the sufferings which made the cross appalling. After some two hours, He withdrew Himself completely from the outer world and turned His face towards the eternal world. At the same time a strange darkness overspread the land, and Jerusalem trembled beneath a cloud whose murky shadows looked like a gathering doom. Golgotha was well-nigh deserted. He hung long silent amidst the darkness without and the darkness within, till at length, out of the depths of an anguish which human thought will never fathom, there issued the cry, "My God, my God, why hast Thou forsaken Me?" It was the moment when the soul of the Sufferer touched the very bottom of His misery.

But the darkness passed from the landscape and the sun shone forth again. The spirit of Christ, too, emerged from its eclipse. With the strength of victory won in the final struggle, He cried, "It is finished!" and then, with perfect serenity, breathed out His life on a verse of a favorite psalm: "Father, into Thy hands I commend My spirit."

The Resurrection and Ascension

There never was an enterprise in the world which seemed more completely at an end than did that of Jesus on the last Old Testament Sabbath. Christianity died with Christ, and was laid with Him in the sepulcher. It is true that when, looking back at this distance, we see the stone rolled to the mouth of the tomb, we experience little emotion; for we are in the secret of Providence and know what is going to happen. But when He was buried, there was not a single human being that believed He would ever rise again before the day of the world's doom.

The Jewish authorities were thoroughly satisfied of this. Death ends all controversies, and it had settled the one between Him and them triumphantly in their favor. He had put Himself forward as their Messiah, but had scarcely any of the marks which they looked for in one with such claims. He had never received any important national recognition. His followers were few and uninfluential. His career had been short. He was in the grave. Nothing more was to be thought of Him.

The breakdown of the disciples had been complete. When He was arrested, "they all forsook Him and fled." Peter, indeed, followed Him to the high priest's palace, but only to fall more ignominiously than the rest. John followed even to Golgotha, and may have hoped against hope that, at the very last moment, He might descend from the cross to ascend the Messianic throne. But even the last moment went by with nothing done. What remained for them but to return to their homes and their fishing as disappointed men, who would be twitted during the rest of their lives with the folly of following a pretender, and asked where the thrones were which He had promised to seat them on?

Jesus had, indeed, foretold His sufferings, death, and resurrection. But they never understood these sayings; they forgot them or gave them an allegorical turn; and, when He was actually dead, these yielded them no comfort whatever. The women came to the sepulcher on the first Christian Sabbath, not to see it empty, but to embalm His body for its long sleep. Mary ran to tell the disciples, not that He was risen, but that the body had been taken away and laid she knew not where. When the women told the other disciples how He had met them, "their words seemed to them as idle tales and they believed them not." Peter and John, as John himself informs us, "knew not the

Scripture, that he should rise from the dead." Could anything be more pathetic than the words of the two travelers to Emmaus, "We trusted that it had been He which should have redeemed Israel?" When the disciples were met together, "they mourned and wept." There never were men more utterly disappointed and dispirited.

But we can now be glad that they were so sad. They doubted that we might believe. For how is it to be accounted for that in a few days afterwards these very men were full of confidence and joy, their faith in Jesus had revived, and the enterprise of Christianity was again in motion with a far vaster vitality than it had ever before possessed? They say the reason of this was that Jesus had risen, and they had seen Him. They tell us about their visits to the empty tomb, and how He appeared to Mary Magdalene, to the other women, to Peter, to the two on the way to Emmaus, to ten of them at once, to eleven of them at once, to James, to the five hundred, and so forth. Are these stories credible? They might not be, if they stood alone. But the alleged resurrection of Christ was accompanied by the indisputable resurrection of Christianity. And how is the latter to be accounted for except by the former? It might, indeed, be said that Jesus had filled their minds with imperial dreams, which He failed to realize; and that, having once caught sight of so magnificent a career, they were unable to return to their fishing nets, and so invented this story, in order to carry on the scheme on their own account. Or it might be said that they only fancied they saw what they tell about the Risen One. But the remarkable thing is that, when they resumed their faith in Him, the were found to be no longer pursuing worldly ends, but intensely spiritual ones; they were no longer expecting thrones, but persecution and death; yet they addressed themselves to their new work with a breadth of intelligence, an ardor of devotion, and a faith in results which they had never shown before. As Christ rose from the dead in a transfigured body, so did Christianity. It had put off its carnality. What effected this change? They say it was the resurrection and the sight of the risen Christ. But their testimony is not the proof that He rose. The incontestable proof is the change itself—the fact that suddenly they had become courageous, hopeful, believing, wise, possessed with noble and reasonable views of the world's future, and equipped with resources sufficient to found the Church, convert the world, and establish Christianity in its purity among men. Between the last Old Testament Sabbath and the time, a few weeks afterwards, when this stupendous change had undeniably taken place, some event must have intervened which can be regarded as a sufficient cause for so great an effect. The resurrection alone answers the exigencies of the problem, and is therefore proved by a demonstration far more cogent than perhaps any testimony could be. It is a happy thing that this event is capable of such a proof; for, if Christ be not risen, our faith is vain, but if He be risen, then the whole of His miraculous life becomes credible, for this was the greatest of all the miracles; His divine mission is demonstrated, for it must have been God who raised Him up; and the most assuring glance which history affords is given into the realities of the eternal world.

The risen Christ lingered on earth long enough fully to satisfy His adherents of the truth of His resurrection. They were not easily convinced. The apostles treated the reports of the holy women with scornful incredulity; Thomas doubted the testimony of the other apostles; and some of the five hundred to whom He appeared on a Galilean mountain doubted their own eyesight, and only believed when they heard His voice. The loving patience with which He treated these doubters showed that, though His bodily appearance was somewhat changed, He was still the same in heart as ever. This was pathetically shown too by the places which He visited in His glorified form. They were the old haunts where He had prayed and preached, labored and suffered—the Galilean mountain, the well-beloved lake, the Mount of Olives, the village of Bethany, and, above all, Jerusalem, the fatal city which had murdered her own Son, but which He could not cease to love.

Yet there were obvious indications that He belonged no more to this lower world. There was a new reserve about His risen humanity. He forbade Mary to touch Him, when she would have kissed His feet. He appeared in the midst of His own with mysterious suddenness, and just as suddenly vanished out of sight. He was only now and then in their company, no longer according them the constant and familiar intercourse of former days. At length, at the end of forty days, when the purpose for which He had lingered on earth was fully accomplished and the apostles were ready in the power of their new joy to bear to all nations the tidings of His life and work, His glorified humanity was received up into that world to which it rightfully belonged.

Conclusion

No life ends even for this world when the body by which it has for a little been made visible disappears from the face of the earth. It enters into the stream of the ever-swelling life of mankind, and continues to act there with its whole force forevermore. Indeed, the true magnitude of a human being can often only be measured by what this afterlife shows him to have been. So it was with Christ. The oldest narrative of the Gospels scarcely prepares us for the outburst of creative force which issued from His life when it appeared to have ended. His influence on the modern world is the evidence of how great He was; for there must have been in the cause as much as there is in the effect. It has overspread the life of man and caused it to blossom with the vigor of a spiritual spring. It has absorbed into itself all other influences, as a mighty river, pouring along the center of a continent, receives tributaries from a hundred hills. And its quality has been even more exceptional than its quantity.

But the most important evidence of what He was, is to be found neither in the general history of modern civilization nor in the public history of the visible Church, but in the experiences of the succession of genuine believers, who with linked hands stretch back to touch Him through the Christian generations. The experience of myriads of souls, redeemed by Him from themselves and from the world, proves that history was cut in twain by the appearance of a Regenerator, who was not a mere link in the chain of common men, but One whom the race could not from its own resources have produced—the perfect Type, the Man of men. The experience of myriads of consciences, the most sensitive to both the holiness of the

Divine Being and their own sinfulness that the world has ever seen yet able to rejoice in a peace with God, which has been found the most potent motive of a holy life, proves that in the midst of the ages there was wrought out an act of reconciliation by which sinful men may be made one with a holy God. The experience of myriads of minds, rendered blessed by the vision of a God who to the eye purified by the Word of Christ is so completely Light that in Him there is no darkness at all, proves that the final revelation of the Eternal to the world has been made by One who knew Him so well that He could not Himself have been less than Divine.

The life of Christ in history cannot cease. His influence waxes more and more; the dead nations are waiting till it reach them, and it is the hope of the earnest spirits that are bringing in the new earth. All discoveries of the modern world, every development of juster ideas, of higher powers, of more exquisite feelings in mankind, are only new helps to interpret Him; and the lifting-up of life to the level of His ideas and character is the program of the human race.

Imago Christi

The Example of Jesus Christ

Introduction

The author of the following volume is one of the most eminent of the younger ministers of the Free Church of Scotland. Educated in his native land, he spent some time in Germany, prosecuting there such studies as he judged to be best fitted to prepare him for his lifework in the ministry of the gospel.

He began his pastoral labors in Kirkcaldy, Fifeshire, and while there attracted wide attention by his eloquence as a preacher and his excellence as an expositor of the Word of God. Two or three years ago he was called to Free St. Matthew's Church, Glasgow, where by all he is "esteemed very highly in love for his work's sake." He occupies there a place of commanding influence, and by his labors among young people and his active sympathy with evangelistic work, he is proving himself eminently useful.

All who were present at the Belfast meeting of the Presbyterian Alliance recognized his ability in dealing with a difficult subject; and his volumes on the *Life of Christ* and the *Life of St. Paul*, though issued under the unpretending title of handbooks, are remarkable for their originality of method, clearness of style, comprehensiveness of view and suggestiveness of matter.

The same qualities are conspicuous in his treatment, in *Imago Christi*, of the example of Christ, a subject which he has handled in a way entirely his own and in a spirit of devoutest reverence. We commend the work as equally fitted to be a companion for the closet and a directory for the life.

WM. M. TAYLOR

NEW YORK, NOV. 23, 1889

Preface

IF it were permissible, I could truly describe the origin of this book in the very words of Bunyan:

> When at the first I took my pen in hand
> Thus for to write, I did not understand
> That I at all should make a little book
> In such a mode; nay, I had undertook
> To make another; which, when almost done,
> Before I was aware, I this begun.

While writing my *Life of Christ*, and reading extensively on the subject, the conviction was borne in upon me that no desideratum more urgently needs to be supplied in our theology than a work on the *Mind* or *Teaching of Christ*. For several years I have been working at this task. But, as I went on, my progress was impeded by the fact that, especially in the department of ethics, Jesus seemed to teach as much by His example as by His words; whereas it was my intention to derive His teaching from His words alone. I commenced accordingly to write a little on His example, merely for the purpose of clearing the surplus material out of the way, and without any thought that it would extend beyond a chapter or two. But, as I wrote, it grew and grew, till, almost unawares, the plan of a new book shaped itself in my mind. Recurring to the quaint and pithy language of Bunyan, I may say:

> Having now my method by the end,
> Still, as I pulled, it came; and so I penned
> It down; until it came at last to be,
> For length and breadth, the bigness which you see.

The plan of this book, as it thus, so to speak, made itself, is — to divide the circle of human life into segments, each of which represents an extensive sphere of experience and duty, and then to follow our Lord through them one after another, in order to see how He conducted Himself in each and thereby learn how to conduct ourselves in the same. It is thus a kind of Christian Ethics with a practical and devotional aim. By making the segments smaller, the chapters might easily have been increased in number, but perhaps no very important part of life has been entirely overlooked.

Each chapter has been written in full view of the whole of our Lord's behavior, as far as it has been recorded, in the department of human life to which it refers; and it was at one time my intention to print in full, from the Gospels, all the evidence on each head. I soon found, however, that this would be impracticable, for the evidence turned out to be far more voluminous than I had any conception of; and to print it in full would have swelled the book to double its size. It has been to me a continual astonishment to find how abundant are the materials for tracing out our Lord's example even in what may be considered the less important parts of life; and I thankfully confess that I have derived from this study a new impression of the wealth which is packed into the narrow circumference of the Four Gospels. On the flyleaf of each chapter I have noted a number of the more important passages; and this list, although in no case complete, may serve as a starting point to those who may wish to collect the evidence for themselves.

I am persuaded that there are many at present in all the churches who are turning earnest eyes to the Example of Christ, and who desire an account, derived directly from the records, of how He lived this earthly life which we are living now. They have awakened to the value and solemnity of time, and feel that the one thing needful is to fill our few and swiftly passing years with a life large and useful and ever more abundant. But it must be a life like Christ's, for His was the best; and any life, however filled with excitement or success, of which He disapproved, would not seem to them worth living. For such I have written this guide to the imitation of Christ, and I send it forth with the earnest hope that they may be able to find in it, in some degree, the authentic features of the image of the Son of man.

GLASGOW, *September 2, 1889*

But Thomas à Kempis?—the name had come across her in her reading, and she felt the satisfaction, which everyone knows, of getting some ideas to attach to a name that strays solitary in the memory. She took up the little old clumsy book with some curiosity: it had the corners turned down in many places, and some hand, now forever quiet, had made at certain passages strong pen-and-ink marks, long since browned by time. Maggie turned from leaf to leaf, and read where the quiet hand pointed. . . .

A strange thrill of awe passed through her while she read, as if she had been wakened in the night by a strain of solemn music, telling of beings whose souls had been astir while hers was in stupor. . . . She knew nothing of doctrines and systems—of mysticism or quietism, but this voice out of the far-off middle ages was the direct communication of a human soul's belief and experience, and came to her as an unquestioned message.

I suppose that is the reason why the small old-fashioned book, for which you need only pay sixpence at a bookstall, works miracles to this day, turning bitter waters into sweetness; while expensive sermons and treatises, newly issued, leave all things as they were before. It was written down by a hand that waited for the heart's prompting; it is the chronicle of solitary, hidden anguish, struggle, trust, and triumph—not written on velvet cushions to teach endurance to those who are treading with bleeding feet on the stones. And so it remains to all time a lasting record of human needs and human consolations.

GEORGE ELIOT, *The Mill on the Floss*

1

Introductory:
Thomas à Kempis' Imitation of Christ

No religious book perhaps, outside the canon of Scripture, has attained so wide a diffusion in the Christian Church as *De Imitatione Christi* of Thomas à Kempis. The only other book which may possibly compete with it in popularity is the *Pilgrim's Progress*. But the hold on Christendom of the older work is probably more extensive than even that of Bunyan's masterpiece; for while the picture of Giant Pope must be an obstacle to the access of the *Pilgrim* to sensitive Catholics, the *Imitation* is as much read among Protestants as in the Church which claims it as its own, and in the Greek Church it is as popular as in either of the communions of the West.

I

To Protestants it has a peculiar interest from the very fact that it was not written by the pen of a Protestant. It belongs to the beginning of the fifteenth century, and its author flourished a hundred years before Luther. It thus belongs to the age which must be accounted the darkest in the whole history of Christianity, when the light of God was wellnigh extinguished by the errors of men. Protestants, indeed, hardly think of the century before the Reformation as a time when Christianity existed at all; so vast is the accumulation of corruptions which meets the eye, that the religion of Christ almost seems to have disappeared. But this single book corrects this impression. The *Imitation of Christ* is a voice rising out of the darkness to remind us that the Church of Christ never ceased to exist, but that God had His witnesses and Christ His lovers even in the ear of deepest decay.

The *Imitation* itself, indeed, bears marks of the evil time in which it arose. There are elements of superstition in it which the modern mind rejects. But these relics of a corrupt age only make the profoundly Christian tone of the whole the more surprising. It throbs throughout with a devotion to Christ which will find its way to the hearts of Christians in every age:

> O my Beloved Spouse Christ Jesus, most pure Lover, Ruler of all creation, who will give me the wings of true liberty to fly and repose in Thee? O Jesus, Brightness of the eternal glory, Comfort of the pilgrim soul, with Thee are my lips without a voice, and my very silence speaks to Thee.
>
> How long delays my Lord His Coming? Let Him come to me, His poor servant, and make me glad. Come, come, for without Thee there will be no glad day nor hour; for Thou art my gladness, and without Thee my table is unspread.
>
> Let others seek, instead of Thee, whatever else they please; nothing else please me, or shall please me, but Thou, my God, my Hope, my Eternal Salvation.

The book overflows with love to the Savior expressed in this impassioned strain; and one very remarkable thing is that, on the whole, the soul goes straight to Christ without halting at those means of grace which were at that time so often substituted for the Savior or feeling any need of the intercession of the Virgin or the saints, on which so much stress is laid in Catholic books of devotion. This is the healthiest feature of the whole production and must be welcome to everyone who wishes to believe that even in that age, when the spirit was buried beneath the forms of worship, there were many souls that reached up through all obstacles to contact with the living Savior.

II

Obscure as is the external history of the author of the *Imitation*[*] the reader comes to be on the most intimate terms with him. He is a

---

[*] "The writer of the *Imitation Christi* is not known, and perhaps never will be known, with absolute certainty. The dispute about the authorship has filled a hundred volumes, and is still so undecided that the voice of the sweetest and hum-

mere shadow to the scientific historian, but to the devout student his personality is most distinct; his accent is separate and easily detected; and, notwithstanding the flight and passion of his devotion, there is in him something homely and kindly that wins our affection. Above all, we feel as we open the book that we are entering into communion with one who has found the secret of life. Here is one who, after weary wanderings, such as we perhaps are still entangled in, and many conflicts, such as we may still be waging, has attained the peace of God; and he takes us aside and leads us by the hand to view the land of rest. This is the enduring charm of the book. We all carry in our hearts a secret belief that somewhere in the world there exists a paradise unvexed with the cares by which we are pursued and watered by the river of God; and whenever one appears whose air assures us that he has lived in that Eden and drunk of that river, we cannot help welcoming him and listening to his message.

But where is this happy land? It is not far away. It is in ourselves: "The kingdom of God is within you." Men seek happiness out of themselves—in riches or learning or fame, in friendships and family connections, in talking about others and hearing news. They roam the

---

blest of books has come to us mingled, for the last two and a half centuries, with one of the most bitter and arrogant of literary controversies. . . . Of the nine or ten saints and doctors to whom at different times the work has been attributed, the pretensions of three alone can be now said to possess the least germ of probability. These three are a certain Gersen de Cahanis, Thomas Hemerken of Kempen, and Jean de Charlier de Gerson; and the claims of the first of the three . . . may now be considered to be set at rest.

"The two, then, between whom rests the glory of the authorship—though in truth earthly glory was the last thing for which the author would have wished—are *Thomas à Kempis*, sub-prior of the monastery of St. Agens, in the diocese of Cologne, and *Jean Gerson*, Chancellor of the University of Paris, and one of the grandest figures of his time.

"The lives of both these saints of God fell in the same dreary epoch. It was that "'age of lead and iron,' of political anarchy and ecclesiastical degradation, of war, famine, misery, agitation, corruption, which marked the close of the fourteenth and the beginning of the fifteenth century. Thomas à Kempis, born in 1379, died at the age of ninety-two; Gerson, born in 1363, died at the age of sixty-one. They were thus contemporaries for forty-five years of their lives. But the destinies of the two men were utterly different. [*continued*]

world in search of adventures; they descend to the bottom of the sea and tear out the bowels of the earth in pursuit of wealth; they are driven forth by turbulent passions in search of excitement and novelty; they fight with one another, because everyone, dissatisfied himself, believes that his brother is making away with his share. But all the time they are stumbling over their happiness, which lies among their feet; they fly to the ends of the earth in search of it, and lo it is at home.

> Whensoever a man desires anything inordinately, he is presently disquieted within himself. The proud and covetous are never at rest. The poor and humble in spirit live in abundance of peace.
>
> We might have such peace, if we would not busy ourselves with the sayings and doings of others, and with things which are no concern of ours.
>
> How can he remain long in peace who entangles himself with the cares of others; who seeks occasions of going abroad, and is little or seldom inwardly recollected?
>
> First keep thyself in peace, and then thou wilt be able to bring others to peace.

"Thomas, the son of an artisan, a quiet recluse, a copier of manuscripts, was trained at Deventer, and was received into a monastery in the year 1400 at the age of twenty-one. In that monastery of St. Agens—*valde devotus, lebenter solus, nunquam etiosus*—he spent seventy-one years of perfect calm, unbroken except by one brief period, in which he fled from his cell rather than acknowledge an archbishop to whom the Pope had refused the pallium. This was almost the sole event of a life in which we are told that it was his chief delight to be alone *in angello cum libello*.

"Far different from this life, 'in a little corner with a little book,' was the troubled, prominent, impassioned life of *Jean Gerson*, the *Doctor Christianissimus*. Rising while yet young to a leading position, he was appointed Chancellor of the University of Paris before the age of thirty, and, struggling against popes and councils, and mobs and kings, became the stormiest champion of a stormy time . . . And when all his life seemed to have culminated in one long failure . . . then forced to see how utterly little is man even at his greatest, and how different are the ways of man's nothing-perfectness from those of God's all-completeness, the great Chancellor, who has been the soul of mighty councils and the terror of contumacious popes, takes obscure refuge, first in a monastery of Tyrol, afterwards under the rule of his brother at Lyons, and there, among the strict and humble Celestine monks, passes his last days in humility and submission. Far other thoughts than those of his tumultuous life had been revealed to him as he wandered, in danger and privation, among the mountains of Bavaris—or, rather, those earlier objects

> A good peaceable man turns all things to good. Such a one is
> conqueror of himself, and lord of the world, a friend of Christ, and
> an heir of heaven.

These counsels sound like many that the world has heard from others of its teachers. They sound like the doctrines of the Stoic philosophers, which ended in making self an arrogant little god; they sound like the teaching of some in modern times who, looking on the raising of "the pyramid of their own being" as the chief end of existence, have sacrificed to culture the rights of others and the most sacred obligations of morality. The doctrine that the interior man is the supreme object of care may turn into a doctrine of arrogant selfishness. But à Kempis has guarded well against this perversion. He has no maxims more pungent than those directed against the undue exaltation of self. When he advises us to turn away from outward things to seek the true wealth and happiness within, it is not in ourselves we are to find it, though it is within ourselves. We have to make an empty space within, that it may be filled with God, who is the only true satisfaction of the soul:

> Know that the love of thyself doth hurt thee more than anything else in the world.
> On this defect, that a man inordinately loves himself, hangs almost all in thee that thou hast to root out and overcome; and, when this evil has been once conquered and brought under, soon will there be great peace and tranquility.
> Christ will come to thee, holding out to thee His consolation, if thou prepare Him a fit dwelling within thee.

---

had faded from the horizon of his soul like the burning hues of a stormy sunset; but as, when the sunset crimson has faded, we see the light of the eternal stars, so when the painted vapors of earthly ambition had lost their coloring, Gerson could gaze at last on those 'living sapphires' which glow in the deep firmament of spiritual hopes. He had been a leader among the schoolmen, now he cares only for the simplest truths. He had been a fierce gladiator in the arena of publicity, now he has passed into the life of holy silence. At his hottest period of strife he had cried out, 'Peace, peace, I long for peace,' now at last there has fallen on his soul—not as the world giveth—that peace that passeth understanding"—FARRAR in *Companions of the Devout Life*.

Many a visit does He make to the interior man; sweet is His communication with him, delightful His consolate, great His peace, and His familiarity exceedingly amazing. Give place, then, for Christ, and deny entrance to all others.

When thou has Christ thou art rich, and He is sufficient for thee. He will provide for thee and faithfully supply thy wants in all things, so that thou needest not trust to men.

"Son," says Christ to us, "leave thy self, and thou shalt find Me."

III

The merits of à Kempis are inimitable and imperishable; yet the book is not without defects more or less inseparable from the time and the circumstances in which it was written.

1. There is a defect of the *Imitation* which lies on the surface and has been often pointed out. Its author was a monk and needed a rule only for the little, monotonous world of the cloister; we live in the freedom and amidst the perils of a larger world, which needs an example more universal. To à Kempis and his brethren this world was the territory of the Evil One, from which they had fled; they wished to have no dealings with it and had no hope of making it better. "Thou oughtest," he says, "to be so far dead to the affections of men as to wish, as far as thou canst, to be without any human company." Even life itself appeared to him an evil: in one of this gloomiest pages he says expressly, "It is truly a misery to live upon earth." This happily is not our creed.

> The world is not a blank to us,
> Nor blot; it means intensely, and means good.

To us it is God's world; and our vocation is to make God's will be done in all departments of its life and to make His Word run on all its highways and byways. Monasticism was a confession on the part of Christianity of being beaten by the world, but today Christianity is planting its standard on every shore and going forth conquering and to conquer.

2. Another blemish which has been attributed to it is thus dealt with by Dr. Chalmers in one of his published Letters: "I have been

reading Thomas à Kempis recently on the Imitation of Jesus Christ—
a very impressive performance. Some would say of it that it is not
enough evangelical. He certainly does not often affirm, in a direct and
ostensible manner, the righteousness that is by faith. But he proceeds
on this doctrine and many an incidental recognition does he bestow
upon it; and I am not sure but that this implies a stronger and more
habitual settlement of mind respecting it than when it is thrust forward
and repeated, and re-repeated with a kind of ultra-orthodoxy, as if to
vindicate one's soundness, and acquit oneself of a kind of exacted
homage to the form of sound words."*

This is both a generous and a just statement of à Kempis' position;
though a simpler explanation of it lies in the fact that he lived a hundred years before the republication, at the Reformation, of this cardinal
doctrine of the Pauline theology. But it is a point of the greatest practical importance to emphasize that in experience the true order is, that
the imitation of Christ should follow the forgiveness of sins through
the blood of His cross.†

3. There is another great Pauline doctrine which hardly perhaps
obtains in à Kempis the prominence which belongs to it in connection with his subject. This is the doctrine of union with Christ, which
may be called the other pole of St. Paul's system. St. Paul's whole teaching revolves between the two poles of righteousness through the death
of Christ for us and holiness through the life of Christ in us. The latter truth is not absent from the pages of the *Imitation*, but its importance is not fully brought out.

For, beautiful as the phrase "the imitation of Christ" is, it hardly
indicates the deepest way in which Christ's people become like Him.
Imitation is rather an external process: it denotes the taking of that
which is on one and putting it on another from the outside. But it is
not chiefly by such an external copying that a Christian grows like
Christ, but by an internal union with Him. If it is by a process of
imitation at all, then it is imitation like that of a child copying its
mother. This is the competentest of imitations. The child reproduces

---

* *Correspondence of Rev. Thomas Chalmers, D. D.*, p. 81.
† On this point see the singularly lofty and weighty statement of Martensen, On
the Imitation of Christ and Justifying Faith, in his *Christian Ethics*, Vol. 1.

the mother's tones, her gestures, the smallest peculiarities of her gait and movements, with an amazing and almost laughable perfection. But why is the imitation so perfect? It may be said it is because of the child's innumerable opportunities of seeing its mother, or because of the minuteness of a child's observation. But everyone knows that there is more in it than this. The mother is in her child; at its birth she communicated her own nature to it; and it is to the working in the child of this mysterious influence that the success of the imitation is due. In like manner we may carefully copy the traits of Christ's character, looking at Him outside of us, as a painter looks at his model; we may do better still—we may, by prayer and the reading of the Word, live daily in His company, and receive the impress of His influence, but, if our imitation of Him is to be the deepest and most thorough, something more is necessary: He must be in us, as the mother is in her child, having communicated His own nature to us in the new birth.*

IV

There is, however, a defect in the *Imitation* which the reader of today feels more than any of these: it lacks the historical sense, which is the guide of the modern mind in every kind of inquiry. Though the spirit of Christ pervades the book and many of its chapters are so full of the essence of His teaching that they might be appended as invaluable comments to His sayings, yet it presents no clear historical image of Him.

This would seem, however, to be the one thing needful for successful imitation. If we are to try to be like Christ, we must know what He was like. No painter could make a satisfactory copy of a figure of which he had himself only a vague conception. Yet no exact image of Christ will be found in à Kempis. To him Christ is the union and sum of all possible excellences, but he constructs Christ out of his own notions of excellence, instead of going to the records of His life and painting the portrait with the colors they supply. He specifies, indeed, certain great features of the Savior's history—as, for instance, that in becoming man He humbled Himself, and therefore we ought

---

* "Christ's example is more than a barren, cold example of virtue; it is a warming, inspiring, living relationship"—KÖGEI, *Predigten*, i. 86.

to be humble; or that He lived a life of suffering, and therefore we ought to be willing to suffer, but he does not get beyond these generalities.

Now, it is possible to construct out of the Gospels a more lifelike portrait than this. It is possible at present as it has never been in any former age. Our century will be remembered in the history of Christian thought as the first which concentrated its attention on the details of the Life of Christ. The works written on this subject in recent times have been without number, and they have powerfully affected the mind of the age. The course of Christ's life on earth has been traced from point to point with indefatigable patience and illustrated with knowledge from every quarter; every incident has been set in the clearest light; and we are now able to follow Him as it has never been possible to do before into every department of life—such as the family, the state, the Church, the life of prayer, the life of friendship, and so on—and to see exactly how He bore Himself in each. This is the method of knowing Him which has been granted to our age; and to be content to know Him merely as a vague image of all possible excellences would be to us like painting a landscape in the studio from mere general conceptions of mountains, rivers and fields, instead of going direct to nature.

Of course it is easy to exaggerate the value of a method. Infinitely more important always are the mind and heart working behind the method. The glowing love, the soaring reverence, the range and sublimity of thought in à Kempis, have brought the object home to him with a closeness and reality which fill every sympathetic reader with a sacred envy and will always enchain the Christian heart.* Yet, though an improved method is not everything, it is something, and, if we feel our own devotion to be cold, and the wing of our thought feeble in comparison with others, all the more ought we to grasp at whatever advantage it may be able to supply. The imitation of Christ is a sub-

---

* In reading the Psalms, who has not coveted the nearness to God which their authors attained, and the splendid glow of feeling which contact with Him produced in them? Who has not questioned whether he has ever himself penetrated so far into the secret of the Lord? Yet this does not blind us to the superior freedom and fullness of access to the divine presence allowed under the New Testament.

ject which is constantly calling for consideration; for the evolution of history and the progress of knowledge place people on new points of view in relation to it. Each generation sees it in its own way, and the last word on it can never be spoken. The historical method of handling it is the one which falls in with those habits of thought which have been worn into the mind of our age by its vast conquests in other directions; and, though it will not make up for the lack of faith and love, it is a *charisma* which the Church is bound to use, and on the use of which God will bestow His blessing.

V

It can hardly be said that evangelical thought has hitherto claimed this subject cordially enough as its own. The evangelical heart, indeed, has always been true to it. I have sometimes even thought that among the causes of the popularity of à Kempis' book not the least potent is its mere name. The Imitation of Christ! The very sound of this phrase goes to the heart of every Christian and sets innumerable things moving and yearning in the soul. There is a summons in it like a ravishing voice calling us up sunny heights. It is the sum of all which in our best moments and in our deepest heart we desire.

But, whilst to Christian experience the imitation of Christ has always been inexpressibly precious, it has held, in evangelical preaching and literature, on the whole, only on equivocal position. The Moderatism which in the last century nearly extinguished the religion of the country made much of the example of Christ. But it divorced it from His atonement, and urged men to follow Christ's example, without first making them acquainted with Him as the Savior from sins that are past. The Evangelicals, in opposition to this, made Christ's atonement the burden of their testimony and when His example was mentioned, were ever ready with, Yes, but His death is more important. Thus it happened that the two parties divided the truth between them, the example of Christ being the doctrine of the one and His atoning death that of the other. In like manner, when Unitarianism seemed for a time, through the high character and splendid eloquence of Channing, to be about to become a power in the world, it derived nearly all the attractiveness it ever possessed from the eulogies in which its preaching abounded of the pure, lofty and self-sacrificing humanity of Christ. The evangelical Church answered with demonstrations of His divinity, scriptural and irresistibly logical no doubt, but not always very captivating. And thus a division was again allowed to take place, the humanity of Christ falling to the one party as its share and His divinity to the other.

It is time to object to these divisions. Both halves of the truth are ours, and we claim the whole of it. The death of Christ is ours, and we rest in it our hopes of acceptance with God in time and in eternity. This is what we begin with, but we do not end with it. We will go on from His death to His life and, with the love begotten of being redeemed, try to reproduce that life in our own. In the same way, while glorying in His divinity, we will allow none to rob us of the attraction and the example of His humanity; for, indeed, the perfection of His humanity, with what this implies as to the value of His testimony about Himself, is the strongest bulwark of our faith that He was more than man.

Matthew 8:14, 15; 9:18–26; 17:18; 18:1–6; 19:13–15; Mark 4:18, 19; 12:18–25; Luke 7:11–15; 11:27, 28; John 8:1–11; 19:25–27.

Matthew 12:46–50; Luke 9:57–62.

Matthew 1; 2; Luke 1:26–56; 2; 3:23–38.

Matthew 13:55–58; Luke 4:16, 22; John 6:42.

Mark 3:21; John 7:3–9.

2

Christin the Home

THE institution of the family affords striking illustrations both of what may be called the element of necessity and of what may be called the element of liberty in human life.

There is in it a mysterious element of necessity. Everyone is born into a particular family, which has a history and character of its own, formed before he arrives. He has no choice in the matter; yet this connection affects all his subsequent life. He may be born where it is an honor to be born or, on the contrary, where it is a disgrace. He may be heir to inspiring memories and refined habits, or he may have to take up a hereditary burden of physical and moral disease. A man has no choice of his own father and mother, his brothers and sisters, his uncles and cousins; yet on these ties, which he can never unlock, may depend three-fourths of his happiness or misery. The doorbell rings some night, and, going out, you see on the doorstep a man who is evidently a stranger from a strange land. You know nothing of him; he is quite outside the circle of your interest; he is ten thousand miles away from your spirit. But, if he can say, "Don't you know me? I am your brother," how near he comes—ten thousand miles at one step! You and he are connected with an indissoluble bond; and this bond may either be a golden clasp which is an ornament or an iron clamp which burns and corrodes your very flesh. This is the element of necessity in the institution of the family.

Jesus could not touch humanity without being caught in this fetter of necessity. He entered its mysterious circle when He was born of a woman. He became a member of a family which had its own traditions and its own position in society; and He had brothers and sisters.

These circumstances were not without importance to Him. That His mother exercised an influence upon His growing mind cannot be doubted. We have not, indeed, the means of tracing in much detail how this influence acted, for few notices of His early years have come down to us, but it may be noted as one significant fact that Mary's hymn, the so-called Magnificat, in which, at her meeting with Elizabeth, she poured forth the sentiments of her heart, embodies thoughts which are echoed again and again in the preaching of Jesus. This production proves her to have been a woman not only of great grace, but of rare natural gifts, which had been nourished from God's Word, till she naturally spoke the very language of the prophets and the holy women of old. We may not ascribe too much to her and Joseph, but we can say that the holy childhood of Jesus was reared in a home of pious refinement, and that there were marks of this home on Him after He left it.

Besides this influence, He was born to a long pedigree; and this was not a matter of indifference to Him. He was of the seed of David; and the Gospel narrative takes pains to trace His descent in the royal line—a procedure which may be regarded as an echo of His own feeling. *Noblesse oblige*; there is a stimulus to noble action supplied by noble lineage; and Milton is not perhaps overstepping the bounds of legitimate inference when, in *Paradise Regained*, he represents the mind of the youthful Savior as being stirred to noble ambition by the memories of His ancestors:

> Victorious deeds
> Flamed in My heart, heroic acts—one while
> To rescue Israel from the Roman yoke;
> Then to subdue and quell o'er all the earth
> Brute violence and proud tyrannic power,
> Till truth was freed and equity restored.

There can at least be no hesitation in believing that His royal descent pointed out His way to the work of the Messiah.

He had, however, also to feel the galling of the ring of necessity. He bore the reproach of mean descent; for, although His remoter ancestry was noble, His immediate relatives were poor; and, when He appeared on the stage of public life, sneering tongues asked, "Is not this the carpenter's son?" His life is the final rebuke to such shallow respect of persons, and will remain forever to the despised and lowly-born a guide to show how, by worth of character and wealth of service to God and man, they may shut the mouths of gainsayers and win a place in the love and honor of the world.

The element of liberty which belongs to human life is exhibited no less conspicuously than the element of necessity in the family, and is equally mysterious. Of his own choice a man enters the married state and founds a family; and by this act of his will the circle is fashioned which in the next generation will be enclosing other human beings in the same bonds of relationship into which he has himself been born.

Of course the nature of the case prevented Jesus from being the founder of a family; and this has sometimes been pointed to as a defect in the example He has left us. We have not, it is said, His example to follow in the most sacred of all the relationships of life. Undeniably there seems to be a certain force in this objection. Yet it is a singular fact that the greatest of all precepts in regard to this relationship is taken directly from His example. The deepest and most sacred word ever uttered on the subject of marriage is this: "Husbands, love your wives, even as Christ also loved the Church, and gave Himself for it; that He might sanctify and cleanse it with the washing of water by the Word, that He might present it to Himself a glorious Church, not having spot, or wrinkle, or any such thing, but that it should be holy and without blemish."*

II

Jesus honored the institution of the family all through His life.

In His day there prevailed in Palestine a shameful dissolution of the domestic ties. Divorce was rife and so easily procured that every trifle was made an excuse for it; and by the system of Corban children were actually allowed to compound by a payment to the Temple for the neglect of their own parents. Jesus denounced these abuses with unsparing indignation and sanctioned for all the Christian ages

---

* Eph. 5:25ff.

only that law of marriage which causes it to be entered on with fore-thought,* and then, when the relationship has been formed, drains the deepest affections of the heart into its sacred channel.

His own love of children, and the divine words He spoke about them, if they cannot be said to have created the love of parents for their children, have at all events immensely deepened and refined it. The love of heathen mothers and fathers for their offspring is a rude and an-imal propensity in comparison with the love for children which reigns in our Christian homes. He lifted childhood up, as He raised so many other weak and despised things, and set it in the midst. If the pat-ter of little feet on the stairs and the sound of little voices in the house are music to us, and if the pressure of little fingers and the touches of little lips can make us thrill with gratitude and prayer, we owe this sunshine of life to Jesus Christ. By saying, "Suffer the little children to come unto Me," He converted the home into a church, and parents into His ministers; and it may be doubted whether He has not by this means won to Himself as many disciples in the course of the Christian ages as even by the institution of the Church itself. Perhaps the lessons of mothers speaking of Jesus, and the examples of Christian fathers, have done as much for the success of Christianity as the sermons of eloquent preachers or the worship of assembled con-gregations. Not once or twice, at all events, has the religion of Christ, when driven out of the Church, which had been turned by faithless ministers and worldly members into a synagogue of Satan, found an asylum in the home; and there have been few of the great teachers of Christendom who have not derived their deepest convictions from the impressions made by their earliest domestic environment.

---

* "He who attacks marriage, he who by word or deed sets himself to undermine this foundation of all moral society, he must settle the matter with me; and, if I don't bring him to reason, then I have nothing to do with him. Marriage is the begin-ning and the summit of all civilization. It makes the savage mild; and the most highly cultivated man has no better means of demonstrating his mildness. Marriage must be indissoluble; for it brings so much general happiness, that any individual case of unhappiness that may be connected with it cannot come into ac-count. . . . Are we not really married to our conscience, of which we might often be willing to rid ourselves because it often annoys us more than any man or woman can possibly annoy one another?" — BLACKIE, *The Wisdom of Goethe.*

Many of the miracles of Jesus seem to have been prompted by regard for the affections of the family. When He healed the Syro-Phoenician's daughter, or gave the daughter of Jairus back to her mother, or raised the widow's son at the gate of Nain, or brought Lazarus from the dead to keep the family circle at Bethany unbroken, can it be doubted that the Savior experienced delight in ministering to the domestic affections? He showed how profound was His appreciation of the depth and intensity of these affections in the Parable of the Prodigal Son.

But it was by His own conduct in the family that He exhibited most fully His respect for this institution. Though the details of His life in Mary's home are unknown to us, every indication shows Him to have been a perfect son.

There is no joy of parents comparable to that of seeing their child growing up in wisdom, modesty and nobility; and we are told that Jesus grew in wisdom and stature and in favor with God and man. If He knew already of the great career before Him, this did not lift Him above the obedience of a child; for, even when He was twelve years of age, we are told, He went down to Nazareth with His parents and was subject unto them. It is generally supposed that soon after this Joseph died, and on Jesus, as the eldest son, fell the care of supporting the family. This is uncertain, but the very close of His life is marked by an act which throws the strongest light back on the years of which no record has been preserved, for it reveals how deep and deathless was His affection for His mother. While hanging on the cross, He saw her and spoke to her. He was at the time in terrible agony, every nerve tingling with intolerable pain. He was at the point of death and anxious no doubt to turn away from all earthly things and deal with God alone; He was bearing the sin of the world, whose maddening load was crushing His heart; yet, amidst it all, He turned His attention to His mother and to her future, and made provision for her by asking one of His disciples to take her to his home and be a son to her in His own stead. And the disciple He selected for this service was the most amiable of them all—not Peter, the headlong or Thomas the melancholy, but John, who could talk with her more tenderly than any other about the one subject which absorbed them both, and who was perhaps more able than any of the rest, on account of the comfort of his worldly condition, to support Mary without allowing her to feel that she was a burden.

III

Sacred as is the parent's right to the obedience of the child, there is a term to it. It is the office of the parent to train the child to independence. As the schoolmaster's aim ought to be to train his pupils to a stage where they are able to face the work of life without any more help from him, so parents have to recognize that there is a point at which their commands must cease and their children be allowed to choose and act for themselves. Love will not cease; respect ought not to cease, but authority has to cease. Where exactly this point occurs in a child's life it is difficult to define. It may not be the same in every case. But in all cases it is a momentous crisis. Woe to the child who grasps at this freedom too soon! This is often the ruin of the young; and among the features of the life of our own time there are none perhaps more ominous than the widespread disposition among the young to slip the bridle of authority prematurely and acknowledge no law except their own will. But parents also sometimes make the mistake of attempting to exert their authority too long. A father may try to keep his son under his roof when it would be better for him to marry and have a house of his own; or a mother may interfere in the household affairs of her married daughter, who would be a better wife if left to her own resources.*

---

* "A child's duty is to obey its parents. It is never said anywhere in the Bible, and never was yet said in any good or wise book, that a man's or a woman's is. When, precisely, a child becomes a man or a woman, it can no more be said, than when it should first stand on its legs. But a time assuredly comes when it should. In great states children are always trying to remain children, and the parents wanting to make men and women of them. In vile states the children are always wanting to be men and women, and the parents to keep them children. It may be — and happy the house in which it is so — that the father's at least equal intellect, and older experience, may remain to the end of his life a law to his children, not of force, but of perfect guidance, with perfect love. Rarely it is so; not often possible. It is as natural for the old to be prejudiced as for the young to be presumptuous; and in the change of centuries, each generation has something to judge of for itself" — RUSKIN, *Mornings in Florence*, Vol. 3, p. 72.

Mary, the mother of Jesus, erred in this respect. She attempted again and again to interfere unduly with His work, even after His public ministry had commenced. It was her pride in Him that made her do so at the marriage in Cana of Galilee; it was anxiety about His health on other occasions. She was not the only one who ventured to control His action in an undue way. But, if anything could arouse the indignation of Jesus, it was such interference. It made Him once turn on Peter with, "Get thee behind Me, Satan"; and on more than one occasion it lent an appearance of harshness even to His behavior to His mother. The very intensity of His life to His friends and relatives made their wishes and appeals sore temptations to Him, for He would have liked to please them had He been able. But, if He had yielded, He would have been turning way from the task to which He was pledged; and therefore He had to rouse Himself even to indignation to resist temptation.

On no other occasion had His conduct so much appearance of unfilial harshness as when His mother and brethren came one day in the midst of His work desiring to speak with Him, and He retorted on the person who told Him, "But who is My mother, and who are My brethren?" and, looking round on the disciples seated in front of Him, added, "Behold, My mother and My brethren! For whosoever shall do the will of God, the same is My brother, and sister, and mother." It cannot be denied that those words have a harsh sound.* But they are probably to be read with what goes immediately before them in the Gospel of St. Mark, where we are told that His friends made an attempt to lay hold of Him, saying, "He is beside Himself." So absorbed was Jesus at this period in His work that he neglected even to eat; so rapt was He in the holy passion of saving men that to His relatives it appeared that He had gone mad; and they conceived it to be their duty to lay hands on Him and put Him in restraint. If Mary took part in this impious procedure, it is no wonder that there should have fallen on her a heavy rebuke. At all events she evidently came to Him thinking that He must at once leave everything and speak to her. But He had

---

* The very fact, however, that Jesus compared the relation between Himself and those who do the will of God to the connection between Himself and His mother and brethren implies that the latter held a high and sacred place in His mind.

to teach her that there are even higher claims than those of domestic affection: in doing God's work He could recognize no authority but God's.

There is a sphere into which even parental authority may not seek admittance—the sphere of conscience. Jesus not only kept this sacred for Himself, but called upon those who followed Him to do so too. He foresaw how in the progress of time this would often sever family ties; and to one who cherished so high a respect for the home it must have been a prospect full of pain: "Think not," He said, "that I am come to send peace on earth, but a sword. For I am come to set a man at variance against his father, and the daughter against her mother, and the daughter-in-law against her mother-in-law. And a man's foes shall be they of his own household." This must have been to Him a terrible prospect, but He did not shrink from it; to Him there were claims higher than even those of home: "He that loveth father and mother more than Me is not worthy of Me, and he that loveth son or daughter more than Me is not worthy of Me."

This sword still cuts. In heathen countries where Christianity is being introduced, especially in countries like India, where the domestic system is extensively developed, the chief difficulty in the way of confessing Christ is the pain of breaking family connections, and often it is nothing less than an agony. Even in Christian lands the opposition of worldly parents to the religious decision of their children is sometimes very strong, and occasions extreme perplexity to those who have to bear this cross. It is always a delicate case, requiring the utmost Christian wisdom and patience, but, when the issues are clear to mind and conscience, there can be no doubt which alternative is the will of Christ: we must obey God rather than man.* How happy are they who are in precisely the opposite case: who know that their full

---

* There is a very important caution hinted at in the words of Martensen on this subject (*Christian Ethics*, Vol. 2): "Whatever doubtful and difficult circumstances may hereby arise, and however mistakenly those members of a family may act, who are awake to Christian truth, but whose Christianity is often made an unseemly display of, and whose whole behavior is one fret and ferment, still the fact itself, that *ordinary* and *worldly* family life is disturbed by the Gospel, is one quite in order, and in conformity with the divine economy."

decision for Christ and frank confession of Him would fill their homes with joy unspeakable!

IV

In every home, it is said, there is a skeleton in the cupboard; that is to say, however great may be its prosperity and however perfect the appearance of harmony it presents to the world, there is always inside, some friction or fear, or secret, which darkens the sunshine.

This proverb may be no truer than many other wide generalizations which need to be qualified by the acknowledgment of innumerable exception. Yet there is no denying that home has its pains as well as its pleasures, and the very closeness of the connection of the members of a family with one another gives to any who may be so disposed the chance of wounding the rest. Under the cloak of relationship torture may be applied with impunity, which those who inflict it would not dare to apply to an outsider.

Jesus suffered from this: He had His peculiar domestic grief. It was that His brethren did not believe on Him. They could not believe that He who had grown up with them as one of themselves was infinitely greater than they. They looked with envy on His waxing fame. Whenever they intervene in His life, it is in a way to annoy.

How great a grief this must have been to Jesus will be best understood by those who have suffered the like themselves. There have been many of God's saints who have had to stand and testify alone in ungodly and worldly homes. Many in such circumstances are suffering an agony of daily petty martyrdom which may be harder to bear than public persecution, for which widespread sympathy is easily aroused. But they know at least that they have the sympathy of Him who alluded so pathetically to His own experience in the words: "A prophet is not without honor save in his own country and in his own house."

How He met His brethren's unbelief—whether He reasoned and remonstrated with them or was silent and trusted to the testimony of His life—we cannot tell. But we may be certain that He prayed for them without ceasing; and happily we know what the issue was.

His brethren, it would appear, continued unbelieving up to the time of His death. But immediately thereafter, in the first chapter of the Book of Acts, we find them assembled as believers with His apostles in Jerusalem (Acts 1:14). This is an extraordinary circumstance; for at this very time His cause was, if we may so speak, at the lowest ebb. Events seemed to have demonstrated that His pretensions to the Messiahship had been false; yet those who had disbelieved in Him at the height of His fame were found among the believers in Him when apparently His cause had gone to pieces. How is this to be accounted for?

The explanation lies, I believe, in a passage of First Corinthians, where, in enumerating the appearances of our Lord to different persons after His resurrection, St. Paul mentions that he appeared to James (1 Cor. 15:7). This was apparently the Lord's brother; and, if so, is there not something wonderfully striking in the fact that one of the first acts of the risen Savior was to bring to His unbelieving brother the evidence which would conquer his unbelief? James, it may be presumed, would communicate what he had experienced to the other members of Mary's family. The result was of the happiest description; and two of the brothers, James and Jude, lived to be the penmen of books of Holy Scripture.

I venture to think that the presence of these brethren of Jesus among the believers in Him at such a crisis is even yet one of the strongest proofs of the reality of the resurrection, but in the meantime we will rather think of it as a signal proof of the unwearied persistence with which He sought their salvation, and as an example to ourselves to pray on, hope on, work on for those of our own flesh and blood who may yet be outside the fold of Christ.

Matthew 9:1; 13:54; 17:24–27; 20:17–19; 23:37–39; 26:32.
Luke 4:16–30; 13:16, 34, 35; 19:9.

Matthew 2; 4:3–10; 9:9, 27; 21:1–11; 22:15–21; 26:47–68; 27.
Luke 2:11, 29, 32, 38; 13:31–33; 23:7–12.
John 6:15; 11:48.

Matthew 18:1–3; 19:28; 20:20–28.
John 18:36, 37; 19:14, 19, 20.

3

Christ in the State

In the mind of the average Christian of the present day the idea of the state does not perhaps occupy a prominent position. Many of his duties appear to him more important than those he owes as a citizen. He probably considers that the most important question which can be asked about him is, What is he in himself, in his secret soul and inward character? Next to this in importance he might perhaps consider the question of what he is as a member of the Church, charged with sustaining its honor and sharing in its work. The third place he might give to the question of what he is in the family, as son, husband, father. But much less important than any of these would appear to him the fourth question—what he is as a citizen of the state.

On the whole, perhaps this is the right way of judging; probably it is the Christian way.* But it is the exact opposite of the view of the whole ancient world. The great thinkers of Greece, for example, put the state before the individual, the home and the Church. To them the

---

* The relative importance of these different ways of considering man affords scope, however, for endless discussion and difference of opinions. Rothe's ethical speculations were powerfully influenced by deference to the ancient view of the priority of the state. Martensen holds that a theory of society must start from the family. Ritschl and his school have re-emphasized the ethical and religious importance of the Church. Among ourselves several causes are contributing at present to give prominence to the social aspects of religion. It is impossible to overestimate these, unless they are put above its individual aspects. I can entertain no doubt that in the mind of Jesus the individual was the *prius*. Indeed, one of the most decisive steps forward taken in His moral teaching was the substitution of the individual as the unit for the nation or the Church.

supreme question about every man was, What is he as a citizen? The chief end of man they believed to be to make the state great and prosperous, and to the interests of the state they sacrificed everything else. Whether the individual was good and happy, whether the family was pure and harmonious, was not what they asked first, but whether the state was strong.

Jesus changed this. He was the discoverer, so to speak, of the individual. He taught that in every man there is a soul more precious than the whole world, and that the best product of this world is a good and noble character. Instead of its being true that individuals do not matter if the state is strong, the truth is that the state and the Church and the family are only means for the good of the individual, and they are tested by the kind of man they produce.* In this, as in many other respects, Christianity turned the world upside down, and put the first last and the last first.

But, although the state does not hold the place in Christian teaching which it held in heathen philosophy, it would be a great mistake to suppose that to Christianity the state is unimportant. Though the primary aim of Christ's religion is to make good men, yet good men ought to be good citizens.

II

It is natural to a healthy human being to love the land of his birth, the scenery on which his eyes have first rested, and the town in which he resides; and it is part of the design of providence to utilize these affections for the progress of man and the embellishment of the earth, which is his habitation. Every inhabitant of a town ought to wish to promote its welfare and adorn it with beauty; and there is no feeling more worthy of a youthful heart than the desire to do something—by making a wise plan, or writing a good book, or singing a noble lay, or expunging a national blot—to add to the fair fame of his native country.

> I mind it weel, in early date,
> When I was beardless, young and blate,

---

* "The test of every religious, political, or educational system is the man which it forms"—*Amiel's Journal*, Vol. 1, p. 49.

And first could thresh the barn.

*　　*　　*　　*　　*　　*

Ev'n then a wish (I mind its power),
A wish that to my latest hour
　　Shall strongly have my breast:
That I for poor auld Scotland's sake
Some usefu' plan or beuk could make
　　Or sing a sang at least.

BURNS

Some countries have had an exceptional power of awakening these sentiments and of binding their own children to their service. Palestine was one of these. It was loved with a fervent patriotism. Its charm lay partly in its beauty. It may have lain partly in its very smallness, for feeling contract an impetuous force when confined within narrow limits, as highland rivers become torrents in their rocky beds. But it is the memory of great and unselfish lives lived on its soil that chiefly excites patriotic sentiment in the inhabitants of any country;* and Palestine possessed this source of fascination in unparalleled measure, for its history was crowded with the most inspiring names.

Jesus felt this spell. Can anyone read in His words the images of natural beauty gathered from the fields of Galilee without being convinced that He looked on these landscapes with a loving eye? The name of the village He was brought up in clings to Him to this day, for He is still Jesus of Nazareth. He vindicated Himself for healing a woman on the Sabbath on the ground that she was a daughter of Abraham; and the publicans and sinners were dear to Him because they were the lost sheep of the house of Israel. Jerusalem, the capital of the country, had always laid a strong hold on Jewish hearts. The bards of the nation used to sing of it, "Beautiful for situation is Mount

---

* Says Novalis: "The best of the French monarchs had it for his purpose to make his subjects so well off that every one of them should be able on Sundays to have roast fowl to dinner. Very good. But would not that be a better government under which the peasant would rather dine on dry bread than under any other on roast fowl, and, as grace before meat, would give God thanks that he had been born in such a country?"

Zion"; "Let my tongue cleave to the roof of my mouth if I forget thee, O Jerusalem." But all such tributes of affection were surpassed by Jesus, when He addressed it, "O Jerusalem, Jerusalem, how often would I have gathered thy children together even as a hen gathereth her chickens under her wings!" This feeling survived even the transformation of the grave, for, in giving instructions, after He was risen, to His apostles about the evangelization of the world, He said, "Begin at Jerusalem." He lived in the closest sympathy with the great figures of His country's past and with the work done by them. Such names as Abraham and Moses, David and Isaiah, were continually on His lips; and He took up the tasks which they had left unfinished and carried them forward to their fulfillment. This is the truest work of patriotism. Happy is that country whose best life has been drained into some ideal cause, and whose greatest names are the names of those who have lavished their strength on this object. The deeds and sayings of these heroes ought, next to the Bible, to be the chief spiritual nourishment of her children; and the young ambition of her choicest minds should be concentrated on watering the seeds which they sowed and completing the enterprises which they inaugurated.

III

There was one task of patriotism in Christ's day and country which seemed to lie to the hand of anyone born with a patriotic spirit. Palestine was at that time an enslaved country. In fact, it was groaning under a double servitude; for, while several of its provinces were ruled over by the tyrannical race of the Herods,* the whole country was subject to the Roman power.

Was it not the duty of Jesus to free His country from this double tyranny and restore it to independence, or even elevate it to a place of sovereignty among the nations? Many would have been willing to welcome a deliverer and to make sacrifices for the national cause. The whole of the Pharisaic party was imbued with patriotic sentiment, and

---

* Herod the Great, the founder of this dynasty, was an Idumean, but tried to conciliate the national sentiment by marrying a Jewish princess.

a section of it bore the name of the Zealots, because they were willing to go all lengths in sacrifice or daring.*

Jesus seemed to be designated for this very service. He was directly descended from David through the royal line. When He was born, wise men came from the East to Jerusalem inquiring, "Where is He that is born King of the Jews?" One of His first disciples,† on being introduced to Him, saluted Him as "the King of Israel"; and, on the day when He rode in triumph into Jerusalem His adherents called Him by the same name, no doubt meaning that they expected Him to be literally the king of the country. These, and many other incidents which they will recall, are indications that it was His destiny not to be the private man He was, but to be the head of an emancipated and glorious state.

Why was this destination not fulfilled? This is the most difficult question that can be asked. It occurs often to every careful reader of the Gospels, but lands us as often as we ask it in a sea of mysteries. Did He ever intend to be the king of His native country? Was Satan appealing to the favorite fancies of His youth when he showed Him all the kingdoms of the world and the glory of them? If the Jewish people, instead of rejecting, had welcomed Him, what would have happened? Would He have set up His throne in Jerusalem and made the whole world subject to it? Was it only when they had made it impossible for Him to reign over them that He turned aside from what appeared to be His destiny and limited Himself to a kingdom not of this world?

It is impossible to read Christ's life intelligently without asking such questions as these; yet it is vain to ask them, for they cannot be answered. We are asking what would have been, if something which did happen had not happened; and only omniscience is equal to such a problem.

We may, however, say with certainty that it was the sin of man which prevented Jesus from ascending the throne of His father David. His offer of Himself to be the Messiah of His country was a *boná fide* offer. Yet it was made on conditions from which He could not depart:

---

* One member of this party, Simon Zelotes, joined the discipleship of Jesus.
† Nathanael

He could only have been king of a righteous nation. But the Jews were thoroughly unrighteous. They once tried to take Him by force and make Him a king, but their zeal was unhallowed, and He could not yield to it.

Then the tide of His life turned and rolled back upon itself. Instead of the expeller of tyrants, He became the victim of tyranny. His own nation, which ought to have raised Him on its shields as its leader, became His prosecutor at the bar of the alien government, and He had to stand as a culprit before both the Roman and the Herodian rulers of the land. As a subject of the country, He yielded with al submissiveness, telling His followers to put up their swords. And the law officers of the state made a malefactor of Him, crucifying Him between two thieves. His blood fell on the capital of the country as a deadly curse; and in less than half a century after His murder the Jewish state had disappeared from the face of the earth.

It is a terrible commentary on the imperfection of the state. The state exists for the protection of life, property, and honor—to be a terror to evildoers and a praise to them that do well. Once, and only once in all history, it had to deal with One who was perfectly good; and what it did was to adjudge Him a place among the very worst of criminals and put Him to death. If this were a specimen of the law's habitual action, the state, instead of being a divine institution, would have to be pronounced the most monstrous evil with which the world is cursed. So the victims of its injustice have sometimes pronounced it, but happily such opinions are only the excesses of a few. On the whole, the laws framed by the state, and the administration of them, have been a restraint on sin and a protection to innocence. Yet the exceptions in every age have been numerous and sad enough. Not everything is righteous which the law of the land sanctions, nor are those all unrighteous whom the administrators of the law condemn. It is of the utmost consequence in our day to remember this, because, in the changed arrangements of the modern state, we are not only subjects of the government, but, directly or indirectly, makers and administrators of the law. Through the exercise of the municipal and the parliamentary franchises, we have a part in appointing those who make and who administer the laws, and thus we have our share in the responsibility of bringing up the laws to the standard of the divine justice and placing the wise and the good upon the judgment seat.

IV

The life of Jesus appeared to miscarry. He who was meant to be a king was held unworthy to live even as a subject; instead of inhabiting a palace, He was consigned to prison; instead of being seated on a throne, He was nailed to a tree.

But, although this was a miscarriage insofar as it was due to the wicked will of men, it was no miscarriage in the wisdom of God. Looked at from man's side, the death of Christ was the blackest spot on human history, a mistake and a crime without parallel, but, looked at from God's side, it is the grandest scene in the history of the universe; for in it human sin was expiated, the depths of the divine love were disclosed, and the path of perfection opened for the children of men. Jesus was never so completely a king as at the moment when His claims to kingship were turned into ridicule. It was in savage jest that the title was put above His cross, "This is Jesus, the King of the Jews." Pilate wrote these words in ridicule, but, when we look back at them now, do they appear ridiculous? Do they not rather shine across the centuries with inextinguishable splendor? In that hour of uttermost shame He was proving Himself to be the King of kings and the Lord of lords.

Jesus had all along had a conception of His own kingship which was distinct, original and often repeated. He held that to be a true king is to be the servant of the commonweal, and that he is most kingly who renders the most valuable services to the greatest number. He was well aware that this was not the world's view of kingship, but precisely the reverse of it. The world's view is that to be a king is to have multitudes in your service, and the greater the numbers ministering to his glory or pleasure the greater is the king. So He said: "The princes of the Gentiles exercise dominion over them, and they that are great exercise authority upon them." "But," He added, "it shall not be so among you: but whosoever will be great among you, let him be your minister; and whosoever will be chief among you, let him be your servant." Such was Christ's conception of greatness; and, if it is the true one, He was never so great as when, by the sacrifice of Himself, He was conferring on the whole world the blessings of salvation.

But this conception of greatness and kingliness was not meant by Jesus to be applied to His own conduct alone; it is of universal application. It is the Christian standard for the measurement of all dignities in the state. He is greatest, according to the mind of Christ, who renders the greatest services to others.

Alas! this is as yet but little understood; it makes but slow progress in the minds of men. The old heathen idea is still the governing one of politics—that to be great is to receive much service, not to render it. Politics has been a game of ambition, if not a hunting ground for rapacity, rather than a sphere of service. The aim of the governing classes hitherto has been to get as much as possible for themselves at the expense of the governed; and it has yet to be seen whether the new governing class is to be swayed by a better spirit.

Still, the Christian idea is growing in this department also of human affairs. The common heart responds to Christ's teaching, that the kingliest is he who sacrifices himself most willingly, works the hardest and achieves the most for the weal of all; and, although the quaint old saying of the Psalmist is still too true, that "men will praise thee when thou doest well to thyself," yet the number of those is daily growing who feel that the greatness of a ruler is measured, "not by the amount of tribute he levies on society, but by the greatness of the services he renders it."

Matthew 3:13–15; 8:4; 9:35; 13:54; 21:12, 13.
Mark 3:1–6; 6:2; 12:41–44.
Luke 2:21–24, 39, 41–49; 4:16–32, 44; 22:53.
John 4:22; 5:1; 8:20; 10:22, 23.

Matthew 9:10–17; 12:1–14; 15:1–9; 16:6; 23.
Luke 10:31, 32.
John 2:13–22.

Matthew 24:1, 2; 26:17–30; 28;19, 20.
John 20:22, 23.

4

Christ in the Church

IN some respects the Church is a narrower body than even the family; for one member of a family may be taken into it and another left out, but in other respects it is wider even than the state; for members of different nations may be members of the same Church.

The family and the state are institutions developed out of human nature by its own inherent force and according to its own inherent laws, but the Church is a divine institution, planted among men to gather into itself select souls and administer to them supernatural gifts. It is not, indeed, without a natural root in human nature, but this root consists of those feelings in man which make him aspire to an enjoyment and satisfaction which are not to be found in this world of which he is lord, but can only be got as the pure gift of Heaven. Without revelation there is no Church. As the edifice of the Church rises above the homes of men, amidst which it is erected, and its spire, like a finger, points to the sky, so the Church as an institution is an expression of man's aspirations after a heavenly life—a life in God and in eternity, which only the condescending grace of God can supply.

I

Jesus was born in a country in which there was already a true Church, founded on revelation and administering the grace of God. He was a child of that nation to which "pertained the adoption and the glory, and the covenants, and the giving of the law, and the service of God, and the promises." He was admitted into the fellowship of the Church by the ordinary gateway of circumcision; and a few weeks thereafter He was in the Temple, like any other Jewish child, in acknowledgment that He belonged to the Lord. Thus, before He was Himself conscious of it, He was, through the wishes of His earthly parents, shut in by holy rites within the visible Church of God.

In our day, all Christian parents devote their children to God, but too many of them show no disposition in maturity to desire for themselves to be connected with the house of God. Jesus, on the contrary, as soon as He became fully capable of self-conscious action, adopted the pious wishes of His parents as His own and developed a passionate love for the house of God. When His parents lost Him in Jerusalem at twelve years of age, they found Him again in the Temple; and, when they told Him how long and how widely they had sought Him, He asked in surprise how they could have expected Him to be anywhere else than there.* He was without a doubt a regular frequenter of the synagogue during His silent years at Nazareth; and strange it is to think of Him being preached to Sabbath after Sabbath for so long.†

When He quitted the privacy of Nazareth and began His public work, He was still a regular frequenter of the synagogue. This was in fact the center from which His work developed itself. "He wrought miracles in the synagogues of Galilee." Nor was He neglectful of the other center of Jewish worship—the Temple at Jerusalem. He regularly attended the feasts; He sat down with His disciples in Jerusalem to eat the Passover; and He preached in the courts of the Temple. Even so secular a part of divine service as the giving of money He did not overlook: He sent Peter to fetch out of the fish's mouth a coin to pay for Him the Temple tax; and He passed a glowing eulogium on the widow who cast her mite into the Temple collecting box.

---

* "Wist ye not that I should be in My Father's house?" So the Revised Version, correctly.

† What was the man like who did it? Was he a wise man, who guided the footsteps of the Holy Child into pastures of the Word and supplied Him with the language in which His own thoughts afterwards expressed themselves? Or was he an embodiment of all that Jesus had afterwards to denounce in Pharisee and scribe? No portion of a congregation is more awe-inspiring to a minister than the children. Any Sunday there may be sitting before us one who is already revolving the thoughts which will dominate the future and supersede our own.

It is thus evident that Jesus was a passionate lover of the house of God. He could say with holy David, "How amiable are Thy tabernacles, O Lord of hosts; my soul longeth, yea, even fainteth for the courts of the Lord. A day in Thy courts is better than a thousand."

One sometimes hears even professedly religious people at the present day disparaging public worship, as if religion might flourish equally well without it; and, for trifling reasons or for no reason at all, they take it upon themselves to withdraw from the visible Church as something unworthy of them. This was not the way in which Jesus acted. The Church of his day was by no means a pure one; and He, if anybody, might have deemed it unworthy of Him. But He regularly waited on its ordinances and ardently loved it. There are few congregations less ideal perhaps than that in which He worshiped in wicked Nazareth, and few sermons are less perfect than those He listened to. But in that little synagogue He felt Himself made one with all the piety of the land; as the Scripture was read, the great and good of former ages thronged around Him; nay, heaven itself was in that narrow place for Him.

The Church is the window in the house of human life from which to look out and see heaven; and it does not require a very ornamental window to make the stars visible. The finest name ever given to the Church, outside the Bible, is Bunyan's Palace Beautiful. Yet the churches which he was acquainted with were only the Baptist meeting houses of Bedfordshire; and in an age of persecution these were certainly as humble structures as have ever served for places of worship. No better than barns they seemed to common eyes, but in his eyes each of them was a Palace Beautiful because, when seated on one of its rough benches, he felt himself in the general assembly and Church of the firstborn; and the eye of his imagination, looking up through the dingy rafters, could descry the gorgeous roof and shining pinnacles of the Church universal. It is the sanctified imagination that invests the Church building, whether it be brick meeting house or noble cathedral, with true sublimity; and love to God, whose house it is, can make the humblest material structure a home of the spirit.

II

Although the Church of Christ's day was of divine origin and He acknowledged it to be the house of God, it was frightfully full of abuses. Though an institution comes from God, many may add to it that which is his own; and by degrees the human addition may become so identified with the divine institution that both are supposed to be of a piece and equally divine. The human additions grow and grow, until it is almost impossible to get at what is God's through that which is man's. Some successful souls, indeed, still find their way through to the reality, as the roots of trees seek their way to the sustenance of the soil between the crannies of the opposing rocks, but multitudes are unable to find the way, and perish through trying to satisfy themselves with what is merely human, mistaking it for what is divine. At last a strong man is raised up to perceive the difference between the original structure and the human addition; and he tears away the latter, breaking it in pieces, amidst the wild outcries of all the owls and birds of darkness that have built their nests in it, and discloses once more the foundation of God. This is the Reformer.

In Christ's day the accumulation of human additions to the religion which God had instituted had grown to a head. No one knows how it had begun; such things sometimes begin innocently enough. But it had been immensely developed by a misconception which had crept in as to what the worship of God is. Worship is the means by which the empty human soul approaches God in order to be filled with His fullness, and then go away rejoicing, to live for Him in the strength thus received. But there is always a tendency to look upon it as a tribute we pay to God, which pleases Him and is meritorious on our part. Of course, if it is tribute paid to Him, the more of it that can be paid the better; for the more of it there is, so much the greater grows the merit of the worshiper. Thus services are multiplied, new forms are invented, and the memory of God's grace is lost in the achievements of human merit.

This was what had happened in Palestine. Religion had become an endless round of services, which were multiplied till they became a burden which life was unable to bear. The minister of religion heaped them on the people, whose consciences were so crushed with the sense of shortcoming that the whole joy of religion was extinguished. Even the ministers of religion themselves were not able to perform all the orders they issued; and then hypocrisy came in; for naturally they were supposed to be doing those things which they prescribed to others. But they said and did not; they bound heavy burdens and grievous to be borne on other men's shoulders, while they themselves would not touch them with one of their fingers. It was high time for a reformer to appear, and the work fell to Jesus.

The first outburst of His reformatory zeal was at the outset of His ministry, when He drove the buyers and sellers out of the Temple. Their practices had probably commenced with good intentions: they sold oxen and doves for sacrifice to the worshipers from foreign countries, who came in tens of thousands to Jerusalem at the feast and could not easily bring these animals with them; and they exchanged the coins of Jerusalem for those of foreign countries, in which the strangers of course had brought their money. It was a necessary thing, but it had grown to be a vast abuse; for exorbitant prices were charged for the animals and exorbitant rates of exchange demanded; the traffic was carried on with such din and clamor as to disturb the worship; and it took up so much room that the Gentiles were elbowed out of the court of the Temple which belonged to them. In short, the house of prayer had become a den of thieves. Jesus had no doubt noted the abuse with holy anger many a time when visiting the Temple at the feasts; and, when the prophetic spirit descended on Him and His public ministry began, it was among His first acts to clear it out of the house of God. The youthful Prophet, with His scourge of cords, flaming above the venal crowd, that, conscious of their sin, fled, amidst tumbling tables and fleeing animals, from before His holy ire, is a perfect picture of the Reformer.

It is said that the high-priestly families derived an income from this unholy traffic, and it is not likely that they felt very kindly to One who thus invaded their vested interests. In like manner He aroused the resentment of the Pharisaic party by turning into ridicule their long and pretentious prayers and the trumpets they blew before them when they were giving alms. He could not but expose these practices, for the people had learned to revere as the flower of piety that which was the base weed of vulgarity and pride. He had to consent to be frowned upon as a man of sin because He neglected the fasts and the Sabbatic extravagances which He knew to be no part of religion; and still more because He mingled with publicans and sinners, though He knew this to be the very course of divine mercy. He was compelled at last to pluck the cloak of hypocrisy entirely away from the religious characters of the day and expose them in their true colors as blind leaders of the blind and whited sepulchers, which appeared fair outside, but inwardly were full of dead men's bones.

Thus He cleared away the human additions piled about the house of God and let the true Temple once more be seen in its own fair proportions. But He had to pay the penalty. The priests, the stream of whose sinful gains He had stopped, and the Pharisees, whose hypocrisy He had exposed, pursued Him with hatred that never rested till they saw Him on the cross. And so, in addition to the name of reformer, He earned the name of Martyr, and Himself became the leader of the noble army of martyrs which in a thin line deploys through the centuries.

Not a few of that army have also been reformers. They have risen against the abuses of the Church of their day and perished in the attempt. For the New Testament Church is no more free than was the Old Testament Church from the danger of being a scene of abuses. The condition of the Christian Church at the time of those men of God to whom we are wont specially to apply the title of the Reformers was remarkably like the state of the Old Testament Church in the time of Christ: man's additions had completely overlaid God's handiwork; religion had been transformed from an institution for the administration of God's grace into a round of forms and ceremonies for procuring God's favor by human merit; and the ministers of religion had become blind leaders of the blind. By the Reformation God delivered His Church from this state of things; and never since, we may hope, has there been anything like the same need of reform. It would be vain, however, to suppose that in our time or in the section of the Church to which we may belong there are no abuses needing the reformer's fan. Though we may be insensible of them, this is no proof that they do not exist; for the Church even in its worst days has been unconscious of its own defects, till the proper man has appeared and pointed them out; and in all ages there have been those who have believed themselves to be doing God service when resisting the most necessary changes.*

III

The name Reformer, where it is truly deserved, is a great one in the Church, but to Jesus belongs one much greater for He was the Founder of the Church.

The old Church in which He was brought up was ready to vanish away. It had served its day and was about to be taken down. He Himself prophesied that of the Temple there would soon not be left one stone above another; He told the woman of Samaria that the hour was coming when they would neither in Gerizim nor yet on Mount Zion worship the Father, but the true worshipers everywhere would worship Him in spirit and in truth; and, when He died, the veil of the Temple was rent in twain from the top to the bottom.

---

* Schism is the caricature of Reform. But Schismatic is often merely a nickname given to the true Reformer; and even real schism nearly always indicates the need for reform, as Schleiermacher has proved in the profound discussion of Church Reform in his *Christliche Sitte*. He says:

"In order, therefore, to prevent unsuccessful attempts, instruction in the proper understanding of the Scriptures is of foremost importance. In addition to that, consciousness must always be raised to the fact that a complete understanding of the Scriptures is not possible through any other method than through the path of taught knowledge. Had both of these been more properly present, many abnormalities would not have arisen. In addition to that comes something else. It is only too often the case that the reverence that the layman has for the scholar as such and for the office of those who represent the church is completely undone by the lack of personal reverence invoked by members of this representation in whom otherwise historic life is manifested. How could the layman reconcile the two, on the one hand the knowledge that he was about them with regards to morality and religious strength, and on the other hand, to subordinate himself to their greater level of cognizance. Spiritual pride would therefore not arise within the individual if it was not constantly furthered, on the one hand, by the imperfection of the organization, and on the other hand, by the lack of efforts that are being made to further proper knowledge of the Scriptures. The multitude of failed attempts in our church is a certain thermometer for the condition of the whole in this regard. We cannot gain control of this evil, therefore, until the roots of the same have been resolved."

He founded the Church of the New Testament in His own blood. By the shedding of His blood He abolished the imperfect relation between God and men mediated by the blood of bulls and of goats, and established a new and better relationship. So He said in instituting the Lord's Supper, "This is the new covenant in My blood." The new house of God is illuminated with the perfect revelation made by Him of the Father; and in it are administered the new and richer blessings purchased by His life and death.

But in building the new house of God its Founder did not wholly discard the materials of the old.* He instituted the Lord's Supper in the very elements with which on the evening of its institution He and His disciples were celebrating the Passover. The forms of worship and office bearers of the Christian Church bear a close resemblance to those of the synagogue. Above all, the Scriptures of the Old Testament, with the figures of their saints and heroes, form part of the same volume as the Scriptures of the New.

Jesus Himself did not draw out in detail the plan of the New Testament Church. He contented Himself with laying its foundation, which none else could have done, and sketching the great outlines of its structure. He entrusted it to His Gospel, with the sacred charge to preach it to every creature; He gave it to the twelve apostles, whose labors and inspired teachings might serve as the second course of foundation stones laid above the foundation which He had laid Himself; He empowered its officers to admit to, and exclude from, its fellowship; He instituted the sacraments of baptism and the Lord's Supper; and, above all, He left with His Church the promise, which is her star of hope in every age: "Lo, I am with you always, even to the end of the world."

---

* The apparent contradiction between speaking of Christ both as the Reformer of the old and the Founder of the new is partly due to the contradiction, expounded in the preceding chapter, between the will of God and the will of man. To finite eyes it cannot but seem that He was striving earnestly for ends which were not realized, and that the results of His life were different from His intentions. Besides, *old* and *new* are terms which may both be applicable to the same object at the same time. It is more orthodox to speak of the Christian Church as the same with that of the Old Testament; but it is perhaps more scriptural to speak of it as a new Church. That is to say, orthodoxy emphasizes the element which is common to both dispensations, while Scripture emphasizes what is distinctive in the new.

This foundation-laying work of Christ was done once for all and cannot be repeated. Men dream sometimes of the Christian Church passing away and something more advanced taking its place. But "other foundation can no man lay." Only the building up of the Church on this foundation is now left to us. This, however, is part of the same work and may be done in the same spirit in which He laid the foundations.

In the first place, those who undertake it require to see to it that they build straight on the foundation. There is much that passes for Christian work that will not in the end be acknowledged by Christ, because it is not building on the foundation which He has laid. If that new covenant in His blood be ignored in which He declared His own work to consist, or if the foundations laid by His apostles in His name are not recognized, we may build a church of our own, but He will not recognize our labor.

All who take part in this work ought to build with His holy ardor. He thought it worthwhile to die for the sake of redeeming the souls of men; what sacrifices are we prepared to make in contributing to the same end? He gave His life; will we give up our ease, our effort, our money? It was because He believed every single soul was more precious than a world that He died to save the souls of men. Are they precious in our eyes? Does their fate haunt us? Does their sin grieve us? Would their salvation fill us with aught of the joy that thrills the angels in heaven when one sinner is converted?*

There is needed, however, not only zeal, but consecrated originality as well, in building this edifice. As I said, Jesus did not prescribe the minute details of the organization of the Church. He largely left it to human ingenuity to find out how best His work may be done; and the Church is only finding out still. New problems arise for her to solve, new tasks to be performed, and therefore she needs inventors and

---

* "Christianity would sacrifice its divinity if it abandoned its missionary character and became a mere educational institution. Surely this Article of Conversion is the true *articulus stantis aut cadentis ecclesiae*. When the power of reclaiming the lost dies out of the Church, it ceases to be the Church. It may remain a useful institution, though it is most likely to become an immoral and mischievous one. Where the power remains there, whatever is wanting, it may still be said that 'the tabernacle of God is with men'" —*Ecce Homo*.

pioneers to devise the plans for her new enterprises and open up the way to new conquests. It is impossible, for example, to measure the blessing which that man conferred on the Church who instituted Sabbath schools. He was no dignitary of the Church nor perhaps in any way a remarkable man, except in this—that he saw a vast work needing to be done and had originality to discover the best way of doing it. He led the way into the children's world, and ever since he has been supplying the best of work for the myriads of willing reapers who have followed him into that most attractive portion of the harvest field. There are plenty of other tasks awaiting solution from sanctified Christian genius; and I know no prize more to be coveted than that of being the first to show how Christian thought may exploit some new mine of spiritual knowledge, or Christian character rise to a new level of spiritual attainment, or Christian zeal reach the spiritual wants of some neglected section of the community.

Matthew 10:2–4; 11:7–11; 17:1, 2; 21:17; 26:14–16, 37, 38, 40, 50; 27:3–5, 55–61.
Mark 5:37; 13:3, 4.
Luke 8:1–3; 10:38–42; 12:4.
John 1:35–51; 11; 12:1–7; 13:1–5, 23; 15:13–15; 19:27.

5

Christ as a Friend

I.

IT has been advanced as an objection to the New Testament that it never recommends friendship, and, while supplying rules for the behavior to one another of husbands and wives, parents and children, brothers and sisters, gives none for the intercourse of friend with friend.*

Various reasons have been suggested to account for this singular omission. But, before entering upon these, it would be well to make sure that the omission itself is a reality. Is it true that the New Testament omits all reference to friendship?

I venture, on the contrary, to affirm that the New Testament is the classical place for the study of this subject. The highest of all examples of friendship is to be found in Jesus; and His behavior in this beautiful relationship is the very mirror in which all true friendship must see and measure itself.

It is objected indeed, that this instance is inadmissible, because Jesus sustained to those who may be called His friends the higher relationship

---

* In an argument designed to prove that Christianity is unfavorable to friendship, the fact might be adduced, that the best book on the subject is from the pen of a heathen. From the classical age of English theology we have two treatises on the subject, one from the Royalist side by Jeremy Taylor, the other from the Puritan side by Richard Baxter; but neither possesses the exquisite flavor of Cicero's *De Amicitiâ*. The *Lysis* of Plato is interesting, as opening some of the difficulties of the subject, but it is not an important dialogue. Shakespeare also has discussed some of the difficulties in *Two Noble Kinsmen* and *Two Gentlemen of Verona*, and he has given the whole subject an exquisite embodiment in *The Merchant of Venice*. But the glory of English literature in this department is *In Memoriam*.

of Savior; and between those standing on such different levels, it is contended, real friendship was impossible.

But He Himself called the Twelve His friends: "Henceforth I call
you not servants, but friends." From among the Twelve He made
special companions of three—Peter, James and John; and of these
three John was specially the disciple whom Jesus loved. We are told that
"Jesus loved Martha and her sister and Lazarus"; and this notice
surely implies that He stood in an attitude of peculiar friendliness towards the members of the family of Bethany. Merely as the Savior, He
is hardly to be thought of as loving one of those He has saved more
than another; He loves them all alike. But in the cases just quoted He
showed preferences for some of His followers over others; and this
seems to prove that within the wider and higher relationship between
Savior and saved there was scope for the strictly human tie of friendship.

II

Among those who have written on the subject of friendship it
has been discussed whether the best friend is he who loves most or he
who bestows the greatest benefits.

Much may be said on both sides; for, on the one hand, there is an
infinite solace in the sincere affection of even the humblest friend,
however unable he may be to render any material service; and, on the
other hand, in the perplexities and misfortunes of life, which come to
all, it is an unspeakable advantage to have one with a sound judgment
and a helpful hand, who will interest himself in our affairs as if they
were his own, because he is our friend. Yet I venture to think that neither of these is the pearl of friendship; there is something in it more
valuable than either.

Let anyone who has drunk deeply of this wellspring of happiness
look back and ask what has been the sweetest ingredient in it: let
him recall the friend of his heart, whose image is associated with the
choicest hours of his experience; and then let him say what is the secret and the soul of his satisfaction. If your friendship has been of a
high order, the soul of it is simply the worth of him you are allowed
to call your friend. He is genuine to the core; you know him through

and through, and nowhere is there any twist or doubleness or guile. It may be a false and disappointing world, but you have known at least one heart that has never deceived you; and amidst much that may have happened to lower your estimate of mankind, the image of your friend has enabled you always to believe in human nature. Surely this is the incomparable gain of friendship—fellowship with a simple, pure and lofty soul.

If it is, what must have been the charm of the friendship of Jesus? If even the comparatively common and imperfect specimens of human nature we have known can make impressions so delightful, what must it have been to see closely that heart which was always beating with the purest love to God and man, that mind which was a copious and ever-springing fountain of such thoughts as have been preserved to us in the Gospels, that character in which the minutest investigation has never detected a single spot or wrinkle! As we read the records of the great and good, we cannot help sometimes wishing it had been our lot to follow Plato in his garden, or to hear the table talk of Luther, or to sit with Bunyan in the sunshine of the streets of Bedford, or to listen to Coleridge bodying forth the golden clouds of his philosophy. But what would any such privilege have been in comparison with that of Mary,* who sat at Jesus' feet and heard His words; or that of John, who leaned on His bosom and listened to the beating of His heart?

III

If that which has just been mentioned is the prime excellence of friendship, love holds in it the second place.

---

* The heathen held woman to be unfit for this relationship, and too many Christian thinkers have followed in their footsteps, alleging such pleas as that a woman cannot keep a secret or that she cannot give counsel in affairs of difficulty. But Jesus "loved Martha and her sister"; some of His friends were women. Thus He vindicated the right of women to this honorable position, and hundreds of the best and manliest of His servants have since experienced the solace and strength springing from the friendship of good women; and, as one of them (Jeremy Taylor) has said, "a woman can love as passionately, and converse as pleasantly, and retain a secret as faithfully, and be useful in her proper ministries; and she can die for her friend as well as any Roman knight."

Friendship is not the mere claim which one man may make on another because he was born in the same village or sat on the same bench at school; it is not the acquaintance of neighbors who have learned to like one another by daily gossiping from door to door, but would, if separated, forget one another in a month; it is not the tryst of roisterers, or the chance acquaintance of fellow travelers, or the association of the members of a political party.* In real friendship there is always the knitting of soul to soul, the exchange of heart for heart. In the classical instance of friendship in the Old Testament, its inception is exquisitely described: "And it came to pass, when he had made an end of speaking unto Saul, that the soul of Jonathan was knit with the soul of David, and Jonathan loved him as his own soul." A union like this is formed not to be broken, and, if it is broken, it can only be with the tearing of the flesh and the loss of much blood.

I cannot, however, agree with those who maintain that true friendship, like wedded love, can have but one object at a time. One of the finest spirits of our century, a thinker conversant with all the heights and depths of man's relationships with man,† has argued strongly in favor of this position, and he silences all objectors by replying that, if you think you have more friends than one, this only proves that you have not yet found the true one. But this is to misinterpret the nature of this affection, and force on it a rule belonging to quite a different passion. At all events, the example of Christ appears to support this view, and to prove that in friendship there may be different degrees, and that the heart is capable of enjoying several friendships at the same time.

---

*For beloved friendship it is not enough
To raise one's glass to closer ties,
To have sat side by side throughout school,
To have often met in a cafe,
To have politely conversed in the street,
To have sung the same songs in a club,
To be publishers of the same political conviction,
Or to praise one another in the press.
BAGGESEN, quoted by Martensen.

† Rothe. See his *Ethic*, Vol. 4, pg. 67. Germany is fortunate in having such examples of friendship among its greatest men as that of Luther and Melanchthon, and that of Goethe and Schiller.

IV

The love of friends is an active passion, and delights in rendering services and bestowing benefits.

So sensible of this were the ancients that, in discussing the duties of friendship, what they asked was, not how much one friend ought to do for another, but where the limit was at which he ought to stop. They took it for granted that he would do, suffer and give all he could for his friend's sake; and they only prescribed to him to restrain himself at the point where his zeal might clash with some still higher obligation to his family, his country or his God. In accordance with this they represented friendship in art as a young man bareheaded and rudely attired, to signify activity and aptness for service. Upon the fringe of his garment was written *Death and Life*, as signifying that in life and death friendship is the same. On his forehead was inscribed *Summer and Winter*, meaning that in prosperity or adversity friendship knows no change except in the variety of its services. The left shoulder and the arm were naked down to the heart, to which the finger of the right hand pointed at the words *Far and Near*, which expressed that true friendship is not impaired by time or dissolved by distance.*

Of this feature in the friendships of Jesus it would be easy to give examples, but none could be more striking than His behavior at the death and resurrection of Lazarus. Every step of His on this occasion is characteristic. His abiding two days still in the place where He was, after receiving the news of His friend's death, in order to make the gift He was about to bestow more valuable; His venturing into Judea in spite of the dangers He was exposed to and the fears of the Twelve; His fanning into flame of Martha's weak faith; His secret sending for Mary, that she might not miss the great spectacle; His sympathy with the emotions of the scene, so intense that He wept and the spectators exclaimed, "Behold, how He loved him"; His preparation of the sisters, by His prayer, for the shock of seeing their brother emerging from the sepulcher in his graveclothes; and then the benefaction of his resurrection—all these are traits of a love that was delicate as a woman's heart, strong as death and bountiful as heaven.

---

* From Jeremy Taylor's treatise on *Friendship*.

But friendship can sometimes show its strength as much by the readiness with which it accepts benefits as by the freedom with which it gives them. It proves by this its confidence in the love on the other side. Jesus gave such a proof of the depth of His friendship for John when, hanging on the cross, He asked the beloved disciple to adopt Mary as his own mother. Never was there a more delicate expression given to friendship. Jesus did not ask him if he would; He took his devotion for granted; and this trust was the greatest honor that could have been conferred on the disciple.

V

It is a well-known characteristic of friendship that friends enjoy being in each other's company and hearing each other talk, and that they admit one another to the knowledge of secrets which they would not reveal to the world at large.

It is the commonest saying about two very intimate friends, that if you are seeking the one, you will do best to resort to the abode of the other. In each other's company they are at peace; speech between them is hardly necessary, for they have a subtler way of divining thought and feeling, and it is a precious privilege of friends to be silent in each other's company without awkwardness. Yet, when the gates of speech are opened, there is an outpouring of the mind's wealth such as takes place in no other circumstances. For nothing needs to be concealed. The shy thought, which scarcely ventured to show its face even to its own creator, is tempted out; the hardy opinion utters itself without fear; confidence is responded to with confidence; like two coals, burning feebly apart, which, when flung together, make a merry blaze, so mind and mind burn as they touch, and emit splendors which nothing but this contact could evoke. He is ignorant of one of the most glorious prerogatives of manhood who does not carry, treasured in his mind, the recollection of such golden hours of the feast of reason and the flow of soul.

Jesus expressly chose the Twelve "that they might be with Him." For three years they were His constant companions; and often He would take them away into uninhabited spots or on distant journeys for the express purpose of enjoying with them more uninterrupted intercourse. In the Gospel of St. John we have notes of these conversations, and from the wide contrast between the sayings of Jesus in this Gospel and those reported in the Synoptists, which rather represent His addresses to the people at large, we may perceive how fully in these interviews He opened to the Twelve His secret mind. And the kind of impressions which they received from these confidences may be learned from the saying of the two with whom He conversed on the way to Emmaus: "Did not our heart burn within us as He talked with us by the way, and as He opened to us the Scriptures?"

The minds of the most favored apostles especially carried in subsequent years the priceless memory of many great hours like this, when, with hearts lost in wonder, they gazed into the vast and mystic realm of the thoughts of Christ. And they were vouchsafed a few hours even greater, when He took them away with Him to pray; as He did, for instance, when they beheld His glory in the Holy Mount, or when He invited them to watch with Him in Gethsemane. Never surely was He so unmistakably the human friend as when, on the latter occasion, He threw Himself on their sympathy, entreating them to be near Him in His agony.

These scenes excite our wonder that any should have been admitted so far into His secret life. Were not these hours of prayer especially too sacred for any mortal eyes to see? That His friends were admitted to them proves that it is a prerogative for friendship to be admitted far into the secrets of religious experience.

It is a truncated and most imperfect friendship when the gateway of this region is closed; for it means that the one friend is excluded from the most important province of the other's life. Hence it may be affirmed that friendship in its highest sense can exist only between Christians;* and even they only taste the bloom on this cup when they have arrived at the stage of free and frequent converse on those themes which were native to the mouth of Christ.

* "The most intense type of friendship is a religious friendship; the chosen attraction of friends to one another is based on the chosen relationship of their religious individualities. Due to the central position of faith in the essence of man, religion-specific sympathy of the individuals is sympathy specific to the very essence of the same, after the totality of their ethical individuality, after the total innermost part of the same" — ROTHE, *Christian Ethic*, Vol. 4, p. 68.

VI

Friendship, like everything else, is tested by results. If you wish to know the value of any friendship, you must ask what it has done for you and what it has made you.

The friendship of Jesus could stand this test. Look at the Twelve! Consider what they were before they knew Him, and think what His influence made them and what position they occupy now! They were humble men, some of them, perhaps, with unusual natural gifts, but rude and undeveloped everyone. Without Him they would never have been anything. They would have lived and died in the obscurity of their peasant occupations and been laid in unmarked graves by the blue waters of the Sea of Galilee. They would never have been heard of twenty miles from home, and would all have been forgotten in less than a century. But His intercourse and conversation raised them to a place among the best and wisest of the sons of men; and they now sit on thrones, ruling the modern world with their ideas and example.

Our friendships, too, must submit to this test. There are friendships so called which are like millstones dragging down those who are tied to them into degradation and shame. But true friendship purifies and exalts. A friend may be a second conscience. The consciousness of what he expects from us may be a spur to high endeavor. The mere memory that he exists, though it be at a distance, may stifle unworthy thoughts and prevent unworthy actions. Even when the fear of facing our own conscience might not be strong enough to restrain us from evil, the knowledge that our conduct will have to encounter his judgment will make the commission of what is base intolerable.

Among the privileges of friendship one of the most valuable is the right of being told our faults by our friend. There are ridiculous traits of character in every man which all eyes see except his own; and there are dangers to character which the eye of a friend can discern long before they are visible to ourselves. It requires some tact to administer such reproof, and it requires some grace to take it gratefully, but "faithful are the wounds of a friend," and there are few gifts of friendship more highly to be prized than words of wise correction.

While, however, we estimate the value of the friendships we enjoy by their influence on us, it is no less important to remember that our own conduct in this relationship has to stand the same test. Is it good for my friend that I am his friend? In the maturity of his fully-formed judgment will he look back on the connection with approval? At the judgment seat and in eternity will he prize it? A man will hesitate to answer these questions, but surely there is no object worthier of intense desire and earnest prayer than that our friendship may never be detrimental to him we love—that it may never pull him down, but help to raise and sustain him. Would it not be a prize better than any earthly distinction, if in the distant years, when we are old and grey-headed, or perhaps beneath the sod, there were one or two who could say, "His influence was a redeeming element in my life; he made me believe in goodness and think highly of human nature; and I thank God I ever knew him"?

There is no way in which we can have any guarantee of exerting such an influence except by keeping ourselves in contact with the great source of good influence. Christ was the friend of Peter and John and James, of Martha and Mary and Lazarus, in Palestine long ago. But He is still the friend of men; and, if we wish it, He will be ours. There are those who walk with Him and talk with Him. They meet Him in the morning when they awake; He is with them in the street and at their work; they tell Him their secrets and appeal to Him in every time of need; they know Him better than any other friend. And these are they who have found the secret of existence and keep alive the faith of mankind in the reality of the life of Christ.

Matthew 6:16–19.
Luke 15:1, 2; 19:5–7; 24:41–43.

Luke 11:37–44; 14:1–24.

Matthew 26:6–13.
Luke 7:36–50.
John 2:1–11; 12:1–8.

Matthew 14:15–21; 26:26–30.
Luke 24:29–31.
John 13:1–15.

6

Christ in Society

BEYOND the narrow circle of those whom we properly call our friends, there is a large circle of acquaintances, brought into connection with us in various ways, which may be designated by the vague term Society. Our intercourse with those to whom we are thus related raises questions which are not free from difficulty, but they receive light from the study of the conduct of Jesus.

I

In this relationship there was a remarkable contrast between our Lord and His forerunner, the Baptist. John shunned society, living in the desert far from the abodes of men. His clothing was unsuited for the house or the town, and he confined himself to the ascetic fare of a hermit. The Savior, on the contrary, descended among His fellowmen. Instead of waiting, like the Baptist, till people went out to Him, He came to them. In village and city, in street and marketplace, in synagogue and Temple—wherever two or three were gathered together, there was He in the midst of them. He entered beneath men's roofs, to rejoice with them when they were rejoicing and to weep with them when they wept. It is astonishing how often we read of His being at feasts. He began His ministry by attending a wedding. Matthew made Him a feast, and He went and sat down among the publican's motley guests. He invited Himself to the house of Zacchaeus, another publican. Indeed, His eating with this class of persons came to be notorious. But, when people from the other end of the social scale invited Him, He accepted their hospitality with equal readiness and sat down as frankly with scribes and Pharisees as among publicans and sinners. St. Luke mentions at least three occasions when He dined with Pharisees. Thus, "the Son of man came eating and drinking." Indeed, so free was His conduct in this respect, that sour and narrow-souled critics were able to call Him a gluttonous man and a winebibber. False as these nicknames were, they derived a color of truth from His way of living; none would ever have dreamed of applying them to the Baptist.

This contrast is remarkable between two so closely associated as John and Jesus. Both were religious teachers, whose disciples imitated them, but in this particular their examples led in opposite directions. The disciples of John fasted, while Christ's disciples feasted. Could these opposite courses both be justified?

The Baptist no doubt had reasons for his conduct which satisfied himself. There are dangers in society. The lust of the flesh and the lust of the eyes and the pride of life are there. Company is the ruin of many a man and of many a family. There are social circles in which religion would not be tolerated, and there are others in which those who profess it are under sore temptation to hide their colors. The Baptist felt that these influences were so predominant in the society of his day that neither he nor his followers could bear up against them. The only alternatives between which they had to choose were either, on the one hand, to flee from society and keep their religion pure and entire or, on the other, to enter it and lose their religion; and there could be no doubt which was the path of duty.* Jesus, on the contrary, could go into society not only without striking His colors, but for the purpose of displaying them. So completely was His religious character the whole of Him, and so powerful and victorious were His principles, that there was no fear of any company He might enter obscuring His testimony for God. And He lent His followers the same power: He filled them with an enthusiasm which wrought in them like new wine; they moved through the world with the free and glad bearing of wedding guests;

---

* John was well aware, however, of the imperfection of his own standpoint. "He pointed across to the sweetness, freedom and glory of the new dispensation, as Moses from Pisgah saw the land of promise."—SCHLEIERMACHER, *Predigten*, Vol. 4. In this volume there are four discourses which may be called a kind of sketch of what has been attempted in this book. They are entitled—Christ as a Teacher; Christ as a Miracle Worker; Christ in Social Life; Christ among His disciples.

and therefore wherever they went they gave the tone to society; their enthusiasm was so exuberant that it was far more likely to set others on fire than to be extinguished by worldly influences.

Here we seem to find the true answer to the perplexing questions often raised as to how far the people of God ought to venture into society and take part in its engagements. What is its effect on your religious life and profession? Does it silence your testimony? Does it cool down your enthusiasm? Does it secularize you and render you unfit for prayer? If so, then you must adopt the Baptist's line of conduct and keep away from it, or seek for company in which your principles will be safe. But there are those who can venture far into the world and yet everywhere be true to their Savior; they are known as Christians wherever they appear, and people respect their position; they would not go anywhere if they knew that their mouths were to be stopped on the subjects lying nearest their hearts; the energy of Christ in them is so glowing and victorious a force that they mold the society in which they are, instead of being molded by it. This may be a difficult attainment, but there can be no doubt that it is the attitude towards the world most worthy of Christ's followers and like to His own.

II

It has been mentioned how often He is recorded to have been present at feasts. This part of His conduct was of a piece with all the rest; for nothing He ever did, however trivial it might seem to be, was unconnected with the grand mission upon which He had come to the world. This mission was to make known the love of Heaven and to awaken and foster love on earth. He lived to increase the love of man to God and the love of man to man; and nothing which could serve either of these ends was unimportant in His eyes.

He encouraged hospitality because it promotes one of these ends: it helps to break down the obstacles which separate men and to bind them together in the bonds of goodwill. When men meet one another, the misconceptions and misunderstandings which have caused estrangement dissolve in the light of better acquaintance. How often we come away from a first conversation with one against whom we have entertained a prejudice with the remark that he is not a bad fellow after all; and not unfrequently after a social rencontre we carry away an enthusiastic admiration for a character which we have previously considered proud, or formal, or shallow. Our dislikes and suspicions breed and grow great at a distance, but they die at the touch of actual acquaintance.

Jesus did not regard even the courtesies of life as beneath His notice and encouragement. These foster respect between man and man, causing us to think of one another as personalities, not as things to be neglected or trampled on. Once He was invited to dine at a house where the hose neglected to show Him the ordinary Oriental courtesies. The man had no real regard for his Guest, but invited Him for a selfish purpose of his own. He wished to gratify his curiosity by examining at leisure one who was the talk of the country and to honor himself by having the distinguished man under his roof. But he felt it to be a condescension, and he showed this by omitting the courtesies which he bestowed on the guests of his own standing. Jesus felt the slight; and, before leaving the table, He exposed Simon's little and loveless heart, enumerating one by one, in tones of scathing indignation, the courtesies he had grudged Him. He could not enjoy a loveless feast.

Where, on the contrary, love was, He would not have it controlled. When, at the feast of another Simon, His gentle disciple Mary poured her costly treasure on His head and brought down on herself the reproaches of narrow hearts that grudged the extravagance, Jesus defended her against the pretended champions of the poor and insisted on love having its way.

It is a violation of the sacrament of hospitality when any other motive underlies it but love. Jesus pointed the finger of condemnation at those who extend hospitality only to guests who, they hope, will extend it to them in turn, thus degrading it to a business transaction. It is, if possible, a meaner motive still to make it only an opportunity of selfish display. Cumbrous luxury is the death of true hospitality. It narrows the scope of it; for even the wealthy can indulge but seldom in such extravagance, and people of humbler means are not able to face it at all except at the risk of ruin. This is one of the growing evils of the present day. With the money spent on a single tiresome feast, half a dozen simple and frugal entertainments might be furnished forth, and thus the scope of hospitality widened.* Instead of gorging the wealthy, who have too much already, influential entertainers might occasionally open their doors to those younger and humbler than themselves, and parents might assemble often round their tables suitable company for their children, instead of driving them to public places to seek occupation for their hours of leisure. There is a mission of social kindness still remaining to be opened up as one of the agencies of Christianity.

III

Though the encouragement of hospitality, and through it of love, was one reason for which Jesus went to the tables of those who invited Him, He carried there a still higher purpose. When He went to dine at the house of Zacchaeus, He said, "Today is salvation come to this house"; and salvation came to many a house when He entered it. Hospitality affords unrivaled opportunities of conversation, and Jesus made use of these to speak words of eternal life. If you carefully examine His words, you will be surprised to find how many of them are literally table talk—works spoken to His fellow guests at meal. Some of His most priceless sayings, which are now the watchwords of His religion, were uttered in these commonplace circumstances, such as, "They that are whole have no need of a physician, but they that are sick"; "The Son of man is come to seek and to save that which was lost"; and many more.

This is an instance of how Jesus dignified life and found golden opportunities of doing good in those elements of it which are often

---

* "Hospitality is threefold:—for one's family, this is of necessity; for strangers, this is courtesy; for the poor, this is charity.

"To keep a disorderly house is the way to keep neither house nor lands. For whilst they keep the greatest roaring, their state steals away in the greatest silence. Yet, when many consume themselves with secret vices, then hospitality bears the blame; whereas it is not the meat but the sauce, not the supper but the gaming after it, doth undo them.

"Measure not the entertainment of a guest by HIS estate, but THINE OWN. Because he is a lord forget not that thou art but a gentleman; otherwise, if with feasting him thou breakest thyself, he will not cure thy rupture, and (perchance) may rather deride than pity thee"—FULLER, *The Holy and Profane State.*

treated as mere waste. The talk and hilarity of the table are a snare. Men of social charm often use their gift to their own undoing and to the injury of others. The meeting place of boon companions is to many the vestibule of ruin. Even where sociality is not permitted to degenerate into temptation, the conversation of the table is too often allowed to lapse into triviality and stupidity; and the meetings of friends, which might give intellectual stimulus and kindle noble purpose, become a weariness and satisfy nobody. It is a rare gift to be able to lift conversation out of the ditch and lead it to manly and profitable themes.

There have, however, been servants of God who in this respect have followed very closely in the footsteps of their Master. They have made conversation a delightful and profitable art; and to enjoy their company in the free interchange of social intercourse has been an education in everything good and true. A man of note recently deceased, son of a father still more notable, has left a striking picture of the circle of scholars and men of God who used to be assembled round his father's hospitable table, and of the wonder and delight with which he and his brothers, then only children, used to listen to the discussions and pick up the crumbs of wisdom.* No parent can do his children a better service than by making his house a resort of the wise and good, in whom the keen observation of childhood may see examples of noble manhood and womanhood. "Be not forgetful," says the Epistle to the Hebrews, "to entertain strangers, for thereby some have entertained angels unawares"; on which one of the wise has thus commented: "By exercising hospitality—by treating with sympathy and hearty interest those who are still in many respects strangers to us—by showing ourselves kindly and opening our houses to them, as circumstances permit and op-

---

* "Here almost every night, for long years, came Professors Dod and Maclean, and frequently Professors J. W. Alexander, Joseph Henry, and the older professors, A. Alexander, and Samuel Miller, President Carnahan, and frequently, when visiting the town, Professors Vethake and Torrey, and Dr. John W. Yeomans. Thus, at least in the eyes of the young sons gleaming out from the corners, from the shadows of which they looked on with breathless interest, this study became the scene of the most wonderful debates and discourses on the highest themes of philosophy, science, literature, theology, morals, and politics"—Rev. Dr. A. A. Hodge in *Princetoniana*, by Rev. C. A. Salmond, M. A.

portunities offer—it may also happen to us to entertain angels; that is, men in whom we must recognize messengers sent to us from God, or from the world of mind and ideas, and whose sojourn in our house, whose conversation, whose influence on our souls, may bring us a blessing far outweighing all we can do for them."*

IV

We have been looking at our Lord as the guest of others, but He comes before us in the Gospels also as Himself an entertainer.

Jesus never, indeed, had a house of His own to which He could invite people. But on the two occasions when He fed the five thousand and he four thousand He acted as entertainer on a colossal scale.

It was a character in which He was thoroughly Himself; for it displayed His consideration for the common wants of man. Spiritual as He was and intent on the salvation of the soul, He never undervalued or overlooked the body. On the contrary, He recognized on it the stamp and honor of its Maker, and He knew quite well that it is often only through the body that the souls can be reached. The great majority of His guests were doubtless poor, and it gratified His generous heart to confer a benefit on them. It was, indeed, but common fare He gave them;† the table was the ground, the tablecloth was the green grass, and the banqueting hall was the open air, but never did His guests enjoy a better meal, for love presided at the table, and it is love that makes an entertainment fine.

As we see Him there, beaming with genial delight over the vast company, it is impossible not to think of such words of His as these: "I am the bread of life"; "The bread which I shall give is My flesh, which I will give for the life of the world." In His teaching He delighted to represent the gospel as a feast, to which He invited all the sons of men in the beautiful spirit of a royal host.

But nothing else shows so strikingly how characteristic of Him this spirit was as the fact that the memorial by which He has chosen to be remembered to all generations is a feast. He might have selected ; of

---

* MARTENSEN, *Christian Ethics*, Vol. 3.
† "Barley loaves," the bread of the poor.

a hundred other mementos. He might, for instance, have instituted among His followers a periodical fast. But this would have been a thoroughly unsuitable memorial of Him; for His is a gospel of abundance, joy and union. He chose what was fitting and truly significant; and so throughout all ages at the head of His own table the Savior sits in the character of Entertainer, His face radiant with goodwill and His heart overflowing with generosity; and over His head, on the wall behind where He sits, these words are written, "This Man receiveth sinners, and eateth with them."

Matthew 11:25, 26; 14:19; 19:13; 21:12, 13; 26:53.
Luke 9:18; 11:1.
John 6:23; 14:16, 17; 17.

Matthew 14:23.
Mark 1:35; 14:22, 23.
Luke 5:16.

Matthew 26:36–44.
Luke 6:12, 13.

Luke 3:21, 22; 9:28, 29.
John 11:41, 42.

7

Christ as a Man of Prayer

I.

THERE is surely a mystery in the prayers of Jesus. If, as we believe, He was no less than God, how could God pray to God, or what need could there be in His nature for the satisfaction of which He required to pray?

It may be a partial answer to this question to say that all prayer does not consist of petitions arising from the sense of need. Prayer, indeed, is often spoken of, especially by those who wish to bring it into ridicule, as if it consisted of nothing but a series of demands addressed to God—to give fine weather, or to take away disease, or in some other way to alter our circumstances in accordance with our wishes. But it is not by those who pray that prayer is thus spoken of. In the prayers of those who pray most and best, petitions proper, I venture to say, occupy only an inconsiderable place. Much of prayer expresses the fullness of the soul rather than its emptiness. It is the overflow of the cup. Prayer at its best is, if one may be allowed the expression, conversation with God, the confidential talk of a child who tells everything to his father. There is a remarkable example of this in the *Confessions* of St. Augustine. This great book is in the form of a prayer from beginning to end; yet it narrates its author's history and expounds the most important of his opinions. Evidently the good man had got into the habit of doing all his deepest thinking in the form of conversation with God.

If this be what prayer is, it is not difficult to understand how the Eternal Son should have prayed to the Eternal Father. Indeed, it is easy to see that, in this sense, He must have prayed without ceasing.

But this does not altogether clear up the mystery of the prayers of Jesus; for many of them were undoubtedly expressions of the sense of want. "In the days of His flesh, He offered up prayers and supplications with strong crying and tears unto Him that was able to save Him from death, and was heard in that He feared" (Heb. 5:7). How can we explain a statement like this? There is but one explanation of it; and it is His true humanity. It is only by accepting this truth in the fullest sense that we can understand this aspect of His life. Christ was not half a God and half a man, but perfectly God and perfectly man. There are things about Him, and there are statements of His own, to which justice cannot be done without categorically calling Him God. We may hesitate to utter this confession, but the facts, unless we flinch from them, will compel us to make it. On the other hand, there are other things about Him which compel us in the fullest acceptation of the term to call Him a man; and we are not honoring but dishonoring Him if we do not accept this truth also in all its fullness and in all its consequences.

He prayed, then, because He was a man. Humanity even at its best is a feeble and dependent thing; it can never be self-sufficient. Even in Him it was not sufficient for itself, but dependent on God from day to day; and He expressed His sense of dependence by praying. Does this not bring Him very near us? Verily He is our brother, bone of our bone and flesh of our flesh.

But there is another lesson in it, and a graver one. Although a man, Jesus was a sinless man. At every stage of development His manhood was perfect. He had no sinful past to weaken the force of present effort. Yet He needed prayer and resorted to it continually. What a commentary on our need of it! If He needed it, being what He was, how must we need it, being what we are.

II

The life of prayer is a secret life, and everyone who really loves prayer has habits of it known only to himself. Much of the prayerfulness of Jesus must have lain beyond the observation of even His disciples, and therefore is altogether unrecorded in the Gospels. But some of His habits have been preserved, and they are extremely interesting and instructive.

He liked, when about to pray, to escape from the house and from the town and go away out into the natural solitudes. We read, "He went out and departed unto a solitary place, and there prayed." Elsewhere it is said, "He withdrew Himself into the wilderness, and prayed." He seems to have especially loved mountains as places of prayer. When the statement is anywhere made that He went up to a mountain to pray, commentators try to find out, by examining the vicinity in which He was sojourning at the time, which mountain it was He ascended for this purpose. But in this, I think, they are on the wrong track. In Palestine, as in many parts of Scotland, there is mountain everywhere. A mile or two from any town you are out on it. You have only to quit the houses, cross a few acres of cultivated ground, and your feet are on the turfy pastures, where you can be absolutely alone. Jesus had, if we may so speak, made the discovery that He could obtain this solitude anywhere; and, when He arrived in a town, His first thought was, which was the shortest road to the mountain, just as ordinary travelers inquire where are the most noted sights and which is the best hotel.

There is a solitude of time as well as a solitude of space. What mountains and wildernesses are to towns and cities, the night time and the early morning are to the day time and the early night. Jesus frequented this solitude too for prayer. We heard of Him continuing the whole night in prayer to God; or it is said that He "rose up a great while before day, and departed into a solitary place to pray."

It may partly have been because, on account of His poverty, He could not easily find solitude in the houses in which He lodged that Jesus cultivated this habit,* and this may give His example a special

---

* Many of us may be able to be quite alone in our own homes. Jesus recognized this when He said: "Enter thou, when thou prayest, into thy closet; and, when thou has shut thy door, pray to thy Father which is in secret." The essential thing is to have the world shut out and to be alone with God. It is for this reason that we shut our eyes in prayer: it is that our attention, being withdrawn from all sights and sounds without, may be concentrated on the vision and the voices within. We may even so familiarize ourselves with the inward world that we shall acquire the habit of transporting ourselves into it at will at any hour of the day and in any circumstances. Amidst the whir of machinery, in the bustle of the street, even in the midst of conversation, we may be able mentally to disappear out   [*continued*]

interest for any whose circumstances expose them to the same difficulty. But it is a discovery which might immensely enrich us all if we
were to realize how easy it is to get into the natural solitudes. There is
scarcely a town out of which you cannot escape in a very few minutes
and find yourself quite alone—on a bit of shore, or on a mountain, or
in a pasture or a wood. The town or city may be thundering away quite
near, with its imprisoned multitudes bound on the treadmill of its toils
or its amusements, but you are out of it and alone with God.

There is more than mere solitude in such a situation to assist
prayer. There is a ministry of nature which soothes the mind and dis-
poses it to devotion. Never did I feel more strongly that in this habit
Jesus had laid bare one of the great secrets of life than one day when
I climbed all alone a hill above Inveraray and lay on the summit of it,
musing through a summer forenoon. On every hand there stretched a
solitary world of mountain and moorland; the loch below as gleaming
in the sun like a shield of silver; the town was visible at the foot of the
hill, and the passengers could be seen moving in the streets, but no
sound of its bustle reached so high. The great sky was over all; and God
seemed just at hand, waiting to hear every word. It was in spots like this
that Jesus prayed.

He prayed, however, in company as well as in solitude. We hear
of Him again and again taking two or three of His disciples away to pray
with them, and sometimes of Him praying with them all. The Twelve
were a kind of family to Him, and He assiduously cultivated family worship. He spoke too of the value of united prayer, "I say unto you,
that if two of you shall agree on earth as touching anything that they
shall ask, it shall be done for them of My Father which is in heaven."
United prayer acts on the spirit very much in the same way as conversation acts on the mind. Many a man's intellect, when he is alone,
is slow in its movements and far from fertile in the production of
ideas. But, when it meets with another mind and clashes with it in conversation, it is transformed: it becomes agile and audacious, it burns

---

of time and stand for an instant in eternity face to face with God; and few prayers
are more precious than the momentary ejaculations offered in the course of daily
occupations. He who has acquired this habit has a strong tower into which he can
retreat in every time of need.

and coruscates and brings forth ideas out of its resources which are a surprise even to itself.* So, where two or three are met together, the prayer of one strikes fire from the soul of another; and the latter in his turn leads the way to nobler heights of devotion. And lo, as their joy increases, there is One in their midst whom they all recognize and cling to. He was there before, but it is only when their hearts begin to burn that they recognize Him; and in a true sense they may be said to bring Him there—"Where two or three are met together in My name, there am I in the midst of them."

III

The occasions which call for prayer are innumerable, and it would be vain to attempt to count them. Jesus undoubtedly had, as we have ourselves, new reasons for praying every day, but some of the occasions on which He prayed are specially instructive.

1. We find Him engaged in special prayer just before taking very important steps in life. One of the most important steps He ever took was the selection from among His disciples of the Twelve who were to be His apostles. It was an act on which the whole future of Christianity depended; and what was He doing before it took place? "It came to pass in those days that He went into a mountain to pray, and continued all night in prayer to God; and, when it was day, He called unto Him His disciples, and of them He chose twelve, whom He also named apostles." It was after this nightlong vigil that He proceeded to the choice which was to be so momentous for Him and for them and for all the world. There was another day for which, we are told, He made similar preparation. It was that on which He first informed His disciples that He was to suffer and die.

Thus it is evident that, when Jesus had a day of crisis or of difficult duty before Him, He gave Himself specially to prayer. Would it not

---

* "Certain it is, that whosoever hath his Mind fraught with many Thoughts, his Wits and Understanding do clarify and break up, in the communicating and discoursing with Another: he tosseth his Thoughts more easily; he marshalleth them more orderly; he seeth how they look when they are turned into Words; finally, he waxeth wiser than himself, and that more by an Hour's Discourse than by a Day's Meditation"—*Bacon's Essays*, 27: Of Friendship.

simplify our difficulties if we attacked them in the same way? It would infinitely increase the intellectual insight with which we try to penetrate a problem and the power of the hand we lay upon duty. The wheels of existence would move far more smoothly and our purposes travel more surely to their aims, if every morning we reviewed beforehand the duties of the day with God.*

2. Jesus appears to have devoted Himself specially to prayer at times when His life was unusually full of work and excitement. His was a very busy life; there were nearly always "many coming and going" about Him. Sometimes, however, there was such a congestion of thronging objects that He had scarcely time to eat. But even then He found time to pray. Indeed, these appear to have been with Him seasons of more prolonged prayer than usual. Thus we read: "So much the more went there a fame abroad of Him, and great multitudes came together to hear and to be healed by Him of their infirmities, but He withdrew Himself into the wilderness and prayed."

Many in our day know what this congestion of occupations is: they are swept off their feet with their engagements and can scarcely find

---

* In Nicoll's *Life of Jesus Christ*, pp. 178–180, an important consideration is added: "Jesus Christ not only prayed before great and decisive acts, but He prayed after them. . . . This teaches us much which it is easy but fatal to miss. When we have done some great work by immense expenditure of force, we are tempted to say our part is done—we cannot accomplish more. Many a man desires to end and crown his public life amidst the shoutings of applause for some victory or achievement. He would retire to boast of it, and live all the rest of his days upon that proud memory. Better it is to pray—to pray, if it be God's will, for new strength, for new if humbler efforts, and, if that is denied, for blessing on what has been attempted or done. Jesus Christ did not boast, He did not give up, but He recruited Himself for new service by continuing in prayer to God. Another temptation is to pride. We are lifted above the simplicity and humility in which we lived before. Our hearts swell, and we are tempted to think our previous life mean and insignificant. Never are we further from God than when intoxicated by pride. In the pride of their hearts the wicked angels fell, and we may fall too unless we are delivered from their sin. Nothing will avail more effectually to allay and silence our pride than prayer. In communion with our Father our pride is chilled and destroyed. A kindred temptation after great achievements is the temptation to profound depression. When one has done one's utmost, and put forth the whole force of life, one feels completely spent, as if work were over. Men who have preached with power to multitudes of people have told us of the terrible languor which succeeds a full outburst

time to eat. We make this a reason for not praying; Jesus made it a reason for praying. Is there any doubt which is the better course? Many of the wisest have in this respect done as Jesus did. When Luther had a specially busy and exciting day, he allowed himself longer time than usual for prayer beforehand. A wise man once said that he was too busy to be in a hurry; he meant that, if he allowed himself to become hurried, he could not do all that he had to do. There is nothing like prayer for producing this calm self-possession. When the dust of business so fills your room that it threatens to choke you, sprinkle it with the water of prayer, and then you can cleanse it out with comfort and expedition.

3. We find Jesus engaging in special prayer when about to enter into temptation. The greatest scene of prayer in His life is undoubtedly Gethsemane. As we enter that garden after Him, we fear almost to look on the scene—it is so sacred and so passes our understanding; and we tremble as we listen to the prayers rising from the ground where He lies. Never were prayers heard like these. We cannot fathom them; yet much may be learned from them. Let one lesson, however, suffice in the meantime: He prayed on this occasion before entering into temptation; for at the gate of the garden, after the agony was over, He said, "This is your hour and the power of darkness." It was the commencement of His final conflict with the powers of wickedness in earth and hell. But He had equipped Himself for the conflict by the prayer in the garden beforehand, and so He was able to go through all that followed with unruffled dignity and with perfect success. His strength was the strength of prayer.

What an illustration of contrast was presented on that occasion by the weakness of the disciples! For them also that hour and the power of darkness began at the gate of Gethsemane, but it was an hour of disaster and ignominious defeat. Why? Because they were sleeping when they ought to have been praying. "Watch and pray," He had said,

---

of the heart. They have told us how they felt as if their life went from them in that supreme effort, and could never be regained. That is natural; and we may learn from Jesus Christ how it is to be met. Let us pray that by prayer and service we may be taught to feel that our wellsprings are in God, and that He who strengthened and filled us for that achievement, which we fear we can never repeat, can gird us, if He will, for new and nobler work."

bending over their prostrate forms, "lest ye enter into temptation." But they heeded not; and so, when the hour of temptation came, they fell. Alas! their experience has often been ours also. The only armor in which temptation can be successfully met is prayer; and, when the enemy is allowed to come upon us before we have buckled it on, we have not a chance of standing.

4. If any scene of prayer in our Lord's life may compete in interest with this one, it is the last of all. Jesus died praying. His last words were words of prayer. The habit of life was strong in death. It may seem far off, but this event will come to us also. What will our last words be? Who can tell? But would it not be beautiful if our spirit were so steeped in the habit of prayer that the language of prayer came naturally to us at the last? Many have died with Christ's own words on their lips. Who would not covet them for his own? "Father, into Thy hands I commend My spirit."

IV

If anyone were to go through the life of Christ seeking for answers to His prayers, many of them, I am persuaded, could be found. But I shall at present refer only to two on which the Word itself lays emphasis, and which are specially instructive.

The Transfiguration was an answer to prayer. This is how it is introduced in one of the Gospels: "And it came to pass about an eight days after these sayings, He took Peter and John and James, and went up into a mountain to pray. And as He prayed, the fashion of His countenance was altered, and His raiment was white and glistering. And, behold, there talked with Him two men, which were Moses and Elias." I do not say that He was praying for this alteration in His countenance and raiment, or even for the privilege of talking with these wise and sympathetic spirits about the work which He was about to accomplish at Jerusalem. But yet, I say, all this was in answer to the prayer He was offering when it came. There are some who, disbelieving in the direct virtue of prayer to obtain from God what it asks, yet believe in what they call the reflex influence of prayer: they allow it does you good to pray, even if you get nothing directly by it, and even if there is no God to hear you. This, taken as the whole theory of prayer, is a mockery, as the simplest mind must perceive. But it is none the less true that there is a most blessed reflex influence of prayer. Prayers for goodness and purity in a sense answer themselves; for you cannot pray for these things without in some measure receiving them in the very act. To lift up the soul to God calms and ennobles it. It was this, I imagine, that was the beginning of Christ's transfiguration. The absorption and delight of communion with His Father overspread His very face with beauty and glory; and through this outlet the inner glory leapt forth. In some degree this happens to all who pray, and it may happen in a high degree to those who pray much. Moses, after being forty days in the mount with God, shone with the same kind of light as the disciples saw in their Master on the Holy Mount; and there is a spiritual beauty bestowed in some degree on all God's saints who pray much which is of the same nature and is the most precious of all answers to prayer. Character flows from the wellspring of prayer.

The other answer to prayer given to Jesus to which I desire to call attention took place at His baptism. Here is St. Luke's account of it: "Now when all the people were baptized, it came to pass, that Jesus also being baptized, and praying, the heaven was opened, and the Holy Ghost descended like a dove upon Him." It was when He was praying that the Spirit was sent down upon Him, and in all probability it was this which at the moment He was praying for. He had just left His home in Nazareth to begin His public work; and He was in immediate need of the Holy Spirit to equip Him for His task. It is a forgotten truth that Jesus was filled with the Holy Ghost, but it is one most clearly revealed in the Gospels. The human nature of Jesus was from first to last dependent on the Holy Ghost, being thereby made a fit organ for the divine; and it was in the strength of this inspiration that all His work, as preacher, miracle worker, and atoner, was done.* And if in any measure our life is to be an imitation of His—if we are to help in car-

---

* "The Holy Spirit, in a peculiar manner, anointed Him with all those *extraordinary powers and gifts* which were necessary for the exercise and discharging of His office on earth. Is. 61:1: 'The Spirit of the Lord God is upon Me; because the Lord hath anointed Me to preach good tidings unto the meek: He hath sent Me to bind up the brokenhearted, to proclaim liberty to the captives, and the   [*continued*]

rying on His work in the world or in filling up what is lacking in His sufferings—we must be dependent on the same influence. But how are we to get it? He has told us Himself: "If ye then, being evil, know how to give good gifts unto your children, how much more shall your heavenly Father give the Holy Spirit to them that ask Him." Power, like character, comes from the fountain of prayer.

---

opening of the prison to them that are bound.' It is the prophetical office of Christ, and His discharge thereof in His ministry on the earth which is intended. And He applies these words unto Himself with respect unto His preaching of the Gospel (Luke 4:18, 19); for this was that office which He principally attended unto here in the world, as that whereby He instructed men in the nature and use of His other offices. . . . Hereunto was He fitted by this unction of the Spirit. And here, also, is a distinction between the 'Spirit that was upon Him,' and His being 'anointed to preach,' which contains the communication of the gifts of that Spirit unto Him. . . . And this collation of extraordinary gifts for the discharge of His prophetical office was at His baptism (Matt. 3:17). They were not bestowed on the Head of the Church, nor are any gifts of the same nature in general bestowed on any of His members, but for use, exercise, and improvement. And that they were then collated appears; for,—

"1. Then did He receive the *visible pledge* which confirmed Him in, and testified unto others His calling of God to, the exercise of His *office*; for then 'the Spirit of God descended like a dove, and lighted upon Him: and, lo, a voice came from heaven, saying, "This is My beloved Son, in whom I am well pleased" ' (Matt. 3:16, 17). Hereby was He 'sealed of God the Father' (John 6:27) in that visible pledge of His vocation, setting the great seal of heaven to His commission. And this also was to be a testimony unto others, that they might own Him in His office, now He had undertaken to discharge it (chap. 1:33).

"2. He now entered on His public ministry and wholly *gave Himself up* unto His work; for before He did only occasionally manifest the presence of God with Him, somewhat to prepare the minds of men to attend unto His ministry, as when He filled them with astonishment at His discourses with the doctors in the Temple (Luke 2:46, 47). And although it is probable that He might be acted by the Spirit in and unto many such extraordinary actions during His course of a private life, yet the fullness of gifts for His work He received not until the time of His baptism, and therefore before that He gave not Himself up wholly unto His public ministry.

"3. Immediately hereon it is said that He was 'full of the Holy Ghost' (Luke 4:1). Before, He was said to 'wax strong in spirit,' (πληρούμενος σοφίας), chap 2:40, 'continually filling'; but now He is (πλήρης Πνεύματος) ('full of the Holy Ghost'). He was actually possessed of and furnished with all that fullness of spiritual gifts which were any way needful for Him or useful unto Him, or which human nature is capable of receiving"—OWEN, *On the Holy Spirit.*

Matthew 4:4, 7, 10; 5:17, 48; 6:29; 7:12; 8:4, 11; 9:13; 10:15; 11:21, 24; 12:3–7, 39–42; 13:14, 15; 15:7–9; 19:8, 18, 19; 21:16, 42; 22:29–32; 35–40; 43–45; 24:37–39; 26:30, 31, 53, 54; 27:46.

Luke 4:16–27; 8:21; 16:29, 30; 23:46; 24:27.

John 5:39, 45, 46; 6:32, 45, 49; 7:19, 22; 8:17, 37; 10:34, 35; 13:18; 17:12, 14, 17.

8

Christ as a
Student of Scripture

I.

IT is probable that Jesus knew three languages.

The language of His country was Aramaic; and some fragments of it, as they fell from His lips, have been preserved to us in the Gospels, such as *Talitha, cumi*, the words with which He raised the daughter of Jairus. But it is not likely that He read the Scriptures in this His native tongue. Sometimes, indeed, the quotations of the Old Testament in the New do not tally exactly with any form of the Old Testament now in our hands, and the conjecture has been hazarded that in such cases the quotations are taken from an Aramaic version then in existence, but this is no more than conjecture.

Another language He spoke was Greek. In Galilee, where He was brought up, there were so many Greek settlers that it was called "Galilee of the Gentiles"; and Greek was the language of commerce and of the more cosmopolitan kind of social intercourse. A boy brought up in Galilee in those days would have the same chance of learning Greek as in our day a boy brought up in the Highlands of Scotland has of learning English. Now in Greek there existed in Christ's time a version of the Old Testament Scriptures. We still possess it, under the name of the Septuagint, or Seventy, the supposed number of the translators who executed it in Egypt between two and three hundred years before the Christian era. It was extensively circulated in Palestine. The New Testament writers very frequently quote from it, and there is little doubt that our Lord read it.

The third language which He probably knew was Hebrew. This can only be stated as a probability; for, though Hebrew was the language of the Jews, it had ceased before Christ's time to be the spoken language of Palestine. Languages sometimes decay even in the countries to which they are native, and become so mixed with foreign elements as to lose their identity. A modern example is seen in Italy, where Latin is now a dead language, having been transmuted by slow degrees into the course of centuries into Italian. Though Italian bears considerable resemblance to the ancient tongue, the boys of Italy today have to learn Latin just as our own boys do. The same thing had taken place in Palestine. The Hebrew language, in which the Old Testament was written, had degenerated into Aramaic; and Jews who desired to read the Scriptures in the original tongue had to learn the dead language. There is reason to believe that Jesus acquired it. In some of His quotations from the Old Testament, scholars have observed, He purposely diverges from the Greek and reverts to the exact terms of the original. It will be remembred also that in the synagogue of Nazareth He was asked to read the Scriptures. Now it is probable that in the synagogue roll the writing was in Hebrew, the reader having first to read it in that language and then to translate it into the language of the people.* If this be so, it is surely interesting to think of Jesus learning the dead language in order to read the Word of God in the tongue in which it was written. Remember, His condition in life was only that of a mechanic; and it may have been in the brief intervals of toil that He mastered the strange letters and forms that were to bring Him face to face with the Psalms as David wrote them and with the prophecies as they flowed from the pen of Isaiah or Jeremiah. In our own country the same sacred ambition is not unknown. At all events, a generation ago there were working men who learned Greek with the grammar stuck on the loom in front of them, that they might read the New Testament in the language in which it was written; and I have spoken with the members of a group of businessmen in Ed-

---

* "Verse by verse, taking turns with the translator, the appointed individual read the text and the translator spoke the Targum, that is, the Aramaic paraphrase"— HAUSRATH, *History of the New Testament*.

inburgh who met every Saturday to read the Greek Testament. Certainly there is a flavor about the Bible, when read in the language it was written in, which it loses more or less in every translation; and it is perhaps surprising that in our day, when the love of the Bible is so common and the means of learning are so accessible, the ambition to read it thus is not more widely spread.

It is pathetic to think that Jesus never possessed a Bible of His own, but there can be no doubt of the fact. The expense of such a possession in those days was utterly beyond the means of one in His condition; and besides, the bulkiness of the rolls on which it was written would have prevented it from being portable, even if He could have possessed it. Possibly in His home there may have been a few of the precious rolls, containing the Psalms or other favorite portions of the Holy Writ, but it must have been by frequenting the synagogue and obtaining access to the books lying there, perhaps through ingratiating Himself with their keeper, as an enthusiastic musician may do with the organist of a church in order to be permitted to use the instrument, that He was able to quench His thirst for sacred knowledge. We can procure the Holy Book for next to nothing, and every child possesses a copy. May its cheapness and universal currency never make it in our eyes a common thing!

Of course it was only the Old Testament Jesus had to read. It may be worthwhile to recall this as a reminder of how much more reason we have to love and prize our larger Bible. When I read in the Psalms such outbursts of affection for the Word of God as these: "Oh how I love Thy law: it is my study all the day"; "How sweet are Thy words to my taste; yea, sweeter than honey to my mouth"; "More to be desired are they than gold, yea, than much fine gold; sweeter also than honey and the honeycomb," — I say, when I read such outbursts of holy feeling, and recollect that they came from the lips of men who possessed only the Old Testament, perhaps only a fragment of it — men in whose Bible there were no Gospels, or Epistles of Paul, or Apocalypse, who had never read the Sermon on the Mount or the Prodigal Son, the seventeenth of John or the eighth of Romans, the thirteenth of First Corinthians or the eleventh of Hebrews, I ask what my feelings are towards the much larger Bible I possess, and I say to myself that surely in modern times the heart of man has become ossified, and the fountains of gratitude have dried up, and the fires of admiration and enthusiasm have been put out, so tame, in comparison, is our affection for the far more perfect Book.*

II

There is the most indubitable evidence that Jesus was an assiduous student of the Word of God. This is furnished, not by repeated statements to this effect, but by proofs far more impressive. His recorded sayings abound with quotations from it. These are sometimes express references to the book and the verse, but oftener they are allusions to Old Testament events and personages or unexpressed quotations so woven into the warp and woof of His own statements as to show that the Old Testament drenched His mind through and through, supplied the scenery in which His imagination habitually worked, and molded the very language in which He thought and spoke.

If His quotations are examined, it will be found that they are derived from every part of the book, showing His acquaintance not only

---

* No nobler tribute has ever been paid to the Divine Word than Edward Irving's *Orations for the Oracles of God*. We quote a few sentences from the first of them: "There is no express stirring up of faculties to mediate her high and heavenly strains—nor formal sequestration of the mind from all other concerns on purpose for her special entertainment—nor pause of solemn seeking and solemn waiting for a spiritual frame, before entering and listening to the voice of the Almighty's wisdom. Who feels the sublime dignity there is in a saying fresh descended from the porch of heaven? Who feels the awful weight there is in the least iota that hath dropped from the lips of God? Who feels the thrilling fear or trembling hope there is in words whereon the eternal destinies of himself do hang? Who feels the tide of gratitude swelling within his breast, for redemption and salvation, instead of flat despair and everlasting retribution? Or who, in perusing the Word of God, is captivated through all his faculties, transported through all his emotions, and through all his energies of action wound up? . . .

"Oh! if books had but tongues to speak their wrongs, then might this book well exclaim—Hear, O heavens! and give ear, O earth! I came from the love and embrace of God, and mute nature, to whom I brought no boon, did me rightful homage. To man I came, and my words were to the children of men. I disclosed to you the mysteries of the hereafter, and the secrets of the throne of God. I set open to you the gates of salvation, and the way of eternal life, heretofore unknown.

with its prominent features, but with its obscurest corners; so that we ourselves need not travel anywhere among the Old Testament writings without the assurance that His blessed feet have been there before us. It is, however, peculiarly enjoyable in the reading of Scripture to be able to halt at a text and know for certain, from His quoting it, that out of this very vessel, which we are raising to our lips, Jesus drank the living water. There are even texts which we may without irreverence call His favorites, because He quoted them again and again. And there are books of Scripture which seem to have been specially dear to Him, Deuteronomy, the Psalms, and Isaiah being the chief.

Not long ago it fell to my lot to look over the papers of a deceased friend. As all who have had the same duty to perform must know, it is a pathetic task. There is a haunting sense of desecration in rifling the secrets kept hidden during life and learning exactly what the man was beneath the surface. My friend had been a man of the world, exposed to many of the temptations of those who have to do its business and mingle with its company, but he had sustained the character of a religious man. I had now the means of finding out whether this was something put on from the outside or growing from within. It was with deep awe that, as I advanced, I came upon evidence after evidence of an inner life with even deeper and fresher roots than I had ventured to hope for. When I opened his Bible especially, it told an unmistakable story; for the marks of long and diligent use were visible on

---

Nothing in heaven did I withhold from your hope and ambition; and upon your earthly lot I poured the full horn of divine providence and consolation. But ye requited me with no welcome, ye held no festivity on my arrival: ye sequester me from happiness and heroism, closeting me with sickness and infirmity; ye make not of me, nor use me for your guide to wisdom and prudence, but press me into your list of duties, and withdraw me to a mere corner of your time; and most of ye set me at naught, and utterly disregard me. I came, the fullness of the knowledge of God: angels delighted in my company, and desired to dive into my secrets. But ye, mortals, place masters over me, subjecting me to the discipline and dogmatism of men, and tutoring me in your schools of learning. I came not to be silent in your dwellings, but to speak welfare to you and to your children. I came to rule, and my throne to set up in the hearts of men. Mine ancient residence was the bosom of God; no residence will I have but the soul of an immortal; and if you had entertained me, I should have possessed you of the peace which I had with God."

every page—the leaves well worn, the choice texts underlined, short breathings of the heart noted on the margins. In some parts the marks of use were peculiarly frequent. This was the case especially with Psalms, Isaiah and Hosea in the Old Testament and the writings of St. John in the New. I now knew the reality of the life that was ended and whence its virtues had sprung.

Thus the very aspect of a man's Bible may be a record of his most secret habits and remain to those who come after him a momentum of his religion or irreligion. To the living man himself there is perhaps no better test of his own religious condition than a glance through its pages; for by the tokens of use or neglect he may learn whether or not he loves it. I copied from the flyleaf of my friend's Bible a few words which perhaps explain the source of true love to the Word: "Oh, to come nearer to Christ, nearer to God, nearer to holiness! Every day to live more completely in Him, by Him, for and with Him. There is a Christ; shall I be Christless? A cleansing; shall I remain foul? A Father's love; shall I be an alien? A heaven; shall I be cast out?"

III

There are different methods of studying the Scriptures with profit. On these we have no express teaching from the lips of Christ, but from the records of His conduct we can see that He practiced them.

According to the method by which it is studied, God's Word serves different uses in spiritual experience; one method being serviceable for one kind of use, and another for another. Jesus displayed perfect proficiency in all the ways of using it; and from this we are able to infer how He studied it.

There are especially three prominent uses to which we find Him putting the Bible, and these are very important for our imitation.

1. *For Defense.*

The very first use we find Him making of the Word is as a defense against temptation. When the Wicked One came to Him and tempted Him in the wilderness, He answered every suggestion with, "It is written." The Word was in His hands the sword of the Spirit, and He turned with its edge the onsets of the enemy.

In like manner He defended Himself with it against the assaults of wicked men. When they lay in wait for Him and tried to entangle Him in His talk, He foiled them with the Word of God. Especially on that great day of controversy immediately before His end (Matt. 22), when all His enemies set upon Him and the champions of the different parties did their utmost to confuse and confute Him, He repelled their attacks one after another with answers drawn from the Scriptures; and at last silenced them and put them to shame in the eyes of the people by showing their ignorance of the Scriptures of which they were the chosen interpreters.

There was yet another enemy He met with the same weapon. It was the last enemy. When the terrors of death were closing round Him, like a dark multitude pressing in upon a solitary man, He had recourse to His old and tried weapon. Two at least, if not more, of His seven last words from the cross were verses out of His favorite book of Psalms. One of them was His very last word, and with it He plucked His soul out of the jaws of death: "Father, into Thy hands I commend My spirit."

For this use of Scripture the practice of committing it to memory is essential. In every case I have mentioned Jesus was able to recur to the contents of a memory stored with texts of Scripture and find at once the necessary weapon for the occasion. Often, when temptation comes, there is no time to search for the word to meet it; everything depends on being already armed, with sword in hand. This shows how necessary it is to fill the memory, while it is plastic, with stores of texts; we do not know what use we may get of them in future days of trial and weakness. In daily reading, when we have gone through a chapter, it is an excellent plan to select a single verse and commit it to memory. Not only does this sharpen the attention on the whole chapter, but it lays up ammunition for future battles.

2. *For Inspiration.*

It is easy from Christ's Old Testament references to see that He dwelt much among the great spirits of the past whose lives the Old Testament records. His earthly environment was unsympathetic in the extreme. In His own home He was not believed in. In His own country there was living an evil generation, as He often said, irresponsive to every motive that most profoundly affected Him. His own followers were, in mind and spirit, but children whom He was only training to comprehend His ideas. His overcharged heart longed for companionship, and He had to seek it among the great figures of the past. In the silent walks and groves of Scripture He met with Abraham and Moses, with David and Elijah and Isaiah, and many more of kindred spirit. These men had lived for aims similar to His own. They had suffered for them as He was suffering; He could borrow the very words of Isaiah about his contemporaries to describe His own. If Jerusalem was persecuting Him, she had always been the city that slew the prophets. So near did He get in His reading of the Word to these departed spirits, so alive in His meditations did they become, that at last two of them, the greatest of all, Moses and Elias, were actually drawn back across the boundary of visibility and appeared conversing with Him in the Holy Mount. But this conversation was only the culmination of hundreds He had held before with them and with the other prophets in the pages of Holy Writ.

To enjoy this use of the Bible a different kind of study of it is necessary from that which makes it useful for defense. For defense the verbal memory of single texts is what is necessary; for inspiration our study must take a wider sweep. It must embrace the life of a man from beginning to end; it must understand the time which produced him and the circumstances against which he had to react. We must read about the man till we see the world of his day, and him moving in it; we must learn to catch his tone and accent. Then he is ours; he will walk with us; he will speak to us; he will be our companion and friend. This is the privilege of the Christian who knows his Bible: whatever be his surroundings in the actual world, he can transport himself at will into the best of company, where the brow of everyone is crowned with nobleness, every eye beams encouragement, and the air is redolent of faith and hope and love.

3. *For Guidance.*

Jesus used His Bible as the chart of His own life. Learned men, ay, and reverent men, have discussed the question at what age He became fully aware that He was the Messiah, and by what degrees He became possessed of a distinct knowledge of the path which He was to pursue: at what point, for example, He learned that He was to be not a victorious but a suffering Savior; and they have supposed that He came to the knowledge of these things by the study of the prophecies of the Old Testament about Himself. I have never felt myself fit for such speculations; these things seem to me to be hidden behind the curtain of the mystery of His person as God and man in one. But it is easy in His words to see that He did follow His own course with intense interest in Old Testament prophecy, as in a chart. Again and again it is said He did this and that, that such and such a prophecy might be fulfilled. To the deputation sent from the Baptist, and to others, He pointed out how literally His way of life corresponded with the portrait of the Messiah sketched by Isaiah and other prophets. His intercourse with His disciples after His resurrection seems to have been mainly devoted to showing them from Moses and all the prophets that His life, sufferings and death were the exact fulfillment of all that had been foretold.

To use Scripture thus requires a method of study far more advanced than is necessary for the uses of defense or inspiration already explained: it requires the power of taking a bird's eye view of Scripture as a whole, of discerning the main currents flowing through it from first to last, and especially of tracing clearly the great central current to which all the others tend and into which they finally empty themselves.

Evidently this was Christ's way of studying the Bible: He could lift it up and wield it as a whole. One sees this even in His mode of using single texts. He rarely quotes a text without revealing in it some hidden meaning which no one had suspected before, but which shines clearly to all eyes as soon as it has been pointed out.* Some rare men in all ages have had this power. You occasionally hear a preacher who can quote a text so that it becomes transfigured and shines in his

---

* "Lord, this morning I read a chapter in the Bible, and therein observed a memorable passage, whereof I never took notice before. Why now, and no sooner, did I see it? Formerly my eyes were as open, and the letters as legible. Is there not a thin veil laid over Thy Word, which is more rarefied by reading, and at last wholly worn away? . . . I see the oil of Thy Word will never leave increasing whilst any bring an empty barrel. The Old Testament will still be a New Testament to him who comes with a fresh desire of information. . . . How fruitful are the seeming barren places of Scripture. Bad plowmen, which make balks of such ground. Wheresoever the surface of God's Word doth not laugh and sing with corn, there the heart thereof within is merry with mines, affording, where not plain matter, hidden mysteries"—FULLER, *Good Thoughts in Bad Times*.

argument like a gem. What gives this power? It comes when the mind can go down and down through the text till it reaches the great lake of light that lies beneath all the texts, and a jet from that fiery sea comes up and burns on the surface.

We are too easily satisfied with enjoying isolated texts. The shock and stimulus which a single text can give is very valuable, but a whole book of Scripture can give a far more powerful shock, if we read it from beginning to end and try to grasp its message as a whole. From this we may advance to groups of books. Sometimes we might take a single subject and go through the whole Bible to find out what is taught on it. And why should we not at last make the attempt to grasp all that the Bible has to teach, for faith on the one hand and for conduct on the other?

The best guide to the fullness of Scripture is to search it, as Jesus did, as the chart of our own life. In a different way, indeed, from that in which He found His life prefigured there, yet in a perfectly legitimate way, we shall find the exact form and image of our own. In precept and promise and example we shall see every deed we have to do, every resolution we have to form, every turn in life we have to take, laid down; and, if we act as it is written, we shall be able to follow up what we do by saying, as He so often did, "This has been done that the Scripture might be fulfilled."

Such a course earnestly followed will, however, bring us still nearer to His method of studying the Scriptures; for it will inevitably land us in the great central current which runs through the whole of Scripture from the first to last. What is this? It is nothing but Christ Himself. The whole stream and drift of the Old Testament moves straight to the cross of Christ. The whole New Testament is nothing but the portrait of Christ. Let a man seek the true course of his own life in the Word, and inevitably it will land him at the cross, to seek mercy as a perishing sinner in the Savior's wounds; and let him, starting afresh from this point of departure, seek his true course still father, and inevitably what he will see will be, rising upon him in the distance, astonishing and enchaining him, but drawing him ever on, the image of perfection in the man Christ Jesus.

Matthew 4:24; 8:16, 17; 9:35; 11:1, 4, 5; 12:15; 13:2; 14:13, 14, 35, 36; 15:30; 19:1, 2.

Mark 2:2; 3:20; 6:31, 54–56; 13:34; 14:8.

Luke 6:19; 10:2; 12:1; 13:32, 33.

John 2:4; 4:32–34; 7:6, 8; 9:4; 12:23; 17:4; 19:30.

9
Christ as a Worker

THERE are two ideals as to work—the one to do as little, and the other to do as much, as possible. The former may be called the Oriental, the latter the Occidental, ideal. The child of the East, living in a warm climate, where movement or exertion soon tires, counts idleness the height of enjoyment, and passes his time, if he can, in a lazy dream. His very clothing is an index of his tastes—the capacious garment, the loose slipper. The son of the West, on the contrary, is apt to be a stirring being; he likes the excitement of endeavor and the exultation of achievement. His clothing is the least elegant in the world, but it has one virtue which in his eyes is a sufficient compensation: it is suitable for movement and work. His very pastimes are strenuous: while the Oriental after work stretches himself on a divan, the Briton spends his leisure in football or hunting.

Even in the West, indeed, there are great differences in the tastes of individuals. People of lethargic temperament are slow to work and prone to laziness, while those of the choleric temperament sometimes carry the enthusiasm for exertion to such extremes that they do not feel right unless they are in a kind of tempest of occupation. Among certain classes the goal of ambition is to be in a position to be able, if you choose, to do nothing; this is called being a gentleman. But the shrewder heads perceive that the pleasures of such a position, when it is won, seldom come up to the expectations of its possessor, unless, when released from a bread-winning calling, he voluntarily devotes himself to some of those invaluable services to the community or the Church which the leisured can best discharge, and on which the welfare of modern society so much depends.

Such are the differences which prevail among men when choosing only according to taste or temperament, but on this subject, as elsewhere, our Lord has set before us, in His teaching and example, the will of God.

I

In its bearing on this question there is endless significance in the fact that Jesus was born in the cottage of a working man and spent the greater part of His life doing the work of a village carpenter. It is impossible to believe that this happened by chance; for the minutest circumstances of the life of Christ must have been ordered by God. The Jews expected the Messiah to be a prince, but God decreed that He should be born a working man. And so Jesus built the cottages of the villagers of Nazareth, constructed the wagon of the farmer, and mended perhaps the plaything of the child.

This sheds immortal honor upon work. The Greeks and the Romans despised manual labor, accounting it only fit for slaves; and this pagan notion easily slips back into the minds of men. But the example of the Son of man will always protect the dignity of honest labor; and the heart of the artisan will sing at his work as he remembers that Jesus of Nazareth stood at the bench and handled the tools of the carpenter.

The virtue of work is manifold. It stamps the brute earth and the raw materials taken out of it with the signature of mind,* which is the image and superscription of Him who is the Supreme Reason. It is a contribution to the happiness of the race, and it brings the individual into cooperation with all his fellow creatures in the common task of taking possession of their habitation. It reacts too on the worker. It is a daily school of patience, sympathy and honesty. The man who scamps his work degrades himself.

Our age has learned these truths well, because they have been expounded to it by several of its favorite and wisest teachers; and there

---

* Compare Schleiermacher's definition of Ethics, as "the collective operation of active human reason upon nature," and of the aim of moral effort as "the perfect interpenetration of reason and nature, a permeation of nature by reason" — WUTTKE, *Christian Ethics*, Vol. 1, pg. 48.

is no healthier element in the literature of our century than this Gospel of Labor, as it is called. It has taught many a man to do his work thoroughly, not merely because he is paid for it, but because he delights in it for its own sake and respects himself too much to pass off for work what he knows to be sham.

II

Although the commonest work well done is honorable, every kind of work is not of equal honor. There are some callings in which a man can contribute far more directly and amply than in others to the welfare of his fellow creatures, and these stand highest in the scale of honor.

It was on this principle that Jesus acted when He quitted the bench of the carpenter to devote Himself to preaching and healing. Than these two there are no callings more honorable, the one ministering directly to the soul and the other to the body. By adopting them, however, Jesus stamped a fresh dignity on the work both of the preacher and of the physician; and, ever since, many in both professions have gone about their duties with intenser ardor and enjoyment because they have been conscious of walking in His footsteps.

But, though His work had changed, He was not less a worker than He had been before. It is a common theme of discussion between manual and professional laborers whether the toil of the hand or that of the brain is the more severe. The artisan thinks that his well-clothed neighbor, who does not need to touch rough materials or lift heavy loads, has an easy time of it; while the professional man, harassed with anxiety and responsibility, sighs for the regular hours, the well-learned task and the freedom from care of the working man. This is a controversy which will never be decided. But it is certain, in the case of Jesus at least, that it was when He entered on His new career that the real hard work of His life began. His three years of work as preacher and healer were years of unexampled toil. Wherever He went multitudes followed Him; when He went into any new region, they sent into all the country round about and brought unto Him all that were diseased in mind or body; the crowds about Him sometimes swelled to such dimensions that the people trod one upon another; and sometimes He had not time even to eat. Such was the pressure and congestion of work with which He was beset. It is the kind of life which many have to live in this busy age, but we can look to Jesus and see in what spirit to carry the burden.

III

In Christ's teaching there are many sayings on the responsibility of devoting our time and strength to the work of the world. We are servants, to every one of whom the Divine Taskmaster has given his own work; and, when He returns, He will rigidly require an account of whether or not it has been done.

The most solemn utterance of this kind is the great parable of the talents. The master, going into a far country, leaves each of his servants with a certain amount of money, one with more, another with less; it is to be well employed in his absence; and, when he comes back, he looks to receive not only the principal, but the additional money it has gained. Those who have made use of their trust diligently enter into the joy of their lord, but the servant who has done nothing with his talent is cast into utter darkness. It is a parable of truly awful solemnity. It evidently means that at the last judgment God will expect us to produce work done equivalent to the talents and opportunities He has conferred upon us; and merely to have done nothing with them, as the man with the one talent did, will be enough to condemn us. it is not necessary to waste our time and squander our strength, money and other gifts on bad objects: merely to have failed to expend them on the work of life will incur the extreme penalty of the law.*

---

* "And who art thou that braggest of thy life of Idleness; complacently showest thy bright gilt equipages; sumptuous cushions; appliances for folding of the hands to mere sleep? Looking up, looking down, around, behind or before, discernest thou, if it be not in Mayfair alone, an *idle* hero, saint, god, or even devil? Not a vestige of one. In the Heavens, in the Earth, in the Waters under the Earth, is none like unto thee. Thou art an original figure in this Creation; a denizen in Mayfair alone, in this extraordinary Century or Half-Century alone! One monster there is in the world: the idle man. What is his 'Religion'? That Nature is a Phantom, where cunning beggary or thievery may sometimes find good victual. That God is a life; and that Man and his life are a lie.—Alas, alas, who of us *is* there that can say, I have worked? The faithfullest of us are unprofitable servants; the faithfullest of

This is an exceedingly severe view of life, but it is the view by which Jesus lived Himself. He did not preach what He did not practice. He was doubtless conscious of possessing vast powers and of being capable of exerting an influence which would produce enormous changes both on individuals and in history. But the time allowed Him for putting this influence forth and impressing it on the world was very brief. He knew this, and He always acted like one who has a great work to do and little time to do it. Every hour of His time seemed to be apportioned to its own part of the task, for, when asked to do anything sooner than He intended, He would say, "Mine hour is not yet come." Everything with Him had its own hour. This made Him bold in the face of danger, for He knew that He was immortal till His work was done. As He said, there are twelve hours in the day of a human life, and, till these are spent, a man walks in safety beneath the shield of Providence. The edge of earnestness on His spirit grew keener as time went on; the purpose of life burned more within Him, and He was straightened till it should be accomplished. On His last journey to Jerusalem, as He went before His disciples in the way, "they were amazed, and, as they followed, they were afraid." "I must work the work of Him that sent Me," He would say, "while it is day; the night cometh, when no man can work."

IV

There is intense joy in work when it is done and well done. The humblest mechanic feels this pleasure, when he sees the article he has been making passing out of his hands perfect. The poet surely feels it when he writes Finis at the end of the work into which he has poured the full force of his genius. What must it have been to William Wilberforce to hear on his deathbed that the cause to which he had devoted the toil of a lifetime had triumphed, and to know that, when

us know that best. The faithfullest of us may say, with sad and true old Samuel, 'Much of my life has been trifled away!' But he that has, and except 'on public occasions' professes to have, no function but that of going idle in a graceful or graceless manner, and of begetting sons to go idle; on what iron spikes is he rushing?"—CARLYLE, *Past and Present.*

On this subject the professional philosophers are no less severe. See DORNER, *Christliche Sittenlehre*, p. 460.

he died, there would not be a single slave breathing in any of the dependencies of Britain!

Jesus drank deeply of this well of pleasure. The work He was doing was done perfectly at every stage; and it was work of the most beneficent and enduring kind. As He saw part after part of it falling accomplished behind Him, as He saw hour after hour receding into the past filled with its God-appointed work, He whispered to Himself, "My meat is to do the will of Him that sent Me, and to finish His work." And in the article of death, as He saw the last fold of the grand design unrolled, He passed out of the world with the cry on His lips, "It is finished!" He uttered this cry as a soldier might do on the battlefield, who perceives, with the last effort of consciousness, that the struggle in which he has sacrificed his life has been a splendid victory. But the triumph and the reward of His work never come to an end; for still, as the results of what He did unfold themselves age after age, as His words sink deeper into the minds of men, as His influence changes the face of the world, and as heaven fills with those whom He has redeemed, "He shall see of the travail of His soul, and shall be satisfied."

V

Rest is as necessary a part of life as work. Even for work's sake it is necessary; for it restores the worker to himself, putting him in possession of all his powers and enabling him to do his best.

Jesus knew how to rest as well as how to work. Though there was constant haste in His life, there was no hurry; though there was much pressure, there was no confusion. Nothing was more conspicuous in Him than His unvarying dignity, calmness and self-possession.

He never did anything unprepared. As He never did anything before the time, so He never did anything after it. One-half of the worry and confusion of life arises from doing things at the wrong time, the mind be it either weakened by borrowing today the trouble of tomorrow or exhausted by having on hand not only today's work but that which ought to have been done yesterday. God never wants us to do more in a day than we have time for; and the day will be found to have room enough for its own work if it is not encumbered with the work of the day past or the care of the day to come.*

Jesus was ready for every duty because He came up with it strengthened by the perfect discharge of the duty preceding it. His work in the carpenter's shop was a preparation for the work of preaching. It acquainted Him with human nature and human life, initiating Him especially into the joys and sorrows of the poor, to whom it was afterwards His boast to preach. Many a preacher misses the mark because, though he knows books, he does not know men. But Jesus "knew what was in man, and needed not that any should teach Him." He did not quit this school of experience till He was thirty years of age. Eager as He must have been for the work which lay before Him, He did not rush into it prematurely, but waited hidden in the country, till mind and body were mature and everything fully ripe; and then He came forth traveling in the greatness of His strength and did His work swiftly, surely, perfectly.

But in the midst of His work also He took means to preserve His independence and peace of mind. When the multitude pressing on Him grew too large and stayed too long, He withdrew Himself into the wilderness. Neither the desire to go on preaching nor even the appeals of the sick and dying could detain Him when He felt He needed to preserve His own calmness and self-possession. After days of too crowded work He would disappear, to refresh His body by casting it on the bosom of God. When He saw His disciples becoming exhausted or excited, He would say, "Come ye yourselves apart into a desert place and rest a while." For even in the holiest work it is possible to lose oneself. One may resign oneself so completely to the appeals and needs of men as to have no leisure for communion with God. The enthusiastic minister, consumed with zeal and willing to please everybody, neglects his study and allows his mind to become starved; and

---

* "Aesthetically we may say that want of time is want of genius; for genius accomplishes in a very short time, and in right time, what others cannot accomplish in an unlimited time. But ethically expressed, it is this: want of time is want of moral energy and wisdom"—MARTENSEN, *General Ethics*, p. 426.

the result is inevitable. He becomes stale, flat and unprofitable; and those whose importunities have induced him to sacrifice his true self are the first to turn round and complain that he has disappointed them.

For the great mass of the world's workers the principal opportunity of rest is the Sabbath.* Jesus threw His shield over this institution, maintaining that it was made for man, and therefore none had the right to take it from him. In His day those who tried to take it away were the Pharisees, who converted it from a day of sacred delight into a day set with thorns to wound the conscience. This danger is not yet past, but in our day the attack comes more from the other side—from the Sadducees rather than the Pharisees. The movements against the Sabbath originate at present almost entirely with the idle rich, who naturally, after spending six days in a round of pleasure and dissipation, have no taste for a day of quietness, when they might have to look within and face themselves. If they obeyed the first part of the fourth commandment, "Six days shalt thou labor," they would have more comprehension of the second. They generally profess, indeed, to be

---

* "The importance to a statesman of refusing to be hurried was recognized by Talleyrand. He had drawn up a confession of faith, which was to be sent to the Pope on the day of his death. On the day before he died he was supposed to be at the point of death, and he was asked whether the paper should be sent off. His reply was addressed to the Duchesse de Dino, who repeated it to the first Lord Ashburton, from whom I heard it: '*Attendez jusqu' à d demain. Toute ma vie je me suis fait une régle de ne jamais me presser, et jai toujours été à temps.*'

"With a view to promote thorough calmness, orderliness—and with higher views also, though these have respect to the man rather than exclusviely to the statesman—it were to be wished that he should set apart from business, not only a sabbatical day in each week, but, if it be possible, a sabbatical hour in each day. I do not here refer to his devotional exercises exclusviely, but to the advantage he may derive from quitting the current of busy thoughts, and cutting out for himself in each day a sort of cell for reading or meditation—a space resembling one of those Lights or incurvations in the course of a rapid stream (called by the Spaniards resting places), where the waters seem to tarry and repose themselves for a while. This, if it were only by exercising the statesman's powers of self-government—of intention and remission in business, of putting the mind on and taking it off— would be a practice well paid; for it is to these powers that he must owe his exemption from the dangers to mind, body, and business of continued nervous

acting in the interest of the poor, but they take the name of the poor in vain, for the poor know better. They know that, wherever the sacredness of the Sabbath is overridden, the poor man has seven days to toil instead of six. Wherever the continental Sunday prevails, the noise of mill and foundry is heard on Sabbath as well as Saturday; and, should the working classes of this country ever yield to a movement for secularizing the Lord's Day, they will find it true that, while they that honor God are honored, those who despise Him shall be lightly esteemed.

It is, however, a problem always requiring fresh consideration, as the conditions of life change, how to observe the Sabbath. The day of rest is not rightly spent unless it is a delight to man as well as holiness to the Lord. But surely the best security for reaping all the fruits it was intended to yield is to spend it in the spirit and the company of Him after whom it is called the Lord's Day.

---

excitement. But to a statesman of a high order of intellect such intermissions of labor will yield a further profit; they will tend to preserve in him some remains of such philosophic or meditative faculties as may be crumbling under the shocks and pressures of public life. One who shall have been deeply imbued in his early years with the love of meditative studies, will find that in any such hour of tranquility which he shall allow himself, the recollection of them will spring up in his mind with a light and spiritual emanation, in like manner (to resume the similitude) as a bubble of air springs from the bottom of the stayed waters" — SIR HENRY TAYLOR, *The Statesman*, pp. 275, 276.

Matthew 2:13–18; 4:1; 8:16, 17, 20; 9:3; 11:19; 12:24; 13:54–58; 16:21; 17:22, 23; 20:17–19; 26; 27.

Mark 3:21, 22; 8:17–21; 9:19; 14:50.

Luke 4:28, 29; 6:7; 11:53, 54; 16:14.

John 6:66; 7:7, 12, 19, 20, 32, 52; 9:16, 22, 29; 10:20; 12:10, 11, 27; 15:18; 17:14; 18:22.

10
Christ as a Sufferer

I.

WORK is but one half of life; suffering is the other. There is a hemisphere of the world in the sunshine of work, but there is another in the shadow of suffering.

Not, indeed, that in any life these states alternate with anything like the same regularity with which the earth rolls out of darkness into light, and back again from light into darkness. Nothing is more mysterious than the proportions in which the two elements are distributed in different lots. Some enjoy the exhilaration of successful exertion nearly all their days, and know little or nothing of illness, bereavement or defeat. Others appear to be marked out by suffering for its own. All through life they are "acquainted with grief"; they are scarcely ever out of mourning, because ever and anon death is knocking at their door to claim their dearest; their own health is precarious; and, whatever dreams of high and sustained achievement may visit them, they know, as soon as the excitement subsides, that they have not physical strength to carry out their vision.

If you are a child of fortune, scarcely ever knowing a day's ill health and delighting in your work, whose results you see day by day waxing greater and more imposing behind you, go and stand by the bedside of an invalid laid down with incurable disease. There you may recognize a mind more capable than your own, a heart as fit as yours for love and enjoyment, but an invisible chain is wound round the limbs and holds them fast; and, though the martyrdom may last for ten or twenty years, that figure will never rise with its own strength from where it lies. What does your philosophy make of such a sight? Yet it is only an extreme instance of what is occurring in a thousand forms. The children of sorrow are numerous, and no man knows how soon his own life of work may be changed into a life of suffering. Any moment a bolt may break from the blue and alter everything. A cloud no bigger than a man's hand may wax and spread till it drapes the sky in blackness from horizon to horizon. And, even if no such awful calamity come, time brings to all their own share of suffering.

> There is no flock, however watched and tended,
> But one dead lamb is there;
> There is no household, howsoe'er defended,
> But has one vacant chair.

Suffering, then, is not an element of life that can be ignored. If we need one to show us how to work, not less do we need one to teach us how to suffer. And here, again, the Son of man does not fail us. While He is the great Captain of work, calling out the young and the energetic to dare and to achieve, He is also the sufferer's Friend, round whom are gathered the weak, the disappointed and the agonized. When on the cross He cried, "It is finished," He was referring not only to the work of His life successfully accomplished, but also to the cup of suffering drunk out to the last drop.

II

1. Jesus suffered from what may be called the ordinary privations of humanity. He was born in a stable and laid in a manger, thus at the very outset of His career stepping into the dark hemisphere of suffering. We know little of the social condition in which He was brought up: we cannot tell whether or not in Mary's home He dwelt much in the shadow of want and misfortune. But at a later state, we know from Himself, "foxes had holes and the birds of the air had nests, but the Son of man had not where to lay His head." It is not often that one of the children of men is reduced so low as thus to have to envy the beast its lair and the bird its nest. As a rule the end of human life, when the habitation in which the soul has tabernacled is broken up, is attended with more or less of suffering, but the physical suffering which He endured at the last was extreme. We need only recall the

bloody sweat of Gethsemane; the scourging, when His body, bent over a short post, was beaten with all the force of cruel soldiers; the thrusting of the crown of thorns on His head; the complicated tortures of crucifixion. We may not be able to assert that none ever suffered so much physical agony as He, but this is at least probable; for the exquisiteness of His physical organism in all likelihood made Him much more sensitive than others to pain.

2. He suffered keenly from the pain of anticipating coming evil. When great sorrow or pain comes on suddenly, there is sometimes a kind of bewilderment in it which acts as an anodyne, and it may be over before the sufferer thoroughly realizes it. But to know that one is in the grasp of a disease which in, say, six months will develop into intolerable agony before carrying one away, fills the mind with a horror of anticipation which is worse than even the reality when it comes. Jesus foreknew His sufferings and foretold them to His disciples; and these communications grew more and more vivid and minute month by month, as if they were taking ever stronger hold of His imagination. This horror of anticipation culminated in Gethsemane; for it was the dread of what was coming which there produced in His mind such a tumult of amazement and agony that the sweat fell like great blood drops from His face.

3. He suffered from the sense of being the cause of suffering to others. To persons of an unselfish disposition the keenest pang inflicted by their own weakness or misfortunes may sometimes be to see those whom they would like to make happy rendered miserable though connection with themselves. To the child Jesus how gruesome must have been the story of the babes of Bethlehem, whom the sword of Herod smote when it was seeking for Him! Of, if His mother spared Him this recital, He must at least have learned how she and Joseph had to flee with Him to Egypt to escape the jealousy of Herod. As His life drew near its close, this sense that connection with Himself might be fatal to His friends forced itself more and more upon His notice. When He was arrested, He tried to protect the Twelve from His own fate, pleading with His captors, "Let these go their way." But He foresaw too clearly that the world which hated Him would hate them also, and, as He said, that the time would come when whosoever killed them would

think that he was doing God service. He had to see the sword piercing the heart of His mother when she gazed up at Him dying a death more shameful in that age than death on the gallows is in ours.

4. The element of shame was all through a large ingredient in His cup of suffering. To a sensitive mind there is nothing more intolerable; it is far harder to bear than bodily pain. But it assailed Jesus in nearly every form, pursuing Him all through His life. He was railed at for the humbleness of His birth. The high-born priests and the educated rabbis sneered at the carpenter's son who had never learned, and the wealthy Pharisees derided Him. He was again and again called a madman. Evidently this was what Pilate took Him for; and, when He appeared before Herod, the gay monarch and his men of war "set Him at nought." The Roman soldier adopted an attitude of savage banter towards Him all through His trial and crucifixion, treating Him as boys torment one who is weak in the mind. They spat in His face; they blindfolded Him, and then, smiting Him, asked, "Prophesy who struck thee!" They made Him a mock king, with the cast-off coat of a soldier for a mantle, a reed for a scepter, and the thorns for a crown. Under such indignities had His godlike mind to burn. He heard Barabbas preferred to Himself by the voice of His fellow countrymen, and He was crucified between thieves, as if He were the worst of the worst. A hail of mockery kept falling on Him in His dying hours. The passersby made faces of derision at Him, adding with their lips the vilest insults; and even the thieves who were crucified with Him cast contempt in His teeth. Thus had He was conscious of irresistible strength to submit to be treated as the weakest of weaklings, and He who was the Wisdom of the Highest to submit to be used as if He were less than a man.

5. But to Jesus it was more painful still, being the Holy One of God, to be regarded and treated as the chief of sinners. To one who loves God and goodness there can be nothing so odious as to be suspected of hypocrisy and to know that he is believed to be perpetrating crimes at the opposite extreme from his public profession. Yet this was what Jesus was accused of. He was believed to be in collusion with the powers of evil and to cast out devils by Beelzebub, the prince of the devils. He to whom the name of God was as ointment poured forth was balled a blasphemer and a Sabbath breaker. His very best acts were mis-

construed; and for going to seek the lost where alone they could be found He had to submit to be called a glutton and a winebibber, a friend of publicans and sinners. In claiming to be the Messiah He was thought by the majority of all classes to be an unscrupulous pretender; the authorities, both ecclesiastical and secular, decided so in solemn court. Even His own disciples at last forsook Him; one of them betrayed Him; and the foremost of them all cursed and swore that he did not know Him. Possibly there was not a single human being, when He died, who believed that He was what He claimed to be.

6. If to the holy soul of Jesus it was painful to be believed to be guilty of sins which He had not committed, it must have been still more painful to feel that He was being thrust into sin itself. This attempt was often made.* Satan tried it in the wilderness, and, although only this one temptation of his is detailed, he no doubt often returned to the attack. Wicked men tried it: they resorted to every device to cause Him to lose His temper and speak unadvisedly with His lips: "They began to urge Him vehemently, and to provoke Him to speak of many things, laying wait for Him and seeking to catch something out of His mouth." Even friends, who did not understand the plan of His life, endeavored to divert Him from the course prescribed to Him by the will of God—so much so that He had once to

---

* "Common usage, I cannot but think, has fallen into a serious error in speaking of *the* temptation in the wilderness. Men speak, if they do not think, as if this temptation stood alone in the life of Christ. Nothing can be a greater mistake. Our Lord's whole life was one continued temptation. We have but to read the memoirs, which the Holy Ghost has caused to be written for our learning, in order to recognize in almost every page how the Lord Jesus Christ was exposed to ceaseless temptations. He was subjected to trials of temper, trials of character, trials of principle; He was harassed by temptations caused by nervous irritability, or want of strength, or physical weakness, or bodily weariness; unfair opposition was constantly urging Him to give way to undue anger and unrestrained passion; or rejection and desertion would, had it been possible, have betrayed Him into moodiness or cynical despair. The machinations of His foes, the fickleness of the mob, even the foolishness of His disciples, were scarcely ever wanting to try His spirit, and would often goad Him beyond endurance. All the continually recurring trials, which are ever betraying man into faults he has bitterly to deplore, and into sins of which he has to repent in sorrow, were present in the life of the Lord Jesus Christ"—BERNARD, *The Mental Characteristics of the Lord Jesus Christ.*

turn on one of them, as if he were temptation personified, with "Get thee behind Me, Satan." Nothing could prove more clearly than such a saying, so unlike Him who uttered it, how keenly He felt the point of temptation, and what horror awoke in Him at the danger of transgressing by a hairsbreadth the will of God.

7. While the proximity of sin awoke such loathing in His holy soul, and the touch of it was to Him like the touch of fire on delicate flesh, He was brought into the closest contact with it, and hence arose His deepest suffering. It pressed its loathsome presence on Him from a hundred quarters. He who could not bear to look on it saw it in its worst forms close to His very eyes. His own presence in the world brought it out; for goodness stirs up the evil lying at the bottom of wicked hearts. The sacredness of the Person with whom they had to do intensified the virulence of Pharisees and Sadducees, and the crimes of Pilate and Judas. What a sea of all the evil passions in human nature He was gazing over when, as He hung on the cross, His eye fell on the upturned faces of the multitude!

It was as if all the sin of the race were rushing upon Him, and Jesus felt as if it were all His own. In a large family of evildoers, where the father and mother are drunkards, the sons of jailbirds and the daughters steeped in shame, there may be one, a daughter, pure, sensible, sensitive, living in the home of sin like a lily among thorns. And she makes all the sin of the family her own. The others do not mind it; the shame of their sin is nothing to them; it is the talk of the town, but they do not care. Only in her heart their crimes and disgrace meet like a sheaf of spears, piercing and mangling. The one innocent member of the family bears the guilt of all the rest. Even their cruelty to herself she hides, as if all the shame of it were her own. Such a position did Christ hold in the human family. He entered it voluntarily, becoming bone of our bone and flesh of our flesh; He identified Himself with it; He was the sensitive center of the whole. He gathered into His heart the shame and guilt of all the sin He saw. The perpetrators did not feel it, but He felt it. It crushed Him; it broke His heart; and He died under the weight of the sin of others, which He had made His own.

Thus we try to bring home to our thoughts the mystery of Gethsemane and the awful cry of Golgotha, "My God, My God, why hast

Thou forsaken Me?" But it is still a mystery. Who can draw near to that figure prostrate beneath the olive trees in the garden, or listen to that voice sounding from the cross, without feeling that there is a sorrow there whose depths we cannot fathom? We draw as near as we may, but something calls to us, "Hitherto shalt thou come, but no further." Only we know that it was sin which was crushing Him. "He was made sin for us who knew no sin, that we might be made the righteousness of God in Him.*

III

The Results of the sufferings of Christ are the principal theme of the Gospel, but only a few words on the subject can be said here.

1. The Epistle to the Hebrews says that "the Author of our salvation was made perfect through suffering"; and, again, that "He learned obedience through the things which He suffered."

These are mysterious statements. Was He imperfect that He needed to be made perfect, or disobedient that He required to learn obedience? They cannot surely mean that the smallest iota was ever wanting to complete His character in either sense. No, but simply because He was a man, with a human history and a human development, He had to ascend a stair, so to speak, of obedience and perfection, and, although every step was surmounted at its own precise time, and He emerged upon it perfect, yet every new step required a new effort and, when surmounted, brought Him to a higher stage of perfection and into a wider circle of obedience.† We see the progress of this effort

---

* George Herbert's *Sacrifice*, with its piercing refrain, "Was ever grief like Mine?" is too long to quote. It gives a detailed and most moving enumeration of the sources of the Savior's sufferings.

† "His divine nature was not unto Him in the place of a soul, nor did immediately operate the things which He performed, as some of old vainly imagined; but, being a perfect man, His rational soul was in Him the immediate principle of all His moral operations, even as ours are in us. Now, in the improvement and exercise of these faculties and powers of His soul, He had and made a progress after the manner of other men; for He was made like unto us 'in all things,' yet without sin. In their increase, enlargement, and exercise there was required a progression in grace also; and this He had continually by the Holy Ghost (Luke 2:40)"—OWEN, *On the Holy Spirit*.

with great clearness in Gethsemane, where in the first access of suffering He says, "Father, if it be possible, let this cup pass from Me," but at the last is able to say in deep tranquillity, "O My Father, if this cup may not pass away from Me except I drink it, Thy will be done."

This was the perfection He attained through suffering. It was complete comprehension of the will of God and absolute harmony with it. This is our perfection too; and suffering is the great means of bringing it about. Many of us would never have thought much of God's will unless we had first felt it as a violent contradiction of our own. We wondered at it, and rebelled against it, but, when we learned, after Jesus, to say, "Not my will, but Thine, be done," we found that this is the secret of life, and the peace which passeth all understanding came into our souls. Or at least we have seen the process in others. I daresay to some of us the most priceless of all memories is that of one of the sons or daughters of affliction made beautiful by submissions to the will of God. There had perhaps been a struggle once, but it was over; and God's will was accepted, not only with submission, but with a holy joy which glorified the whole being. And, as we have watched the pure and patient face on the pillow, we have felt that here was one who by surrender had won the victory, and we have confessed that our own life, with all its storm and stress of activity, might be far less valuable to either God or man than this one lying bound and motionless:

They also serve who only stand and wait.

2. St. Paul, in one of the most confidential passages of his writings, tells of a lesson which he learned from suffering. "Blessed be God," he says, "the Father of mercies and God of all comfort, who comforteth us in all our tribulation, that we may be able to comfort them which are in any trouble by the comfort wherewith we ourselves are comforted of God" (2 Cor. 1:3, 4). He was glad that he had suffered, because he had learned thereby how to deal with sufferers. How like his big heart was the sentiment! And it is profoundly true. Suffering gives the power to comfort. Indeed, there is no other way of acquiring the art. To one in deep trouble there is all the difference in the world between the words of the heart-whole, who have never themselves been

in the fire, and the tender grasp and sympathetic tones of those who have personally suffered. Those, therefore, who are in the furnace of bereavement or pain may take to themselves the inspiring suggestion. Perhaps this is my apprenticeship to the sacred office of the comforter. Jesus thus acquired the art; and the tried and tempted of every generation come to Him with a confidence which is born of the knowledge of how He personally explored all the recesses of this kind of experience. "We have not a high priest which cannot be touched with the feeling of our infirmities, but was in all points tempted like as we are, yet without sin."

3. The results of the sufferings of Christ enter still more deeply into His work as the Savior. He foresaw them Himself and spoke often about them. "Except a corn of wheat," He said, "fall into the ground and die, it abideth alone, but, if it die, it bringeth forth much fruit"; "I, if I be lifted up from the earth, will draw all men unto Me"; "As Moses lifted up the serpent in the wilderness, even so must the Son of man be lifted up, that whosoever believeth on Him should not perish, but have eternal life."

When He died, His cause seemed to be lost. Not a single adherent was left clinging to it. But, when this eclipse was over and He came forth from the grave, His adherent awoke to discover that they possessed in Him a hundred times more than they had before been aware of; and the new glory in which He shone was that of the suffering Savior.

In every age His sufferings attract to Him the hearts of men; for they prove the boundless extent of His love, His absolute unselfishness, and His loyalty to truth and principle even unto death. Thus they have power with men.

But they have also power with God. "He is the propitiation for our sins; and not for ours only, but also for the sins of the whole world." Because He died we need not die. God has put into His hands the forgiveness of sins to be bestowed as a free gift on all who receive Him. Because He humbled Himself, God hath highly exalted Him. He is seated now at the right hand of power, a Prince and a Savior, and He carries at His girdle the keys of hell and of death.

Matthew 4:23, 24; 8:16, 17; 9:35, 36; 10:1, 8; 11:4, 5; 14:13, 14, 36; 15:30–32; 19:21; 21:14; 25:34–40; 26:8–11.

Mark 6:54–56; 10:21.

Luke 10:12–17.

John 13:29.

11

Christ as a Philanthropist

I.

PHILANTHROPIST may be thought too light a name to apply to Christ. And it must be confessed that it has a secular sound.

Some words are unfortunate: in common usage they are degraded, and their original meaning is lost. The word "charity" is a well-known instance. Originally meaning "love," it had at one time a good chance of being the technical term for the very highest kind of love—that passion which is kindled by union with Christ. This is its meaning in the thirteenth of First Corinthians, and the authority of so great a chapter might have been expected to determine forever the usage of Christendom. But somehow the word missed this honor and suffered degradation; and now "charity" is another name for "alms." In like manner, "philanthropy" has been brought down by usage to denote work done on behalf of men's bodies and temporal condition, as distinguished from work done for their spiritual good. But originally it was not so restricted, but meant simply to love men.

In this wide sense, it is ascribed in Scripture to God Himself. Thus, in a well-known passage in the Epistle to Titus, the literal rendering is, "But after that the kindness and philanthropy* of God our Savior appeared, not by works of righteousness which we have done, but according to His mercy He saved us, by the washing of regeneration and renewing of the Holy Ghost, which He shed on us abundantly through Jesus Christ our Savior." Here, it will be perceived, philanthropy denotes, not God's kindness to the bodies of men, but His

---

* A.V., "love of God our Savior towards men."

grace to their souls; for it displayed itself in bestowing the washing of regeneration and the renewing of the Holy Ghost.

It was in the same way that the philanthropy of Christ also primarily manifested itself, His work and sufferings being gone through with a view in the first place to the salvation of men's souls, while the relief of their bodily wants and ailments came in only in the second place. Nor is it easy to understand why work done for the soul's sake should not be called philanthropy as much as work for the body's. From the Christian standpoint at least it is a far greater kindness; and none can deny that it often involves far-reaching temporal advantages. In both foreign and home missions the success of the Gospel, when it saves men's souls, generally includes, as a secondary but inevitable accompaniment, the sweeping away of masses of cruelty, poverty and ignorance.

If, indeed, the improvement of men's temporal condition be dignified with the name of philanthropy, and sharply dissociated from spiritual aims, the name of Philanthropist must be denied to Jesus. He unfolded the utmost consideration for the physical necessities of men, but always in subordination to the higher wants of the soul. His love extended to the whole man—body and soul together. His love to God and His love to man were not two passions, but one. He loved man because He saw God in him—God's handiwork, God's image, the object of God's love.

This must ever be the pulse of a powerful philanthropy—to see God in man; or, as Christians more naturally phrase it, to see Christ in man. "Inasmuch as ye did it unto the least of these ye did it unto Me," are Christ's own words. When I touch the body of a man, I am touching what was made to be a temple of the Holy Ghost. In the humblest—ay, in the most sinful—human being we see one whom God loves, whom the Savior died for, and who may be a heir of the glory of Christ. These are the deep wells of conviction out of which a strong philanthropy is nourished.

II

It cannot be said that an active philanthropy has always been a characteristic of those professing godliness. Jesus Himself gave a significant hint of this in the Parable of the Good Samaritan. The priest and the Levite passed the poor maltreated wayfarer by, whereas the milk of human kindness was found in the common, unordained man. History supplies too many instances to confirm the parable. Often has the untrained heart of humanity noted and branded a wrong, and the uncovenanted hand sprung forth to the relief of misery, when those expressly called by their offices to the service have remained silent and supine. It would even seem sometimes as if intense sympathy with God destroyed sympathy with man. But one of the greatest services of Jesus to the world was to harmonize religion and morality. He would not allow neglect of man to be covered by zeal for God, but ever taught that he only loves God who loves his brother also.

At present we see these things, which He joined, put asunder from the other side. One of the novelties of our own age is an atheistic philanthropy. There are those who do not believe in God or the God-man, or in the spiritual and eternal world, but yet make a life of sacrifice for others the sum of morality. They confess that it was Jesus who brought their ideal into the world, and that it was established in the convictions of mankind by His authority, but now, they maintain, it is able to dispense with His support, and they call on us to love man, not for Christ's sake, but for his own. They profess to see in man himself, apart from God, enough to inspire hourly and lifelong effort on his behalf; and in the very brevity of his existence, which comes completely to an end at death, they find a pathetic motive for instant activity, because he must be helped now or never.

Insofar as any may be induced by such motives to embrace the life of self-denial and really grapple with the problems of poverty and crime, Christians need not hesitate to wish them Godspeed. This is a wide world, affording room for experiments; and it is a world of such fearful misery that there is little need to forbid anyone who from any motive may feel inclined to lend it a helping hand. We may even recognize some to be for Christ who believe themselves to be against Him. But, where the opposition is radical and final, we are hardly justified either by reason or the facts of the case in expecting very much from such a movement.

No doubt there is in the natural heart a love of man for man, which, if blown up by a favorable wind, may now and then do wonders; and the kindness of those who make no profession of religion sometimes puts Christians to shame. But, on the other hand, the force which the philanthropic spirit has to overcome is one of the mightiest in nature. It is the force of selfishness—that universally diffused instinct which makes the individual seek his own interest and happiness whatever comes of others, which makes the strong domineer over the weak and the many tyrannize over the few. This force lodges in every human breast; it pervades communities as well as individuals; it is embodied in customs and laws; it evolves new forms of wrong in every age; and many would say that it rules the world. This is the force which philanthropy has to overcome. It is not easily dislodged. It will not be conquered by fine words. There is needed, to overcome it, a change which only God can work by communicating to us His own nature, which is love.

> 'Is there a reason in nature for these hard hearts?' O Lear,
> That a reason out of nature must turn them soft seems clear.

In the teaching of Christ man is so dignified by his connection with God and by his immortal destiny, that everyone who really believes this creed must feel himself condemned if he treats his brother ill. But strip man, as Agnosticism does, of all the greatness and mystery with which Christianity invests him—cease to believe that he comes from God, that he is akin to beings greater than himself who care for him, and that his soul is of infinite worth because it has before it an unending development—and how long will it be possible to cherish for him the reverence which wins him consideration and help? The brevity of man's existence gives him, according to the present teaching of Agnosticism, a pathetic claim to instant help, but who knows whether in a society given over to unbelief the argument might not tell the other way, the selfish heart reasoning that sufferings which must end so soon do not matter?

It was in the generation preceding the French Revolution that atheistic philanthropy took its rise. The prophets of the time were predicting an age of peace and brotherhood, when selfish passion should disappear and cruelty and wrong no more vex the world. But, when their teaching had done its work, its fruit appeared in the Revolution itself, whose unspeakable inhumanities afforded our race such glances into the dark depths of its own nature as can never be forgotten. It is painful to recall that Rousseau himself, the most eloquent and, in some respects, the noblest apostle of the new faith, while preaching universal brotherhood, sent his own children one by one, as they were born, to the Foundling Hospital, to save himself the trouble and expense of their support. The Revolution did much destructive work for which the hour had come, but it was a gigantic proof that the love necessary for the work of reconstruction must be sought in a superhuman source.*

We are living at present in a state of society in which there is an afterglow of Christian sentiment even in minds that have ceased to name the name of Christ, which develops beautiful manifestations, but

---

* "The practical paradox, that the age in which the claims of humanity were most strongly asserted is also the age in which human nature was reduced to its lowest terms — that the age of tolerance, philanthropy, and enlightenment was also the age of materialism, individualism, and skepticism — is explicable only if we remember that both equally spring out of the negative form taken by the first assertion of human freedom.

"As the individual thus fell back upon himself, throwing off all relations to that which seemed to be external, the specific religious and social ideas of earlier days lost power over him; and their place was taken by the abstract idea of God and the abstract idea of the equality and fraternity of men — ideas which seemed to be higher and nobler because they were more general, but which for that very reason were emptied of all definite meaning, as well as of all vital power to hold in check the lusts and greeds of man's lower nature. Thus the ambitious but vague proclamation of the religion of nature and the rights of man was closely associated with a theory which was reducing man to a mere animal individual, a mere subject of sensations and appetites, incapable either of religion or of morality. For an ethics which is more than a word, and a religion which is more than an aspiration, imply *definite* relations of men to each other and to God, and all such relations were now rejected as inconsistent with the freedom of the individual. The French Revolution was the practical demonstration that the mere general idea of religion is not a religion, and that the mere general idea of a social unity is not a state; but that such abstractions, inspiring as they may be as weapons of attack upon the old system, leave nothing behind to build up the new one, except the unchained passions of the natural man" — E. CAIRD, *Ilegel*, pp. 19, 20.

those who know human nature will demand very strictly where Agnosticism is to get the light and the glow which will keep back the onrushing force of dark and selfish passion, when Christianity is removed. There is a remnant of Christianity in many who think they have got quit of it, but it remains to be seen how long this will last when cut off from its source. A sheet of ice holding on to the edges of a pool may maintain its position even after the water on whose surface it has been formed has been drawn off, but it will not maintain it long, and it will not bear much weight. The facts with which philanthropy has to deal are excessively disagreeable to face, and the temptation as to spare oneself and enjoy the world are insistent. Not long ago, when the bitter cry of outcast London grew so piercing as to attract universal attention, the heart of the West End was stirred, and the sons and daughters of fashion left their frivolities to go "slumming," as it was called, in the East End. But already, I am told, this is nearly all over; and the work of relieving the wretched is left, for the most part, to the humble followers of Christ, who were at it before. If strict inquiry were made, I imagine it would be found that there are very few philanthropic institutions of any dimensions in our midst that would not go down if they were deprived of the support of those who give not only for the sake of man, but for the sake of the Savior who has redeemed them.

III

The actual forms in which the philanthropy of Christ manifested itself were mainly two.

One of these was the giving of alms to the poor. This was, it is evident, a constant habit of His—so much so, that when, on the night of the betrayal, He said to Judas, who had the bag, "That thou doest do quickly," the rest of the disciples thought that the message the betrayer had received was to visit and relieve with a gift of money someone in distress. How the bag was filled we do not know very well. Jesus may have put into it savings of His own which He had laid by, when working as a carpenter, in view of the life He had in prospect. The Twelve may have done the same; and the holy women who followed Him contributed to it. But there is no reason to think that it was ever very full, but the contrary. When Jesus gave alms, it was the poor giving to the poor; yet He kept up the practice to the very end.

There have been good men who have seen so much peril in this form of philanthropy that they have pronounced against it altogether, but the example of Jesus supports it. There can be no doubt, however, that it requires caution and consideration. To give to the professional beggar generally does more harm than good, and too facile yielding to his importunities is to be accounted a vice rather than a virtue.* But there are deserving poor. They are known to those whose work lies among them; and the wealthy might with advantage make these workers their almoners. But it is not difficult to find them out, if we are willing to go on our own feet into the abodes of poverty. To many, indeed, this is an unexplored world, though it is at their doors. But it is not difficult to discover. Once enter it with a loving heart, and progress is easy. You will find in it honest men, on whom illness or temporary want of work has fallen, and whom a gift may help honorably over the time of need. You will find the aged, who have fought the battle manfully, but now can fight no more; and surely it is a honor to have a few of these dependent on our bounty. Among the poorest there are princes of God, who at a future stage of existence may be in a position to patronize us.†

The other form of His philanthropy was healing. Because He healed by miracle we naturally think of it as easily done, but perhaps it was more an effort than we suppose. On one occasion, when a woman touched Him and was healed, without wishing Him to know, He did know, because, it is said, He perceived that virtue had

---

* Compare Dorner, *Christliche Sittenlehre*, p. 469: "There is something holy in poverty. The poor are the altar of the Church. But there is no holiness in beggary."
† "Those are ripe for charity who are withered by age or impotency—especially if maimed in following their calling; for such are industry's martyrs, at least her confessors. Add to these those that with diligence fight against poverty, though neither conquer till death make it a drawn battle. Expect not, but prevent, their craving of thee; for God forbid the heavens should never rain till the earth first opens her mouth, seeing some grounds will sooner burn than chap!

"The House of Correction is the fittest hospital for those cripples whose legs are lame through their own laziness"—Fuller, *The Holy and Profane State*.

gone out of Him. And there are other indications that these cures must have cost Him an expenditure of nervous sympathy and emotion which imparts a deep pathos to the saying of St. Matthew, "Himself took our infirmities and bare our sicknesses." But, in any case, the work of healing was a congenial one in which His loving nature rejoiced; and He as never more at home than in a crowd composed of persons suffering from every kind of disease and infirmity of body and mind, among whom He moved benignly, touching one here into health, speaking to another the word of power, and letting glances of kindness and good cheer fall on all. The joy radiated far and wide, when the father returned to his home to be no longer its burden but its breadwinner, the son to be no more a care but a pride, the mother to resume the place and the work from which illness had dislodged her. The best help to the poor and needy is that which enables them to help themselves; and this was the kind of help which Jesus gave by His miracles.

We of course do not possess miraculous powers, but in their place we have others, which may be put to the like uses and are capable of working wonders as far beyond what could be achieved in His day through natural causes as His miracles are beyond us.

We possess, for instance, the power of science. There is no form of philanthropy perhaps more Christ-like than that which puts at the disposal of the poor and the ignorant first rate medical skill. Our infirmaries and dispensaries are the continuation of Christ's healing activity. Medical missionaries carry to the heathen a commission singularly like that with which Jesus sent forth the apostles. The Church is beginning to employ trained nurses in mission work. And in every part of the country there are medical men who are daily rendering to the poorest the best efforts of their art, for which they receive little or no remuneration, but which they give with even greater inward delight than they feel in working for their best-paying patients, because they are serving Christ in His members.

There is also the power of politics. Of this the early Christians had no control; they had no influence whatever in the State. But this power is now in the hands of all. The work of a Wilberforce or a Shaftesbury shows what use can be made of it in putting an end to wrong and misery. It enables us to ascend the stream and cut great evils off at their sources. Christian men are only learning how to use it yet; some are even shy of touching it, as if it were unholy. But they will yet prize it as one of the most powerful instruments put by Providence into their hands for doing good. We shall not always be content with a philanthropy that picks up the victims as they fly broken from the wheel of oppression; we will stop the wheel itself.*

These are only specimens of the powers with which Christian philanthropy is arming itself; and the strange word of Christ is coming true, "Verily, verily, I say unto you, he that believeth on Me, the works that I do shall he do also; and greater works shall he do, because I go unto My Father."

IV

There is nothing more certain than that our Lord left this part of His work as an example to His followers. In the distribution of alms

---

* "The obligation of philanthropy is for all ages, but if we consider the particular modes of philanthropy which Christ prescribed to His followers, we shall find that they were suggested by the special conditions of that age. The same spirit of love which dictated them, working in this age upon the same problems, would find them utterly insufficient. No man who loves his kind can in these days rest content with waiting as a servant upon human misery, when it is in so many cases possible to anticipate and avert it. Prevention is better than cure, and it is now clear to all that a large part of human suffering is preventible by improved social arrangements. Charity will now, if it be genuine, fix upon this enterprise as greater, more widely and permanently beneficial, and therefore more Christian than the other. It will not, indeed, neglect the lower task of relieving and consoling those who, whether through the errors and unskillful arrangements of society or through causes not yet preventible, have actually fallen into calamity. But when it has done all which the New Testament enjoins, it will feel that its task is not half fulfilled. When the sick man has been visited and everything done which skill and assiduity can do to cure him, modern charity will go on to consider the causes of his malady, what noxious influence besetting his life, what contempt of the laws of health in his diet or habits, may have caused it, and then to inquire whether others incur the same dangers and may be warned in time. When the starving man has been relieved, modern charity inquires whether any fault in the social system deprived him of his share of nature's bounty, any unjust advantage taken by the strong over the weak, any rudeness or want of culture in himself wrecking his virtue and his habits of thrift"—*Ecce Homo.*

from the common bag He associated the Twelve with Himself, giving the bag in charge to one of them. To one who wished to join the company of those who followed Him, He said, "Go and sell all that thou hast and give to the poor, and thou shalt have treasure in heaven, and come and follow Me"; and in other cases He may have imposed the same condition of discipleship. He associated the Twelve with Himself in like manner in the work of healing. "Heal the sick," He said, as He sent them forth, "cleanse the lepers, raise the dead, cast out devils: freely ye have received, freely give."

But the most impressive evidence of all is His great description of the last judgment, where the King says to those on His right hand, "Come, ye blessed of My Father, inherit the kingdom prepared for you from the foundation of the world: for I was a hungered, and ye gave Me meat; I was thirsty, and ye gave Me drink; I was a stranger, and ye took Me in; naked, and ye clothed Me; I was sick, and ye visited Me; I was in prison, and ye came unto Me," but to those on His left hand, "Depart from Me, ye cursed, into everlasting fire, prepared for the devil and his angels: for I was a hungered, and ye gave Me no meat; I was thirsty, and ye gave Me no drink; I was a stranger, and ye took Me not in; naked, and ye clothed Me not; sick, and in prison, and ye visited Me not."

Are there any Christians who realize that this is the test by which at the final review their Christianity is to be tried? Do the habits of Christendom accord with our Lord's plainest teaching? There are, indeed, a few who follow Him along this path. And, though it is a path of self-denial, they find it one of flowers; for on the way to the homes of the destitute they see the marks of His footsteps, and, in handling the bodies of the bedridden and suffering, their fingers touch His hands and His side. Thus, while losing their life, they find it. But is this a practice of the average Christian? Do his feet know the way to the homes of the blind, the tortured and the friendless? There is a day coming when many of us shall wish that every penny we have given to the poor had been a pound; when those who have begged from us on behalf of the suffering and the ignorant, but of whose importunities we have often complained, will be accounted our best benefactors; and when it will be more valuable to us to remember one hour passed in the garret of the poor than a hundred spent at the tables of the rich. "Inasmuch as ye have done it unto one of the least of these My brethren, ye have done it unto Me."

Matthew 1:21; 4:18–22; 9:10–13.

Luke 4:43; 7:36–50; 15; 19:1–10, 41, 42; 22:39–43.

John 2:23; 3; 4; 7:31, 37; 9:35–38; 10:11; 12:21, 22.

12

Christ as a Winner of Souls

I.

I HAVE heard that one of the diamond fields of South Africa was discovered on this wise. A traveler one day entered the valley and drew near to a settler's door, at which a boy was amusing himself by throwing stones. One of the stones fell at the stranger's feet, who picked it up and was in the act of laughingly returning it, when something flashed from it which stopped his hand and made his heart beat fast. It was a diamond. The child was playing with it as a common stone; the peasant's foot had spurned it; the cart wheel had crushed it; till the man who knew saw it and recognized its value.

This story comes often to my mind when I am thinking of the soul. Was it not the same careless treatment the soul was receiving when Jesus arrived in the world and discovered it? A harlot's soul, sunk in the mud and filth of iniquity! Why a Pharisee would not stain his fingers to find it. A child's soul! The scribes used to discuss in their schools whether or not a child had a soul at all.

Even yet there is nothing else of less account in the eyes of the majority than the soul. It is flung about, it is ignored, it is crushed by the careless foot, just as the undiscovered diamond was. A new soul, fresh out of eternity, enters an earthly home, but in most cases the family sin on as if it were not there; they are visited by no compunctions lest it should be corrupted by their example. By-and-bye it goes out into the world and is brought into contact with the multifarious influences of social life, but here there is, if possible, still less sense of its value; there is no fear of misleading it, no reverence for its high origin or its

solemn destiny. If it remains undeveloped, or if it is lost and rushes unprepared upon its doom, the majority heed not; its fate is no business
of theirs, and they do not even remember that it exists.

Our common language betrays that to the majority the soul is as
undiscovered as the diamond was to the settler and his children.
When the *employees* are pouring out of a factory at the meal hour, we
say, What a number of hands! Hands! not souls; as if the body and the
power of work in it were the whole of the man. Even the Church
speaks of the population of the East End as the masses; as if they
only counted in the bulk, and were not separable into units, in each
of which there is that which touches heaven above and hell beneath.
As we watch the multitude pouring along a crowded street, what is it
we see? Only so many figures interesting or uninteresting for their
looks, their dress and the like; or embodied spirits, that have come from
God and are going to God?

If we have the power of seeing the latter, we have learned it from
Christ. He lifted the soul up out of the mud and from among the tram-
pling feet, and said, Behold the diamond! "What shall it profit a man
if he gain the whole world and lose his own soul?"

Mankind believed, indeed, in the souls of the great—the soul
that could distinguish itself by force or wisdom—the soul of Socrates,
the soul of Caesar.* But Jesus taught it to believe in the common
soul—the soul of a child, of a woman, nay, of a publican or a sinner.
This is His immortal discovery. In every child of Adam He perceived
the diamond. The rags of the beggar could not hide it from His eyes,
nor the black skin of the savage, nor even the crimes of the evildoer.
It was true the soul was lost sunk deep in ignorance and unrighteousness. But this only made it the more interesting; it only stimulated
His desire to rescue and cleanse it, and set it where it might shine. To
a physician who are interesting? Not that they are whole, but they who
are sick; and among all his patients the most absorbing case is that
which most needs his help. It haunts him day and night; it runs away

---

* "Contempt of men is a ground feature of heathenism, which goes side by side
with the deification of men, and we can trace this twofold extreme down to the heathenism of our own days"—MARTENSEN, *Christian Ethics*.

with nine-tenths of his thinking; he visits it thrice a day; and, if the disease is overcome, this case is the triumph of his art. So Jesus taught, explaining His own feelings and conduct.

Yet there is a mystery in this estimate of the soul. Is it really true that one soul—that of the thief lying today in prison or of harlequin who was grinning last night in the circus—is more precious than the gold of California or the diamonds of Golconda? To multitudes, if they would confess the truth, such an assertion has no meaning. Yet it was made by Him who, while living here below in time, lived also aloft in eternity and could look clearly along the track of the future, seeing all that the soul can become—both the splendid possibilities it may develop and the depths to which it may fall.

This unique estimate of the soul was the secret spring of his work as a soul winner; and it is this faith, kindling mind and heart, which makes the soul winner always. A man has no claim to this office under any of its forms if he does not believe in the soul more than in money, or physique, or success, or any earthly thing, and unless the saving of a single soul would be to him a greater prize than all Greek and Roman fame.*

---

* "There is one power which lies at the bottom of all success in preaching; its influence is essential everywhere; without its presence we cannot imagine a man as making a minister of the Gospel in the largest sense. Under its compulsion a man becomes a preacher, and every sermon he preaches is more or less shaped by its presence. That power is the value of the human soul felt by the preacher, furnishing the motive and inspiration of all his work. The other motives for the minister's work seem to me to stand around this great central motive as the staff officers stand about the general. They need him, they execute his will; but he is not dependent on them as they are on him. Any one of them might fall away, and he could fight the battle out without him. Pleasure of work; delight in the exercise of power; love of God's truth; the love to study; gratification in feeling our life touch other lives; the perception of order; love of regular movement; insight into the lives and ways of men; and, lastly, the pleasure of seeing right ideas replace wrong ideas—these are the noble members of the staff of the great general. But how the motive which they serve towers above them all!" From a noble lecture on the value of the soul, with which Dr. Phillips Brooks closes his *Yale Lectures on Preaching*. The *locus classicus*, however, on this subject is Baxter's *Reformed Pastor*, through which the thought of the danger and the preciousness of the soul sounds like the bell of eternity.

II

There is another motive perhaps even more essential. It is the sense of a divine call. The soul winner must be conscious that he is doing God's work, and that it is God's message he bears to men.

Enthusiasm for humanity is a noble passion and sheds a beautiful glow over the first efforts of an unselfish life. But it is hardly stern enough for the uses of the world. There come hours of despair when men seem hardly worth our devotion. They are so base and ungrateful, and our best efforts are able to change them so little, that the temptation is strong to throw up the thankless task. Those for whom we are sacrificing ourselves take all we can do as a matter of course; they pass us by unnoticed, or turn and rend us, as if we were their enemies. Why should we continue to press our gifts on those who do not want them? Worse still is the sickening consciousness that we have but little to give: perhaps we have mistaken our vocation; it is a world out of joint, but were we born to put it right? This is where a sterner motive is needed than love of men; our retreating zeal requires to be rallied by the command of God. It is His work; these souls are His; He has committed them to our care; and at the judgment seat He will demand an account of them.

All prophets and apostles who have dealt with men for God have been driven on by this impulse, which has recovered them in hours of weakness and enabled them to face the opposition of the world. Most of them have experienced a crisis in which this call has come and clearly determined their life work. It came to Moses in the wilderness and drove him into public life in spite of strong resistance; and it bore him through the unparalleled trials of his subsequent career. It came to Isaiah in a vision which colored all his after history; and it revolutionized St. Paul's life in a hour. Jeremiah felt the divine message like a sword in his bones and like a fire which consumed him till he cast it forth among the people.*

This was one of the strongest motives of Christ's life also. It gave to it its irresistible momentum; it strengthened Him in the face of op-

---

* The difficult question of what constitutes a call to the ministry is discussed with great good sense in Blaikie's *For the Work of the Ministry*, and with racy wisdom in Spurgeon's *Lectures to My Students*.

position; it rescued Him from the dark hour of despair. He was never weary of asserting that the works He did were not His own, but God's; and that so were the words He spoke. His comfort was that every step He took was in fulfillment of the divine will.

But He had no hour at which His life was broken in twain by a moral crisis, and the task of living for others imposed on Him. This vocation was inwoven with the very texture of His being; the love of men was as native to His heart as it is to the nature of God; the salvation of men was the primary passion of His soul; and, though He claimed that His works and words were given Him by God, yet so identified were His own deepest wishes with the purposes of the divine love, that He could say, "I and My Father are one."

III

The name of Soulwinner which I have ventured to apply to the Savior is a scriptural one; for we read in Scripture that "he that winneth souls is wise." It is a word which indicates the delicacy and the difficulty of the work of seeking the lost. This work requires tact and skill in him who undertakes it. Souls have to be *won*; and this requires a winning way—a kind of winsomeness—in those who seek them.

Jesus Himself did not use this word, but He made use of one suggestive of the same truth. When calling His disciples to take part with Him in this work, He said to them, "Follow Me, and I will make you fishers of men." Every fisher with the rod knows how much knowledge of the weather and the water, how much judgment, keenness of eye and lightness of touch fishing requires. Probably it was of net fishing Christ was thinking, but this requires no less experience, alertness, tact and perseverance.

All these qualities are needed in winning souls. Jesus was the perfect model of this art; and the best guide to its acquisition is to watch His methods.

1. He made use of His miracles as stepping stones to reach the soul. All the acts of kindness and mercy described in the foregoing chapter were introductions to the development of the higher and more spiritual aims which were always in His mind. I do not say that this was their only purpose; for His miracles had many meanings. But it was one

of them: they often opened the door to spiritual dealing which could not have taken place without them. For example, in the ninth of St. John we read of a man whom He cured of blindness, without making Himself known to him. The man conceived a passion of gratitude and went about praising and championing his unknown friend; till Jesus, meeting him, made Himself known, when the man at once exclaimed, "Lord, I believe," and worshiped Him. This is a clear case in which the bodily cure was a prelude to the cure of the blindness of the soul. In numberless other instances it must have served the same end; and, if it be remembered that the miracles were often nearly as valuable to the relatives of those who were healed as to themselves, it will be understood how many minds must have been conciliated by this means to a favorable hearing of His divine message.

Philanthropy may serve us also as a stepping stone to higher work. Kindness opens hearts; and through the open door salvation may be introduced. There lurks danger, indeed, on either hand; for, on the one hand, charity may be robbed of all true human kindliness by the proselytizer's zeal, and, on the other, a hypocritical pretense of piety may be put on by the receiver of temporal advantages, as a payment for the accepted dole. But, while these dangers need to be avoided, the principle itself has the highest authority, and in earnest Christian work it is receiving at present many happy applications. Zeal for the soul often awakens consideration for the body also, and produces deeds which smell as sweetly to the Savior of men as did the ointment with which Mary anointed him.

2. Preaching was one of the principal means by which Christ sought the lost. As a separate chapter occurs below on Jesus as a Preacher, the subject need not here be dwelt upon. Only let it be noted how attractive His preaching was—how well-fitted to win men. He invested the truth with every charm of parable and illustration, though He well knew that such gay clothing is not truth's native garb. Truth is plain and simple; and those who know it love to have it so. But Jesus had to deal with those to whom in itself it had no attraction; and therefore He administered it to them as they were able to bear it, trusting that, if once it had won them and they had learned its worth, they would welcome it in any garb.

So powerful a means of winning men to God is preaching still, that it is no wonder that the desire to preach is often born at the same time as the desire of saving souls, but perhaps it is a wonder that of those who preach so few exert themselves, as Jesus did, to attract men by presenting their message in beautiful and winsome forms.*

3. Of course only a small proportion of those who burn to save the lost can become preachers, but with His preaching Jesus combined another method, which it is more open to all to imitate—the method of conversation. We have illustrations of His use of this method in His conversation with Nicodemus and His talk at the well with the woman of Samaria, which are models, intended to serve to all time, of this mode of winning souls. If the two cases be compared together, it will be seen with what perfect tact He adapted Himself to the circumstances of His interlocutors, and how naturally, while meeting them on their own ground, He led the conversation to the point He aimed at, always descending full upon the conscience.

This is a difficult art; for religious conversation must be natural—it must well up out of a heart full of religion—or it is worse than useless. Yet it is of priceless value, and no trouble is too great to be spent in acquiring it. I am not sure but we are more in need of those who can talk about religion than of those who can preach about it. A sermon is often applied by the hearers to one another, while each puts its message away from himself, but conversation goes straight to its mark. If it is supported by an impressive and consistent character, he who can wield it carries a blessing with him wherever he goes; in homes in which he has been a visitor his memory is cherished as that of one who has made religion real; and, though his name may be little heard of on earth, his track through the world is marked by a line of light to the eye of Heaven.

---

* "One is surprisingly in error if one thinks that that which sounds the way the people speak among themselves during their working hours is that which they most dearly like to hear. They put on their Sunday best when they go to church, so it does them good, if the sermon they hear maintains the formal trappings."—From the Preface of Tholuck's *Predigten*, where will be found some of the most remarkable pages on Preaching ever written.

Jesus did not, however, need always to be the aggressor when employing this instrument. In many cases those whom He conversed with about the concerns of the soul introduced the subject themselves. Persons who were anxious about religion sought Him out; for they instinctively felt that He knew the way after which they were groping. The passing of Jesus through the country was like the passing of a magnet over a floor where there are pieces of iron: it drew the souls which had affinity for the divine life to itself. And in all Christian communities there are some who, in greater or less degree, discharge the same function. They are known to possess the secret of life; those passing through the deepest experiences of the soul are confident that they will understand them; burdened consciences seek their sympathy. Surely this is the most precious privilege of the soul winner: he is never so effectively seeking the lost as when the lost seek him.

IV

As our subject in these chapters is the imitation of Christ, we naturally dwell on those aspects of His life and work in which it is possible for us to imitate Him. But ever and anon we need to remember at what a height He is above us. It is only with distant and faltering steps we can follow Him at all; and in many places He passes quite beyond our reach.

It is so at this point. In some respects, such as those just mentioned, we can imitate Him in winning souls, but He went, in this quest, where we cannot go: He came not only to seek but to save the lost. He compared Himself, as a soul winner, to the shepherd going after the lost sheep and bringing it home on his shoulders rejoicing; and thus far we may venture to compare our own soul winning to His, but He carried the comparison further: "The good shepherd giveth his life for the sheep." He followed sinners to their earthly haunts, and so may we, but He followed them further—down to the gates of hell, where He plucked the prey from the hands of the mighty. He entered a supernatural region, where He conquered for us, made atonement for us, opened for us the gates of immortality. Of these transactions we can but dimly know, for they were done in a region which we have not seen. Only we now that they were greater—more pathetic and solemn

—than all our thoughts. The outward sign and symbol of them which we can see is Golgotha—His body broken for us, His blood shed for us. And this is the highest symbol of soul winning love.

Here we rather bow down and adore than think of imitation. Yet here too there are lessons which all must learn who wish to be expert in this art. No one will have power with men who has not power with God for men; the victory may seem to be won while we persuade men, but it has to be previously won in the place of intercession. This place was to Jesus a place of agony and death; and there is no soul winning without pain and sacrifice. St. Paul said that he filled up that which was lacking in the sufferings of Christ for His body's sake, which is the Church; and all who will be partakers of Christ's joy in the redemption of the world must first be partakers in His sufferings.

V

If the art of the soul winner is difficult and accompanied with much pain, its reward is correspondingly great. I have known an eminent portrait painter, who, when the crisis of his picture came at which it was to be determined whether or not he had produced a likeness of the features only, or a picture of the soul and character of his subject, used to fall into perfect paroxysms of excitement, weeping, wringing his hands and groveling on the ground, but, when it was over and the true likeness stood embodied on the canvas, gave way to equally extravagant exultation. And it must be a strange sensation to see an image of beauty, out of nothing so to speak, gradually developing itself on the canvas and living there. But what is this compared with seeing a soul emerging from death into life—its wings freeing themselves from the hard, ugly chrysalis of its natural condition, to flutter forth into the sunshine of eternity?

Of the effect of this sight on Jesus we have an authentic glimpse in the wonderful parables of the fifteenth of St. Luke—the shepherd calling his friends together and saying, "Rejoice with me, for I have found my sheep which was lost," and the father of the prodigal crying, "Let us eat and drink and be merry." He has told us Himself what this rejoicing means: "Verily I say unto you, There is joy in the presence of the angels of God over one sinner that repenteth." And that joy in the faces of the angels is only a reflection of the joy of the Lord of angels, on whose face they are ever gazing.

In His earthly life we see very clearly on at least one occasion this holy excitement in His heart.* When He had won the wicked woman of Samaria to God and holiness, His disciples, arriving where He was with provisions which they brought from the town, prayed Him, saying, "Master, eat." But He could not eat; He was too delighted and absorbed; and He answered, "I have meat to eat that ye know not of." Then, looking towards the city, whither the woman had gone to bring more souls to Him to be won, He continued in the same enraptured strain, "Say not ye, There are yet four months, and then cometh harvest? Behold, I say unto you, Lift up your eyes, and look on the fields; for they are white already to harvest." It was the same deep passion in another phase, when He beheld the city which He had in vain attempted to win and in which so many souls were perishing, and wept over it.

In these sacred emotions all soul winners partake in their degree; and there are no higher emotions in this world. They are the signature and patent of a nobility derived directly from Heaven; for the humblest Christian worker, who is really pained with the sin of men and rejoices in their salvation, is feeling, in his degree, the very passion which bore the Savior of the world through His sufferings, and which has throbbed from eternity in the heart of God.

---

* I have heard the late Brownlow North say that, though on one side of His nature Jesus was the Man of Sorrows, on another He was the happiest of all the children of men.

Matthew 4:16, 23–25; 5 — 7; 9:4, 13, 35–38; 10:7, 19, 20, 27; 13; 16:14.

Mark 1:38, 39; 2:2; 4:33; 6:1–6.

Luke 4:16–32; 5:17; 7:16; 8:1–8; 11:27, 28.

John 3:34; 7:14–16, 26, 40, 45, 46; 8:1, 2.

13

Christ as a Preacher

I.

IF, in the course of a lifetime, we have been fortunate enough to hear once or twice an orator of the first rank, we talk of it all our days; or, if we can remember a preacher who first made religion real to us, his image is enshrined in our memory in a sacred niche. What, then, must it have been to listen to Him who spoke as never man spoke? What must it have been to hear the Sermon on the Mount or the Parable of the Prodigal Son issuing, for the first time, fresh from the lips that uttered them?

For thirty years Jesus had kept silence. During this period the waters of thought and conviction had been accumulating in His mind; and, when the outlet was opened, forth they rushed in copious volume. He began in Nazareth and Capernaum, the places of His abode, to preach in the synagogues on the Sabbaths. But He soon extended His activity to the neighboring villages and towns. Nor were the Sabbaths and the synagogues and the customary hours of worship sufficient for His zeal; by-and-bye He was preaching every day, and not only in the synagogues, but in streets and squares, and in the more picturesque temple of the hillside or the seashore.

The enthusiasm of those whom He addressed corresponded with His own. Almost as soon as He began to preach His fame spread over the whole of Syria, bringing hearers from every quarter; and from this time onwards we are constantly hearing that great multitudes followed Him, the crowd becoming sometimes so dense that they trode one upon another. Thy detained Him when, wearied out with His efforts, He wished to escape into solitude; and, if at length He got away for a little, they were waiting for Him when He came back.

All classes were to be found in His audiences. Not infrequently the preacher who can move the populace is neglected by the educated, while he who can satisfy the cultured few is caviar to the general. But at the feet of Jesus you might have seen Pharisees and doctors of the law sitting, who were come out of every town of Galilee and Judea and Jerusalem; while, on the other hand, the common people heard Him gladly; and even the class below the line of respectability—those who in general cared nothing for synagogues and sermons—were roused for once to frequent the public religious assemblies: "Then drew near unto Him all the publicans and sinners for to hear Him."

Wherein lay the secret of this intense and universal interest? The ancients represented the orator in works of art as drawing men after himself with golden chains issuing from his mouth. What were the chains of attraction by which Jesus drew all men unto Himself?

II

When the standard of religious life and of preaching is conspicuously low in a country or neighborhood, the appearance of a man of God who preaches the Word with power is made remarkable by contrast; the darkness of the background making the light more visible.

A darkness of this kind, which may be compared to that of midnight, was brooding over Galilee when Jesus opened His career as a preacher; and St. Matthew, who lived on the spot, describes the contrast by quoting these words of prophecy: "The people that sat in darkness saw great light; and to them who sat in the region and shadow of death light is sprung up." In the same way, the first criticism passed on the new Preacher by all who heard Him was a surprised expression of the difference they felt between Him and their accustomed teachers: "The people were astonished at His doctrine; for He taught them as one having authority, and not as the scribes."

The scribes were their accustomed teachers, who harangued them week by week in the synagogues. No doubt there must have been differences among them; they cannot all have been equally bad, but, taken as a whole, they were probably the most barren and unspiritual set of men who have ever held sway over the mind of a nation. In the collection of Jewish books called the Talmud, which has come down to us and is, indeed, at present in process of being translated into the English language, we have specimens of their teaching, and those who have studied them declare that they are the driest products of the human mind. To read them is like traveling through endless galleries of lumber, where the air is darkened and the lungs are well-nigh asphyxiated with the rising dust.

The people in their criticism of Jesus exactly hit the principal defect of their teachers. He, they said, taught with authority, and not as the scribes; that is, the scribes taught without authority. This is the leading characteristic of these Talmudic writings. No teacher speaks as if he had ever been in touch with God Himself or seen the spiritual world with his own eyes. Everyone quotes some earlier teacher, to whose authority he appeals; they are all leaning upon one another. This is a fatal kind of preaching, though it has often prevailed and sometimes loudly arrogated to itself the name of orthodoxy. Have you never heard God spoken of as if He had existed hundreds of years ago, in Bible times, but no longer moved and worked in the life and history of today? Have you never heard joy in God, the happiness of forgiveness, the fullness of the Spirit, and the other higher experiences of the spiritual life, spoken of as if they had, indeed, been experienced by the saints of the Bible, but were no longer to be looked for in these modern centuries? The Bible can be converted into a prison in which God is confined, or a museum in which the spiritual life is preserved as an antiquarian curiosity. But those who came to hear Jesus felt that He was in direct contact with the spiritual world and brought to them news of What He had Himself seen and felt. He was not a mere commentator, repeating some faint and far-derived echo of the message received from on high by men long dead. He spoke like one who had just come from the abode of the Highest, or rather who was still in it, seeing what He was describing. He was not a scribe, but a prophet, who could say, "Thus saith the Lord."

So the fame of Him traveled from Dan to Beersheba; men said to one another, with kindling looks, "A great prophet is risen up among us"; and the shepherd left his sheep in the wilderness, the husbandman his vineyard, and the fisher his nets by the shore, to go and hear the new

Preacher; for men know they need a message from the other world, and they instinctively recognize the authentic voice when they hear it.

III

Preaching sometimes acquires an extraordinary influence from the personality of the preacher. Those who have merely read the sermon are told by those who have heard it that they have no conception of what it was: "You should have seen the man." It is well known that the posthumously published discourses of some of the greatest pulpit orators have entirely disappointed the world, posterity asking in surprise where the influence can have lain. It lay in the man—in the peculiarity of his personality—in the majesty of his appearance, nor his passionate earnestness, or his moral force.

It cannot be said that the printed words of Jesus are disappointing: on the contrary, their weightiness and originality must have attracted attention however they had been spoken. But yet in this case, also, as can easily be perceived from the criticism of His hearers, the Preacher told as well as the sermon.

We do not, indeed, know how Jesus looked—whether His appearance was attractive, His voice pleasant, or the like; the traditions about such things which have come down to us not being trustworthy. But we do know in some respects the nature of the impressions which He made on His hearers.

Though for many generations the only preachers whom His countrymen had heard were dry-as-dust scribes, yet one of the proudest traditions of the Jewish people was the memory of great speakers for God whose voices had sounded throughout the land in days gone by, and whose characteristics were indelibly imprinted on the national memory; and, as soon as Jesus commenced to preach, it was recognized at once that the great order of the Prophets had revived in Him. They said He spoke as one of the prophets.

But they went further: They actually believed that one or other of the old prophets had risen from the dead and resumed his work in the person of Jesus. In indulging this fancy, they were divided between two of the ancient prophets, and the selection of these two clearly shows what characteristics they had specially remarked in Him. The two were

Jeremiah and Elijah: some said He was Jeremiah, others that He was Elijah.

Now these were both great prophets; perhaps the very greatest in the popular estimation; so that it was to their very greatest that they compared Him. But the two were of types so diametrically opposite to one another that it may seem impossible that their characteristics should have been united in one personality.

Jeremiah was the soft, pathetic prophet—the man of heart, who wished that his eyes were a fountain of tears to weep for the misfortunes of his people. It is not surprising that Christ's hearers discovered a resemblance to him; for it must have been evident at the first glance that Jesus was a man of heart. The very first sentences of His Sermon on the Mount were words of compassion for the poor, the mourners, the oppressed. The most insignificant among His hearers must have felt that He took an interest in him and would take any trouble to do him good. Although He addressed all classes, His boast was that He preached the Gospel to the poor; while the scribes flattered the wealthy and coveted cultivated audiences, the common man knew that Jesus considered his soul as precious as that of the wealthiest of His hearers. The sight of a multitude moved Him with a strange compassion. And, like Jeremiah, He was such an intense lover of His country and His countrymen, that even the publican or harlot was dear to Him because belonging to the seed of Abraham.

Elijah was in every respect a contrast to Jeremiah: he was a man of rock, who could rebuke kings and queens to their faces and stand alone against the world. It did not seem possible that one who exhibited the traits of Jeremiah should also exhibit those of Elijah. Yet the people recognized in Jesus an Elijah. And they were not mistaken. It is an entire misapprehension to suppose that Jesus was all softness and gentleness. There was a sternness in many of His utterances not surpassed even by Elijah's rebukes of Ahab, and the bold denunciation of wrong was one of the most imposing elements of His power. There has never been in this world a polemic so uncompromising and annihilating as His against the Pharisees.

The truth is, both characteristics, His softness and His sternness, had a common root. As in the poorest peasant He saw and revered a man, so in the wealthiest noble He saw no more than a man. As the rags of Lazarus could not conceal from Him the dignity of the soul, so the purple of Dives could not blind Him to its meanness. He knew what was in man—the height and the depths, the glory and the shame, the pathos and the horror; and men felt, as they faced Him, that here was One whose manhood towered above their own and yet, stooping down, embraced it and sympathized with it through and through.

IV

No preacher has perhaps ever made a profound impression on the general mind who has not studied the form in which to put what he has had to say; or perhaps the fact might be more correctly stated by saying, that the true messenger from God to the people instinctively clothes his message in attractive and arresting words. Beginners in preaching, I observe, are apt to neglect this: they think that, if only they have something good to say, it does not matter how they say it. As well might a housewife suppose that, if only she has something good to give her guest to eat, it does not matter how it is cooked.

The teaching of Jesus owed its attractiveness, and owes it still, in no small degree, to its exquisite form. The common people do not, I think, as a rule remember so well the drift of an argument or a long discourse as remarks here and there expressed in pithy, pointed, crystalline words. This is the form of most of the sayings of Jesus. They are simple, felicitous and easily remembered; yet every one of them is packed full of thought, and the longer you brood over it the more do you see in it. It is like a pool so clear and sunny that it seems quite shallow, till, thrusting in your stick to touch the pebbles so clearly visible at the bottom, you discover that its depth far exceeds what you are trying to measure it with.

But the discourse of Jesus had a still more popular quality: they were plentifully adorned with illustrations. This is the most attractive quality of human speech. The same God being the Author of both the world of mind and the world of matter, He has so fashioned them that the objects of nature, if presented in a certain way, become mirrors in which are reflected the truths of the spirit; and we are so constituted that we never relish truth so well as when it is presented in this way. Nature contains thousands of these mirrors for exhibiting spiritual truth which have never yet been used but await the hands of the masters of speech who are yet to be born.

Christ used this method of illustrating truth so constantly that the common objects of the country in which He resided are seen more perfectly in His words than in all the historians of the time. The Jewish life of Galilee in the days of Christ is thus lifted up out of the surrounding darkness into everlasting visibility, and, as on the screen of a magic lantern, we see, in scene after scene, the landscapes of the country, the domestic life of the people, and the larger life of the cities in all their details. In the house we see the cup and the platter, the lamp and the candlestick; we see the servants grinding the meal between the millstones and then hiding the leaven in it, till the whole is leavened; we see the mother of the family sewing a piece of cloth on an old garment and the father straining the wine into the skin bottles; we see, at the door, the hen gathering her chickens under her wings and, in the streets, the children playing at marriages and funerals. Out in the fields we see the lilies in their stately beauty rivaling Solomon's, the crows picking up the seed behind the sower, and the birds in their nests among the branches; the doves and the sparrows, dogs and swine, the fig tree and the bramble bush. Looking up, we see the cloud carried over the landscape by the south wind, the red sky of evening promising fair weather for the morrow, and the lightning flashing from one end of heaven to the other. We see the vineyard with its tower and winepress; the field adorned with the tender blade of spring or sprinkled with the reapers among the yellow grain of autumn; the sheep, too, yonder on their pastures, and the shepherd going before them or seeking the lost one far over hill and dale. Are there any figures of our own streets with which we are more familiar than the Pharisee and the Publican at prayer in the Temple; or the Priest and the Levite and the Good Samaritan on the road to Jericho; or the gorgeous Dives at his daily banquet and Lazarus lying at his gate with the dogs licking his sores? Nor were these pictures less striking to the audiences of Jesus, though they were familiar; for—

> We're made so that we love
> First, when we see them painted, things we've passed
> Perhaps a hundred times, nor cared to see.

It was because Jesus had exquisite love and consideration for His hearers that He thus sought out acceptable words to win their minds. But there was a reason in Himself besides. It is when the mind of a preacher is acting on the truth with intense energy and delight that it coruscates in such gleams of illustration. When the mental energy is only smoldering in a lukewarm way inside the subject, then you have the commonplace, prosaic statement; when the warmth increases and pervades the whole, you get the clear, strong, impressive statement, but, when the glow has thoroughly mastered the mass and flames all over it, then come the gorgeous images and parables which dwell forever in the minds of the hearers.

V

However important the form of preaching may be, the supremely momentous thing is the substance of it. The form is only the stamp of the coin, but the substance is the metal. What is that—is it gold or silver, or only copper? Is it genuine or counterfeit? This is the all-important question.

Never has the substance of preaching been more trivial than among the Jewish scribes. The Talmudical books show this. The topics they deal with are in their triviality beneath contempt. The religion of the scribes was a mere round of ceremonies, and their preaching was almost wholly occupied with these: the proper breadth of phylacteries, the proper length of fasts, the articles on which tithe ought to be paid, the hundred and one things by which one might be made ceremonially unclean—these and a thousand similar minutiae formed the themes of their tiresome harangues. There have been times in the history of the Church since then when the pulpit has sunk almost to as low a level. In our own country immediately before the Reformation the sermons of the monks were, if possible, even worse—more trivial and low in tone—than those of the scribes in the time of Christ. Similarly in Germany in the last century, when Rationalism was at its lowest, the pulpit had reached an almost incredible stage of degradation.* The truth is, there is a necessity in these things. When the minds of preachers grow cold, they move away insensibly from the central things and drift to those on the circumference; and at length they go over the circumference.

Of course the subjects which formed the substance of Christ's preaching cannot here be enumerated. It must suffice to say that His matter was always the most solemn and vital which can be presented to the human mind. He spoke of God in such a way that His hearers felt as if to their eyes God was now light and in Him was no darkness at all. As He uttered such parables as the Lost Sheep and the Prodigal Son, it seemed as if the gates of heaven were thrown open and they could see the very beatings of the heart of the divine mercy. He spoke of man so as to make every hearer feel that till that moment he had never been acquainted either with himself or with the human race. He made every man conscious that he carried in his own bosom that which was more precious than worlds; and that the passing hours of his apparently trivial life were charged with issues reaching high as heaven and deep as hell. When He spoke of eternity, He brought life and immortality, which men before then had only vaguely guessed at, fully to light, and described the world behind the veil with the graphic and familiar force of one to whom it was no unknown country.

Is it any wonder that the crowds followed Him, that they hung spellbound on His lips and could never get enough of His preaching? Intoxicated as men are with the secularities of this world, they know, deep down, that they belong to another, and, interesting as the knowledge of this world is, the questions about the other world will always be far more fascinating to the spirit of man. Whence am I? What am I? Whither am I going? Unless preaching can answer these questions, we may shut our churches. That voice which sounded on the Galilean mountainside and which spoke of these mysteries so familiarly, we, indeed, shall never hear, till we hear it from the great white throne. But the heart and the spirit that embodied themselves in these sounds never die; they live and burn today as they did then. Whenever a preacher strikes correctly a note of the eternal truth, it is

---

* "The days of coffee and cowpox sermons" is wittily named by Tholuck, referring, I fancy, to the subjects of some notorious sermons.

Christ that does it. Whenever a preacher makes you feel that there is a world of realities above and behind the one you see and touch; whenever he lays hold of your mind, touches your heart, awakens your aspiration, rouses your conscience — that is Christ tying to grasp you, to reach you with His love, to save you. "Now then we are ambassadors for Christ; as though God did beseech you by us, we pray you in Christ's stead, be ye reconciled to God."

Matthew 4:18, 19; 9:9, 14–17; 10; 12:1–3, 49; 13:10, 11, 16–36; 15:15, 16, 23, 24, 32, 36; 16:5–28; 17; 18:1–3, 21, 22; 19:13–30; 20:17–19, 20–28; 26:21, 22, 26–36, 56; 28:7, 10, 16–20.

Mark 3:1; 4:34; 6:30–32; 9:35–41; 16:7.

Luke 9:54–56; 10:1–17; 11:1; 24:36–51.

John 2:11, 22; 4:2; 13–17.

14

Christ as a Teacher

THE function of the teacher is a more limited one than that of the preacher. The preacher addresses the multitude; the teacher concentrates his attention on a select few. The audiences to whom Jesus preached numbered thousands; the men to whom He acted as teacher numbered only twelve. Yet perhaps in its results His work in the latter capacity was quite equal in value to His whole work as a preacher.

The teacher's office had many remarkable occupants before Christ. In the schools of Greek philosophy, Socrates, Plato, Aristotle and other famous masters stood in a relation to their disciples similar to that which Jesus sustained to His. Among the Jews also this relationship was not unknown. In the schools of the prophets, in the Old Testament, the "men of God" were the teachers of "the sons of the prophets." John the Baptist, besides preaching to the multitude, had disciples who followed him.

The standing phrase in Greek for the disciples of any master is "those about him": the disciples of Socrates, for example, are "those about Socrates." Similarly it is said in the Gospels that Jesus chose the Twelve "that they should be with Him." This circumstance alone must have limited the number of those who were His disciples in the strict sense; for few could give up their work and home in order to follow Him. His habits were itinerant; and this made the separation of those about Him from settled occupations more absolute. It seems, indeed, that some attached themselves to Him temporarily and intermittently; for we hear on one occasion of as many as a hundred and twenty disciples, and on another of seventy, but those whom He chose out to give up all and be with Him continually were only twelve.

There was, however, another reason for the strict limitation of their number. A teacher has to know his disciples individually and study them, as a mother has to study the temperament of each of her children separately in order to be to them a good mother. While the preacher, addressing a crowd, draws the bow at a venture, not knowing whom he may hit, and has carefully to avoid references to particular persons, the teacher addresses every question and remark straight to individuals; and therefore he must know the precise mental condition of everyone before him. This is why the names of the Twelve are so exactly given in evangelist after evangelist, and their relations to one another indicated. Perhaps they included as great a variety of disposition and experience as will ever be found among the same number of men, but they were not too numerous for separate treatment, and there is the completest evidence that their Master studied everyone of them till He knew him through and through, and carefully adapted His treatment to each particular case. His affectionate way with John exactly suited the temperament of that disciple; and equally adapted to the case was His patient and delicate handling of Thomas. But His treatment of Peter was the crown and glory of His activity in this character. How completely He knew Him! He managed the tumultuous and fluctuating elements of his character as a perfect rider does a high-mettled horse. And how successful He was! He transformed a nature unstable as water into the consistency of rock; and on this rock He built the Church of the New Testament. Similar results were achieved in the whole apostolic circle. With the exception of the traitor, every one of the Twelve became, by means of the Master's teaching, able to be a pillar in the Church and a power in the world.

Jesus combined the work of the preacher and that of the teacher. The former was most fascinating, and it could easily have absorbed His whole time and strength. The multitudes were clamorous to have Him, and their needs spoke urgently to His heart. Yet He saved most of His time for the training of twelve men. We love numbers too much. We measure ministerial success by them; and many servants of God expend on them their whole strength. It is true, indeed, that no preacher who has the heart of Jesus in his breast can join in the depreciation of the multitude which sounds so wise, but is so cheap. Yet the example of Jesus teaches us also a different lesson. It is a saying of one of the wise, that the difference between being a marsh and being a stream; and the quaint remark has a bearing on the present case. If a moderate quantity of force, such as may be in us, is distributed over too wide a surface, it may have no more effect than the inch deep water of a marsh, but, concentrated on a more limited task, it may be like a stream which sings along its narrow channel and drives the mill. Get a multitude and distribute your influence over it, and everyone may receive but little, but throw yourself on twelve men or six or even one, and the effects may be deep and everlasting. There are those quite unfit to address a multitude who might teach a small number; and it may turn out in the end that they have done as much as if they had been endowed with the more coveted gift.

II

In some respects Christ's methods of teaching the Twelve were similar to those which He pursued with the multitude. They heard all His addresses to the multitude, for they were always with Him; whereas the majority of his hearers can only have heard Him once or twice. Besides, they heard from Him in private many a discourse not dissimilar in its structure to His public sermons. In the same way, they witnessed all His miracles, because they accompanied Him wherever He went; whereas the majority saw only the miracles performed in one or two places. Besides, He wrought some of His very greatest miracles—such, for example, as the stilling of the tempest—in their presence and for their benefit alone. This constant repetition of great impressions was an incalculable advantage.

But that which was distinctive in His method of dealing with them was the permission He gave them to put questions, which He answered. Whenever there was anything in His public discourses which was obscure, they asked Him in private what it meant, and He told them. Or, if they had hesitation about the truth or wisdom of anything He stated, they were at liberty to propound their doubts, and He solved them. Thus, at the beginning of His ministry, we find them asking why He spoke in parables, and again and again afterwards they

requested Him to explain a parable which they had not fully understood. When they heard His severe teaching on divorce, they said to
Him, "If the case of the man be so with his wife, it is not good to marry,"
and drew from Him a fuller statement on the subject. In the same way,
when they heard Him say that it is easier for a camel to go through the
eye of a needle than for a rich man to enter into the kingdom of
God, they exclaimed, "Who then can be saved?" and thus led Him on
to a copious discourse on the subject of riches. In short, we are told that,
"when He was alone, He expounded all things to His disciples."

But He pursued this method further: He not only allowed them to
ask questions, but provoked them to do so. He deliberately wound His
statements in obscurity and paradox to excite the questioning propensity. He Himself gave this explanation of His habit of speaking parables.
The parable was a veil cast over the face of the truth for the very purpose of tempting the hearers to lift it and see the beauty which it half
concealed and half revealed. A teacher has done nothing unless He
awakens the mind to independent activity. As long as it is merely passive, receiving what is poured into it but doing nothing more, true education has not commenced. It is only when the mind itself begins to
work on a subject, feeling within itself difficulties to which the truth
supplies the answers, and wants to which it gives satisfaction, that
growth commences and progress is made. What Christ said set the
minds of His disciples in a ferment; it was intended to raise in them all
sorts of perplexities, and then they came to Him for their solution.

The method of Socrates, the wisest of heathen teachers, was similar. In his teaching also questioning played a prominent part. When
a disciple came to him, Socrates would ask a question on some important subject, such as righteousness, temperance or wisdom, about
which the disciple believed himself to be perfectly well-informed.
His answer would be replied to by another question, designed to
make him doubt whether it was correct or sufficient. Then Socrates
would go on asking question after question from twenty different
sides and angles of the subject, till the disciple was made to see that his
own opinions about it were, as yet, nothing but a confused bundle of
contradictions, and probably also that his mind itself was a mass of
undigested pulp.*

---

* Description by Dr. Chalmers of a foolish preacher; story still remembered in
Kirkcaldy.

Both methods had the same end—to excite the mind to independent activity. Yet there is a subtle and profound distinction between them. Socrates asked questions which his disciples tried to answer; Jesus provoked His disciples to ask questions which He answered. On the whole, what was aimed at in the school of philosophy was the mental gymnastic; the answers to the questions did not matter so much. Indeed, many philosophers have avowed that the chief end of their work is the mental investigation obtained in the pursuit of truth;[*] and the saying of one of them is well known, that, if the Deity were to offer him in one hand the pursuit of truth and in the other the truth itself, he would unhesitatingly choose the former. This may be a wise saying in the region of philosophy, but no wise man would make it in the region of religion. It was saving truth of which Jesus was a teacher. The pursuit of this also disciplines the mind, but we dare not be satisfied with the pursuit alone; we must have the answers to the great questions of the soul. Therefore, while Socrates questioned, Jesus answered; and to Him, after wandering in the obscurities of doubt and inquiry, men will always have at last to come for the solution of the problems of the spirit. "Lord, to whom shall we go? Thou hast the words of eternal life."

III

If we were to express the aim of Christ in the training of the Twelve by saying that it was to provide successors to Himself, we should be using too strong a word; for of course in His greatest and most characteristic work—the working out of redemption by His sufferings and death—He had, and could have, no successor. He finished the work leaving nothing for anyone else to do.

But, this being understood, we may perhaps best express what He did as a teacher by saying that He was training His own successors. When He was taken from the earth, much that He had been wont to do, and would have continued to do had He remained here, fell to them. They had to undertake the championing of the cause which He

---

[*] Compare the witty remark of NOVALIS (*Schriften*, Vol. 3, p. 196): "The philosopher lives on problems just as mankind lives on food. An unsolvable problem is like undigestagble food. A problem is only truly solved when it is destroyed as such. So it is also with food. The profit with both is the activity caused by both. However, there are also nourishing problems just as there is nourishing food, the elements of which develop my intelligence."

had founded, and its guidance in the world. From the very beginning of His own activity He had had this in view; and, in spite of preoccupations, which would, if He had allowed them, have entirely absorbed Him, He devoted Himself to the preparation of those who should take His place after His departure.

He employed them at first in subordinate and ministerial branches of His own work. For example, it is expressly said that "Jesus baptized not, but His disciples." After they had been longer with Him and attained to some degree of Christian maturity, He sent them forth to labor on their own account. They made tours, perhaps of no great extent, preaching and healing, and then returned to tell Him "all things, both what they had done and what they had taught," and to receive instructions for further operations. In this way the ground was sometimes broken up by the disciples before the Master came to sow it with the seed of eternal life; and perhaps regions were overtaken which He had not time to visit in person. But above all, their powers were being developed and their faith strengthened in view of the day, which He foresaw, when they would find themselves left alone face to face with the task of founding the Church and conquering the world in His name.

It is one of the characteristics of genuine Christianity, that it gives us an interest not only in the great events of the past, but also in the history of the future. The average man cares little for the future, except so far perhaps as his own offspring may be concerned: if he is happy, what does it matter to him what the state of the world will be after he is dead? But to a Christian it does matter. The faith and love in his heart bind him to the saints yet unborn. He is interested in a cause which is to go on after he has left it, and which he is to meet and take up again at a subsequent stage of his existence. It is almost as important to him how the work of Christ will be prospering when he is in his grave as how it is prospering now. This ought to make us think anxiously of those who are to be doing our work after we have left it. Christ thought of this from the very commencement of His own activity; and it was not too soon.

A man may do more for a cause by bringing younger forces into its service and training them to their work than by lavishing on it every moment of his own time and every atom of his energy. I was recently reading a monograph on the history of a particular branch of medicine; and intensely interesting it was to trace the progress from the beginning of knowledge among the Greek naturalists down through the Arab physicians of the Middle Ages, till one came to the vast and daily multiplying discoveries of modern science. But the name in the whole succession which chiefly arrested my attention was that of one whose contributions had been very large, but who acknowledged that they had not been strictly his own. He was always surrounded by a group of young physicians whom he inspired with enthusiasm for his subject; then he was in the habit of giving them single points of obscurity to investigate; and it was by the accumulation of these detailed studies that he was able to make vast additions to science. We need nothing more pressingly in the Christian Church at present than men who will thus guide the young and the willing to their work, showing what needs to be done and adapting talent to task. By taking up this function of the teacher, many a man might bring into the service of Christ those whose contributions would far surpass his own, as Barnabas did when he brought into the Church the services of Paul.

IV

Perhaps in our modern life the work most closely resembling the work of Jesus as a teacher is that of a professor of divinity.* The students in our theological seminaries and colleges are at the same stage as the

---

* In *The Public Ministry and Pastoral Methods of our Lord* Professor Blaikie heads a chapter, "The College of the Twelve." He also suggests another analogy: "A young minister, for example, may try to multiply himself by means of the young men of his flock. Some have a rare gift of finding out the most susceptible of these—getting them about them in classes and meetings, and perhaps sometimes in walks and at meals—explaining to them their plans, infusing into them their enthusiasm, enlisting their sympathies, and drawing out their talents. Dr. Chalmers in Glasgow, gathering young men around him, pouring his own views and spirit into them, rousing them to aid in his territorial schemes, and thus training the youths who in after years became the *élite* of the Christian laity of the west, comes as near as may be on a mere common level to the example of Christ and His Twelve."

Twelve were before they were sent forth on their independent course; and the intercourse between Christ and the Twelve, if carefully studied, would throw much light on the relationship between professors and students.

To the Twelve the most valuable part of their connection with Christ was simply the privilege of being with Him—of seeing that marvelous life day by day, and daily receiving the silent, almost unobserved, impress of His character. St. John, reflecting on this three years' experience long afterwards, summed it up by saying, "We beheld His glory!" The word he uses denotes the shekinah that shone above the mercy seat. In those lonely walks through Phoenicia and Perea, in those close talks on the hills of Galilee, they often felt that the holy of holies was being opened to them, and that they were gazing on the beauty that is ineffable.

The chief defect perhaps of theological training, as it is practiced at present, is the lack of this close intercourse between the teacher and the taught. Few professors have attempted it on any considerable scale. It would, indeed, be trying work. No eyes are so keen as those of students. If admitted close to a man, they take immediate stock of his resources. They are hero worshipers when they believe in a professor, but their scorn is unmeasured if they disbelieve in him. They can be dazzled by a reputation, but only massiveness of character and thoroughness of attainment can be sure of permanently impressing them.

I know of only one man in recent times who threw himself without fear or reserve into the most intimate relations with students. His conduct was so Christ-like and is so great an example, that it is worthy of being commemorated here.

Professor Tholuck is well known, by name at least, to all who have any tincture of theological knowledge. His numerous works in exegesis and apologetics give him a high place among the evangelical theologians of the century. He ranks still higher as a reforming force. What Wesley did for the Church of England, and Chalmers for the Church of Scotland, and Vinet for the Church of Switzerland, he may be said to have done for the Church of Germany: he fought down and annihilated the old Rationalism, which corresponded to our Moderatism, and during the first decades of this century made evangelical religion a respected and waxing power in the land.*

But the method by which he chiefly accomplished this is what will entitle him to lasting remembrance in the Church of God. No sooner was he converted and settled down to his work as an academic teacher, than he at once began to seek intercourse with his students of a kind most unusual in Germany. Not satisfied with merely lecturing from his chair, he made himself personally acquainted with them all, with the view of winning them to Christ. He invited them to walk with him; he visited them in their lodgings; he gathered them in his rooms two evenings a week for prayer, study of the Scriptures and reports of missionary enterprise. As time went on and his classes grew, this became a task of portentous dimensions. But his devotion to it never relaxed. At the busiest period of his life, when he was preparing lectures which filled his classroom with crowds of students and publishing the books which won him a worldwide reputation, he regularly spent four hours a day walking with students, besides having one student at dinner with him and another at supper.

It was not superficial work. It bore no resemblance to the method of some who think they have dealt with a man about his spiritual concerns when they have once forced the subject of religion into conversation without preparation. He often found the approaches to the mind of the student very difficult and had to begin far out on the circumference of things. He was full of geniality and overflowed with humor; he tried the students' wits with the oddest questions, and those who had enjoyed the privilege of walking with him would retail for weeks afterwards the quips and sallies in which he had indulged. He was full of intellectual interest, knew how to draw every man out

---

* The great name of Schleiermacher will doubtless occur to many as deserving to occupy this place, and it would be difficult to overestimate the profundity and extent of his influence. But to me at least the Life of Tholuck (by Witte, 1886) has been a revelation as to what were the real sources of the Evangelical Revival in Germany. Schleiermacher intellectualized the movement and became the scientific guide of those who had been spiritually quickened; but the quickening itself, on which in the last resort all depended, was largely due to humbler instrumentalities.

on the subjects with which he was acquainted, and could give invaluable hints on books and methods of study. He endeavored to rouse and stimulate the mind from every side, and many owed to him their mental as well as their spiritual awakening. He did not neglect the body either: no professor in Germany did so much to help on poor students. Yet, all the time, he had his eye on one object and was drifting steadily towards it—the personal salvation of every student with whom he had to deal.

He had his reward. It was known in his lifetime that his success had been great, but it is only by the publication of his biography that it has been made known how great it was. Among his papers were found hundreds of letters from students and ministers owning him as their spiritual father; and it turns out that among his converts were some of the most illustrious names in the German literary history of the century. In the pulpits and professorial chairs of Germany there are at present hundreds working for the evangel who owe their souls to him.

Why does such a life seem to us so original and exceptional? Why is it not repeated in other spheres—in the office, the shop and the school, as well as in the Church and the university? Tholuck explained the secret of his life in a single sentence: "I have but one passion, and that is Christ."

Matthew 5:21–48; 9:10–13; 12:24–45; 15:1–14; 16:1–4; 19:3–12; 21:23–46; 22; 23.

Luke 7:36–50; 10:25–37; 11:37–54; 12:1; 13:11–17.

John 2:18–20; 5; 6:41–65; 7:10–53; 8:12–59.

15

Christ as a Controversialist

THE ministers of the temple of truth, it has been said, are of three kinds: first, those stationed at the gate of the temple to constrain the passersby to come in; secondly, those whose function is to accompany inside all who have been persuaded to enter, and display and explain to them the treasures and secrets of the place; and, thirdly, those whose duty is to patrol round the temple, keeping watch and ward and defending the shrine from the attacks of enemies. We are only speaking very roughly if we say that the first of these three functions is that of the Preacher, the second that of the Teacher, and the third that of the Controversialist.

I

At the present time controversy has an evil name; the mere mention of it excites alarm; and the image of the controversialist, in most people's minds, is anything but an amiable or admired figure. He who is called in providence to undertake the function of controversy can reckon less than almost any other servant of Christ on the sympathy and appreciation of Christ's people; for even those who agree with his view of the truth will be sorry that he has allowed himself to enter the atmosphere of strife, and regret that he has not rested content with other kinds of work. This temper of mind of the Christian public has had its natural result. Able men are shy of undertaking work of this kind, easily finding employment for their talents in other directions, where labor is more appreciated. Controversy has accordingly fallen to a large extent into the hands of inferior practitioners; and it would be easy to mention controversies acknowledged to be of vital consequence to the welfare of the Church which do not receive the support of the champions whose advocacy would lend them dignity in the eyes of men.

It would be interesting to trace this state of public feeling back to its causes; for without doubt there are good reasons for it. It would probably be found to be a reaction from the temper of a time when controversy was carried to excess; for, although an important function at the Church, controversy is far from being the most important; and that which in due proportion is wholesome may in excess be poisonous. In their zeal for truth good men have sometimes forgotten to be zealous for charity. Controversy has raged round small points, on which Christians might well agree to differ, with a heat and violence which would only have been justified had the hearths and altars been at stake. When men thus indulge their passions, they lose from their own minds the sense of proportion, and, having expended their superlatives on objects of trifling importance, they have not the use of them when subjects emerge to which they would be really applicable. They also lose their hold on others; for the public mind, having been flogged into fury over questions which it afterwards discovers were not worth fighting about, refuses to stir even when the citadel is in danger. Thus has the Church to expiate her mistakes.

Yet it is no good sign of the times that controversy should be looked down upon. As has been mentioned in the Preface to this book, we have had to refrain from printing in full the evidence, from the Gospels, of the conduct of Jesus in the different departments of life, but, had this been done, the bulkiest of all these bodies of evidence would have been the appendix to the present chapter. In the records of His life we have page upon page of controversy. It may have been far from the work in which He delighted most to be engaged, but He had to undertake it all through His life, and especially towards the close. The most eminent of His servants in every age have had to do the same. St. Paul may not have been indisposed by nature to throw himself into controversy, but St. John had to enter into it with equal earnestness. It is scarcely possible to mention a representative man in any section of the Christian Church in any age who has been able altogether to avoid it.

The spirit of the true controversialist is the joyful and certain sense of possessing the truth, and the conviction of its value to all men, which makes error hateful and inspires the determination to sweep it away.* It was the King of Truth† that Christ carried on controversy, and He was borne along by the generous passion to cut His fellowmen out from their imprisonment in the labyrinth of error.

II

There are differences, indeed, in the present feeling of the public mind to different kinds of controversy. One of the tasks of controversy is to combat error outside of the Church. Christianity is incessantly assailed by forms of unbelief, which arise one after another and have their day. At one time it is Deism which requires to be refuted, at another Pantheism, at another Materialism. To defend the temple of Christian truth from such assailants is popular enough and meets with perhaps even excessive rewards. This kind of controversy is accordingly much cultivated and sometimes may be indulged in where it is not needed. When it is of the right quality, however, its value cannot be overestimated; and at the present moment it requires the very highest talent, for the apologetic problems of our century have not yet been solved.

It is controversy within the Church which excites alarm and aversion. Yet the controversy which our Lord waged was inside the Church; and so has been that carried on by the most eminent of His followers. It would, indeed, be well if the sound of controversial weapons were never heard in the temple of peace, but only on condition that it is also

---

* Late in life he (Mozley) speculated on the controversial temper with an evident though unacknowledged sense of experience. He did not appear to estimate it over-highly, further than as he considered it now to be rare. The contrary temperament was dealt with tenderly—the one that really needs the agreement of those around it, that has a sense of discomfort and privation without it, that must act with others; but the true controvrsial spirit, that which, strong in the feeling of possession, of a firm hold of its own view, rises with opposition or neglect, which can stand alone, ready as it were for all comers, this was the temper that, as he defined it, his nature evidently responded to"—Introduction to *Mozley's Essays*.

† John 18:37.

a temple of truth. In the time of Christ it was the stronghold of error; and not once or twice since then it has been the same. Jesus had to assail nearly the whole ecclesiastical system of His time and a large body of the Church's doctrines. To do so must, to a thoughtful mind, in any circumstances be an extremely painful task; for the faith reposed in their spiritual guides by the mass of men, who have little leisure or ability to think out vast subjects to the bottom, is one of the most sacred pillars of the edifice of human life; and nothing can be more criminal than wantonly to shake it. But it sometimes needs to be shaken, and Jesus did so.

Of course the opposite case may easily occur: the Church may have the truth, and the innovator may be in error. Then the true place of the Christian controversialist is on the side of the Church against him who is trying to mislead her. This also is a delicate task, requiring the utmost Christian wisdom and sometimes likely to be repaid with little thanks; for, while he who defends the Church against error coming from the outside is loaded with honors as a savior of the faith, he who attempts to preserve her from more menacing danger within may be dismissed with the odious and withering title of heresy hunter. But it is not easy to see what ethical standing ground there is to the competent Christian man between either, on the one hand, attacking the Church himself as heretical or, on the other, being prepared to defend her from accusations of not teaching the truth.

III

Christ and the Jewish teachers with whom He contended had a common standard and test of controversies to which they appealed. Both acknowledged the Scriptures of the Old Testament to be the Word of God. As this gave a peculiar coloring to all His work among the Jewish people, whom He addressed as He could not have preached to any other nation, so also it immensely simplified His work as a controversialist. His superiority consisted in His more intimate familiarity with this standard to which they both appealed. They were, indeed, the learned men of the nation, and the Old Testament was their textbook; while He, as they liked to remind Him, had never learned. But His intense love for the Word of His Father and His lifelong diligence in searching it made Him far more than a match for them on their own ground. Out of the stores of memory He could fetch the passage which was needed on every occasion; and, as He brought forth the word which was to overthrow their argument, He would sometimes taunt them, who boasted of their acquaintance with the Bible, by beginning His quotation with the question, "Have ye never read?" At other times, in a more solemn mood, He would tell them plainly, "Ye do err, not knowing the Scriptures."

He did not, however, trust merely to His knowledge of the letter of Scripture. This is the method of the small controversialist, who is satisfied if he can always meet text with text and if at the end he has one text more than his opponent. Such controversy is barren as the sand of the sea driven with the wind and has no more value than the bickerings of kites and crows. It is this kind of controversy which has brought the controversial function of the Church into contempt. In the true controversialist there is more than mere familiarity with the text of Scripture: he has a grasp of scriptural principles, a religious experience of his own which interprets the Scripture, and a nearness to God which imparts earnestness and dignity to his work.

The mind of Jesus stood thus above the mere letter of Scripture and handled it with consummate ease and freedom. This was why He scarcely ever quoted a text of the Old Testament without revealing a new meaning in it. It was as if His touch split it asunder and showed the gem flashing at its heart. Sometimes He would gather a principle from the general scope of Scripture which seemed to dissolve and even contradict the mere letter.* While loving and reverencing the Word of His Father with His whole soul, He knew Himself to be the organ of a revelation in which the older one was to be merged, as the light of the stars is lost in the dawn of the morning.

But it was not with Scripture alone that Jesus operated as a controversialist. There is an appeal to the common sense and to the reason of men—an appeal away from the mere pedantry of learning and the citation of authorities—which every controversialist of real mark must be able to make. And, if it can be made in a flash of wit or

---

* *e.g.*, Matthew 5:31, 33.

in an epigram which stamps itself instantly on the memory, the effect is irresistible, when the controversy is carried on before popular judges. Jesus possessed this power in the highest degree, as many of His sayings show. One of the most striking is this, at which "they marveled, and left Him, and went their way": "Render unto Caesar the things which are Caesar's and unto God the things which are God's."

IV

In any exposition of the ethics of controversy at the present day, a prominent place would be given to the duty of treating opponents with consideration. However severely their arguments may be handled, their persons ought to be treated with respect, and they should receive credit for honorable motives.

No rule could be more reasonable. We know but little of our fellowmen at the best, and, when anything inflames us against them, it is easy to be blinded by prejudice to their excellences. On the other hand, we know so much about ourselves that we may well hesitate to cast stones at others. No man has all the truth, and an opponent may be seeing a side of it which we cannot see. God sometimes gets the whole truth given to the Church only by the halves of it, held by different minds, meeting at first in conflict. The fire generated by their collision united them at last in perfect fusion.*

Yet, excellent as this rule is, it is not without exceptions; for Jesus broke it. We have not enough information to know whether or not at the beginning of His career He treated His opponents with more

---

* "They that purify silver to the purpose put it in the fire again and again, that it may be thoroughly tried. So is the truth of God; there is scarce any truth but hath been tried over and over again, and still if any dross happen to mingle with it, then God calls it in question again. If in former times there have been Scriptures alleged that have not been pertinent to prove it, that truth shall into the fire again, that what is dross may be burned up; the Holy Ghost is so curious, so delicate, so exact, He cannot bear that falsehood should be mingled with the truths of the Gospel. That is the reason, therefore, why that God doth still, age after age, call former things in question, because that there is still some dross one way or other mingled with them; either in the stating the opinions themselves, or else in the Scriptures that are brought and alleged for them, that have passed for current, for He will never leave till He have purified them"—THOMAS GOODWIN.

consideration, but, towards the end of His life, He exposed them with more and more keenness, and at last He poured on Pharisees, scribes and priests a torrent of scorn never equaled in its withering and annihilating vehemence (Matt. 23).

In point of fact, our estimate of the characters of men exercise an important influence on the value we set on their opinions. We may not be able to express it in public, yet in secret we may know that about an opponent which robs his opinions of all weight. He may be writing or speaking confidently on religious subjects, while we know him to be a thoroughly irreligious man, who has not the very faculty on which true insight in such matters depends, and who could not afford to confess the truth, even if he knew it, because it would condemn himself at every point. It may in certain circumstances be a duty to make this public. Jesus often told the Jewish teachers that it was impossible for them to understand Him, because they lacked moral sympathy with the truth; and the interests of priests and Pharisees were vested in the system of hypocrisy which their arguments were invented to defend. Our judgments in such cases are liable to be mistaken, but He could completely trust His own; and at last He broke all the authority of His opponents by thoroughly exposing their character.

V

In the very rush of the controversial onset, however, Jesus would pause to note and acknowledge a better spirit, if any sign of candor showed itself in an opponent.

There was a day of fierce conflict in His life to which the Evangelists devote close attention. It was one of the days of the last week before He suffered, and a combination of a most formidable character took place among His enemies, to confute Him and put Him down. The scribes and Pharisees were there of course; even the Sadducees, who in general neglected Him, had come out of their haughty retirement; and Pharisees and Herodians, who generally hated one another, were for once united in a common purpose. They had arranged well beforehand the questions with which they were to try Him; they had chosen their champions; and one after another they delivered their assaults upon Him in the Temple. But it was for them a day of disaster and humiliation; for He refuted them so conclusively that "no man was able to answer Him a word; neither durst any man from that forth ask Him any more questions."

In the very midst, however, of this exciting scene a controversialist arose to whom Jesus extended very different treatment than to the rest. The man appears to have known comparatively little about Christ, except that He was one who was everywhere spoken against. But he was a scribe, and, as his party was attacking Christ, he was drawn into the same attitude. He looked upon Him as a misleader of the people, who deserved to be put down, and he had come to do so. Yet the answers which he heard Jesus giving before his own turn came shook him; for they were right answers, which by no means confirmed the impressions of Christ which he had brought to the spot. Some such acknowledgment seems to have been conveyed in the tone of his own question, when he put it.

It was, indeed, but a paltry question, "Which is the first commandment of all?" This was one of the subjects on which in the rabbinical schools they were wont to chop logic, and the man probably considered that it was one on which he was superior to any other rabbi. Jesus, however, had observed something that pleased Him in the man's look or manner, and, instead of merely overthrowing and humiliating him, as He had done to the others, He gave him a full and earnest answer: "The first of all the commandments is, Hear, O Israel; The Lord our God is one Lord: and thou shalt love the Lord thy God with all thy heart, and with all thy soul, and with all thy mind: this is the first commandment. And the second is like, namely this, Thou shalt love thy neighbor as thyself. There is none other commandment greater than these."

To us this is familiar teaching, and it falls on our senses without making much impression. But it is not difficult to conceive with what irresistible power and majesty it may have fallen on a mind which heard it for the first time. It seems to have thrown the man completely out of the caviling attitude into one of intense moral earnestness. It not only smote his arguments down, but burst open the doors of his being and went straight to his conscience, which sent back the echo instantaneously and clearly: "Well, Master, Thou hast said the truth: for there is one God; and there is none other but He: and to love Him with all the heart, and with all the understanding, and with all the soul, and with all the strength, and to love his neighbor as himself, is more than all whole burnt offerings and sacrifices."

This was a noble answer. The man had forgotten the *rôle* he had come to play; he had forgotten his comrades, and what they were expecting of him; he let his heart speak and did homage to the moral dignity of Christ. Jesus marked the change with deep inward satisfaction and said to him, "Thou art not far from the kingdom of God."

This is a great example. To attack them remorselessly in controversy often drives into permanent opposition those who might be won by milder treatment. Men may appear as opponents of Christianity who in their hearts are very near it; and it is Christ-like to detect this sympathy and bring it to expression. To prove to men that they are outside the kingdom is an easy thing in comparison, but it may be far better to let them see that they are only a few steps from its threshold. The triumph of a ruthless polemic may gratify the natural heart, but far more like the Master, where it is possible, is a winning irenicum.

Matthew 8:17; 9:36; 14:14; 15:32; 20:34.
Mark 1:41; 4:33.
Luke 7:11–15.

Matthew 27:34.
Mark 10:13–16, 21; 12:34.
Luke 10:21; 19:41.
John 8:1–11; 12:27; 13:21; 20:16, 17.

Matthew 8:10; 9:2, 28; 11:6; 13:58; 14:31; 15:28; 26:13, 38.
Mark 6:5, 6; 8:12.
Luke 7:9; 17:17.

Matthew 8:4; 9:30; 12:16; 14:22; 16:20; 17:9.
Mark 7:24, 36; 8:26, 30.
John 5:14; 6:15.

Matthew 16:23; 17:17; 26:50, 55.
Mark 1:25; 3:5; 15:3, 5.
Luke 4:35, 39–41.
John 11:33–38.

16

Christ as a
Man of Feeling

So much learning has been expended in the present age on the Life of Christ, and every particle of the record has been so thoroughly sifted, that it may be questioned if mere intellect will now discover much that is new in the subject. There may still, however, be great scope for the divinatory power of feeling.* Jesus was as refined and delicate in feeling as He was wise in speech and mighty in act; and the motives of His conduct are often incomprehensible except to those who possess in some degree the same feelings as He had. He taught mankind to feel finely, and ever since He was in the world there have been increasing numbers who have learned from Him to regard childhood and woman, poverty and service, and many other objects, with sentiments totally different from those with which they were regarded before His advent.

---

* No more brilliant instance of such psychological interpretation could be adduced than the explanation given in *Ecce Homo* of our Lord's conduct when the woman taken in adultery was brought to Him. "He stooped down and wrote on the ground" (John 8:8). Why did He do so? It was because He was ashamed of listening to a foul story. "He was seized with an intolerable sense of shame. He could not meet the eye of the crowd, or of the accusers, and perhaps at that moment least of all the woman. In His burning embarrassment and confusion He stooped down so as to hide His face, and began writing with His finger in the ground." Everyone who reads this explanation feels it to be the true one; it shines with its own light; and, when first heard, gives a shock of delighted surprise.

The author adds, "The effect on Jesus was such as might have been produced upon many men since, but perhaps scarcely upon any man that ever lived before."

The notices in the Gospels of the impressions made on His feelings by different situations in which He was placed are extraordinarily numerous, but a single incident—the raising of the daughter of Jairus —in which the feelings of His heart came conspicuously into view will serve as a sufficient clue.

I

His Compassion was illustrated in this incident.

It was the case of a man whose only daughter was lying at the point of death; and he besought Jesus greatly for her, says St. Mark. The heart of Jesus could not but answer such an appeal. In a similar instance— that of a woman with an only son, the widow of Nain—it is said that, when the Lord saw her following behind the bier, He had compassion on her and said to her, "Weep not." He not only gave the required help in such cases, but gave it with an amount of sympathy which doubled its value. Thus He not only raised Lazarus, but wept with his sisters. In curing a man who was deaf, He sighed as He said, *"Ephphatha."* All His healing work cost Him feeling. There is a great difference between the clergyman or physician who merely calls at the house of sorrow as a matter of duty, to be able to say that he has been there, and him who takes the suffering of the stricken home on his heart and goes away melted and broken down with it.

On this occasion the compassion of Christ was deepened by the fact that it was a child who was ill. "My little daughter" she was called by her father. All the scenes in Christ's life in which children appear are exquisitely touching; and it was His feeling which gave them their beauty and pathos. As you look at them, you feel that He not only knew all that is in a father's and a mother's heart, but sank new wells in the heart of humanity and brought love up from deeper levels than it had sprung from before. Ruskin has observed that there are no children in Greek art, but that they abound in Christian art—an unmistakable token that it was the eye of Christ which first fully appreciated the attractiveness of childhood.

II

A second feeling which Jesus showed in this incident was Sensitivity.

At Jairus' request He went to the house where the dying girl was, but on the way a messenger met them, who told the poor father that all was over, and that he need not trouble the Master any further. Whereupon, without waiting to be appealed to, Jesus turned to him and said, "Be not afraid; only believe."

In this we might see a new instance of His compassion, but it also reveals something else: Jesus was extremely sensitive to the sentiments of trust or distrust with which He was regarded. If any generosity of belief was shown towards Him, His heart filled with gladness, and He acknowledged His gratification without stint. Thus, when another applicant for help, in a situation not unlike that of Jairus, expressed his belief that, if Jesus would only speak a word even at a distance, without going to the house in which the sick person was lying, a cure would ensue, Jesus stood still in the road and, turning to the bystanders, exclaimed, "I have not found so great faith, no, not in Israel." The faith of Jairus, though not so strong as this, had evidently gratified Him, and it was because He could not bear to have it clouded with doubt that He hastened so promptly to strengthen it.

He had, however, many an experience to encounter of the opposite kind, and the feeling thereby occasioned in Him was keen. If now and then He had to marvel at the greatness of faith, He had to marvel far oftener at unbelief. In His own native place, when He visited it, He could do scarcely any mighty works on this account. The rebuff so chilled His heart that the activity of His miraculous power was restrained. His most signal favors were sometimes received with ingratitude, as in the case of the ten lepers, of whom only one returned to give thanks for his cure, causing Him to ask sadly, "Where are the nine?"

III

A third species of feeling which He betrayed on this occasion was Indignation.

When He reached the house, not only was the child dead, but the place had been taken possession of by the mummers who undertook the ghastly ceremonial of mourning. Death, though the most solemn of all events, has in many countries been invested with absurdity through the mourning customs with which it has been associated, but in Palestine this was carried to an extreme. As soon as a death took place, the house was invaded by professional mourners, who filled it with wild ululations and doleful music. This hideous custom was in full operation when Jesus arrived, and to His serene soul it was intolerable. He indignantly enjoined silence, and, when this was not forthcoming, He drove the whole ghastly apparatus forth and cleared the house.

Indignation, though closely allied to sinful anger, is not vicious, but virtuous. It is the sign of an honorable and self-respecting nature. The soul that loves order, uprightness and nobleness cannot but be indignant at disorder, duplicity and meanness. The indignation of Jesus is often mentioned. It could be aroused by unseemly noise and confusion, as on this occasion. When casting out devils, he used angrily to rebuke the outcries of the possessed. He is represented in the same attitude when calming the winds and waves in the storm, presumably because He was counteracting the prince of the power of the air. The whole empire of Satan is the empire of disorder, and every manifestation of its power affected Him in this way. This explains the strange tumult of indignant excitement in which He advanced to the grave of Lazarus: His condition of mind was one of angry vengeance against the ravages of death.*

---

* The story of the raising of Lazarus so abounds with notices of Christ's emotions that we might have taken it for our clue instead of the raisig of the daughter of Jairus. As He approached the grave of Lazarus, it is said "He groaned in spirit, and was troubled"; but the Greek words are much stronger: ἐνεβριμήσατο τω πνεύματι και ἐτά ραξεν ἑαυτόν. The first verb denotes, not groaning, but "visibly expressed indignation, displeasure, or wrath"; and the second denotes the change in His countenance caused by this indignation. "His whole frame was moved. A storm of wrath was seen to sweep over Him." What was the cause of this angry agitation? "He was gazing into the skeleton face of the world, and tracing everywhere the reign of death. The whole earth to Him was but 'the valley of the shadow of death'; and in those tears which were shed in His presence He saw that

'Ocean of Time, whose waters of deep woe
Are brackish wth the salt of human tears.'

"... But this is not all. Behind the presence of death there was the awful reality, not only of sin, 'the sting of death,' but also of him through whom sin came—him who is in this Gospel so frequently called 'the prince of this world.' If then we would rightly understand the true meaning of our Lord's wrath, His visibly expressed

The state of the times in which He lived afforded peculiar occasion for the display of this sentiment. It was because the mourning in the house of Jairus was professional, with no heart in it, that He disliked it so utterly. But the society of Judea at that time was one vast hypocrisy. The holders of sacred offices were self-seekers; the professors of piety were hunting for the praise of men; the teachers of the people laid grievous burdens on other men's shoulders, which they would not themselves touch with one of their fingers; sacred language was a cloak for spoliation and impurity. Jesus burned with indignation against it all and poured His feelings out in philippics against the parties and personalities of the time.

His was holy fire: it was the flame of truth consuming falsehood, of justice attacking wrong, of love burning against selfishness. Too often the crusade against shams and hypocrisy has been inspired by zeal which is unholy. Men have undertaken the office of the censor and satirist whose own hearts have not been pure and whose lives have been inconsistent, plucking the mote out of their brother's eye, and behold a beam was in their own. They have only masqueraded in the garment of indignation. But this robe found in Jesus its true wearer, and He wore it with incomparable dignity. "Are ye come out," He demanded of those about to arrest Him, "as against a thief." "Judas," He asked the traitor, "betrayest thou the Son of man with a kiss?" Before the high priest, Pilate, and Herod, His indignant silence was more eloquent than the most scorching words. He has not put off this garment yet: in heaven still burns "the wrath of the Lamb."

IV

A fourth mode of feeling characteristic of Jesus which was illustrated on this occasion was Delicacy.

Having put the professional mourners out, He went into the room of death, where the little maid was lying on the bed. But He did not go alone, or only with the three disciples whom He had taken into the

---

indignation, we must regard Him here as confronting in conflict the great enemy of His kingdom—the destroyer of the race which He Himself had come to save." See a remarkable paper on this difficult passage by the Rev. John Hutchison, D.D., in the *Monthly Interpreter*, Vol. 2 (T. & T. Clark, 1885).

house with Him: He took with Him the father and mother of the maiden, as being deeply interested in her who was their own and entitled to see all that happened to her.

Then He took her by the hand before pronouncing the resurrection words; for He did not wish her to be startled when she woke, but to feel the support of a sympathetic presence. Many a one in an hour of agitation or when coming out of a swoon has felt how it steadies and strengthens to be held by a firm hand and to look into a calm face.

Thus He did all with perfect tact, not by calculation, but with the instinct of delicate feeling, which guided Him at every turn to do precisely the best thing. Yet there was no straining after refinement. The besetting sin of emotional natures is to overstrain and overdo. But how healthy and manly was the feeling of Jesus! His very next act, after these exquisite touches, was this: "He commanded that something should be given her to eat." In the same way, after days of healing and preaching in the wilderness, during which He had been borne along with the prophetic enthusiasm, it was He who made the proposal that food should be given to the multitude, before they were dispersed, lest they should faint by the way; the disciples, though far less preoccupied, never thinking of such a thing. He excelled them as much in considerateness and practicality as in delicacy of feeling.

V

The last kind of feeling exhibited by our Lord on this occasion was Modesty. After the miracle was performed, "He charged them straitly that no man should know it." This is the sequel to many a work of wonder in His life. "See thou tell no man," He said to a leper whom He had cleansed. "See that no man know it," He said to two blind men whose sight He had restored. He straitly charged those, as a rule, out of whom He had cast devils not to make Him known.

Such notices abound in the Gospels; yet I am not sure that I have ever seen the true explanation of them given. All kinds of elaborate explanations have been attempted. In one case, for example, it is said that He forbade the man who had been healed to mention his cure, lest it should do him harm by puffing him up; in another, because his testimony would have had no weight; in a third, because it was not yet time to acknowledge Himself to be the Messiah; and so on. Such are the suggestions made by learned men, and there may be some truth in them all. But they are too elaborate and recondite; the real explanation lies on the surface. It is simply that, while so great a worker, He disliked to have His good deeds made known. St. Matthew puts this so plainly that it ought not to have been overlooked. After mentioning an occasion when, after healing great multitudes, He charged them that they should not make Him known, the evangelist adds that this was in fulfillment of a prophecy which said, "He shall not strive nor cry, neither shall anyone hear His voice in the street." It is one of the penalties of public work for God that it comes to be talked about, and vulgar people make a sensation of it. We are well acquainted with this at the present day, when nothing is allowed to remain private, and, if a man does anything in the least out of the common, the minutest details of his life are dragged out and exposed to the public eye. But this is contrary to the very genius of goodness and exposes even those occupied with the holiest work to the temptation of playing for the praise of men instead of acting humbly in the eye of God. Jesus detested it. He would have been hidden if He could; and it was a heavy cross to Him that the more He pressed people to say nothing about Him, the more widely did they spread His fame.*

Such was the heart of Christ as it is laid bare in a single story. By taking a wider sweep we might have accumulated more illustrations. But the clue, once seized, can be easily followed in the Gospels, where the notices of how He felt in the different situations in which He was placed was far more numerous than anyone whose attention has not been specially directed to them would believe.

Nor would it be difficult to trace the refining influence which intercourse with Him had on His disciples—how they learned to feel about things as He did. There is no other influence so refining as genuine religion. Where the Gospel is faithfully preached and affectionately believed, there is gradually wrought into the very features of people the stamp of the Son of man. The friendship of Jesus breeds the gentle heart.

---

* There is, however, a shrinking from publicity which is vicious: it may be mere fastidiousness or the cowardice which fears responsibility. And there is an enjoyment of popularity which is nothing but unselfish absorption in the triumph of a good cause.

Matthew 7:28; 8:27; 9:8, 26, 31, 33; 12:23; 13:54; 22:22, 33.
Mark 1:45; 2:1, 2, 12; 7:36, 37; 9:15; 15:5.
Luke 2:47, 48; 4:15, 22, 32, 37.

Matthew 14:1, 2.
Mark 4:41; 10:32.
Luke 5:8, 26; 23:45, 48.
John 18:6.

Mark 1:23–27; 5:6, 7.
Luke 6:11; 13:14.

Matthew 2:1–3; 3:13, 14; 4:19–22; 27:19, 55.
Mark 1:37; 5:18; 12:37.
Luke 1:41; 8:40; 11:27; 22:61, 62; 24:32.
John 6:68; 7.

17

Christ as Man of Influence

In the foregoing chapter we have seen the feelings produced in the sensitive heart of Christ by the persons and things He was brought into contact with. In the present one we have to deal with the feelings which He produced, by His presence and actions, in the hearts of men. If much attention is paid in the records of His life to the depth and variety of the impressions which others made on Him, no less surprising is the number of notices they contain of the impressions which He made on others.

Simeon the aged, when he held the child Jesus in his arms in the Temple, prophesied that by contact with Him the thoughts of many hearts would be revealed; and this was one of the most outstanding features of His subsequent life. None who came near Him could remain indifferent. They might hate or they might love, they might admire or they might scorn Him, but in any case they were compelled to show the deepest that was in them. In the Talmud there is a fable that King Solomon wore a ring engraved with the divine name, and everyone towards whom he turned the inscription was forced to speak out whatever he was thinking at the moment. So Jesus, by His mere presence among men, brought to the surface their deepest thoughts and feelings and made them display the best and the worst which their hearts concealed.

I

The commonest impression which He is narrated in the Gospels to have excited is Wonder. "They marveled at Him"; "they wondered"; "they were astonished with a great astonishment"—such are the phrases which recur continually in the records of His life. Sometimes it was at His teaching that they marveled—at its gracefulness, originality and power—or at the knowledge displayed by one who had never learned. Still more noisy was their wonder at His miracles. People ran together to the spot where a miracle was taking place; those who had been cured spread abroad the fame of what had happened to themselves; and, wherever He went, there rose around Him a cloud of notoriety.

Though this was the commonest impression made on people's minds, it was far from the most valuable. To Himself it was an unpleasant necessity. His soul shrank from the importunities of the crowd, and He gauged the depth of their shallow adulation. The one advantage of it, for the sake of which He submitted to the necessity, was that it brought to Him, among the rest, those who really wanted Him and whom He wanted—as in the case of the woman who came behind Him in the crowd, when He was on the way to the house of Jairus, and touched the hem of His garment, that she might be healed. The crowd was thronging Him, many no doubt touching His very person, but they got nothing from this contact. She came in dire need and trembling faith, and, at her touch, virtue went out of Him and healed her. But she would hardly have been there but for the crowd: it was by the noise and excitement that she was informed that He was near; at all events the crowd supplied her with her opportunity.

This may still be the one advantage which compensates for the many drawbacks of the rumor that rises round religion in some of its forms. The sensation is a bell that rings into church those who need Christ. The appearance of popular preachers is trumpeted abroad, and crowds flock to hear them. When a distinguished evangelist appears or a revival of religion breaks out, the country is moved with wonder. Much of this noise is silly enough, but some may derive advantage from it. While the multitudes throng, one here and there touches. The crowd comes talking and buzzing out of church, but someone, hurrying silently through the throng to escape into solitude, carries away a blessing.

II

Sometimes wonder deepened into Fear. Thus, when He rose from sleep during the storm and rebuked the winds and waves, it is said, "they feared exceedingly"; and, when He raised to life the widow's son at Nain, "there came a fear on all."

From other parts of Scripture also it may be inferred that this was the natural result of witnessing a miracle. A miracle, seen close at hand, produced the sense of the immediate presence of the Almighty; and any unmistakable manifestation of the divine excites fear. A loud and sudden thunder there falls an awe over the spirit; and I have heard those who have experienced an earthquake describe the sensation of terror it awakens as unique and quite beyond the control of the will. It is the sense of being utterly helpless in the grasp of immeasurable power. Those who saw Christ perform a miracle felt that there was in Him that which could do what it pleased with them and with nature round about them; and it was this vague impression of the divine in Him which made them afraid.

But the fear He inspired was at other times a genuine tribute to the majesty of His human character; and we get no more authentic glimpses of the moral stature of Jesus than by observing the impressions which He produced on the minds of others in the great moments of His life. At the gate of Gethsemane, when He encountered the band sent to arrest Him, the traces of the experiences which He had passed through in the garden were still upon Him, and the effect of His rapt and tragic air was extraordinary. At the sight of Him "they went backward and fell to the ground." All through the last six months of His life, indeed, He seems habitually to have been invested, through brooding on His approaching fate, with an awful dignity. His great purpose sharpened His features, straightened His figure and quickened His step; and sometimes, as He pushed ahead of the Twelve, absorbed in His own thoughts, "they were amazed"; and, as they followed, "they were afraid."

Earlier, however, even in the serene beginning of His ministry, there were manifestations of this overpowering moral dignity. When He drove the buyers and sellers out of the Temple, in the first access of His prophetic inspiration, why did they flee crouching before Him? They were many, while He was but one; they were wealthy and influential, while He was but a peasant. Yet there was that in Him which they never thought of resisting. They felt how awful goodness is. There is a majesty in virtue indignant before which the loftiest sinners cower. I have known a youth from the country enter an office in the city, where the daily conversation was so foul and profane that it would almost have disgraced the hulks, but a month after his arrival not a man in the place dared to utter an unchaste word when he was present. Yet he had scarcely spoken a syllable of reproof; it was simply the dignity of manly goodness that quelled conscious iniquity.

III

The fear excited by Jesus sometimes deepened into Repulsion. The fear He caused was the fear of the finite in the grasp of the Infinite. But those who felt themselves helpless in the hands of the Almighty felt themselves at the same time exposed in the sight of the All-seeing and the All-pure.

As the ignorant speak with fluency in the company of the ignorant, but, if introduced among the learned, stammer and become afraid of their own voices; or as the beggar, who is quite unconscious of his rags when moving among his equals, if brought into a drawing room filled with well-dressed people, becomes suddenly aware of every patch on his coat and every hole in his looped and windowed raggedness; so, when confronted with spotless holiness, the human soul turns round upon itself and recognizes its imperfections. It was this which made St. Peter, when he saw the miraculous draft of fishes, put up his hands in deprecation and cry to Jesus, "Depart from me, for I am a sinful man, O Lord." And for the same reason the Gadarenes, when they beheld the miracle which Jesus had wrought in their midst, besought Him to depart out of their coasts. They felt the instinctive shrinking of the guilty from the holy.

In the tragedy of *Faust*, Margaret, who is meant to represent virgin purity, cannot bear the sight of Mephistopheles, though he is disguised as a knight and she has no idea who he really is. She shrinks from him instinctively —

> In all my life not anything
> Has given my heart so sharp a sting
> As that man's loathsome visage.

Christ's presence produced precisely the opposite effect: in the unholy it awoke repulsion and the desire to flee from Him. As He held down His head with burning shame and wrote on the ground, when the sinful woman was brought to Him, her accusers, at length dimly recognizing what was going on in His mind, grew afraid and, "being convicted in their own conscience, went out one by one, beginning at the eldest, even unto the last; and Jesus was left alone, and the woman standing in the midst." When He drew near to possessed persons, His mere proximity threw them into paroxysms of excitement, and they entreated Him to depart and not torment them; for merely to see one so holy was a torment.

The presence of superlative goodness, if it does not subdue, stirs up the wild beasts which lurk in the subterranean caverns of the human heart into angry opposition to itself. Christ made the evil in those who opposed Him show itself at its very worst. Pilate, for example, only applied to the case of Jesus the same principles of administration which he had made use of in hundreds of other cases—the principles of the self-seeker and time-server dressed in the garb of justice, but never did these principles appear in all their ghastly unrighteousness till he released Barabbas and handed over Jesus to the executioner. The inhumanity and hollowness of Sadducee and Pharisee were never seen in their true colors till the light which streamed from Jesus fell on them and exposed every spot and wrinkle of the hypocrite's robe. Christ's very meekness provoked them to deeper scorn of His pretensions; His silence under their accusations made them gnash their teeth with baffled malice; the castigation of His polemic made them cling to their errors with more desperate tenacity.

Thus are hearts hardened by the very excellence of those with whom they have to deal. As Ahab, when he met Elijah, hissed at him, "Hast thou found me, O mine enemy?" so the mere sense that his godly mother is praying for him, or that good people are planning for his spiritual welfare, may excite in one who is going determinedly down the broad road a diabolical scorn and rage. The contempt with which one who bears witness for God is flouted by his comrades is often only an evidence that they feel his presence a reproach to their own evil characters, and it is a real, though undesigned, tribute to his superiority. "Marvel not if the world hate you; ye know that it hated Me before it hated you."

IV

Although the presence of Jesus repelled some, it exerted on others the most powerful attraction, and the most characteristic feature of His character was Moral Attractiveness. He repelled those who were wedded to their sins and unwilling to abandon them, but He attracted all who in any degree were feeling after a new and better life.

Strong as the power of sin is in the soul of man, it never altogether overcomes the opposite principle. There is that in every man which opposes his sin and protests against it. It reminds the prodigal of the Father's house, from which he has wandered, and makes him feel the shame of serving among the swine. It warns him in solitary hours that the sin to which he is attached is his worst enemy, and that he will never be happy till he is separated from it.

This redeeming principle in human nature is the conscience; and without its feeling for what is holy and divine the condition of man would be hopeless. But it exists even in the wicked; who cannot withhold their admiration from the truly good and, though following the worse, approve the better, course. It makes men afraid and ashamed of their own sin, even when they are most abandoned to it. It may be stimulated by denunciations of sin, like those of the Baptist, but it is touched even more effectively by the sight of exceptional purity or by the compassion which pities ungodliness. This reminds man of something he has lost; it causes the sinful enjoyments with which he is occupied to appear cheap and vulgar; it makes him uneasy and dissatisfied.

Jesus naturally exerted this kind of influence in the strongest degree. Wherever there existed any tenderness or susceptibility towards what is high and pure, it was stimulated by His presence. Conscience, hearing His voice in its prison, woke up and came to the windows to demand emancipation. As the presence of a physician armed with a cure for some virulent disease excites a sensation among those afflicted with the malady, who communicate the news of relief to one another with the swiftness of a secret telegraphy, so wherever Jesus went, the heavy-laden and the aspiring heard of Him and found Him.

In publicans and sinners, and even in Pharisees, unaccustomed movements showed themselves: Nicodemus sought Him by night; Zacchaeus climbed into the sycamore tree to see Him; the woman who was a sinner stole to His feet to bathe them with her tears.

Moral attractiveness is of two kinds—the passive and the active.

There is a goodness which draws men by the mere force of its own beauty. It is not thinking of any such effect; for it is inward and self-absorbed; its attention is concentrated on an inner vision and occupied with following a secret law. It would never think of crediting itself with an influence on others; for it is not aware of its own beauty, and that which sets off all its qualities is the ornament of humility. This is the goodness especially of the feminine virtues, and the characters which exhibit it in a marked degree have always a womanly element. "Such have many of us seen—sometimes in humble life, faithful and devoted, loyal to man and full of melody in their hearts to God, their life one act of praise; some in a higher sphere, living amid the pride of life, but wholly untouched by its spells; free and unensnared souls, that had never been lighted up with the false lights and aspirations of human life, or been fascinated by the evil of the world, though sympathizing with all that is good in it, and enjoying it becomingly; who give us, as far as human character now can do, an insight into the realms of light, the light that comes from neither sun nor moon, but from Him who is the light everlasting."*

Of such characters Jesus is the head and crown. His image shines through all the centuries with the beauty of holiness. This is why the eyes of men, sweeping the fields of history in search of excellence, always rest at last on Him as its perfect and final embodiment. This is why none can write of Christ without falling into a kind of rapture and ecstasy of admiration, and even those who are bitter and blustering in their opposition to everything Christian grow hushed and reverent when they speak of Christ Himself. No pen can fully render the impression made on the reader by His life in the Gospels. It is easy to make a catalogue of the qualities which entered into His human character, but the blending and the harmony and the perfection, the

---

* MOZLEY, *University Sermons.*

delight and the subduing charm, who can express? Yet all this walked the earth in the flesh, and men and women saw it with their eyes!

The moral attractiveness of the active sort influences in a different way. There are natures which we call magnetic. People cannot help being drawn to them and following where they go. Whatever such natures do, they act with all their might, and others are drawn into the rush and current of their course. It may be an evil course, and then they are ringleaders in sin; for the kingdom of darkness has its missionaries as well as the kingdom of heaven. Like other forces of human nature, this one requires to be redeemed and consecrated. Then it becomes the spirit of the missionary, the apostle, the religious pioneer.

Nothing in the memoirs of Jesus is more surprising than the apparent ease with which He induced men to quit their occupations and follow Him. John and James are in their ship mending their nets, but, when He calls, they instantly leave the ship and nets and their father Zebedee and go after Him. Matthew is at the seat of custom, and that is a seat not easily left, but no sooner is he called than he forsakes all and follows Jesus. Zacchaeus, who had been an extortioner for a lifetime, was no sooner asked to receive Him into his house than he began to make proposals and promises of the utmost generosity. Jesus was engaged in a splendid work, whose idea and results touched the imagination of all who were capable of anything noble. He was wholly absorbed in it; and to see unselfish devotion always awakens imitation. He was the author and leader of a new movement, which grew around Him, and the enthusiasm of those who had joined it drew others in. The same power has belonged in remarkable measure to all great spiritual leaders—to St. Paul, to Savonarola, to Luther, to Wesley, and many more; who, filled themselves with the Holy Ghost, have been able to lift men above the instincts of pleasure and comfort and make them willing to deny themselves for a great cause. And no earnest life, in which the enthusiasm of Jesus burns, fails to exercise in some degree the same influence.

It is one of the healthiest features of our day that all thinking people are growing sensitive about their influence. To many the chief dread of sin arises from perceiving that they cannot sin themselves without directly or indirectly involving others; and it would be to them the greatest of satisfactions to be able to believe that they are doing good to those with whom they are brought into contact, and not harm.

This is a feeling worthy of the solemn nature of our earthly existence, and it ought certainly to be one of the guiding principles of life. Yet it is not without its dangers. If allowed too prominent a place among our motives, it would crush the mind with an intolerable weight and cause conduct to appear so responsible that the spring of energy would be broken. It might easily betray us into living so much for effect as to fall into hypocrisy. The healthiest influence is unsought and unconscious. It is not always when we are trying to impress others that we impress them most. They elude the direct efforts which we make, but they are observing us when we are not thinking of it. They detect from an unconscious gesture or chance word the secret we are trying to conceal. They know quite well whether our being is a palace fair within or only a shabby structure with a pretentious elevation. They estimate the mass and weight of our character with curious accuracy; and it is this alone that really tells. Our influence is the precise equivalent of our human worth or worthlessness.

A man may strive for influence and miss it. But let him grow within himself—in self-control, in conscientiousness, in purity and submission—and then he will not miss it. Every step of inward progress makes us worth more to the world and to every cause with which we may be identified. The road to influence is simply the highway of duty and loyalty. Let a man press nearer to Christ and open his nature more widely to admit the energy of Christ, and whether he knows it or not—it is better perhaps if he does not know it—he will certainly be growing in power for God with men, and for men with God. "Abide in Me, and I in you: as the branch cannot bear fruit of itself except it abide in the vine, no more can ye except ye abide in Me."

FINIS

The Teaching of Jesus Concerning Himself

Preface
to the First Edition

IN the preface to an early issue of *The Life of Jesus Christ*, and again in the preface to *Imago Christi*, I made public my intention of writing on the Teaching of Christ. But the fulfillment of this purpose has long been delayed. This has not been due to the withdrawal of my attention from the subject, which for more than twenty years has been my favorite study. Again and again I have brought my materials to the verge of publication, but I have shrunk back owing to the impossibility of doing justice to the subject, and to a fear lest my results were not grounded upon a sufficiently thorough exegesis of the Savior's words. At length, however, when the trustees of the Cunningham Lectures did me the honor of asking me to undertake the course for this year, I felt this to be a providential summons to delay no longer but to bring at least a portion of my materials to the maturity requisite for publication. The result is the volume now offered to the public, which deals with a part of the teaching of Jesus complete in itself.

A word may be desirable to indicate the relation of what is here completed to what is left. More prominent than the Christology in the Synoptists is that which may be called the Ethic of Jesus; and these two together—the Christology and the Ethic—pretty well embrace all that the Synoptists offer. The distinction between the two is that, while the Christology sets forth what God has done for man's salvation, the Ethic would cover what man has to do and experience in being saved. Then there remains the teaching of Jesus according to St. John, which, as has been explained in the opening lecture, is a formation by itself demanding separate treatment. Some of my hearers, I have learned, were not satisfied with what I said in the first lecture about St.

John, supposing my statement to be unfavorable to the authenticity of the Fourth Gospel. This, however, was by no means my intention. Supremely as I prize the Synoptists, I feel, after reading them, that there is something still untold. They fail to account fully for the origin of so stupendous a movement as Christianity, in the same way as, after reading Xenophon's *Memorabilia*, one feels that something more requires to be told to make intelligible the influence of Socrates in the history of Greek thought. Whether the teaching of Jesus as recorded by St. John is idealized like that of Socrates in Plato's Dialogues, or in what other way the Teacher depicted in the Fourth Gospel is related to fact, I need not attempt here to define, because it will be seen, from the advertisement at the beginning of this volume, that I look forward to writing both on the Ethic of Jesus as unfolded in the Synoptists and on the Teaching of Jesus as recorded by St. John. But it is astonishing how St. John, after being so often proved to have had nothing to do with the divine picture of the Fourth Gospel, ever and anon reappears as its veritable producer and owner, and, after having had to endure the reproach of fantasticality and incompetence, is loaded again with admiration ad eulogy. There are enigmas in this Gospel which still await explanation, but the world will never rest in the belief either that this intimate record came from anyone but an apostle, or that the disciple whom Jesus loved can have distorted and falsified the image of his Master.

Though each of the three divisions of our Lord's teaching indicated above has its own difficulties, the one treated in this volume is the most difficult of all; for, whereas in expounding the Ethic of Jesus and His Teaching as recorded by St. John, we shall have prolonged and continuous statements to draw upon, here we are dependent on isolated sayings, scattered throughout the Gospels and frequently on this account difficult of interpretation. But it would be rash to draw the inference that, because the teaching of Jesus about Himself in the Synoptists is scanty and inconspicuous, it is, therefore, of subordinate importance. On the contrary, it is the salt of the whole.

Inside the flyleaf of each chapter I have given the entire evidence of texts for what follows; so that every reader may have the means of verifying for himself what is advanced.

When I first began to occupy myself with this subject, the helps were few, and I was thrown back upon the Gospels themselves. In recent years, as is explained in the first chapter, this has altered, and an extensive literature has accumulated, of which a fuller account will be found in this volume than anywhere else, as far as I am aware, in the English language. But, while I have profited by the labors of others, I have adhered principally to the biblical documents, and I hope my pages may still be redolent of the intense delight with which I first found out the actual testimony of Jesus to Himself.

The critical remarks in the first lecture are supplemented in the Appendix by a critical essay, reprinted from *The Expositor*, on the first volume of Wendt's *Lehre Jesu*; and I have to thank Messrs. Nisbet & Co. for permission to reproduce from *The Thinker* an essay on the book of Enoch.

Glasgow, 1899.

1

The Importance of
the Teaching of Jesus

THE present generation is under the impression that it has discovered the teaching of Jesus. It would be absurd, indeed, to speak as if our own age had been the first to appreciate the beauty and the power of our Lord's words; for since the Christian Church began, the sentences of the Sermon on the Mount have found a lodgment in the memory of Christendom more secure than any other words whatever; the Parables have never in any century failed to charm; and the Farewell Discourses in the Gospel of St. John have in every generation been the solace of the Christian heart in its most solemn moods. Nevertheless, in our own day our Lord's words have obtained a prominence never accorded to them before. We now separate them from the rest of Scripture, with which formerly they were indiscriminately mingled, and assign them a commanding authority. Their unique theological value is acknowledged. It is recognized, in short, that Jesus is the best teacher of His own religion.

This change is due to deep causes, to trace which thoroughly would be a long and arduous task.

Perhaps it may be best assigned to one of those mysterious movements in the depths of the human spirit which it is difficult to scrutinize and account for, but by which, under the guidance of Providence, one epoch is made to end and another to begin. Suddenly, you can hardly tell how or why, one way of thinking about things, which has long appeared to be the only possible way, becomes disused, and a new way becomes so easy and universal that people can hardly realize that things have not always been seen in this light. At the Reformation the Pauline mode of conceiving Christianity fitted into the necessities of experience; and the Christian mind rose up to take possession of its heritage as it is unfolded in the Pauline Epistles. The forms of truth there deposited are so priceless that it took long to bring them fully to light; the theological consciousness was aware of profiting by the robust efforts which it had to put forth in the process of acquisition; and so the predominance of this view of Christianity lasted long. But it could not last forever, because the Bible is rich enough to contain other ways of conceiving Christianity; and these were certain, some time or other, to get their turn. What Novalis says of Shakespeare—that in his works "the last and deepest of observers will still find new harmonies with the infinite structure of the universe, concurrences with later ideas, affinities with the higher powers and senses of man"—is far truer of the Bible. Humanity, under the training of history, is always being made ready to understand and appreciate some new portion of the Word of God, and some book or section of Scripture is big with a secret which it can only disclose to those providentially prepared for its reception. Everyone is aware how at present, in the Old Testament, the writings of the prophets, after being long neglected, are coming into such prominence that every young minister of ability is discoursing from them; and in the same way, in the New Testament, we are moving from the Epistles to the Gospels. Rabbi Duncan was one of those lofty and sensitive spirits which catch the first rays of an approaching time, and he foretold this change: "I have certainly," he said, "more of the Pauline Epistles than of the four Gospels in my nature; but, were I a younger man and to begin my studies again, the Gospels would bulk more prominently in my attention than they have done." As has been hinted, there is an overruling Providence in the matter: when the flock have long been in one section of the pasture and have nibbled it bare, the great Shepherd leads them into another, where the grass is lush and uncropped; and there they abide till the fields which they have left have had time to grow again.

It may only be another way of stating the same reason to say, secondly, that the recognition of the importance of the words of Jesus has been prepared for by the extraordinary attention bestowed in the present century on His life. At the Reformation it was on the work of

Christ that the thoughts of men were concentrated; and this long remained the supreme and ruling conception of theology. Ever and
anon, however, His person came into prominence; and in the present
century the most intense study has, owing to a variety of causes, been
directed upon the details of His earthly life. Archaeology, the explo-
ration of Palestine, the history of the century in which He was born,
and many other subsidiary sciences have been pressed into the service;
and the Son of man has been made to walk forth in breathing reality
before the eyes of men, who have eagerly followed every step of His
course from the manger to the cross. But under this close inspection of the records His words could not fail to attract attention. Accordingly everyone who wrote of His life expressed the hope to write
some day on His words likewise. At last the press begins to teem with
this new burden; and in the next fifty years the books on the teaching
of Jesus will probably be as numerous as in the last fifty have been those
on His life. Observers who watch closely the signs of the times in the
theological world are wont to keep an eye on the young Privatdo-
centen in the German universities. When these begin, as if by general
consent, to write on any topic, it may be taken for granted that this subject is in the air, and will be heard of everywhere before long. And of
late they have been taking, in full cry, to the teaching of Christ. The
first monograph on the subject which I remember came form the pen
of a French theologian, M. Meyer, in 1883;* then followed, at a considerable interval of time, *The Kingdom of God* of Dr. Bruce; then
Wendt's *Teaching of Jesus*;† but now it is scarcely possible to take up
a theological catalogue without seeing the announcement of one or
more monographs on the whole or on some special aspect of the
subject. And the demand in the public mind is equally keen; for
multitudes are saying, that they only need to know for certain what
Jesus believed in order to believe the same.

---

* *Le Christianisme du Christ,* dealing only with the words of Jesus recorded by St.
Matthew.
† Dr. Robertson's excellent handbook, in the Guild Series of the Church of Scotland, deserves special notice as the first popular presentation of the subject. See
also that of Dr. D. M. Ross.

Another cause which has stimulated interest in this subject has been the rise of Biblical Theology.* The old view of the Bible was that it is a unit, all its parts forming one glorious whole and conspiring to convey one divine message; and this view expresses an eternal truth. But it is also manifest that the Bible is a library of books, differing enormously as to age, style and contents. If they all convey one message, yet they severally embody different parts and aspects of it; and, if the unity of Scripture is a grand truth, its variety lies more obviously on the surface. To see how revelation grew from simplicity to complexity and how the germ unfolded into leaf, flower and fruit, is to follow the course of a spiritual romance; and it brings Biblical knowledge into line with the ideas of evolution so characteristic of our time in all the other departments of knowledge. In the New Testament we see how elementary conceptions of Christianity, in the Book of Acts and the Epistles of St. James and St. Peter, expand into the comprehensive and philosophical system of St. Paul, and how the development is crowned by the mystic views of St. John. But the question could not but be asked, Where do Christ's own views come in? They stand at the commencement of the volume in the Gospels, but is this their place in the development? Are they really overtopped and overshadowed by the teachings of the Apostles? This was virtually the place assigned them in the older handbooks of Biblical Theology. But, as time has gone one, they have been allowed more and more space, till in the latest specimen—the handbook of Holtzmann†—they obtain nearly half of the whole room to themselves. The question will undoubtedly force itself more and more to the front, Is the teaching of Jesus a rudimentary form of Christianity which the others transcend, or it is the perfect form, which they only supplement?

---

* This is the science which defines the circle of ideas belonging to each prominent writer of Scripture, or group of writers, and, by arranging these types of thought in chronological order, seeks to trace from stage to stage the growth of revelation.

† Since this was penned, Stevens' *Theology of the New Testament* has appeared; and all English-speaking people are to be congratulated on now having in their own tongue a treatise so able and trustworthy. Still later have appeared, in German, works by Schlatter, Feine, Weinel.

Whatever may be the answer given to this question, there can be no doubt that the tendency to attach supreme importance to the words of Christ is a healthy one. It is in accordance with the mind of Christ Himself; for He frequently spoke of His own words in terms the grandiosity of which it would be difficult to surpass. The very first lesson which a student of Christ's teaching should take is to collect the sayings of Jesus about His own words.

In the first place, He took a very high and unusual view of the value of words in general. There is nothing which to the ordinary man appears more trivial than a word. What is it? A breath converted into sound: out it goes on the air, and is carried away by the wind; and there is an end of it. No, said Jesus, it does not end there, and it does not end ever: when once it is called into existence by the creative force of the will, it becomes a living thing separated from our control; it goes ranging through time and space, doing good or evil; and it will confront us again at the last day—"Every idle word that men shall speak, they shall give account thereof at the day of judgment" (Matt. 12:36). At that solemn crisis the influence of our words on our destiny will be extraordinary; for "by the words thou shalt be justified and by thy words thou shalt be condemned" (Matt. 12:37). There is nothing of which the average man is more surely convinced than that his tongue is his own, and that he can at will make it utter words either good or evil. Very different was Christ's estimate: words are inevitable: if the speaker be good, then they are good, but, if he be evil, then they are inevitably evil: for as much control as he seems to have over them, he cannot alter their character unless he first alter his own; for "out of the abundance of the heart the mouth speaketh" (Matt. 12:34).

Such was Christ's conception of words; and such were His own words: they were the overflowings of his heart, an effluence from His character, bits of Himself. No wonder if virtue resided in them. Poets and thinkers have sometimes boasted, half in jest, that their words would survive the most permanent works of man—pyramids of kings and monuments of brass—but Jesus declared, in sober earnest, that His would outlive the most stable works of God—"Heaven and earth shall pass away, but My words shall not pass away" (Luke 21:33).

He spoke of the attachment to His words as attachment to Himself, and as the test of discipleship—"If ye continue in My word, then are ye My disciples indeed, and ye shall know the truth, and the truth shall make you free"; "If a man love Me, he will keep My words, and My Father will love him; and We will come unto him and make Our abode with him. He that loveth Me not keepeth not My sayings; and the word which ye hear is not Mine, but the Father's who sent Me" (John 8:31; 14:23, 24). When Mary was seated at His feet listening to His words, He declared that she was doing the one thing needful (Luke 10:42).

He attributed to His words the power of regenerating and sanctifying the soul—"Now ye are clean through the word that I have spoken unto you"; "The words that I speak unto you, they are spirit and they are life"; "Verily, verily, I say unto you, if a man keep My sayings, he shall never see death." And those who first heard His words confirmed out of their own experience the justice of these claims, when St. Peter said in their name, "Lord, to whom can we go? Thou hast the words of eternal life"; (John 15:3; 8:51; 6:68).

It was only the logical consequence of this when Jesus alleged, that the eternal destiny of His hearers would depend on the attitude they assumed to His words—"He that rejecteth Me and receiveth not My words hath one that judgeth him: the word that I have spoken, the same shall judge him at the last day" (John 12:48). He wound up the Sermon on the Mount with the well-known imagery of incomparable solemnity: "Therefore whosoever heareth these sayings of Mine, and doeth them, I will liken him unto a wise man, which built his house upon a rock: and the rain descended, and the floods came, and the winds blew, and beat upon that house: and it fell not: for it was founded upon a rock. And every one that heareth these sayings of Mine, and doeth them not, shall be likened unto a foolish man, which built his house upon the sand: and the rain descended, and the floods came, and the winds blew, and beat upon that house; and it fell: and great was the fall of it" (Matt. 7:24–27).

I have considered it worth while to quote all these sayings in detail because they show not only how high was the estimate placed by Jesus on His own words, but how frequent a theme of thought and speech this was with Him. He claimed for Himself as a teacher a position far above all who had preceded Him, when He said to His hearers that many prophets and kings had desired in vain to hear the things which they were blessed enough to be hearing from His lips; and still more decisively did He place Himself above all who should come after Him, when He said, "Be not ye called Rabbi, for One is your teacher; and all ye are brethren" (Matt. 23:8; "even Christ" is unauthentic). There could not be a more emphatic warning against placing the apostles on the same level as the Master.

From the point of view of the old doctrine of inspiration an objection might be raised: indeed, I have heard it said, "Why should the words of Jesus be considered more important than the rest of the Bible? All the Scriptures are utterances of God, and what more are the words of Christ?" But even from the old point of view this objection can be met with a decisive answer. It is true that in one sense all sections of Scripture are equally important because they are parts of a whole which would be mutilated, if any of its constituent parts, even the smallest, were absent. In the same sense the smallest joint of the smallest finger is as important in the human body as the head, because it is essential to the perfection of the whole. But manifestly there is another sense in which a finger is by no means as important as the head. The members of the body differ in dignity, the eye being a far more glorious member than the ear, and the majesty of manhood far more fully exhibited in the face than in the foot. In a similar sense some portions of Scripture may be spoken of as more important and glorious than others. This has never been questioned by even the strictest orthodoxy. The nature of God is more fully revealed in the pages of Isaiah than in the lines of Nahum; and no one would think of comparing the message of St. James for glory with that of St. Paul. When God made use of inspired men, He did not destroy their individuality or make them all speak in the same strain, but, like one laying on instruments of different shapes and sizes, He transmitted one element of revelation through one and another through another. He let the light of the knowledge of His glory shine through a great variety of media, but some of these were larger and more transparent than others, and let more of the light of revelation through. If this is recognized, it is impossible to deny a unique value to the words of Jesus; for of all the media ever employed by God for purposes of revelation none can be compared to Him: in no other mind did the spirit of revelation obtain such ample room, and never, either before or after, did it find such perfect channels of outlet as through His organs of thought and speech. This is the very least that must be conceded from even the most orthodox point of view; and it is enough to place the words of Jesus above all human words—even those of revelation.

By some this contrast, however, is carried much further, and it is proposed to convert the teaching of Christ into a standard with which to criticize and to correct the rest of Scripture. Formerly the whole Bible was looked upon as a single authority, but first the Old Testament was dropped and the New adopted as the sole authority; and now the narrowing process is carried further: not the New Testament as a whole, it is contended, is the authority, but the teaching of Christ alone; and some go so far as to draw a circle of exclusion even inside the teaching of Christ, maintaining that the Sermon on the Mount is an ample norm both of faith and practice. This is the position taken up by Dr. John Watson in *The Mind of the Master*. "The religion of Protestants," he says, "or let us say Christians, is not the Bible in all its parts but first of all that portion which is its soul, by which the teaching of Prophets and Apostles must itself be judged—the very words of Jesus"; and he goes on to argue that even of the words of Jesus those contained in the Sermon on the Mount are sufficient.

To suggestions of this sort the reply has often been given, that Jesus expressly intimated at His departure that He had not been able to utter all He had to say, but would find means of conveying it to His Church after He was gone; and that the teaching of inspired apostles was the virtual continuation of His own: "I have yet many things to say unto you, but ye cannot bear them now; howbeit, when He, the Spirit of truth, is come, He shall guide you into all truth; for He shall not speak of Himself; but whatsoever He shall hear that shall He speak; and He will show you things to come; He shall glorify me; for He shall receive of Mine, and shall show it unto you" (John 16:12–15). For one thing, the resurrection and ascension of our Lord entirely altered the point of view. As long as He was on earth, He had perforce to speak from the level of the earth, the minds of the disciples obstinately refusing to take the hint of anything higher, but, after He had risen and ascended, He was to all who believed in Him the Lord of glory; and it is from this point of view that the latter half of the New Testament is written. It is especially contended that within the very extensive promise of illumination quoted above, the full truth about His own death was included, because it was impossible, or at least unnatural, that He should speak fully about this event before it had taken place, and before the minds of the disciples were opened to credit it. Even if Jesus had spoken fully on this subject from His own point of view—that is, the point of view of the Giver of salvation—it would still have been necessary that it should be fully and authoritatively explained from the opposite point of view—that of the receivers of salvation. Jesus might speak of salvation, but He was never Himself saved; and there would have been an intolerable blank in the Bible had not inspired men, when the forces of salvation, in their first freshness, were doing their work in their soul and life, committed their experience to the pages of Holy Writ. This is the value of the writings of St. Paul, St. John and St. Peter, who tell what Christ was to themselves as Savior and Lord.

A still weightier argument is, that Christ Himself is more than His words. Stier, the commentator on our Lord's sayings, calls them "the words of the Word"—a most suggestive title, because it reminds us that Christ Himself is the great and final Word of God, of which His detailed words are only fragments. Even all of these in combination are not equal to Him; for there are other words of the Word: His earthly history, His miracles and His sufferings are all words of the Word, on a level with His spoken words. His association with publicans and sinners was no less significant than were the parables of St. Luke 15; His weeping over Jerusalem was more eloquent than anything He said on patriotism; His sufferings and death were far more suggestive than anything He ever said about sin. We are wont in modern thought to draw a distinction between revelation and inspiration—revelation being the grand, primary fact in God's relation to men, whereas inspiration is subsidiary and ministerial. Revelation did not take place, as the old orthodoxy assumed, through whispers of truth communicated to the prophets, but through the institutions, the events and the personages of a divine history; and inspiration was the power of interpreting this history and putting its meaning into words. Now, that which was perfected in Christ was the revelation: in Him the divine history culminated and the divine love was fully disclosed. It may no doubt be argued that the inspiration culminated in Him likewise, and was adequate to the revelation. But at all events even His inspiration did not exhaust the revelation embodied in Himself, which invited the attention of other inspired personalities, to interpret it from the point of view of their own experience. And this is the reason why, instead of merely collecting His words and commenting on them, the apostles go straight themselves to the revelation made in Christ and give it an original interpretation out of the fullness of their own experience.

There is a double objection to the exaggerated way of putting the matter on which I am commenting. First, it tempts to disparage St. Paul and the other New Testament writers in order to exalt Christ. This temptation Dr. Watson has not escaped. "If," he says, "one may be pardoned his presumption in hinting at any imperfections in the Apostle of the Gentiles, is not his style at times overwrought by feeling? Is not his doctrine often rabbinical, rather than Christian? Does not one feel his treatment of certain subjects—say marriage and asceticism—to be somewhat wanting in sweetness?" In the fancied interest of Jesus, it is not uncommon at present to hit in this style at inspired men. But would Jesus accept such championship? The truth is, Jesus Himself could be criticized in this tone to His disparagement. And this is the other side of the objection: it tempts those who vindicate the apostles to depreciate Jesus, or at least to put Him in the background. "The specifically Christian consciousness," it is argued, "which has to be scientifically developed by the theologian, is not the consciousness of Jesus, it is the consciousness of reconciliation to God through Jesus";* and the teaching of Jesus, being thus, by means of an ingenious def-

---

* These words are from Dr. Denney's Inaugural Lecture on Dogmatic Theology (published in *The Expositor*, December, 1897); perhaps, however, it is scarcely fair to criticize thus a mere *obiter dictum*.

inition of theology, excluded from the immediate materials of the theologian, no specific place is assigned to it at all.

Of course, the decisive question is, whether St. Paul and the other apostolic writers are at variance with their Master. If they are, then undoubtedly they must go to the wall; and Dr. Watson is quite justified when he contends that St. Paul must be read in the light of Christ rather than Christ in the light of St. Paul. Only he and others are constantly taking it for granted that St. Paul cannot stand this test, but that a considerable portion of the apostolic teaching must be cast aside as inconsistent with that of Jesus, although Dr. Watson himself is vague and meager in the extreme, when he comes to particulars. There can be no question that Jesus abolishes a great deal of Moses; for He does so in express terms, but it is gratuitous to assume that He would have done the same to St. Paul. Even in the Synoptists the germs are to found of all that the Epistles contain; and, if St. John be taken into account, the Christian theologian may without hesitation undertake to prove the substantial identity of the teaching of the Master and that of the disciples, He speaking from the point of view of the Savior and they from that of the saved.[*]

I have spoken of the importance of the words of Jesus in themselves, and of their comparative importance when contrasted with the apostolic writings, but I should like to add something about their importance in relation to dogma.

Dr. Watson speaks as if the words of Jesus were the long neglected but rich source of dogmas, where anyone can lay his hand on them, as on the eggs in a discovered nest, and find his creed made-and-ready. In fact, he gathers a creed from them, in half-a-dozen lines, and says that, if only a church could be found to adopt it, men would come from the north and the south, the east and the west, to press into its membership. Experiments have not, however, been wanting to found churches on very abbreviated creeds. Their success has not been conspicuous. And it may be doubted whether articles of belief thus found made-and-ready would be of much utility, whatever might be

---

[*] Compare the preface to the new edition of Dr. Robertson Nicoll's *The Incarnate Savior.*

their origin—even if it were in the words of Jesus. I have found, in preaching, that to tell people how little Abraham believed or what were the precise limits of Isaiah's theology does not affect them much; and that merely to expound a doctrine as having been that of St. Paul or even that of Jesus does not make much impression. Herein lies perhaps the weakness of all Biblical theology, which to a student is in many ways so fascinating: it is apt to become a mere branch of archaeology; whereas the truth which affects the human mind is that which has on it a streak of warm blood. Personal conviction is the soul of religious testimony.*

But, besides, when we go to the words of Jesus for the articles of a creed, is not this to mistake the genus to which these words belong? The difference between religion and theology may be hard to define, but it is not hard to feel; and surely the words of Christ belong not to theology but to religion. They are *kerygma*, not dogma; nature, not science. Rothe denies that there are any dogmas in the Bible;† and perhaps he is right. Many parts, indeed, of the writings of St. Paul approach pretty near to the dogmatic type; yet even they are perhaps best considered as kerygma—warm outbursts of emotion and experience—rather than scientific theology. At all events the words of Jesus are at the opposite pole from scientific statements. Who has not not felt the transition from a confession of faith or a dogmatic treatise to the Parables and the Sermon on the Mount? It is like the change from the atmosphere of a library to the open air, or from a museum, stuffed with skeletons and specimens, into a fair garden, where the flowers are in bloom and the dew of the morning is glistening on every blade of grass.

A strong corroboration of this view may be found in the form in which Jesus left His words. He did not write them down Himself, but entrusted them to the memory of His disciples, although these were

---

* What underlies my friend Dr. Watson's argument, which I have ventured to criticize so freely, is the perfectly just perception, that the teaching of Jesus is so predominantly ethical, and that theology has done no sort of justice to the Ethics of Jesus.

† "I am not disputing that there is religious teaching in the Bible, but I do dispute that the religious teaching in the Bible has already the quality which raises it to the level of a dogma"—*Zur Dogmatik*, p. 18.

not men of literary culture. This was not because He was indifferent on the subject. On the contrary, never has there lived a son of Adam to whom it has been so imperative a necessity to be remembered after death; and He took the most elaborate and farsighted measures to secure this end. But His anxiety was not that of the professor, who dictates the *ipsissima verba* of his paragraphs, or of the jurist, who inscribes his decrees on tables of stone. He could trust the memory even of humble men, supplemented, as He knew it would be, by the living epistle of their life.

There is a widespread desire among theologians at present to find at least the organizing idea of the theological system in the teaching of Christ. Thus in Ritschl's small handbook of Christian Instruction the Kingdom of God is the organizing idea, and this is a favorite notion of the whole Ritschlian school. But although Jesus published His Gospel under the form of a doctrine of the Kingdom of God, it may be doubted whether He did this strictly on His own motion or rather under stress of circumstances, adapting His teaching to the modes of thinking current in His time. Principal Fairbairn takes the Fatherhood of God to be the center of Christ's teaching and proposes to make it the center of theology;* and this is a proceeding which falls in with the tendencies of the modern mind. But, like the Kingdom of God, the Fatherhood of God is a figure of speech of extremely uncertain application, even in the teaching of Christ sometimes describing the relation of all men to God and at other times the peculiar relation of believers. Other great ideas might be lifted from Christ's teaching and made the ruling conceptions of theology. There is Righteousness, for example, which is certainly the ruling idea of the Sermon on the Mount;† and I have been much interested in a work on the teaching of Jesus by Titius,** one of the younger German writers, who proposes to investigate not it only, but the whole teaching of the New Testament, from the standpoint of Blessedness—to my mind a most central and comprehensive idea. Of course all such

---

* In *Christ in Modern Theology.*
† Dante said it was the theme of *The Divine Comedy.*
** *Die N.T. Lehre von der Seligkeit. Erster Theil: Jesu Lehre vom Reiche Gottes.* 1895.

proposals might be tested by their success, when the attempt is actually made to organize by their means the whole mass of theological material, but, if the attempt be successful, this will be due, I venture to think, not to the idea being that of Jesus, but to its being that of the thinker himself.

This desire to find dogmas ready-made in the teaching of Jesus, or at least to borrow from Him the organizing conception of theology, savors too much of the old notion that the Bible is a vast collection of proof-texts, and that the work of dogmatic theology is merely to arrange and systematize them. Dogmatic theology is not, indeed, at present very sure of its own definition, but at all events, since Schleiermacher, it is pretty certain that it has a close relation to Christian experience. Some would define it merely as the science of dogmas, and restrict the material with which it has to deal to the creed of the church to which the theologian belongs; others would make its material to consist rather of the living faith of the Church — that is, of the dogmas modified by opinion — while others still would emphasize most strongly the Christian experience of the dogmatist himself. But at all events dogma is more than the mere datum of Scripture: it is this taken up into the mind of the Church in combination with all the knowledge of which it may at any stage be possessed and viewed under the providential light shining at the time. It is not a mere report by the Church to the world that such-and-such a statement was made by Isaiah or Moses, by St. Paul or Jesus, and, therefore, must be true, but it is an affirmation by the Church of its own present conviction: "I know and declare this to be true, not merely because the Bible says it, but because I have experienced it, and because it is at this moment throbbing in my heart as the power of God unto salvation."

The old view was, that a perfect theology could only have one form, and that the organizing idea must be either the right or the wrong one. But does not the whole history of theology prove that the intention of nature is different? The form is continually changing; and new organizing ideas emerge with every new generation, every spiritual movement, and every original thinker. Even the individual, if his religion be progressive, does not see truth always from the same point of view. John Bunyan's experience is normal in this respect; who, in

Grace Abounding,* tells, that, preaching ever what he saw and felt, he moved every two years or so from one standpoint to another, being now absorbed with the curse and doom of sin, then with the offices of Christ, and again with union to Christ. So the Church at large, if its mind is not stagnating, must quit one point of view and move on to another. This is because its own historical position is shifting. While Scripture is meant to explain all the changing aspects of providence, providence, on the other hand, likewise casts on Scripture an ever-changing light. The organizing thought of theology is with one thinker the Sovereignty of God, with another Justification by Faith, but, if the Church is progressing instead of stagnating, it will neither be the one nor the other forever. In our day the best ruling idea may possibly be the Kingdom of God or the Fatherhood of God, but, if so, it will be, not because this was the supreme conception of Jesus, but because it is the thought which corresponds most intimately to the knowledge and the temper of the age.

The use of Scripture, and especially of the Words of Jesus, is not to supersede the spiritual and intellectual processes of the Church's life by supplying her with dogmas ready-made, but to give stimulus and direction to these processes. The Scriptures have the same relation to the thinking and testimony of the Church as the influences of the atmosphere have to the products of the soil. Let the mind of the Church be continually refreshed with the Law, the Prophets and the Psalms, with the Epistles of St. Paul, the Writings of St. John, and, above all, the Words of Jesus, and it will think both copiously and correctly, but let it cease to absorb into its experience these divine oracles, or let it deal with them carelessly and deceitfully, and its thinking, as well as the other manifestations of spiritual life, will suffer. Thus there is always an appeal from the teaching of the Church to the truth as it is in Jesus, and the Scripture is always above the Church, but not in the sense of a creed or a doctrinal system. The Scripture is like the rain from heaven, without the continual soaking of which through the soil the rivers, lakes and reservoirs would soon dry up and every green thing perish from the face of the earth. And this shows what should be

---

* Pars. 276 to 278.

the aim of a revival of the teaching of Jesus—not to set up a creed of Christ in opposition to the creeds of the churches, which would simply be to revive in the twentieth century the arrogance of those who in the first said at Corinth, "We are of Christ," but to facilitate such a saturation of the Christian mind with the words and the spirit of the Author of Christianity that from the soil, thus nourished, all forms of good thinking as well as all manner of good living may spontaneously spring.

It will be observed that, in this course of lectures, I propose to derive the teaching of Jesus from the Synoptical Gospels, to the exclusion of St. John. One reason for this is the present state of criticism. At one time the Gospel of St. John—the pneumatic gospel, as it was called, or gospel of religious genius—enjoyed singular favor among the most advanced critics, who declared, that in it, if anywhere, was to be found the authentic portrait of Jesus: but at present the pendulum has swung to the opposite extreme, and this gospel is spoken of in terms of great dubiety, if not of condemnation; and in these circumstances, whatever one may think of the merits of the case, it is advisable to adduce the evidence for the teaching of Jesus concerning Himself from the two sources separately. There is, besides, another reason which to my mind is still more cogent: the Gospel of St. John is a work of unique character, in which the shape given even to the teaching of Jesus is due to the peculiarities of the Evangelist; and the whole hangs together so compactly that the parts cannot without some violence be separated from the whole, in order to supplement the outline of the Synoptists. In short, the system of the thoughts of Jesus, as it is presented in St. John, ought always to be developed from its own center. Dr. Wendt, the author of the most important monograph which has yet appeared on the teaching of Jesus, does not follow this course, but gives, under each leading article, first the account supplied by the Synoptists and then the corresponding section from St. John. This is extremely interesting; in fact, it is the most striking feature of Dr. Wendt's performance; and many readers must have been astonished at the identity of thought which he has often been able to demonstrate as existing beneath both the plain language of the Synoptists and the mystic phraseology of the Fourth Evangelist. Yet it must also have been felt that this method scarcely does justice to St. John, whose ideas are torn from their natural connection and not infrequently somewhat distorted in the process.

We have not, however, done with critical questions when we leave St. John out, but, on the contrary, are face to face with the Synoptic Problem, the most perplexing of literary riddles. It is known how interminable has been the controversy about the order of the first three Evangelists and their relation to one another, but it seems to me that those who have contended for the priority of one or another have seldom taken sufficient time to consider what is the precise value of priority, even if it could be made out. As a rule, it is taken for granted that priority must necessarily imply superiority, but to a student of the words as distinguished from the acts of Jesus this must appear a doubtful proposition. Suppose three authors of our own time were to write memoirs of a life belonging to about the middle of the century, would the one who wrote in 1880 have a very great advantage over the one who wrote in 1890, or he over the one who wrote in 1900? Might not any such advantage be far outweighed by superior ability or access to special information? I do not pretend that the cases are exactly parallel, but, on the other hand, I do not know that there is any very great difference, unless we are to assume that in the Christian circles of the first century there was at work a strong mythopoetic propensity, which was engaged in adorning with legendary marvels the memory of Jesus. The distance between St. Mark and St. Matthew, or St. Matthew and St. Luke, is so inconsiderable that the question of priority is of only secondary importance.* Far more worthy of notice are the evidences which the contents of these books themselves supply of special aptitude for investigation or presentation. St. Mark, to whom the priority in time is now generally conceded, has seemed to many to possess a remarkable gift for indicating the movement and energy of the life of Jesus, together with the sequence and articulation of its periods; and through his rough, hasty and graphic sketches there is conveyed an image of the facts which carries on its face the signature of veracity. But St. Mark

---

* The dates given by Harnack in his great work on Christology are — St. Mark 65–85, St. Matthew 70–75, St. Luke 78–93.

has no such gift for rendering the words of Jesus. This belongs to St. Matthew, who inspires me, as a student during many years of the words of Jesus, with the same enthusiasm as students of the events feel for St. Mark. Evidently St. Matthew had a passion for the words, and he diligently searched them out. They were treasured in his mind, where they arranged themselves in the pregnant forms in which he has reproduced them. For he does not render them in chronological order, but in groups, as a goldsmith arranges gems in such settings that one precious stone is set off by another. The supreme instance of this is the Sermon on the Mount, but only less conspicuous are the parables grouped together in chapter 13, the succession of sayings on Offenses in chapter 18, and the discourses on the Last Things in chapters 24 and 25. St. Matthew has penetrated down through the original sayings to the spirit moving beneath them all, and everywhere in his record we feel the height, the wisdom and the subtlety of the mind of Him who spoke as never man spoke. In the Gospel of St. Luke, as a whole, I feel more of the atmosphere of a later time;[*] yet how little the faithfulness of his reporting has been impaired by greater distance from the events may be realized by recalling the parables which we owe to him alone, such as the Good Samaritan and the Prodigal Son.

Of course it would be different if we could get back much nearer to the life of Jesus than the date of the Synoptic Gospels; and at this problem scholarship is laboring at the present time with astonishing enterprise. It is believed that the words of Jesus were the first memorials of Him which His followers collected in written form, and that there existed such a collection from the pen of the Apostle Matthew, upon which the authors of the canonical St. Matthew and St. Luke, and possibly St. Mark, drew in compiling their gospels. By the close scrutiny of the Gospels as we now have them, and especially by gathering together the common element which they exhibit, it has been recently attempted to reproduce this assumed document.[†] In a criti-

---

[*] A striking illustration of this is the frequent occurrence of "the Lord" as a name for Jesus.

[†] Besides the works described in the following sentences, mention should be made also of *The Apostolic Gospel,* by J. Fulton Blair, B.D., 1896; also, Harnack, *Sprüche und Reden Jesu.*

cal volume published by Dr. Wendt before his work on the Teaching of Jesus which has been has been translated into English, this original St. Matthew is printed verse by verse in Greek. Another German scholar, Dr. Resch, well known for his profound studies on the forms in which the words of Jesus appear in the earliest postcanonical literature, has gone further: holding that the original St. Matthew contained, besides discourses, an element of narrative, he has reproduced narrative and *logia* together; and, since Papias, to whose information the idea of the original St. Matthew is due, says that it was written in Hebrew, he has supplied a Hebrew rendering of his own in addition to the Greek.* Finally, Dr. Dalman, an eminent Aramaic scholar, in the first volume, just published, of a work on the Words of Jesus, maintains that the Hebrew of the original St. Matthew was really Aramaic; although he does not propose to retranslate back into that language, but only to make constant use of Aramaic, which he believes to have been the tongue in which Jesus spoke, in order to throw light on the sayings in general and in detail.†

The attempt, not only to prove the existence of a written gospel earlier than the canonical Gospels, but actually to reconstruct the document, must be felt to be of profound interest. Dr. Resch believes that we are thus carried back to a date not later perhaps than four years after the death of Jesus, when, he supposes, St. Matthew committed his recollections to writing, if he did not actually keep notes of his Master's utterances from day to day; though of course this is only the conjecture of a sanguine specialist. It would be gratifying to learn that any of our Lord's words or acts could be traced back, in written records, so near to the confines of His actual life. But the use made of the results thus obtained falls in rather with German ideas than with ours; for it is proposed to employ this gospel above the Gospels as a standard by which to try the other contents of the canonical Gospels. German

---

* *Die Logia Jesu*, 1898. The author holds that the Hebrew, as the sacred and literary language, would in any case have been employed for such a purpose.
† *Die Worte Jesu*, 1898. The impression left on my mind by the arguments of Dalman, who speaks with great contempt of the knowledge of Aramaic possessed by his predecessors, is that there do not exist sufficient remains of the language or dialect spoken by Jesus to make it possible to determine with any great amount of certainty the actual vocables he used.

scholarship, even of a comparatively orthodox type, takes quite naturally to the idea, that even among our Lord's words there must be distinctions made between those the authenticity of which is of first rank and others belonging to a secondary or tertiary formation, in which His actual sentiments are compounded with later elements caught from the atmosphere of the apostolic age. Indeed, a German theologian is never quite happy unless, in dealing with a book of Scripture, he is making use of one portion to test, and generally more or less to invalidate, the rest. In this country scholarship is more modest: we at least keep open the possibility that the application of the test may justify all the sayings. We are not unfamiliar, indeed, even in this country, with the fact that for reasons of edification an evangelist may have omitted words in his possession, and I have already referred to the influence of St. John's genius on his reporting; there may be modifications due to other causes of like kind, but it does not seem to me reasonable to suppose that a first sketch such as is attributed to St. Matthew would contain all that was vital in our Lord's teaching; and I prefer to start with the presupposition that all the sayings are authentic till strong evidence is forthcoming to the contrary.

No other words ever uttered possess in the same degree the power of self-authentication. As a painter of the highest genius, like Raphael or Rubens, has a style of his own by which his work may be recognized, so the words of Jesus are full of peculiarities by which they can be identified.

One of their prominent characteristics is Pregnancy. No other speaker ever put so much into few words. Yet the matter is not too closely packed: all is simple, limpid, musical. This virtue was studied in the rabbinical schools, and it was realized in a high degree in the Wisdom Literature of the Old Testament, where, it may not be irreverent to suppose, Jesus admired and studied it. But in His case it was chiefly due to the cast and habit of His own mind. It is when truth has been long and thoroughly pondered that it embodies itself in brief and memorable language, as it is the ore thoroughly smelted which flows out in an uninterrupted stream and crystallizes in perfect shapes; and such intense and convinced thought was so habitual to Jesus that the most striking sayings were often coined by Him on the spur of the moment, as when He said in controversy, "Render unto Caesar the things which are Caesar's, and unto God the things which are God's." Sentences of this kind stick like goads and nails. No other words have adhered as those of Jesus to the memory of mankind. Let almost any of His sayings be commenced, and the ordinary hearer can without difficulty finish the sentence. But, if we can retain them so easily since they have been written, the first hearers could remember them as easily before they were written.

Another very prominent characteristic is Imaginativeness. The style of Jesus is intensely figurative. He never says, "You ought to exert a good influence on your fellow creatures," but "Ye are the salt of the earth; ye are the light of the world"; never, "All events are ordered by Providence," but, "Are not two sparrows sold for a farthing? Yet one of them shall not fall to the ground without your Father." Never abstract statements or general terms, but always pictures, full of life, movement and color! Of course the use of imagery was a feature of the sacred books He studied. In many a verse, for example, of the Book of Proverbs a moral truth is embodied in a picture borrowed from the realm of nature; and, indeed, the Hebrew word for a proverb means a simile. The psalmists and the prophets have a grasp of nature such as can be found in no other ancient literature. But, whatever influence Jesus may have derived from this quarter, the peculiarity of His language was due, in the fullest sense, to Himself—to His insight into the secret of beauty, His sympathy with every aspect of human life, and His perception of the play of natural law in the spiritual world. It is frequently said that the use of parables is common in the rabbinical schools, as, indeed, it is native to the Oriental mind, but the specimens produced from Indian and Jewish sources only illustrate the perfection of His by contrast; and, although His have been so long before the world, they have never been imitated with even tolerable success. The early Christians have not infrequently been credited with inventing the miracles, but the man would only betray his own intellectual and literary incapacity who ventured to say that they invented the parables.[*]

---

[*] Just and choice remarks on what may be called the Style of Jesus will be found in Wendt's *Teaching of Christ* and Holtzmann's *N. T. Theologie*; also in Jülicher's introductory volume on the Parables. The latter work is a powerful   [continued]

These characteristics, however, are only external; and far more significant are those which concern not the form but the substance of His teaching, such as the sublimity and simplicity of His conception of God, which answers perfectly to the idea sunk at creation in the texture of human nature, and His conception of man, which ennobles while it humbles, at once dwarfing all human attainment and yet opening up boundless vistas of progress. In all great teaching the speaker is more than the word spoken; and this is preeminently true of the teachings of Jesus. Behind the qualities of the words we divine a personality in which they are all united—a personality serene and harmonious, solid and firm at the center and yet shading off at the circumference into the most ethereal nuances of beauty, revealing God so perfectly because of its perfect union with God, and appealing to all that is great and tender in man because of the comprehensiveness of its own human experience.

By characteristics such as these the words of Jesus authenticate themselves; and I am not without the expectation that there may yet be founded on them a powerful apology even for His miracles, because the words are inextricably mixed up with the acts—words so original and characteristic that they must have been His, and, at the same time, so obviously occasioned by the miracles, in the midst of which they stand, that the latter must have been actual also. At all events the words support and vindicate one another; for they bear the stamp of the same incomparable mind, and the study of them as a whole will make it increasingly evident that they form the constituent elements of one harmonious circle of truth.*

---

plea for what is now the recognized method of interpreting the parables—illustration and truth being regarded not as two flat plates, meeting at every point, but as a sphere resting on a plate and touching it at a single point. But the correct theory is carried too far. Jesus Himself uses the word "parable" loosely for any figure of speech, and was probably unconscious of the literary structure of His illustrations. Jülicher writes as if He had never taken His eye off a rhetorical model.

* This brief discussion of the sources is supplemented in Appendix A.

PASSAGES IN WHICH "THE SON OF MAN" IS MENTIONED:
Matthew 8:20; 9:6; 10:23; 11:19; 12:8, 32, 40; 13:37, 41; 16:13, 27, 28; 17:9, 12, 22; [18:11]; 19:28; 20:18, 28; 24:27, 30, 37, 39, 44; 25:[13], 31; 26:2, 24, 45, 64.
Mark 2:10, 28; 8:31, 38; 9:9, 12, 31; 10:33, 45; 13:26, [34], 14:21, 41, 62.
Luke 5:24; 6:5, 22; 7:34; 9:22, 26, 44, [56], 58; 11:30; 12:8, 10, 40; 17:22, 24, 26, 30; 18:8, 31; 19:10; 21:27, 36; 22:22, 48, 69; 24:7.
The square brackets indicate interpolations.

2
The Son of Man

THE name by which Jesus most frequently designated Himself was "the Son of Man," which occurs in St. Matthew thirty-two times, in St. mark fifteen times, in St. Luke twenty-five times, and in St. John twelve times.

How did Jesus come to designate Himself in tnis way?

He never either defines the title or mentions where He found it; so that we have to ascertain its origin and significance for ourselves by examining His mode of using it. This proves to be a difficult inquiry, which has given rise to extraordinary diversity of opinion. A laborious German, writing on the subject, has recently collected a perfectly bewildering enumeration of the different meanings assigned to the term by different writers.[*]

The supposition which would most naturally occur to the unsophisticated mind is that He invented the term Himself. If this was His favorite self-designation, it must, one would suppose, express what was most prominent in His consciousness of Himself, and He must have carefully constructed a phrase to express His own conception; in which case the way for us to arrive at the meaning would be to analyze the words themselves. In sound the title seems to be a most appropriate expression for the human side of His person; and in this sense it has been understood by Christendom. The Greek and Latin Fathers, from Irenaeus downwards, thus employ it; and at the present day probably ninety-nine out of every hundred Christians do the same. To the average man it is a designation for the human side of our Lord's

---

[*] Appel, *Die Selbstbezeichnung Jesu: Der Menschensohn*, 1896. Though rather bewildering, the conspectus of opinions is most interesting.

person, as "the Son of God" is for the divine; and these two phrases, complementing each other, define the God-man.

Merely to read over, however, a continuous list of the passages in which the name occurs will shake anyone's faith in the correctness of this assumption because it will at once be felt that the statements made about "the Son of man" are anything but characteristic predicates of humanity. How, for example, does this assumption harmonize with a saying like the following: "And no man hath ascended up to heaven, but He that came down from heaven, even the Son of man, which is in heaven"; or with this, "When the Son of man shall come in His glory, and all the holy angels with Him, then shall He sit upon the throne of His glory, and before Him shall be gathered all nations, and He shall separate them one from another, as a shepherd divides the sheep from the goats, and He shall set the sheep on His right hand, but the goats on the left"? Many more sayings of a similar strain might be quoted in which things are predicated about "the Son of man," which are the reverse of simply human. This has never escaped the observation of those who have actually looked at the facts; and as early as Origen we find the hermeneutical principle laid down, that throughout the Scripture the divine nature of Christ is mentioned with human characteristics and the human nature adorned with divine attributes. *

In modern times the belief that this title refers primarily to the humanity of our Lord has been represented by many famous names and from different points of view, without its being held, however, that Jesus Himself invented it. Thus Neander interprets it as the ideal man; and he has had a multitude of followers. His beautiful words are well worthy of quotation: "Jesus thus names Himself as belonging to mankind—as one who in human nature has accomplished such great things for human nature—who is man, in the supreme sense, the sense corresponding to the idea—who makes real the ideal of humanity." He supports this definition by reference to such passages as St. Matthew 9:6, where it is said that to the Son of man is given the power on earth to forgive sins; and 12:8: "The Son of man is Lord even

---

* The remark is a common one in subsequent Fathers.

of the Sabbath day."* Others have supposed the view of humanity which the title expresses to be from beneath rather than above — from the side of weakness and lowliness rather than of dignity. This was the view of Baur, and he has had many supporters. "Jesus," he says, "designates Himself by this term as one who is man, with all the attributes which belong to human nature . . . one who takes His share in all that is human, *qui nikil humani a se alienum putat.*" In support of this view he appeals especially to St. Matthew 8:20: "Foxes have holes, and the birds of the air have nests, but the Son of man hath not where to lay His head," which he thus paraphrases, "A child of man, like Me, must endure the very lowest which belongs to the lot of any man."†

One circumstance which might make it doubtful to an observant reader of the Bible whether Jesus invented this phrase Himself is, that it occurs frequently in the Old Testament. Everyone is aware how steeped the mind of Jesus was in biblical phraseology, and, therefore, the suggestion is not unlikely, that He may have adopted this name from one or other of the Old Testament passages in which it is found.

The most famous of these is in the eighth Psalm:

> When I consider Thy heavens, the work of Thy fingers,
> The moon and the stars, which Thou hast ordained;
> What is man, that Thou art mindful of him,
> And the son of man, that Thou visitest him?

Here "man" and "the son of man" are obviously synonyms; and the whole psalm is an incomparable utterance on human nature, bringing out both its lowliness and its loftiness. When contrasted with God, man is nothing: it is a marvel that the Creator of the moon and the stars should condescend to look upon him. Yet, regarded from a different point of view — as a favorite among God's creatures — this being, insignificant in himself, is crowned with glory and honor; he is but a little lower than the divine; and to him has been committed the empire

---

* Also St. John 1:32; 2:13; 5:27; 6:53. —*Leben Jesu*, p. 117.
† *N. T. Theologie*, pp. 80, 81.

over the rest of the creatures, which the psalmist causes to march past, as if in procession, testifying their submission. Thus, in this splendid poem, which seems to have been composed beneath the midnight heavens, both the heights and the depths of human nature are brought to light; and, if the origin of the self-designation of Jesus were found here, both the meaning of the term already quoted from Neander and that quoted from Baur would be united. One distinguished theologian, Keim, was of opinion that it was in this place that Jesus obtained the first hint of the name, but he has not been followed by many.*

There is another instance in the Psalms of the use of the "son of man" as a synonym for "man" which I am surprised has never been referred to as possibly furnishing the seed-thought out of which grew the ideas which Jesus combined in His favorite self-designation. In Psalm 80:17 occur these words:

> Let Thy hand be upon the man of Thy right hand,
> Upon the son of man whom Thou madest strong for Thyself.

The whole psalm is a passionate appeal for national revival. It describes, first, the public defeat and humiliation: the people are fed with the bread of tears, and are given tears to drink in great measure; they are a strife unto their neighbors, and their enemies laugh among themselves. Then comes in the celebrated comparison of the nation to a vine, brought out of Egypt and planted in Canaan, where it grew and flourished, till the hills were covered with the shadow of it and the boughs thereof were like the goodly cedars. Alas, however, days of calamity supervened, when the hedge was broken down and the fair plant defaced: "the boar out of the wood doth waste it, and the wild beast of the field doth devour it." In these circumstances the sacred poet appeals to the Shepherd of Israel to shine forth—to come and save them—and the form in which he anticipates deliverance is indicated in the word quoted above. He expected a hero to be raised up, whom Jehovah would favor and sustain, until He should have accomplished the grand task of emancipating His people. This passage is inter-

---

* *Jesus of Nazara*, iii. 79–92. The whole passage is one of great beauty.

preted messianically in the Targums;* the situation sketched in the psalm is only too faithful a description of the political condition of Palestine during the youth of Jesus; and the picture of a deliverer, under the designation of "the son of man," is such as might well have fired a pious and patriotic mind. Here, it will be observed, the idea is totally different from that in the eighth psalm: in the latter passage "the son of man" is humanity in general, but here the term signifies an individual, chosen from the mass and endowed with special gifts and graces for God's work.

There is another book of the Old Testament in which the phrase "the son of man" occurs no fewer than ninety times. This is the Book of Ezekiel; and the term is always applied to the prophet himself. Thus, in the opening vision, which describes his call to the office of prophet, the very first words addressed to him by Jehovah are, "Son of man, stand upon thy feet, and I will speak to thee." "And," he proceeds, "the Spirit entered into me, when He spoke unto me, and he set me upon my feet, that I heard Him that spoke to me." Then the voice continued, "Son of man, I will send thee to the children of Israel"; and, a little further on, "Son of man, be not afraid of them, neither be afraid of their word . . . thou shalt speak My words unto them, whether they will hear or whether they will forbear." The designation has obviously but one meaning throughout the entire book; and it is not difficult to gather from these first instances of its use what this is. "It expresses the contrast between what Ezekiel is in himself and what God will make out of him, the aim being not exactly to humble the prophet, but to make his mission appear to him not as his own, but as the work of God, and thus to lift him up whenever the flesh threatens to faint and fail. By this form of address God testifies how well He knows what His prophet is in himself, and, therefore, promises to lay no burden upon him without accompanying it with the appropriate equipment."†

Thus there was one before Jesus of Nazareth who bore this name, at least in certain moments of his life, and may have derived from it

---

* See Delitzsch: *Die Psalmen, in loco*
† Nösgen: *Christus der Menschen-und Gottessohn*, p. 16.

some of the support with which it inspired our Savior. It would not have been surprising if other prophets, imitating Ezekiel, had appropriated it to themselves, as a designation of their office, since it expresses so admirably the situation of the prophet, as a man weak in himself but strong in the Lord; and at least one young prophet betrays a disposition to do so; for in Daniel 8:17 we read, "So He came near where I stood; and, when He came, I was afraid and fell upon my face, but He said unto me, Understand, O son of man"; and then follow words calculated to restore the trembling prophet's courage. Weizsäcker[*] and others have suggested that Jesus may at first have used the term to express His claim to be reckoned one of the prophetic line in succession to Ezekiel and Daniel; and it has also been suggested that His frequent employment of it may have led to His being classed among the prophets in popular opinion, but these suggestions are somewhat far-fetched, and they have not commanded any considerable amount of assent.

In the Book of Daniel, besides the passage just quoted, there is another reference to "the son of man" far more famous. It occurs in the seventh chapter, in one of the apocalyptic visions common in this prophet. He sees four beasts coming up out of the sea—the first a lion with eagle's wings, the second a bear, the third a four-headed leopard, and the fourth a terrible monster with ten heads. To the distress of the prophet, in his dream, these beasts bear rule over the earth, but at last the kingdom is taken away from them and given to a fifth ruler, who is thus described: "I saw and, behold, one like the son of man came with the clouds of heaven, and came to the Ancient of days, and they brought him near before Him; and there was given unto him dominion, glory, and a kingdom, that all people, nations and languages should serve him; his dominion is an everlasting dominion, which shall not pass away, and his kingdom that which shall not be destroyed."

This chapter is not a place where one would naturally look for the origin of a name so beautiful as "the Son of man"; for to many minds the imagery of Daniel is anything but attractive, on account of its deficiency in those graces of plastic beauty which distinguish the

---

[*] *Untersuchungen über die Evangelische Geschichte*, p. 429.

Greek from the Hebrew imagination; and even a writer as near to our own time as Schleiermacher speaks of the notion, that Jesus could have derived His favorite designation from this source, as an odd fancy. Yet, since Schleiermacher's time the belief has steadily grown, that this is the classical passage to which we must go back, and this opinion seems destined to become universal. Read the words of Daniel: "Behold, one like the son of man came with the clouds of heaven . . . and there was given unto Him dominion, glory, and a kingdom." Then read the words addressed by Jesus to the high priest in the hour of His condemnation: "Hereafter shall ye see the Son of man sitting on the right hand of power, and coming in the clouds of heaven"; and the echo of the Old Testament words is unmistakable. It is equally indubitable in the following, from the great discourse on the future in the twenty-fourth of St. Matthew: "Then shall appear the sign of the Son of man in heaven; and then shall all the tribes of the earth mourn; and they shall see the Son of man coming in the clouds of heaven with power and great glory; and He shall send His angels with a great sound of a trumpet, and they shall gather together His elect from the four winds, from one end of heaven to the other." There are other passages in which the echo is distinguishable, if not quite so distinct, such as Matthew 13:41: "The Son of man shall send forth His angels, and they shall gather out of His kingdom all things that offend, and them which do iniquity, and shall cast them into the furnace of fire; there shall be wailing and gnashing of teeth," or Matthew 16:27, 28: "For the Son of man shall come in the glory of the Father, with His angels, and then He shall reward every man according to his works. Verily, I say unto you, there be some standing here which shall not taste of death till they see the Son of man coming in His kingdom," or Matthew 19:28: "Verily, I say unto you, that ye which have followed Me, in the regeneration when the Son of man shall sit in the throne of his glory, ye also shall sit upon twelve thrones, judging the twelve tribes of Israel."

In Daniel the kingdom given to "one like unto the son of man" supersedes the kingdom of the beasts; and it is obviously the messianic kingdom, for it is described as universal and everlasting. No mention is, however, made of a personal Messiah: on the contrary, thrice over, in the explanation of the vision supplied in the second half of the chapter, the occupant of the throne is described as "the people of the saints of the Most High." Obviously, therefore, the "one like unto the son of man" is a symbolical figure, representing Israel, just as the lion, the bear, the leopard, and the ten-headed monster represent the world-conquering peoples of that epoch. Jesus, however, by assuming the title, puts Himself in the place of Israel, no doubt on the ground that in Him its attributes culminated and its kingly destiny was fulfilled.

If it is a little disappointing to find the place of origin of this beautiful name in one of Daniel's visions, it will to some minds be even more disappointing to discover what, if this is granted, must be its primary signification; for evidently it describes position, not character: it is an official, not a personal designation. Nevertheless, this is the key which fits the lock.

The passages in the Gospels where Jesus calls Himself "the Son of man," are easily divisible into three classes. First, there is a large number, of which the verses last quoted are specimens, in which functions are attributed to Him above the range of ordinary humanity. These have been explained, by those who hold "the Son of man" to be the ideal man, as describing functions of humanity in its loftier aspects, but they are much more simply explained as functions of the Messiah.* There is a second large class of passages referring to the humiliation, sufferings and death of Jesus, like Matthew 17:22: "The Son of man shall be betrayed into the hands of men, and they shall kill Him, and the third day He shall be raised again," or Matthew 26:24: "The Son of man goeth, as it is written of Him, but woe unto that man by whom the Son of man is betrayed; it had been good for that man if he had not been born." These have been explained, in accordance with another of the theories mentioned already, as descriptive of our Lord's humanity on its lower side, where it was exposed to the trials of the human lot, but they are far more completely and satisfactorily ex-

---

* How awkwardly, on the theory that "the Son of man" designates humanity on its humble and suffering side, comes in the addition in the first of these quotations, that "the third day He shall be raised again"!

plained as descriptive of what was to fall to His lot as Messiah. The point in these numerous passages is the contrast between the great destiny of Jesus as Messiah and His actual experiences during His earthly life—a contrast the pathos of which comes supremely out in the saying that "even the Son of man came not to be ministered unto but to minister, and to give His life a ransom for many." The third class of passages is miscellaneous, and in them different points of view may be contended for, but there is not one of them in which the messianic view does not yield a good and natural sense.

I have discussed the possibility of Jesus inventing this name Himself, and, secondly, that of His borrowing it from the Old Testament, but there remains a third possibility—that He may have derived it from the thought of the time in which He lived, or that, at all events, its transference to His mind from the Old Testament may have been mediated by means of the postcanonical literature of the Jews.

I have already pointed out that the term "son of man," applied by the prophet Daniel to Israel as a nation, is by Jesus applied to Himself as an individual, but the question may be raised, whether this modification was entirely due to Jesus, or whether it may not have been made to His hand. Daniel was a favorite book in the interval between its composition and the commencement of the Christian era; and it is conceivable that the religious mind, brooding on its promises, may have transmuted the prediction of a messianic kingdom into that of a messianic king. By some scholars it is considered that remarkable proof of this having taken place is found in the Book of Enoch.

This book may be roughly said to belong to the second century before Christ; it is apocalyptic in character and strongly influenced by the Book of Daniel; and "the Son of man" plays in it a remarkable *rôle*. To prove this, let me make a few quotations, which might easily be multiplied:

"And there I saw One who had a head of days, and His head was white like wool, and with Him was another being, whose countenance had the appearance of a man, and His face was full of graciousness, like one of the holy angels. And I asked the angel who went with me and showed me all the hidden things concerning that

Son of man, who He was, and whence He was, and why He went with the Head of days. And he answered and said unto me, This is the Son of man, who hath righteousness, with whom dwelleth righteousness, and who reveals all the treasures of that which is hidden, because the Lord of spirits hath chosen Him, and His lot before the Lord of spirits hath surpassed everything in uprightness forever. And this Son of man, whom thou hast seen, will arouse the kings and mighty ones from their couches, and the strong from their thrones, and will loosen the reins of the strong, and grind to powder the teeth of the sinners. And He will put down the kings from their thrones and kingdoms, because they do not extol and praise Him, nor thankfully acknowledge whence the kingdom was bestowed on them."

"And in that hour that Son of man was named in the presence of the Lord of spirits, and His name before the Head of days. And before the sun and the signs were created, before the stars of heaven were made, His name was named before the Lord of spirits. He will be a staff to the righteous, on which they will support themselves and not fall; and He will be the light of the Gentiles and the hope of those who are troubled at heart. All who dwell on earth will fall down and bow the knee before Him, and will bless and laud and celebrate with song the Lord of spirits. And for this reason has He been chosen and hidden before Him, before the creation of the world and forevermore."

"And He sat on the throne of His glory, and the sum of judgment was committed unto Him, the Son of man, and He caused the sinners and those who have led the world astray to pass away and be destroyed from off the face of the earth."

According to this book, "the Son of man" pre-exists with the Ancient of days; at the critical moment He is to be sent forth to destroy the unrighteous and to reign over the righteous forever; and He is the judge by whom the destiny of men is to be decided. If these passages are genuine products of the period between the Old Testament and the New, they are among the most important documents of the life of Christ; for their influence upon His thought and language is unmistakable. But the question of their date and origin is a highly debatable one. The Book of Enoch used to be considered the work of a single author, with possibly a few interpolations, but its latest editor, Mr.

Charles, considers it to be an extremely composite production, made up of at least five documents of different authorship and different dates. Indeed, he says, it is rather a collection of the fragments of an Enoch literature than a literary unity. The passages about "the Son of man" all occur in a portion of it known as the Book of Similitudes, which is a document of peculiar character and uncertain origin. It abounds with acknowledged interpolations, and the passages about "the Son of man" have been regarded by trustworthy authorities as Christian additions.

At the present moment, indeed, the trend of criticism is rather in the opposite direction; and this is not to be wondered at because it falls in with the tendencies of a school, claiming several very able and zealous adherents, which is taking a prominent part in the discussion of the teaching of Jesus, and the watchword of which is, that He is to be understood by studying the conditions of thought and life in the midst of which He grew up.* The old way, they say, was to approach Jesus from the side of St. Paul and the other apostolic writers and to see Him in the light which these cast upon Him, but this was not the light in which He actually lived and moved. The true way is to approach Him from the opposite direction, coming down to Him through the society in which the presuppositions of His life are to be found. No doubt the older theology approached Him in this way too, for it developed with peculiar zeal the Christology of the Old Testament, but, they would say, it leaped from Malachi to St. Matthew without taking any account of the centuries lying between. Yet this interval was as long as from the Reformation to the present day, and the human spirit was not dead then: on the contrary, in Palestine and the other homes of the Jews the keenest intellectual activity was going on; changes were taking place in the beliefs and the language of religion from generation to generation; and a literature exists in which the course of this history can still be traced. Jesus, like every other human being, was a product of His age; and it is to the ideas and customs of the age we must look, if we desire to understand Him.

---

* Baldensperger's *Das Selbstbesusstsein Jesu* is the ablest production of this school.

The adherents of this school speak of their method in the tone of discoverers, and unfold remarkable enthusiasm and assiduity in exploring the records of the two or three centuries immediately before Christ. It is not to such noble productions of this period, however, as *The Wisdom of Solomon* or *Ecclesiasticus* that they chiefly turn their eyes, but to a series of apocalyptic writings, imitations of the spirit and style of the Book of Daniel, lying for the most part outside of the collection know to the common man as the Apocrypha;[*] and among these the largest and most important is the Book of Enoch.

Unquestionably there is a true idea in this movement; and, if in some minds a great deal too much is expected from it, this also belongs to the nature of the case; for it is by such illusions that nature gets the necessary work done in unremunerative fields of inquiry. One is reminded of a literary parallel—the sensation created at one time in the region of Shakespeare criticism by the discovery of the sources from which the poet derived the materials of his plays. For a moment it seemed as if the very secret of Shakespeare had been found out; and to this day no one can read without astonishment for the first time, in the introductions of Mr. Aldis Wright or other able editors, the old plays, the stories from Boccaccio, the extracts from Plutarch, and the other rough materials with which the dramatist worked; for he adheres to them, often for pages at a time, with extraordinary closeness. On second thought, however, everyone perceives that the copiousness of such borrowing only enhances the marvel of that genius which was able to transmute whatever it touched into a product entirely its own. The secret of Shakespeare no more lies in his sources than does the secret of the Parthenon in the quarry out of which it was built. Of late certain editors have been making similar discoveries about Burns, and have been so surprised at them as to express the fear lest the general diffusion of their knowledge might impair the popular faith in the poet's originality; and it certainly does give a shock of surprise to compare, for example, *The Cotter's Saturday Night* for the first time

---

[*] Mr. Charles, in Hastings' *Dictionary of the Bible* gives the following as the leading products of Apocalyptic Literature: Apocalypse of Baruch, Book of Enoch, Book of Secrets of Enoch, Ascension of Isaiah, Book of Jubilees, Assumption of Moses, Testament of the Twelve Patriarchs, Psalms of Solomon, Sibylline Oracles.

with *The Farmer's Ingle* of Ferguson. But they may spare their fears; for authors who can make of foreign materials what Shakespeare and Burns have made of theirs may borrow wherever they can and on any scale they please. It may be that Jesus was more the child of His age than we have been accustomed to suppose; and ideas or phrases may be recovered from apocalyptic literature which have entered into His teaching, but these are no more than the particles of inorganic matter which the plant takes up into its own substance and transmutes into forms of beauty. Indeed, the more the apocalyptic literature is unearthed, the more is the incomparable originality of Jesus enhanced; for nothing else in the whole range of human records is more utterly wearisome and worthless. The sneer of the great scholar, Lightfoot, about rabbinical literature might be applied to it with at least equal justice—*Lege, si vacat, et si per taedium et nauseam potes.**

As for the Book of Similitudes, my belief, after many readings, is, that the passages on "the Son of man" are derived from Christianity. The whole book is strewn with interpolations, and must always have invited interpolation on account of the excessive looseness of its texture. Whatever definite connection it has is interrupted by these passages, which bear a stamp of their own quite different from the adjacent materials. At all events their literary character is too doubtful to permit of

---

* Those who insist so much more than is meet on the influence of the later Judaism on the teaching of Jesus might ponder, with profit to themselves, some words of Carlyle on a kindred subject: "Show our critics a great man, they begin to, what they call, 'account for him.' He was 'the creature of the time,' they say; the time called him forth; the time did everything, he nothing. This seems to me but melancholy work. The time call forth? Alas, we have known times call loudly enough for their great man, but not find him when they called. He was not there, Providence had not sent him. The time, calling its loudest, had to go down to confusion and wreck because he would not come when called. I liken common times, with their unbelief, distress, perplexity, their languid doubting character, impotently crumbling down through even worse distress to final ruin, all this I liken to dry, dead fuel, waiting for the lightning out of heaven that shall quicken it. The great man, with his free, direct force out of God's own hand, is the lightning. All blazes now around him. The critic thinks the dry, moldering sticks have called him forth. They wanted him greatly, no doubt. But as to calling him forth! They are critics of small vision who think that the dead sticks have created the fire."

any really scientific conclusions being built upon them (see Appendix B). Those who champion their genuineness suppose that the Enoch literature enjoyed an extensive circulation and was well-known in the circles in which Jesus grew up; one proof of which is that his brother, St. Jude, quotes one of the opening verses of the Book of Enoch—"And Enoch also, the seventh from Adam, prophesied of these, saying, Behold, the Lord cometh with ten thousands of His saints, to execute judgment upon all; and to convince all that are ungodly among them of all their ungodly deeds which they have ungodly committed, and of all their hard speeches which ungodly sinners have spoken against Him." The name of "the Son of man," as a messianic title, was, therefore, in the atmosphere which Jesus breathed; and it may have been thence, rather than directly from the Book of Enoch, that He derived it. But the phenomena of the Gospels are not in harmony with these assumptions. In the book called by his name Enoch is a heroic figure; he is the prophet of prophets; once, at least, he is even identified with the Messiah. But in the Gospels he is never once mentioned, and, even when all kinds of conjectures are being made as to who Jesus is, it is never once suggested that He is Enoch, though this might have been expected to be the very first suggestion, if Enoch had held the position supposed in the popular mind. That "the Son of man" was in any degree a current name for the Messiah is contradicted by the fact, which lies on the very surface of the Gospels, that, while Jesus called Himself "the Son of man" in all audiences, He continued, almost to the very end, to forbid His disciples to make Him known as the Christ. And the form of His question to the Twelve in the critical interview at Caesarea Philippi, "Whom do men say that I, the Son of man, am?" shows that the knowledge of Him as "the Son of man" was not identical with the knowledge of Him as the Messiah. To His own mind this was the meaning of the title; and it was destined sometime to convey the same meaning to others, but it more than half concealed the secret till it was ripe for disclosure.[*]

---

[*] Baldensperger speaks with so much assurance of the sayings about the Son of man as original parts of the Enoch literature that in this country also some are affecting to take this for granted; but I am glad to find that Bousset, one of the younger and certainly one of the ablest members of the same school, in his work

Thus we have passed in review the possible sources of this name, with the result that the indications point strongly to the passage in Daniel. And the place of origin determines the sense to be messianic; though it does not seem to me at all unlikely, but the reverse, that the other Old Testament passages in which it occurs may have contributed to enrich its significance in the consciousness of Jesus.

Our conclusion is established by the linguistic structure of the phrase. The Greek is full-sounding—ὁ υἱὸς τοῦ ἀνθρώπου—with the definite article before each of the nouns, literally "the son of the man." The Fathers used to discuss the question, who "the man" was of whom He was the son. It was frequently held, that the reference was to the Virgin Mary, because of course "man" is equivalent to "human being." Other suggestions were David, Abraham, Adam. But some even of the Fathers were aware, that in the circle of thought in which Jesus moved "man" and "son of man" were synonymous, and that, therefore, the article before "man" is generic; and this is now the accepted opinion. The other article, before "son," in all probability points directly back to the passage in Daniel, indicating that the "son of man" intended is the famous one referred to there. †

entitled *Jesu Predigt in ihrem Gegensatz zum Judenthum*, takes the same view as I have done; and the general tone in which he speaks of the postcononical literature is identical with that which I have used. His reasons for looking upon the passages in question as interpolations are three. First, they interrupt the connection, which is restored when they are removed; secondly, the view of the Son of man which they represent is non-Jewish, such an uplifting of the Messiah to equality with God and to the position of Judge of the world being totally unlikely on Jewish soil; thirdly, in the development of Jewish Apocalyptic there is no tendency towards giving such a prominence to the Messiah: the tendency is rather the contrary way: the Messiah retreats more and more into the background, by which God's own infinite power alone being looked to as the agency by which the changes of the future are to be brought about; so that the divine figure of the Messiah in this part of the Book of Enoch is neither preceded by anything similar to itself, leading up to it, nor followed by anything which it has produced. Wellhausen also declares it to be incredible that Jesus can have picked up His favorite title in the Book of Enoch: see *Israelitische und Jüdische Geschichte*, p. 312, note.

† A very thorough discussion of the Greek words will be found in Holsten's famous article on *Die Bedeutung der Ausdrucksform ὁ υἱὸς τοῦ ἀνθρώπου im Bewusstsein Jesu* in *Zeitschrift für wissenschaftliche Theologie*, 1891, pp. 46 ff.   [continued]

The force of such linguistic deductions has been entirely called in question on the ground that the language spoken by Jesus was Aramaic, in which, it is argued, no phrase exists, or can have existed, equivalent to this Greek one. It is assumed, that the phrase employed by Jesus was *barnash*, which, instead of being a definite and dignified phrase like ὁ υἱὸς τοῦ ἀνθρώπου, is in the highest degree vague and indefinite, meaning only "man" in the most general sense, or rather "anyone." Wide attention has been drawn to this suggestion through Wellhausen having lent it the support of his great name; and a young scholar, Hans Lietzmann, has recently devoted an entire book to the development of the theory. His conclusions are, that Jesus never made use of the phrase at all, but that it came into use as a messianic title in Asia Minor not later than the middle of the second century. To English-speaking people such a theory will hardly appear serious enough for discussion, but will be thought one of those *tours de force* by which the German Privatdocent seeks to attract public attention. It may, however, be worthwhile to show wherein its weakness lies. One point of weakness is the dogmatic assertion, that the Aramaic language was incapable of supplying an equivalent to the Greek phrase. Evidently, *barnash* is no equivalent, but this only proves that a mistake has been made in assuming this to have been the phrase employed by Jesus. The Greek words have all the appearance of an effort to render something which was not Greek; and the task of scholarship is to find out what this was. But a still greater difficulty is to account for the introduction of the phrase, on so extensive a scale, into the Gospels, if, as is presupposed, these did not originally contain it. To begin to call Jesus "the Son of man" would have excited the strongest suspicion at a time when belief in His godhead was everywhere diffused; and Lietzmann has not allowed himself to realize the difficulty of getting such a form of speech, arising in Asia Minor, introduced so extensively into the Gospels that no copies have remained without it. The author adduces, as one of his strongest arguments the absence of the name from the Epistles of St. Paul and the

---

Beyschlag, following a hint derived from Hupfield, explains the second article from the Hebrew practice of placing the article before the second noun in such a compound phrase as "the son of man."

other New Testament writings; for it occurs only once in the Book of Acts, in Stephen's speech, and twice in the Book of Revelation.* But there may be other reasons for this. For example, the name "Christ" itself had become so universal as to make other equivalents for the Messiah unnecessary. Very likely the chief reason was the fear, just alluded to, of throwing doubt on our Lord's divinity. At all events, if the name had been introduced into the Gospels in the way suggested by Lietzmann, is it not perfectly certain that it would have been inserted in the other New Testament writings as well?†

We hold it, then, to be established that the passage in Daniel is the source of this title, and that its meaning is messianic. But a question of great importance still remains: Why did Jesus appropriate this name as His favorite from among all those which were offered by the Old Testament or which might have occurred to His own mind? It was not, as we have seen, thrust upon Him by its popularity among

---

* The writer of Revelation seems, however, to go back not to the use of the term by Jesus, but to its use by Daniel.

† Wellhausen's statement occurs in a footnote, p. 312 of his *Geschichte Israels*. He assumes that Jesus simply said "man" where the Gospels make Him say "the Son of man." Krop, in his book entitled *Le Royanne de Dieu*, has shown that this theological novelty is nothing more than the resurrection of a notion of the old rationalist Paulus. Great confusion is introduced into Lietzmann's book by the fact that he seems often to be arguing for this hypothesis too. This, however, is not really his drift. He sees that a splendid phrase like ὁ υἱὸς τοῦ ἀνθρώπου cannot have been a rendering of *barnash*. But he is rash in affirming that it cannot have had any equivalent in Aramaic. Dalman, who, I suppose, is the most eminent Aramaic scholar living, sees no such difficulty, and he regards the discovery of Wellhausen as a mare's nest. Mrs. Lewis informs me that in Old Syriac the rendering of "the Son of man" is generally *bareh de ansha* (in Cureton's MS 42 times, in her own palimpsest 65 times), though it is a few times *bareh de gabra*. She does not, however, suppose that this was the form of words used by Jesus; but she adds, with much point, "It seems to me that the Evangelists and the copyists of their text must have been perfectly well acquainted with Syriac idioms and therefore, could not have translated *barnash* by ὁ υἱὸς τοῦ ἀνθρώπου and that some more definite phrase must have been behind the Greek." I am indebted to Mrs. Lewis and her sister, Mrs. Gibson, for their kind courtesy in examining manuscripts and interviewing experts for me on this ticklish point.

His contemporaries; nor, if it had, would this alone have determined His choice: a self-designation so intimate must have had its chief reason in His own mind.

The suggestion has been made, that it commended itself to Him because the figure in Daniel, being of heavenly origin and engaged in high and solemn fellowship with the Ancient of days, before descending to engage in his earthly task, would correspond with His consciousness of pre-existence. Again, the practical reason has been hinted at already, that the name suited His purpose of concealing His messianic claims, while it expressed them to Himself and hinted them to His disciples. But, it seems to me, the deepest reason for His choice of this name must have been the admirable expression which it gives to His connection with the human race. That the sense of His identity with all mankind was one of His master sentiments requires no demonstration. With whatever is high and noble in man's nature or destiny He was in intimate sympathy; and His compassion reached down to everything that is painful or pathetic in the human lot. He is the Brother of all, the Man of men. This is one of the two poles on which His messiahship rests. Without this connection with the race and this universality of sympathy He could not have been the Messiah.

It must be confessed, however, it is surprising in how few of the passages in which "the Son of man" occurs there is direct and undeniable reference to this.[*] It has even been argued, that there is no such reference in any of them at all. But this is an exaggeration. When He says, "The Sabbath was made for man, and not man for the Sabbath," and then adds, "Therefore the Son of man is Lord also of the Sabbath," the force of the inference lies partly in the identity of the Speaker with all the children of men and partly in His supremacy above them. He is the head and representative to whom it belongs to guard and vindicate their rights.[†] When He contrasted Himself with the Baptist by saying that "the Son of man came eating and drinking," He was

---

[*] Of course there is abundant reference to it in His sayings in general; and nearly every incident of His life could be quoted in illustration.

[†] Lietzmann and others take the inference to be that man collectively is Lord of the Sabbath. But would Jesus have made this assertion? I do not think so.

pointing to His sympathy with all simple and natural human enjoyments. Even when He says, "The Son of man is come to seek and to save that which was lost," while He may be describing a function of the Messiah, the great saying gains immeasurably in depth and pathos, if we consider it to express His sense of brotherhood with all men, even the worst. Indeed, even if it be allowed that the primary reference in every saying about "the Son of man" is to messiahship, yet, on the other hand, everyone of them gains in point and power, if this under sense be also remembered.

There must have been a moment in the experience of Jesus when the text in Daniel, so often referred to, suddenly shone forth upon Him as the guiding star of His career; and, if only a record of this incident had been vouchsafed to us, much that is dark would have been made clear. Where did it take place? Was it in Nazareth, some Sabbath, when in the synagogue the Prophets were being read? Or was it later, during one of the nights of communion with His Father on some mountain-top of Galilee, when the words of the sacred Book stood out on the sky of His imagination in letters of fire? To those His experience will not be altogether foreign to whom, in some great spiritual crisis, a word of God, detaching itself from the rest of Scripture, has been given as a pledge of the divine choice, to be kept forever. I have expressed a certain regret and disappointment that our Lord's favorite name is official rather than personal; but I take this back, because I now see, that, when He was standing before the Word of God, to receive the message of destiny, it was meet that this should come to Him not as a reflection upon His own qualities and attributes, but as a summons to a grand work, which was to carry Him out of Himself and absorb all His powers. Or if, in any degree, in that solemn hour there was the consciousness of self, it was the consciousness of His identity with all the children of men, whom He was to seek and to save.[*]

---

[*] During the passage of this book through the press an important essay on "The Son of Man" has appeared in the sixth volume of Wellhausen's *Skizzen und Vorarbeiten*. It adds little to the arguments advanced by Lietzmann for eliminating the phrase from the words of Jesus; but it is much more cautious about determining when and where the name was given to our Lord.

Identity—and yet at one essential point there is no evidence of participation by Jesus in the experience of humanity; for He betrays no consciousness of sin.

The proof of the sinlessness of Jesus is not derived exclusively from the Gospels; and in the Gospels it is not proved exclusively by His own words; nor are the most forcible even of such words in the Synoptists. The Synoptists, indeed, draw frequent attention to the impression of His perfection made on both friends and foes. Thus they tell us, how the centurion at the cross declared, evidently with deep emotion, that Jesus was "a righteous man"; how Pilate and Pilate's wife acknowledged His innocence; how the Baptist affirmed, "I have need to be baptized of Thee, and comest Thou to me?" How St. Peter, in the boat, dazzled with the proximity of perfect moral purity cried out, "Depart from me, for I am a sinful man, O Lord"; and how even Judas confessed that he had betrayed "innocent blood."* But they do not record sayings in which He lays claim to sinlessness.

They even narrate incidents which might be interpreted as acknowledging the reverse. Such is His baptism. Was not the baptism of John the baptism of repentance? Such it was to others, but it need not necessarily have been so to Him; for, besides this negative side, it had also a positive side: it not only symbolized the washing of the nation from sin, but its consecration to a new career of holiness. Jesus knew Himself to be the Leader of this new movement; and, knowing this, He might choose, in His humility, to go through the common door, although the negative virtue of the ordinance was not a necessity to Him. Then, there is His statement to one who hailed Him as "Good Master": "Why called thou Me good? There is none good but One, that is God." Is not this a confession of imperfection? It is an acknowledgment of a certain kind of imperfection—the imperfection of a character that is growing, and has to realize its goodness on every fresh stage of advancement—but this does not necessarily imply a guilty imperfection at any stage.

---

* Luke 23:47, 4; Matthew 27:19; 3:14; Luke 5:8; Matthew 27:4.

It is not, however, for anything which they made Him say positively about His sinlessness that the Synoptists are remarkable, but for the things they do not make Him say. A recent writer has adduced as a fresh proof of His sinlessness that He never prayed in company with others: He taught the Twelve to pray, but He did not pray even with them, the reason being that prayer requires the confession of sin, which He could not make.* On this I lay no stress, because I am doubtful of the fact. It seems to me that He did pray with others when He gave thanks in their name; and may there not be prayer without confession? But the broad fact remains, that Jesus did not confess sin. His habits of prayer are commemorated in the Gospels, and specimens of His prayers are given, but these include no acknowledgments of personal transgression. This is in striking contrast with the other great figures of the Jewish race. Isaiah confesses, "Woe is me, for I am undone, for I am a man of unclean lips, and I dwell among a people of unclean lips." David says, "I was shapen in iniquity, and in sin did my mother conceive me." Job says, "I abhor myself, and repent in dust and ashes." Ezra says, "O my God, I am ashamed and blush to lift up my face to Thee, my God, for our iniquities are increased over our heads, and our trespass is grown up unto the heavens." Our Lord's own apostles make similar acknowledgments. Thus St. Paul groans, "Oh wretched man that I am! who shall deliver me from the body of this death?" And even the saintly St. John confesses, "If we say that we have no sin, we deceive ourselves, and the truth is not in us." Such is the tone of all the men of religious genius who were either the teachers of Jesus or His disciples. If He was merely the supreme religious genius among them all, it would be natural to expect from Him still more agonizing cries of penitence. But nothing of the kind is ever heard from His lips. What is the explanation of this singular phenomenon? It will hardly be interpreted as a defect. Could it be so understood, it would lower Him far beneath such figures as have just been quoted; for what quality of saintliness is more essential than humility? But, if

---

* FORREST, *The Christ of History and of Experience*, c. I. The chapter as a whole is an admirable statement on the sinlessness of Jesus.

it was not a defect, the only alternative is, that He confessed no sin because He had none to confess but was "holy, harmless, undefiled, separate from sinners."*

---

* The proof of the sinlessness of Jesus rests primarily on His own testimony in St. John (see especially John 4:34; 8:29, 46) and the Synoptists, secondly on that of the apostles (see, for example, Heb. 3:15; 7:26; Acts 3:14; 1 Peter 3:18; 1 John 3:5; 2 Cor. 5:21), and thirdly on the prevalence in Christendom of the ideal of holiness. Wherever Christianity exists, holiness exists. Remarkable holiness may be a rare phenomenon; but in every Christian community there are many striving after it, and there are few places in Christendom where there cannot be found some whose holiness impresses others as distinctly a divine creation. Not infrequently the effect is overawing in a high degree—a vision of unearthly beauty. And Christian holiness, which is a well-proportioned mixture of religion and morality, traces itself back to Christ. Its communion with God is founded on reconciliation through Him; it knows itself to spring from a life rooted in Him; it is a never-ending imitation of Him; and it knows Him to be infinitely above itself. But, if He is far above the holiest, must He not have been perfectly holy? The Christian movement towards holiness must have as its *fons et origo* One whose holiness was perfect. Ullmann's book on the Sinlessness of Jesus is one of the most artistic and enduring products of German theology.

PASSAGES IN WHICH JESUS IS CALLED "THE SON OF GOD" BY OTHERS,
   HIMSELF SOMETIMES ADOPTING THE NAME:
Matthew 2:15; 3:17; 4:3, 6; 8:29; 14:33; 16:16; 17:5; 21:37, 38; 26:63,
   64; 27:40, 43, 54.
Mark 1: [1], 11; 3:11; 5:7; 9:7; 14:61, 62; 15:39.
Luke 1:32, 35; 3:22; 4:3, 9, 41; 8:28; 9:35; 20:9; 22:70.

PASSAGES IN WHICH JESUS CALLS HIMSELF "THE SON":
Matthew 11:27 (thrice); 22:2; 27:43; 28:19.
Mark 13:32.
Luke 10:22 (thrice).

PASSAGES IN WHICH JESUS CALLS GOD HIS FATHER:
Matthew 7:21; 10:32, 33; 11:25, 26, 27; 12:50; 15:13; 16:17, 27; 18:10,
   19, 35; 20:23; 24:36; 25:34; 26:29, 39, 42, 53; 28:19.
Mark 8:38; 13:32; 14:36.
Luke 2:49; 9:26; 10:21, 22; 22:29, 42; 23:34, 46; 24:49.

3
The Son of God

THE other self-designation of our Lord is "the Son of God." Jesus does not make use of it Himself in the Synoptists, but it is frequently applied to Him by others, when He accepts it in such a way as to appropriate it to Himself. He makes use sparingly on His own initiative of the abbreviated form, "the Son," evidently with the same force; and He often speaks of God as "the Father," or "My Father," or "My Father who is in heaven," in a way that involves the consciousness that He is the Son of God.

The terms "Son of man" and "Son of God" appear to form a pair; and they describe so aptly the two sides of our Lord's person that it is no wonder that this should have been taken to be their original meaning. So they have been interpreted from very early times; and so they are understood by ordinary readers of the Bible to this day. As, however, we found reason to modify this assumption in the case of "the Son of man," so, in investigating this other term, we must not rashly yield to the impression conveyed by the mere sound of the words.

At all events there is no likelihood that Jesus invented this phrase; for it occurs frequently in the Old Testament, and it has a wide range of application in the Bible.

Thus, first, it is applied to angels. In the Book of Job we read that at the creation of the world "the morning stars sang together, and all the sons of God shouted for joy." In the same book an occasion is mentioned when "the sons of God came to present themselves before the Lord, and Satan came also among them," where it is not quite clear whether Satan is reckoned as one of the sons of God, or whether he is an intruder forcing himself in where he has no right to be (Job 38:7;

1:6; 2:1). The reason why the angels are called by this name may only be that they are creatures of God, as we call a poet's works the children of his imagination; or it may more probably be that, as spiritual beings, they bear a resemblance to God, who is a spirit.

Secondly, the term is applied to the first man. In the third chapter of St. Luke the genealogy of our Lord is traced back from generation to generation, each member of the series being described as the son of his father, till Adam is reached, "who," it is added, "was the son of God" (Luke 3:38: Ἀδὰμ τοῦ θεοῦ). This may mean simply that God was the Author of his being; though it is more likely that there is also a reference to the fact, mentioned so impressively in the first chapter of Genesis, that Adam was made in the image of God. This raises the question, whether all the children of Adam might not be called by this name. It would seem to be in the spirit of Scripture to answer this question affirmatively; and, if many passages cannot be quoted in favor of this application, there is at least one which weighs very heavily—the Parable of the Prodigal Son. The prodigal in the far country is still a son, though a lost one.

Thirdly, the term is applied to the Hebrew nation as a whole. For example, Moses was sent to Pharaoh with this message, "Thus saith the Lord, Israel is My son, even My firstborn, and I say unto thee, Let My son go" (Ex. 4:22). And in Hosea 2:1 Jehovah says, "When Israel was a child, then I loved him, and called My son out of Egypt." These quotations show very clearly the idea at the root of this designation: Israel was the son of God as the object of His special love and gracious choice. The entire Old Testament, however, is pervaded by the correlative idea, that sonship implies likeness, or at all events the obligation to be like the Father. Thus in Malachi 1:6, Jehovah says, "A son honors his father, and a servant his master; if I then be a Father, where is mine honor? And, if I be a Master, where is My fear?" It would be a natural transition from the application of the term to Israel as a whole to apply it to individual Israelites; and this appears to have been effected at least in New Testament times; for, in argument with Jesus, the Jews affirmed (John 8:41), "We have one Father, even God"; and Jesus Himself said of the Jews to the Syrophoenician woman, "Let the children first be filled."

Fourthly, the kings of Israel, or at least some of them, bore this title. Thus Jehovah said of Solomon, "I will be his Father and he shall be to Me a son" (2 Sam. 7:24). In Psalm 89, an ancient oracle is quoted in which Jehovah says of King David, "He shall cry unto Me, Thou art My Father, my God, and the rock of my salvation. Also I will make him My firstborn, higher than the kings of the earth." But the most remarkable expression of this idea is to be found in the second Psalm, where the king of Israel is represented as surrounded by a combination of enemies threatening his throne; whose machinations, however, are interrupted by an oracle, probably conceived as uttered in thunder from the sky, which proclaims "Thou art My son, this day have I begotten thee"; and, before this angry and irresistible declaration of the divine will, the confederated heathen melt away. In this psalm two names occur which were destined to have an extraordinary history— "the Messiah" and "the Son of God"—and the king appears in the closest connection with God, as joint ruler with Him and as the object of His love and choice. His figure is highly idealized, and it may be doubted whether it could ever, as Hupfeld asserts it did, have represented the Israelitish kingship in general. Applied to most of the actual kings it would have been gross and hyperbolic flattery;[*] and, if any rules of sobriety are to be observed in interpretation at all, it is more natural to understand it only of an excellent actual king or, still better, of someone whom the best of the actual kings typified. The reason for designating the kings by this title was, that the nation culminated in them, and perhaps that the great position they held was one in the bestowal of which there was specially manifested the electing love of God.

Fifthly, in the New Testament believers in Jesus Christ are everywhere described by this name—"To as many as received Him, to them gave He power to become the sons of God, even to them that believe in His name." One reason in their case is that they have been born of God—"Being born again not of corruptible seed, but of incorruptible, by the Word of God, which lives and abides forever." A further reason is that they are like God. On this Jesus Himself lays the greatest stress: "Love your enemies, and pray for them that persecute

---

[*] So Nösgen: *Der Menschen-und Gottessohn*, p. 144.

you; that you may be sons of your Father which is in heaven; for He makes His sun to rise on the evil and the good, and sends rain on the just and on the unjust" (John 1:12; 1 Pet. 1:23; Matt. 5:44, 45, R.V.). And to these two has to be added the third reason, that they are objects of God's special and distinguishing love—"Behold, what manner of love the Father hath bestowed upon us, that we should be called the sons of God; therefore the world knoweth us not, because it knew Him not" (1 John 3:1).

Thus, the term is applied to angels, to men, to the Jewish nation as a whole, to the Jewish kings, and to all saints; and the principal ideas which it embodies are, that those bearing the name are derived from God as their Author, that they are the objects of His love and choice, and that they are like Him in character and conduct.

Such being the wide and varied application of the term, the question arises, from which of these points it was that the title was transferred to our Lord. And the almost universal verdict of scholarship is that its application to Jesus arose from its application to the kings of Israel, He being the King to whom these all pointed forward. In short, this term, like "the Son of man," is messianic. Such is the accepted view, which, however, I wish to submit to a thorough examination.

It is commonly asserted that the term is a synonym for the Messiah in the apocryphal books, but for this the evidence is slender. There is a passage in the end of the Book of Enoch where God is made to say "I and My Son" will do something, but it occurs in one of the most meaningless paragraphs of that incoherent production. Two or three references are also usually given to 4 Esdras, but the value of these may easily be estimated from the following specimens: "For My Son Jesus shall be revealed with those who are with Him, and they that remain shall rejoice for four hundred years"; "And it shall come to pass after these years that My Son Christ shall die, and all men that have breath."*

It has already been remarked that in the Synoptists the term is for the most part applied to Jesus not by Himself but by others; and from this circumstance it has been argued that its sense must be messianic,

* Enoch 105:2; 4 Edras 7:28, 29.

because it is manifest that the phrase was diffused among the people as a title of the expected deliverer.[*]

A close study of the instance does not, however, lend this conclusion very clear support.

In the first chapter of St. Luke the angel of the Annunciation calls the Child to be born of Mary by this name, not because He is to be the Messiah, but for the reason stated in these words: "The Holy Ghost shall come upon thee, and the power of the Highest shall overshadow thee; therefore also that Holy Thing which shall be born of thee shall be called the Son of God" (Luke 1:35). The derivation of His human nature from the special creative act of God is here the reason of the name—a reason akin to that on account of which it is also given by St. Luke to Adam. I do not remember any other place in Scripture where this precise point of view recurs.

When the centurion at the foot of the cross said, "Truly this was the Son of God";[†] the likelihood is, that he, a heathen, was thinking of a hero like the sons of divine fathers and human mothers of whom there were many in the mythology of Greece and Rome.

Demoniacs are reported to have cried out to Jesus as "the Son of God"; and it might be supposed that in their mouths this was a popular name for the Messiah, especially as they sometimes addressed Him in so many words as the Messiah. But there is something peculiar about their testimony. The Evangelists evidently look upon their exclamations as proceeding not so much from the possessed human beings as from the demons by whom they were possessed, and we are no judges of the meaning which would be attached to this term by such intelligences, except that Jesus was dreaded by them as the Strong One by whom their power was to be broken. Still less can we narrow down the meaning attached to the name by the prince of devils, when he played with it in our Lord's temptation. [**]

---

[*] Beyschlag, *New Testament Theology*, I. 66: "The occurrence in the mouths of others shows from the outset that the Nem is rooted in the Old Testament, in Israel already commonplace, and so, therefore, to obtain the sense in which Jesus uses it for Himself, one must go back to the Old Testament."

[†] Or, more correctly, "a son of God," Mark 15:39.

[**] Matthew 8:29; Mark 3:11; Luke 4:41; Matthew 4:3, 6.

"They that were in the ship" on the occasion when Jesus stilled the tempest and rescued St. Peter from the waves, "came and worshiped Him, saying, Of a truth Thou art the Son of God" (Matt. 14:33). If by this they meant that He was the Messiah, it was a remarkable anticipation of the confession at Caesarea Philippi, but it looks more like an involuntary recognition of the divine in Jesus, extorted by the overwhelming impression produced by the miracle.

In the confession at Caesarea Philippi, which St. Matthew records two chapters later, St. Peter says, "Thou art the Christ, the Son of the living God"; and it is contended that the second phrase is only a variation of the first, without the addition of anything new such as is involved in the meaning attached by theology to the name. This is rendered the more probable by the fact that St. Mark and St. Luke omit the second title altogether; for is it conceivable that they would have done so if St. Peter had proclaimed his faith not only in the messiahship of Jesus but in His deity? This passage is the strongest support of the view that the name is messianic. Yet many instances might be quoted to prove that arguments based on omission in one or even two Evangelists are far from trustworthy.[*]

Analogous is our Lord's confession before the high priest. According to St. Matthew the high priest asked, "I adjure thee by the living God that Thou tell us whether Thou be the Christ, the Son of God. Jesus said unto him, Thou hast said." Here, it is contended, the very collocation of the words proves that the phrases are equivalent; and, besides, a Jewish high priest could have used the Old Testament phrase in no other sense. On the other hand, St. Luke describes this scene in a way that excites dubiety.

Jesus is asked, "Art Thou the Christ? tell us. And He said unto them, If I tell you, you will not believe; and, if I also ask you, you will not answer Me nor let Me go. Hereafter shall the Son of man sit on the right hand of the power of God. Then said they all, Art Thou then the Son of God? And He said unto them, You say that I am." Here the question, "Art Thou the Son of God?" is separated from the question, "Art Thou the Christ?" and it is not obvious that it means the same

---

[*] Matthew 16:16; Mark 8:29; Luke 9:20.

thing. Perhaps it does, but it looks more as if the reply of Jesus to the first question had suggested to His interrogators that He made a claim beyond even that of being the Messiah. Accordingly they asked, in angry curiosity, if He was the Son of God; and how great was the shock caused by His affirmative answer is shown by their instant and unanimous decision, that He had committed blasphemy. If the claim to be "the Son of God" implied nothing more than a human messiahship, wherein consisted the blasphemy?* Holtzmann, a passionate denier of the traditional theology, says, "The blasphemy can only have been found in this, that a man belonging to the lower classes, one openly forsaken of God, and going forward to a shameful death, should have dared to represent Himself as the object and fulfillment of all the divine promises given to the nation. Such a claim smote in the face all the presuppositions and the conclusions of the Jewish faith and irritated the national susceptibilities to the uttermost."† This is admirable special pleading, yet everyone must recognize that the blasphemy was far more obvious if the phrase meant what this scholar denies.

Besides, it is not to be forgotten that St. John says, "The Jews sought the more to kill Him, because He not only had broken the Sabbath, but said also that God was His Father, making Himself equal with God"; and again, "The Jews answered Him, saying, For a good work we stone Thee not; but for blasphemy; and because that Thou, being a man, make Thyself God" (John 5:18; 10:33). These statements are not, properly speaking, portions of the Johannine theology: they are historical testimonies as to the sense attached by the Jews to their own charge of blasphemy and as to the claim of Jesus to be the Son of God; of course they may be misrepresentations, but there is no ambiguity about them; and it is not a departure from our plan in the present lectures of deriving the teaching of Jesus from the Synoptists alone to quote them here for what they are worth.**

---

* Matthew 26:63, 64; Luke 22:66–71.

† N. T. *Theologie*, I.266.

** Dorner has the weighty words (*Teaching from the Person Jesus*, p. 79): "The term 'Son of God' among the synoptics cannot be traced back to the meaning [*continued*]

To sum up: the meaning attached to this title when applied to Jesus by others is not uniform. In some cases it may be messianic, but the common element seems rather to be the recognition in our Lord of something above the level of ordinary humanity.

The use of the name by Jesus Himself is naturally what interests us most.

From whence did He derive it? Are we to suppose that, like those who applied it to Him, He picked it up from the religious vocabulary of the period or borrowed it from the Old Testament? Another source is conceivable—namely, the voice from heaven at His baptism, repeated in the Transfiguration. In some minds there may exist doubt as to the objectivity of this occurrence, but, even were it supposed to be purely subjective, it would be an accurate indication of what were the sentiments of Jesus at the time. What it most emphasizes is His consciousness of being the object of the divine love. Even if "My Son" means nothing else than "Messiah," yet the adjective, "beloved" is added, together with the phrase, "in whom I am well pleased." Thus the personal predominates over the official.

This is the phenomenon which encounters us everywhere, when we take a survey of His own language; and, it will be observed, it is precisely the reverse of what we found upon a detailed examination of His use of the term "Son of man." The official meaning of that term is the one which makes everything clear, whereas the personal sense is rarely prominent, even if it can with certainty be traced at all, but in the use of this term, while the reference to messiahship is sometimes present as a suggestive undersense, the reference to an interior relation between person and person is uniform. So it manifestly is in the very first recorded saying of Jesus, "Wist ye not that I must be in My Father's

---

of that word in the Old Testament. He is not merely like David or the other kings of Israel, or the faithful of the people or the prophets, a son of God. He does not at all appear as one amongst the others, not as one of the sons of God but rather the Son of God, the only One, the Beloved. In comparison to Him, the greatest men and prophets stand as δοῦλοι before the υἱός." He goes on to describe His sonship as threefold—physical, ethical and official; and of these the second depends on the first, and the third on the first and second.

house?"; and in the last, "Father, into Thy hands I commend My spirit." *

There is one passage in which this intense consciousness of personal relationship to God comes out with peculiar clearness and force, as the sense denoted by Jesus when calling God "the Father" and Himself "the Son." It occurs in a scene commemorated by both St. Matthew and St. Luke; and the two accounts combined enable us to bring the circumstances vividly before our eyes.†

Jesus had been discoursing sadly on the reception He had met with at the hands of His generation, and reproaching the cities in which most of His mighty works were done, when the Seventy returned overflowing with gladness at the success of their mission. And "in that hour Jesus rejoiced in spirit** and said, I thank Thee, O Father, Lord of heaven and earth, because Thou hast hid these things from the wise and prudent, and hast revealed them unto babes. Even so, O Father; for so it seemed good in Thy sight." He had been looking back with bitter disappointment to the refusal of the learned and the influential to have anything to do with His cause, but the appearance of the Seventy, with their enthusiastic report, so brought home to Him the success of His confidence in the honest and good hearts which He had attracted from the ranks of the common people that He was able completely to rise above His depression and rejoice in the whole course of His ministry as the disposition of God. Then He added, as if sunk in a beatific soliloquy—and these are the words which express so wonderfully the intimacy of His relation to God—"All things are delivered unto Me of My Father; and no man knows the Son but the Father, neither knows any man the Father save the Son, and he to whomsoever the Son will reveal Him."

The opening words, "All things are delivered unto Me of My Father," have been very variously interpreted. Some have given them the widest possible scope, understanding Jesus to be claiming lordship and

---

* Luke 2:49; 23:46. In the latter passage Jesus is quoting from the Old Testament; but He adds "Father" to the quotation—a very significant addition.
† Matt 11:25-30; Luke 10:21, 22.
** "In the Holy Spirit" (R.V.).

government over the universe. Modern interpreters restrict them as much as possible—Weiss to the control of all things essential to His messianic work, while Holtzmann thinks they only express the claim that His doctrine is of God. The meaning most consistent with the context seems to be, that all His fortunes are of divine appointment—the disagreeable as well as the agreeable—all are working together for good; and in this assurance His spirit finds rest. But the next words are those which carry us into the sanctuary of His secret life: "No man knows the Son but the Father, neither knows any man the Father save the Son, and he to whomsoever the Son will reveal Him."* These words may be a continuation of the thought just hinted at: God alone knows the course of the Son's career, seeing clearly its glorious issues beyond its present intricacies; and the Son alone knows the Father's design, and, therefore, He can bear without repining the disappointments of apparent failure. But this is only the minimum of meaning which can belong to the words; and their full meaning is probably much more comprehensive. At all events the impressiveness of the parallel between the Father's knowledge of the Son and the Son's knowledge of the Father can escape no one; and the saying is an incomparable expression of mutual intimacy, serene trust and perfect love. No wonder that Jesus burst out of His soliloquy with the memorable words on His lips, "Come unto Me, all ye that labor and are heavy laden, and I will give you rest." He felt in Himself a joy great enough to satisfy the whole word. He held the secret of peace, and could invite all to come and receive it from Him.†

Even the least enthusiastic writers kindle into unwonted warmth in speaking of this utterance, but they hasten to add, that of course the sonship of Jesus was not specifically different from that of all believers. Sonship is the highest expression for the relation to God to which He raises those who receive Him, and it places them on the same platform

---

* βουλήται ἀποκαλύψαι.

† Keim thinks that the great passage must have ended thus: "and he to whom the Father will reveal Him" (the Son). But surely this is also implied. Keim's long exposition of this passage, which he considers the loftiest utterance of the self-conscious Jesus, is very fine. Holtzmann also calls it the pinnacle of Jesus' testimony to Himself.

with Himself. This dogmatic assertion is, however, confronted by the fact, that in all the Gospels Jesus carefully distinguishes His own sonship from that of His disciples. He speaks constantly of "My Father" and of "your Father," but never of "Our Father." Feeble attempts have been make to break down this distinction, but totally without avail. The fact, if substantiated, is a cardinal one, and it is useless, in face of it, to assert that obviously His sonship must be the same as ours.

A similar piece of dogmatism, very common at present, is the assertion that of course the sonship of Jesus was ethical, not metaphysical. Certainly it was ethical, consisting in the harmony of his mind and will with the thoughts and purposes of God, and in the affection and delight felt by Jesus for God and of God for Jesus. But it does not follow in the least that, because ethical, it was not metaphysical. On the contrary, the ethical always rests on the metaphysical; and ethical unity becomes less possible the farther any two beings are metaphysically separated from each other. The sympathy between a beast and a man is imperfect, because they are metaphysically so far apart; on the contrary, the union of man and woman is capable of such completeness because, though between them there exists the difference of sex, yet both partake in the same human nature. Men, as we have seen, may be called the sons of God for a variety of reasons; yet the union between God and man is a distant one; and this not only for ethical reasons, but for the metaphysical one that their natures are distinct. Angelic nature is nearer the divine; yet even here sonship is a figure of speech. No doubt the question whether any higher sonship is possible—a sonship as perfect in the divine region as sonship is in the human—is metaphysical, but to deny this is as pure a piece of dogmatism as to affirm it.

We must rid ourselves of all such preconceptions, if we wish to receive on our minds the simple and natural impression made by the testimony of Jesus about Himself.

In the parable of the Wicked Husbandman He describes the owner of the vineyard as sending first servant after servant to receive the fruits, but then, after much premeditation, as sending his own son, his well-beloved (Mark 12:6); and by this figure, the peculiarity of which consist not in his office, but in his relation to the sender, Jesus obviously intended Himself. It reminds us of His claim elsewhere to be above the kings and the prophets—"A greater than Solomon is here," "A greater than Jonah is here" (Matt. 12:41, 42).

This again recalls the well-known passage where He demands of the scribes, whose son the Messiah is, and, when they reply, "The son of David," immediately demands, why, then, David calls Him Lord (Mark 12:35–37). We shall have to deal on a subsequent page with the notion that Jesus raised this question in order to deny the Davidic origin of the Messiah, but what we are here concerned with is the subtle insinuation that the Messiah is the Son of God in such a sense that He is rightly styled David's Lord. What must this sense be?

There is a saying of Jesus about His own sonship which is frequently quoted as the final refutation of the Church doctrine on the subject, because in it He confesses His ignorance of the date of His second coming—"Of that day and that hour knows no man, no, not the angels which are in heaven, neither the Son, but the Father" (Mark 8:32). This saying does not stand alone: it is akin to many other statements in the Gospels, made by Jesus or about Him, in which His true and proper manhood is clearly brought out, but perhaps there is no other passage which has done so much to keep the mind of the church sound on this great doctrine and to restrain it from extravagance in the statement of the opposite one. It has not by any means been overlooked. On the contrary, in recent times especially it has attracted the attention of theologians; and the most interesting contributions to modern Christology—the so-called Kenotic theories—have been founded on this more than any other text of Scripture, except the saying of St. Paul that the Son of God "emptied" Himself.* That by

---

* Of the *teaching* of Jesus on this subject we can hardly speak, as He offered no explanation of His ignorance. Stated dogmatically, the question is this: How can the omniscience of the Second Person of the Trinity be reconciled with the ignorance of Jesus? The answer of theology is, that there took place at the incarnation a kenosis (from ἑαυτὸν ἐκένωσεν, Phil. 2:7), by which the Second Person of the Trinity emptied Himself of certain of His attributes, till the period of His humiliation was completed. Great diversity of opinion has, however, prevailed as to the manner in which this kenosis ought to be conceived; and all the Kenotic theories, as they are called, have been rejected by some eminent theologians. Full information will be found in Bruce's *Humiliation of Christ*. The problem has recently

these efforts the mystery has been cleared away I do not say, but the church has been anew convinced by them that no theory of our Lord's person can be correct which does not recognize that there is a mystery. In fact, there is no saying of Jesus which makes this more indubitable; for He evidently states it as an astonishing thing that He does not know. He specified four planes of being and of knowledge—that of men, that of angels, that of Himself, and that of God. "Of that day and that hour," He says, "knows no man, no, not the angels, neither the Son, but the Father." Evidently the Son is above not only men but angels, and knows more than they.

The conclusion would seem to be that he is a being intermediate between the angels and God. But this impression is corrected by the greatest of all the sayings in which He calls Himself the Son: "Go you, therefore, and teach all nations, baptizing them in the name of the Father and of the Son and of the Holy Ghost"—where the Son is named

---

received a remarkable access of interest in English theology in connection with the burning question of our Lord's relation to the criticism of the Old Testament. The weightiest utterance is that of Gore in the book entitled *Dissertations*, where the second dissertation is on "The Consciousness of our Lord in His Mortal Life." There is an American book just published—Hall: *The Kenotic Theory*. See also Mason, *The Conditions of Our Lord's Life on Earth*, and Adamson, *Studies of the Mind in Christ*; also the books on the Incarnation by Ottley, Powell and Gifford. During recent discussions a word of Tholuck has often recurred to my mind: "Now human knowledge has two sides, that which amongst greater or lesser external inspiration, develops completely on the inside through thinking and contemplation, and that which is only learned in a human sense and has been imprinted on the memory. If the development of the Savior is therefore just commonly human, then that knowledge which existed within his religious ethical sphere, especially that necessary for interpretation of the Scriptures which can only be memorized, was only known to him and accessible to him in accordance with the education level of his time and the education methods of his upbringing and surroundings. It could be therefore shown also in such questions belonging to well-educated exegesis as those relating to the historic context of a passage to the authorship and historical placement of a book, the historic insight even without the proper school knowledge, could divine the truth. The highest measure of such divine insight can be ascribed to the Savior. But that cannot at all times replace the actual scientific study. The Savior had not appeared to reveal science or even theology to the world, but to speak and live religious, ethical truth to humanity"—*Das alte Testament im neuen Testament*, p. 60.

with the Father and the Holy Ghost in a way that suggests the equality of all three, and an act of worship is directed to them jointly.* This is the verse next to the last of the Gospel of St. Matthew; and of course to those to whom the bodily resurrection of our Lord, with all that follows, is mythical, such words will carry no conviction, but to those who believe in His risen glory, they will appear perfectly congruous with the great occasion on which they were uttered.

Thus it would appear that, while Jesus took this title into His mind either from His religious environment or from the voice from heaven, it became to Him mainly an expression for His own relation to God; and this relationship was not only unique, but reached up beyond the competency of men or angels, till He named Himself in the same breath with the father and the Holy Ghost as an object of worship. It has, I venture to avow, been no effort of mine to find in the name the meaning at which we have arrived. Had the evidence led to a different conclusion, I would have accepted it without hesitation. But I have been led on step by step by the sheer force of Christ's own testimony. It remains to inquire what other testimony on the point His words contain apart from this particular name.

1. There is, in connection with our Lord's miracles, a long series of remarkable utterances, in which He commands the paralyzed to arise, the blind to open their eyes, the demons to depart out of the possessed, the stormy sea to be calm, and so on. Most of them are extremely concise, as "I will, be thou clean," "Peace, be still," "Ephphatha," and the like, but in this very brevity there is a sublime impressiveness, like that of the words in the first chapter of

---

* "It has of course often been made an objection against the originality of this formula, that it is only once mentioned in the New Testament, while, on the other hand, the phrase 'to be baptized in (or into) the name of the Lord Jesus' occurs more than once in the Acts of the Apostles. But, whatever force such an objection may have been supposed to have, has been greatly weakened since the discovery of *The Teaching of the Twelve Apostles.* For that early document, which is sometimes referred to as if it represented a Christianity more original than that of the New Testament, mentions twice over the formula of baptism into the threefold name, and thus interprets the expression which it also uses in common with St. Luke, that of being 'baptized into the name of the Lord' "—GORE, *The Incarnation of the Son of God,* p. 84.

Genesis: "Let there be light, and there was light." Even more impressive are the passages where He conveys the same powers to His disciples, as He sends them forth to preach and heal in His name—such as Matthew 10: 7, 8: "As you go, preach, saying, The kingdom of heaven is at hand; heal the sick, cleanse the lepers, raise the dead, cast out devils; freely you have received, freely give." The fact, indeed, that such powers were exercised by the disciples proves that the working of miracles was not in itself evidence of anything superhuman in the miracle worker. Some of the Old Testament prophets worked miracles too. Yet there is a difference. The scale on which Jesus acted entirely threw the prophets who were before Him into the shade; and the power of the disciples was entirely derivative. In the Book of Acts we have an apostolic miracle described which must have been typical; and, in performing it, St. Peter says to the subject on whom it took place, "Aeneas, Jesus Christ makes thee whole; arise, make thy bed" (Acts 9:34). Words could not betray more clearly that the power with which the apostles acted proceeded from their Master. It may be said that He, in like manner, was only the organ of the power of God working through Him; and this would be true. Yet would it be the whole truth? His miracles frequently produced an overwhelming impression of the divine glory embodied in His person. The exclamation of "those in the ship," when He stilled the storm, has been already quoted; and the terror of St. Peter, when he cried, "Depart from me; for I am a sinful man, O Lord," must have been repeated in many a sensitive mind on similar occasions. Remarking on the state of mind which prompted St. Peter's exclamation, an enlightened modern commentator says: "It burst upon his perception that the Lord God of Israel was beside him in that boat. The claims of Jesus suddenly rose upon Peter's conviction to those of the Highest. He is proved to be both God and Lord."* And, although this may go too far in the way of formulating the apostle's thought, yet it is not too much to say that the apostle received vague and vast impressions which were equivalent to this thought, and were destined in the course of time to condense into it.

---

* Laidlaw: *The Miracles of our Lord, in loco.*

2. Another series of sayings in which our Lord's superhuman self-consciousness betrays itself is that in which He comes forward as the supreme and final Revealer of truth. Frequently such sayings commence with the formula, "I say unto you," or, "Verily I say unto you." This phrase occurs more than thirty times in St. Matthew alone; and everyone will recall instances in which it falls on the ear with an extraordinary weight of authority. He not only sets up His own word in opposition to the authority of the scribes of His time and the traditions of the past, but even to the authority of Moses. With sovereign freedom He declares one law of Moses to be only a concession to the hardiness of heart of his contemporaries; and by His great statement, that not that which goeth into the man defiles but that which comes out of him, He sweeps away at one stroke whole pages of Mosaic legislation.* It may be said that this was only the prophetic function in its most perfect development. And this is true, but is it all the truth? The greatest of the prophets prefaced their oracles with, "Thus saith the Lord," but Jesus deliberately substitutes for this formula the simple claim, "I say unto you." When the most intricate moral and religious questions are submitted to Him, He does not hesitate a moment, because the will of God is perfectly familiar to Him. It is often said that one of the peculiarities of the Johannine Christ is that He is intimate with the secrets of the unseen world, but this characteristic is far from being confined to the Fourth Gospel. In the Synoptists, too, Jesus speaks like one to whom the scenery of the other world is native and familiar. Thus He says, that a sparrow does not fall but God marks it; and that the hairs of those whom He is dissuading from carefulness are all numbered. The angels of children do always behold the face of the heavenly Father. When surrounded by those sent to arrest Him, He declared that, had He but asked it, His heavenly Father would have sent to His rescue twelve legions of angels.† He assured the thief on the cross, "Today shalt thou be with me in Paradise." Many similar sayings might be adduced to show His acquaintance with both the near and the remote future, but these are reserved for a later lecture.

---

* Mark 7:19. Observe the R.V. translation: "This He said, making all meats clean."
† Matthew 10:29, 30; 26:53.

3. A third remarkable series of sayings consists of those in which He lays His claims upon the conscience, and states what will be the consequences of acknowledging or of rejecting these. One of the great and characteristic words of His ministry was, "Follow Me," which He employed with remarkable effect in instances known to all, and which He must have employed in many more that have not been recorded. The power of this form of address doubtless lay in the attraction with which a life in His company drew those who were capable of aspiration, but there lay in it, also, an authority of a more sovereign description which He never attempted to conceal. When one whom He had called asked to be allowed to go first and bury his father, He said, "Let the dead bury their dead." He warned those who might be disposed to follow Him that they must not only sacrifice the prizes of the world, but even hate father and mother, wife and children; and He did not hesitate to forewarn His disciples that they would be brought before principalities and powers, would be stripped and maltreated, and would even lose their lives (Matt. 8:22; Luke 14:26). The one sufficient compensation, however, for every hardship would be that they suffered for His sake. These claims are not embodied in one or two exceptional sayings: they were the daily language of Jesus. Who was He who dared to make such claims? He repeated in every form of expression, that the eternal destiny of His hearers would depend on their attitude to Himself. Even His disciples, when they went forth in His name, carried in their persons the fate of those with whom they came into contact, for whosoever received them received Him, and whosoever received Him received the Father who had sent Him, but whosoever rejected them brought down the contrary doom upon his soul (Matt. 10:14, 40).

4. A very remarkable series of sayings, though not an extended one, is that in which He claims to forgive sins. The most outstanding case was that of the man borne of four who was let down through the roof to be healed. When Jesus pronounced this man's sins forgiven, a charge of blasphemy was instantly raised. The opponents did not believe that the man's sins were forgiven or that Jesus could forgive them (Luke 5:21; 7:49). Of course, however, anyone can pretend to forgive sins, because forgiveness belongs to a region which is beyond

the control of human observation. The reply of Jesus was, that He would do something within the sphere of human observation which He could not do if He was capable of lying, but, if His word took effect in the visible sphere, this would prove that it had taken effect in the world invisible. Thereupon He healed the man. Against the supposition that Jesus in this transaction claimed anything superhuman the argument has been advanced, that He subsequently empowered the apostles to do the same thing. Obviously, however, the forgiveness of sins by them rested on His authority: it was purely declaratory and ministerial. And it may be said that in the same way His forgiveness was no more than the declaration that God had forgiven. He did not say so, however—not even when He was accused of blasphemy and might, by such an explanation have escaped from the charge. The natural sense of His words undoubtedly is, that the authority rested in His own person.

5. There remain a few very great sayings which I need not attempt to include under any rubric. They are well entitled to stand alone and to be separately pondered. They need little exposition or remark.

In the exaltation of mind produced by St. Peter's great confession, Jesus aid to him, "Thou art Peter, and upon this rock I will build My church; and the gates of hell shall not prevail against it. And I will give unto thee the keys of the kingdom of heaven; and whatsoever thou shalt bind on earth shall be bound in heaven: and whatsoever thou shalt loose on earth shall be loosed in heaven" (Matt. 16:18, 19). It is with a kind of bewilderment that one thinks of the claims implied here in every line. No wonder that those who look upon Jesus as no more than a man try to make out that He never uttered the words. But their magnificent assurance fits Him well.

Is there not the same superhuman greatness in the appeal, "O Jerusalem, Jerusalem, thou that kills the prophets, and stones them which are sent unto thee, how often would I have gathered your children together as a hen gathers her chickens under her wings, and you would not" (Matt. 23:37)? Is not this the same voice as that which of old claimed to have borne Israel through the wilderness as an eagle, fluttering over her nest, carries her young upon her wings?

Repeatedly He promised to be with His own in the future, when in bodily presence He would be far away. Thus, when they were confronted with the opposition of the great and powerful, "I will give you a mouth and wisdom, which all your adversaries shall not be able to gainsay nor resist"; and again, when, escaping from the persecution of society, they should meet for fellowship and prayer, "Where two or three are gathered together in My name, there am I in the midst of them" (Luke 21:15; Matt. 18:20).

The greatest saying of all is, appropriately, the last: "All power is given unto Me in heaven and in earth . . . and, lo, I am with you alway, even unto the end of the world" (Matt. 28:18-20). Many attempts have been made to define and confine these extraordinary words, but, like Samson's strength, they burst the withes of definition; and those only know what they mean who, in prayer with their fellow Christians, have felt the personal nearness of Him whom, having not seen, they love.

It is possible to take such great sayings one by one and either discredit them as unauthentic or deplete them of their meaning. The former is habitually done, for example, by Holtzmann, the latter by Wendt. According to Holtzmann such words are the rudimentary beginnings of dogma: that is to say, they did not proceed from the lips of Christ, but were crystallized from the consciousness of the primitive Christians.[†] But our knowledge of primitive Christianity dates very far back; the earliest epistles of St. Paul, as dated by the latest scholarship, stand at but an inconsiderable distance from the death of Christ; and not only is the Christ of St. Paul's earliest writings the very same, in all essentials, as the Christ of his later writings—the same, for example, as He of the Epistle to the Philippians, who, "being in the form of God thought it not robbery to be equal with God," and has "a name which is above every name, that at the name of Jesus every knee should bow of things in heaven and things in earth and things under the earth, and that every tongue should confess that Jesus Christ is Lord to the glory of God the Father"—but St. Paul's Christ was the Christ of primitive Christianity. On other subjects there was fierce controversy

---

† *N. T. Theologie*, I. 352 ff.

in the primitive Church, but on this there was none. Now, is it credible that there should have been such unanimity about a cardinal belief like this, if Christ's own words had contained no hint of it, but rather the reverse? Wendt takes each saying by itself, and having laboriously shown the very least it can possibly have meant, then assumes this to have been the original meaning. But it is often not the natural meaning; and one gets tired of this continual shallowing of everything that Jesus said. The truth is, if Jesus meant no more than Wendt makes Him say, He was the most paradoxical and hyperbolical teacher that has ever appeared, and He alienated His hearers by mystifications, when a few words of common sense, such as Wendt now speaks for Him, would have cleared away all difficulties and conciliated the minds of men.

These divine sayings of our Lord do not look like fragments of a different formation, but are congruous with all His words, of which they form the natural completion. You may attempt to take them from Him and assign them to other minds, or you may suppose that in some way, without the agency of any actual minds, they were crystallized from the atmosphere of the apostolic age, but this is forcework; and, when the hand of violence is removed, they revert to their Author and fill out the lineaments of the great personality which rises upon us in the Gospels. I do not attribute to Jesus dogmatic statements or make Him responsible for the phraseology of the creeds. His utterances were of a totally different character: they were remarks made in passing, hints dropped of which He may sometimes hardly have been conscious, impressions rayed forth from his personality on the minds of others, and fitted at first to produce states of feeling rather than definite beliefs. But what I cannot credit is, that by the time of the earliest Christian records His followers had already distorted and mistaken Him altogether, so that the history of Christianity was built from the very foundation on a misunderstanding and a misrepresentation, behind which we must, after two thousand years, get back, if we are to have a real Christ and a genuine Christianity. "Back to Christ" is the watchword of theology in this generation; and I will repeat it with an enthusiasm born of a lifelong study of His words, but, when I go back to Him, I do not find a Christ who puts to shame the highest which His Church has taught about Him. He is different indeed—far more simple, actual and human—yet in all that is most essential He is the same Son of God as for nineteen centuries has inspired the lives of the saints and evoked the worship of the world.

PASSAGES IN WHICH JESUS REFERS TO HIMSELF AS THE CHRIST:
Matthew 16:20, 22, 42; 23: [8], 10; 24:5, 23, 24; 26:64.
Mark 9:41; 12:35; 13:6, 21; 14:61.
Luke 4:18, 19, 21; 20:41; 21:8; 22:67, 68; 24:26, 46.

PASSAGES IN WHICH OTHERS REFER TO HIM AS THE CHRIST, HE SOME-
    TIMES ASSENTING:
Matthew 1:1, 16, 17, 18; 2:4; 11:2, 3; 16:16; 26:68; 27:17, 22.
Mark 1:1; 8:29; 14:61; 15:32.
Luke 2:11, 26; 3:15; 4:41; 7:19; 9:20; 23:2, 35, 39.

PASSAGES IN WHICH JESUS IS CALLED THE SON OF DAVID:
Matthew 1:1, 6, 17, 20; 9:27; 12:23; 15:22; 20:30, 31; 21:9, 15; 22:42, 45.
Mark 10:47, 48; 11:10; 12:35, 37.
Luke 1:27, 32; 3:3; 18:38, 39; 20:41, 44.

PASSAGES IN WHICH "THE KINGDOM" IS MENTIONED, OR "THE KINGDOM
    OF HEAVEN," OR "THE KINGDOM OF GOD":
Matthew 4:17, 23; 5:3, 10, 19, 20; 6:10, [13], 33; 7:21; 8:11, 12; 9:35;
    10:7, 11, 12; 12:28; 13:11, 19, 24, 31, 33, 38, 41, 43, 44, 45, 47, 52;
    16:19, 28; 18:3, 4, 23; 19:12, 14, 23, 24; 20:1, 21; 21:31, 43; 22:2;
    23:13; 24:14; 25:1, 14, 34; 26:39.
Mark 1: [14], 15; 4:43; 6:20; 7:28; 8:1, 10,; 9:2, 11, 27, 62; 10:9, 11;
    11:2, 20; 12:31, 32; 13:18, 20, 28, 29; 14:15; 16:16; 17:20, 21;
    18:16, 17, 24, 25, 29; 19:11, 12, 15; 21:31,; 22:16, 18, 29, 30;
    23:42.

4
The Messiah

Of all the names of our Lord, with the exception of His birth-name, "Jesus," the one which has stuck most firmly in the memory of the world is "Christ," which is the Greek equivalent for "Messiah," and in English is correctly rendered by the word "Anointed." Indeed, this name may be said to dispute the foremost place with the name "Jesus" itself. Why the ordinary man sometimes says "Jesus" and sometimes "Christ," he could hardly tell; though there appear to be peculiar states of religious feeling which incline towards the one or the other. Of course the original name was "Jesus": this was what His mother called Him, and what He was called in the streets and the workshop of Nazareth; whereas "Christ" was originally a title. Some preachers seem to themselves to be imparting freshness to their sermons by saying "the Christ" instead of simply "Christ"; and undoubtedly this was the original form, but already in the New Testament "Christ," without the article, is a proper name. Very frequently the two names are combined in the form "Jesus Christ" or "Christ Jesus"; and even the Evangelists St. Matthew and St. Mark announce that they are going to write the memoirs of "Jesus Christ."*

In the Old Testament, "the Lord's anointed" is a synonym for "the king"; and in poetical passages the two stand in parallelism, as Psalm 18:50,

> Great deliverance giveth He to His king,
> And sheweth mercy to His anointed.

---

* On the N. T. use there are interesting statistics in Nösgen's *Der Menschen-und Gottessohn*, pp. 118 ff. The combinations "Jesus Christ" and "Christ Jesus" are formed exactly as "Emin Pasha" and "Queen Victoria."

The king was called "the anointed" because at his coronation the sacred oil was poured upon his head, by which he was consecrated to his office. This oil was a symbol of the Spirit of God, from whom the young monarch was supposed to receive the wisdom, dignity and other gifts necessary for the discharge of his functions; as is beautifully brought out in Isaiah 11:1–4: "And there shall come forth a Rod out of the stem of Jesse, and a Branch shall grow out of his roots, and the Spirit of the Lord shall rest upon Him, the Spirit of wisdom and understanding, the Spirit of counsel and might, the Spirit of knowledge and the fear of the Lord; and shall make Him of quick understanding in the fear of the Lord; and He shall not judge after the sight of His eyes, neither reprove after the hearing of His ears, but with righteousness shall He judge the poor and reprove with equity for the meek of the earth; and He shall smite the earth with the rod of His mouth, and with the breath of His lips will He slay the wicked; and righteousness shall be the girdle of His loins and faithfulness the girdle of His reins." This perfect description of a king may well be quoted in full, because, although it does not contain the name "Messiah," it had a great deal to do with shaping the meaning ultimately attached to the term; which was that of an ideal king, who should embody in himself all the attributes and achievements proper to the kingly office and thereby conduct the nation to the full realization of its destiny.

For this ideal personage the title "Messiah" is already used in the second Psalm, though not elsewhere in the Old Testament; in the postcanonical writings of the Jews there occur more frequent instances of its use in this sense;[*] and in our Lord's time "the Messiah" was the regular term for the expected deliverer, as is manifest from the pages of the Gospels. In the palmy days of the ministry of John the Baptist "all men," St. Luke informs us, "mused in their hearts of John, whether he were the Christ, or not" (Luke 3:15). The same Evangelist tells us, a little later, that "devils came out of many, crying out, and saying, Thou art Christ; and He, rebuking them, suffered them not to speak; for they knew that He was Christ" (Luke 4:41). That our Lord

---

[*] Cf. Dalman, Die Worte Jesu, p. 239; Schürer, *The History of the Jewish People in the time of our Lord*, II. ii. 158.

should have disliked testimony coming from such a quarter, and have tried to check it, need occasion no surprise; for, even when the same testimony came from unexceptionable quarters, He was slow to accept it. Yet this does not prove, as some extreme critics of the Gospel history have contended, that He never claimed to be the Messiah of the Jews at all. The evidence to the contrary is as strong as it can be. First there is His declaration in the synagogue of Nazareth:

> The Spirit of the Lord is upon Me,
> Because He hath anointed Me to preach good tidings to
>   the poor:
> He hath sent Me to proclaim release to the captives,
> And recovering of sight to the blind,
> To set at liberty them that are bruised,
> To proclaim the acceptable year of the Lord.
> —Luke 4:18, 19, R.V.

Because these words in their original setting describe the inspiration of a prophet, it may be argued that they express no more than prophetic consciousness, but they are elastic terms, capable of embodying much more than Isaiah put into them, and capable, in fact, of embodying more than even Jesus put into them at Nazareth because they contain the entire program of the ripest Christianity. And, if they be compared with the expectations of the time, as we find them in the hymns, in the first chapters of St. Luke, emitted by those who were waiting for the kingdom of God, and if the exalted and solemn tone be considered in which Jesus uttered them, it can scarcely be doubtful that they are an expression of messianic consciousness. Still less questionable is the reply of Jesus to the deputation from the Baptist, whose inquiry was, "Art Thou He that should come, or do we look for another?" Can there be any reasonable question either which personage was intended by the Baptist or what was the force of our Lord's reply? And with this we may join the fact, that more than once Jesus designated the Baptist as Elias (Matt. 11:14; 17:12)—the figure in the popular creed who was to be the forerunner of the Christ. Next there is the great crisis at Caesarea Philippi, when He drew from the Twelve the acknowledgment that He was the Christ, and manifestly rejoiced in their testimony. Finally, on His trial, "the high priest asked Him and said unto Him, Art

Thou the Christ, the Son of the Blessed? And Jesus said, I am" (Mark 14:61, 62). And a little later Jesus "stood before the governor, and the governor asked Him, saying, Art Thou the King of the Jews? And Jesus said unto him, Thou sayest."* Around the head of Jesus, when He was hanging on the cross, these names, all meaning the same thing—"the Christ," "the King of Israel," "the King of the Jews"—flew, being shot like angry missiles from the mouths of His enemies, till he breathed His last; and the inscription above His head ran thus, "This is Jesus, the King of the Jews" (Mark 15:32; Matt. 27:42, 37).

Another name applied still more frequently by others to Jesus—"the Son of David"—means precisely the same as "the Messiah." It was the unanimous testimony of Old Testament prophecy that the messianic king was to be of David's line. So far does this feature enter into the conception that He is even called "David" pure and simple; not as if it were supposed that the son of Jesse was to rise from the dead and ascend the throne of the country again, but to emphasize the fact that the new king, being of David's seed, was to reproduce the spirit and glory of the original.

Only once did Jesus of His own accord allude to this circumstance, when, on the great day of controversy at the close of His life, after replying to all the entangling questions of His enemies and reducing Pharisees and Sadducees to confusion, He propounded to them the problem, how it could be that in the hundred-and-tenth Psalm David called the Christ "Lord" who was at the same time his son. The school of interpreters who happen at the present moment to be most conspicuous in Germany make this out to be an announcement by Jesus that He did not claim Davidic descent or attach any importance to it. But, if Jesus had declared Himself not to be of David's line, He would have run counter not only to the tradition of the Jewish parties, but to the testimony of the prophets, as well as to the convictions held both then and subsequently by the most intimate of His own friends; for His descent from David is much insisted on by the writers of the New Testament (Rom. 1:3; 2 Tim. 2:8; Rev. 5:5; 22:16).

---

* Matt. 27:11. On the reply Σὺ εἶπας see Dalman, *Die Worte Jesu*, pp. 253 ff., who replies to the doubt which has been started as to whether this was an affirmative answer.

Why, if this was the intention of Jesus, should He have raised the question at all? It could only be because His descent from David was called in question by His enemies, but of this there is not a hint in the evangelic records; and yet nothing can be more certain than that it would have been a prominent and often repeated charge, if it had ever been made at all. The truth is, the question propounded by Jesus had a totally different drift: it was one of the most significant indications ever thrown out by Him of His consciousness of divine sonship in a unique sense; and the only effect of twisting the point of His question in another direction is to obscure the glory of this sublime claim.

We may look upon it, then, as proved that Jesus claimed to be the Messiah, the Son of David; and this turns our attention, which has hitherto been fixed on the Person, to the Work of the Savior, because His messiahship denotes the function which He came to fulfill. Not that these two topics lie far apart; for the loftiness of the person points to a correspondingly important work, and, the grander the work, the greater must the person be who undertakes it. But we have now before us the inquiry, What, according to His own teaching, was the object of our Lord's earthly mission?

The immediate answer to this question is, The Kingdom of God.* If Jesus was the Messiah, the kingdom of God was the realm in which He was to rule;† and He habitually made use of the phrase for the purpose of describing succinctly all the blessings which He had come to bestow.

The ordinary reader of the Gospels hardly realizes how prominent in them is the idea of the kingdom of God. A little attention, however, reveals the fact that it is omnipresent: it is the name for the contents

---

* "The idea of the βασιλεία is found in Matthew 53 times, in Mark 16, in Luke 39, in John 5, in Acts 8, in the Epistles 18, in Mark 16, in Revelation 7. It is absent from Philippians, 1 Timothy, Titus, Philemon, 1 Peter, 1–3 John and Jude." — *Issel: Das Reich Gottes*, p. 27.

† There has been a good deal of discussion as to whether βασιλεία in the mouth of Jesus means the domain in which the Messiah was to rule or the sovereignty which he was to exercise within this domain. It has both meanings, sometimes the one and sometimes the other idea being prominent.

of the Gospel—the name habitually given by Jesus to His own message. If the average man were asked what Jesus spoke and preached about, he would answer without hesitation, "The Gospel"; and in this he would not be wrong; for Jesus did characterize His message as the Gospel, or Evangel, or Glad Tidings. But, if he were further asked what the Gospel which Jesus taught was about, he would answer with equal confidence that it was about Salvation; and in this he would not be so right because, although "the Gospel of Salvation" is a phrase found in the writings of St. Paul, it never occurs in the records of the teachings of Jesus. What we find in place of it is "the Gospel of the Kingdom of God." Sometimes it is merely said that He preached "the Kingdom"; or to this name may be added the qualifying phrase, "of God," or "of heaven." We find all these phrases: that Jesus preached "the Kingdom," "the Kingdom of God," "the Kingdom of heaven," "the Gospel of the Kingdom of God," and "the Gospel of the Kingdom of heaven."[*] In St. Mark 1:14 the commencement of His ministry is described in these terms: "Now, after that John was put in prison, Jesus came into Galilee preaching the gospel of the kingdom of God." Referring to a period a little later, St. Matthew thus describes His activity: "Jesus went about all Galilee, teaching in their synagogues and preaching the gospel of the kingdom" (Matt. 4:23). Later still St. Luke says, "It came to pass afterward, that He went through every city and village, preaching and showing the glad tidings of the kingdom of God" (Luke 8:1). When the Twelve are sent forth, their mission is described in these words: "He sent them to preach the kingdom of God" (Matt. 9:2). The parables of Jesus, which form so large a portion of His teaching, are collectively denominated "the mysteries of the kingdom of heaven" (Matt. 13:11); and, it will be remembered, how many of them begin with the phrase, "The kingdom of heaven is like."

Thus it is evident that "the kingdom of God" formed the watchword of Jesus.[†] But, although it occupied so prominent a place in His

---

[*] Matthew 4:23; 9:35; Luke 4:23; Matthew 10:7; 4:23; Mark 1:15.

[†] In St. Matthew in the majority of passages where it occurs it is called "the kingdom of heaven"; but this is only a variation of phraseology without alteration of sense, for "Heaven" appears to have been in the time of Jesus a not unusual

teaching, it was not a phrase of His own invention. John the Baptist, before Him, summed up his message in the same phrase. In the First Gospel he is thus introduced: "In those days came John the Baptist, preaching in the wilderness of Judea, and saying, Repent ye; for the kingdom of heaven is at hand" (Matt. 3:2). Indeed, the phrase is far older. In the Book of Daniel, the influence of which is known to have been great in the generations immediately before the Advent, the young prophet explains to the monarch the image of gold, silver, iron and clay which, in his dream he has seen shattered by "a stone cut out of the mountain," as a succession of world kingdoms to be destroyed by "a kingdom of God," which will last forever; and in his other famous vision of the Son of man, referred to on a previous page, it is said, "There was given Him dominion, glory and a kingdom; and all people, nations and languages shall serve Him; His dominion is an everlasting dominion which shall not pass away, and His kingdom that which shall not be destroyed" (Dan. 2:44; 7:14).

This is the proximate Biblical source of the phrase, but the idea it represents mounts far higher in history. It will be remembered that at the very origin of the monarchy in Israel the proposal to appoint a king was condemned on the ground that Jehovah was King, and the appointment of Saul was only acquiesced in as a compromise, on account of the difficulty of getting the ideal to work. In David ideal and reality became approximately identical: God was King, and David was His vicegerent, governing in according with His will and purposes, and, therefore, able to make the kingdom great and prosperous in Jehovah's name. In Solomon the approximation was still tolerable, but in the long succession of kings that followed there were few who did not cause the better spirits of the nation to sigh for the kingdom of God as something still unrealized. Never, however, did the conviction die out that Jehovah was the real King, and that the only right and stable kingdom

---

synonym for "God." It is thus used by Jesus in the parable of the Prodigal Son— "I have sinned against Heaven and before thee," says the returning prodigal—and we use it to this day in the same sense in such phrases as "Heaven help them." Of course the phrase may also mean the kingdom which comes from heaven, or which is like heaven, or which will be consummated in heaven. It cannot always be determined with certainty which of these shades of meaning the word expresses.

would be that in and through which His will was done on earth as it is done in heaven. When at last even the form of earthly sovereignty was swept away, on account of its deflection from the ideal having become intolerable, the old faith, so far from perishing, flourished more and more vigorously; and the one hope of the dark days of exile nd oppression was that God would yet restore the kingdom to Israel.* That He would do so, the pious never doubted; for to doubt this would have been to doubt His existence, or at all events His character and His promises. All the prophets predicted that He would soon take to Himself His great power and reign; and they vied with one another in painting the picture of the blessings which would ensue under His government.

To us, with our modern habits of thought, it is astonishing that religious hope should have been so closely associated with political change. But the sense of the value of a well-ordered state to secure the safety and happiness of human life was universal in the ancient world; and there were times when this was felt to be the one thing needful. Even "salvation"—a word which we associate with the most interior experiences of the individual—was a term the significance of which was social and national, and the realization of which was to take place through political means. Only get your state right, it was thought —with perfect laws and a perfect administration—and everything will be right: even sin will disappear; for all injustice will be smitten to the ground, and righteousness will flourish under the protection of authority. The grand difficulty was to find an earthly king—or a succession of kings—pious, able and steadfast enough to be the organ through which the divine wisdom and power might act. At this point failure had constantly taken place; and it was always becoming more and more evident that the only vicegerent of God who could ensure the perfect and enduring prosperity for which pious and patriotic hearts sighed must be One who, while earthly, shared in the perfec-

---

* When Israel lay beneath the shadow of the great world-powers, the pious recognized in these the diabolical counterfeit of what the kingdom of God was to be. In the relation of subordinate rulers, like their own, to the Roman central authority, for example, they saw a dim image of what the relation of the heathen princes and peoples would be to the Messiah, when he should appear.

tion and everlastingness of the supreme Ruler. If they never actually put this conclusion into words, it lay in the line of their hopes to do so.

These messianic hopes continued after the date of the latest Old Testament writings and on to the time of Jesus. The rumor of them spread so far that its echoes are heard even in the Roman historians, Tacitus and Suetonius;* and the post-canonical writings of the Jews themselves abound with descriptions, ranging from the driest prose up through all degrees to the most highly-colored poetry, of the blessings to be anticipated when the kingdom of God begins.† Schürer, the latest historian of this period, putting these passages together, has constructed a kind of messianic creed, which he attributes to the contemporaries of Jesus. Its articles are eleven in number, and the following order indicates also the chronological sequence in which the different phases of the messianic epoch were expected to develop themselves:(1) the last tribulation and perplexity (the night of humiliation and oppression being darkest just before the dawning); (2) Elijah as the forerunner; (3) The advent of the Messiah; (4) The final attack of the hostile powers; (5) The destruction of the hostile powers; (6) The renovation of Jerusalem; (7) The gathering together of the dispersed; (8) The kingdom of glory in Palestine; (9) The renovation of the world; (10) The general resurrection; (11) The last judgment: eternal condemnation and salvation.**

It remains doubtful, however, how far this creed extended, or, at least, to how many it was a living creed. Many Jews were, no doubt, too immersed in the world and too well pleased with their actual condition to care for such dreams. This was the attitude of the Sadducees. Others, imbibing these hopes in a narrow, nationalist spirit, indulged in fantastic imaginings as to the miraculous agencies through which Jehovah would destroy His enemies and bestow felicity on His favorites. Such were the Pharisees, and especially the Zealots. But the true repositories of the messianic hopes were those who, regarding

---

* Quoted by Schürer, II. ii. 149.

† See the valuable texts from postcanonical Jewish literature printed as an appendix in Dalman's Die Worte Jesus, and also published separately.

** Schürer, II. ii. 126 ff.

them from the spiritual and moral side, cultivated them with religious enthusiasm.* Of Joseph of Arimathea it is said that "he waited for the kingdom of God"; and the same was, in all likelihood, true of Nicodemus and of other persons of rank and influence. The majority, however, of those to whom waiting for the kingdom of God was a portion of living piety, belonged to the humbler ranks of society. To their delightful circle we are introduced in the opening pages of the Gospel, which tell of Simeon and Anna, the Shepherds of Bethlehem, and other kindred spirits. In this circle were born both John the Baptist and Jesus; and it is in the songs which, at the time of their birth, burst from the inspired lips of Mary and Elizabeth, Zechariah and Simeon, that we discover the truest image of what the messianic hope actually was. It is infinitely deeper than the creed compiled by Schürer. It is redolent not of the schools of the scribes, but of the inspiration of the prophets. Above all, it is instinct with the humility of broken hearts and of souls passionately longing for salvation. It reflects precisely the state of mind to which our Lord subsequently addressed Himself when He said, "Come unto Me, all you that labor and are heavy laden, and I will give you rest."

---

* These were "die Stillen im Lande"—a beautiful name for the cultivators of a piety of this type. Another name is οἱ προσδεχόμενοι Schnedermann frequently directs attention to the importance of this class in his work on the Kingdom of God. He devotes three volumes (see page 128, *supra*) to the repetition of the single proposition that the Kingdom of God of Jesus was fundamentally identical with the same idea as cherished by God's ancient people. His volumes form amusing reading to a foreigner, because he considers himself not only the owner but even the martyr of this proposition, and warns off all other writers from participation in his property. He appears, however, to excite strong feeling in the scholars of his own country, who resent his claims to originality. His writing is diffuse and paradoxical, yet he makes a number of good points. Such, for example, is his distinction between the "Israelite" and "Jewish" elements in the intellectual atmosphere in which Jesus grew up: though Judaism reigned in the schools of the scribes and held the field to outward appearance, yet an "Israelite" strain of piety and conviction prevailed in a certain section of religious society. Those who walked in the green pastures and beside the still waters of this faith of the heart were in touch with the Prophets and understood all that is deepest in the Old Testament. That this is true and valuable I have no doubt. Another of his striking sayings is that "the kingdom of God" is of fundamental but not of central importance in the teaching of Jesus.

This circle of receptive and prepared souls may have been wider than is generally supposed; for piety of this type, though exercising great influence, makes little noise and receives little notice from contemporary chroniclers. At all events, it would be the whole world to Jesus in the years during which His mind was forming. He may even, on this account, have taken long to realize how widely the spirit and views of the Jewish world at large differed from His own; and this may partly account for what is a difficulty of no inconsiderable magnitude—that He should have given such prominence in His preaching to a term understood so differently by Himself and His hearers.

His use of it has sometimes been spoken of as an accommodation to the usages and the capacities of His contemporaries, but it was the very form in which He thought His own thoughts. It was, indeed, a borrowed garment, and it may from the first have been too scanty for Him; or perhaps His mind eventually outgrew it; yet it was native to Him, and He moved in it without the sense of incongruity. It was besides, a noble form. As the prophets had conceived it, and as it had shaped itself in the pious minds in whose midst He grew up, it was an ideal in which a young soul could revel and rejoice.

It was, therefore, with a great rush of emotion that He first announced the coming of the kingdom. His message was emphatically the "Gospel" of the kingdom of God. He commenced, like John, with announcing simply that the kingdom was at hand (Mark 1:14); and there is no reason to doubt that there existed in the public mind a sufficient amount of messianic sentiment to make this announcement attract attention and excite enthusiasm. At first everyone would interpret it according to his own ideas of the expected kingdom; and so the rumor of the preaching of John and Jesus rang through the land, and all men were in expectation as to the shape in which the promised kingdom would appear.

As soon, however, as Jesus began to explain Himself, it became manifest that the majority of His countrymen and He were expecting the fulfillment of the promise in totally different forms. Both employed the same phrase—"the kingdom of God"—but His countrymen laid the emphasis on the first half of it—"the kingdom"—while He laid it on the second—"of God." They were thinking of the external benefits and glories of a kingdom, such as political emancipation, a throne, a court, a capital and tributary provinces, while He was thinking of the character of the subjects of the anticipated realm and of the doing in it of the will of God, as it is done in heaven.

Jesus had, indeed, Himself felt at one time the glamour of their point of view; for this was the meaning of the Temptation. The account of this experience preserved in the Gospels may be an imaginative rendering of the actual facts; and it is highly instructive as embodying a variety of reflections on temptation in general, as all men have to encounter it, but it is also the record of a crisis in the life of Jesus at a particular point, and it exhibits Him in conflict with the messianic preconceptions of His countrymen. This is clearest in the temptation in which He was offered the kingdoms of the world on condition of compromising with evil; for manifestly this was a temptation to begin at the outside instead of the inside—to begin with the nation instead of the individual—to get the shell of mere appearance first and to fill it with reality afterwards. The temptation to turn stones into bread is generally interpreted as referring to the use of His miraculous power for His own behoove, but it was also, in all probability, directed towards the winning of popularity by creating the necessaries and luxuries of life on a lavish scale—by becoming, in short, a bread-king, like those who in another country courted the popular favor by giving *panem et circenses*.[*] The temptation to cast Himself from the pinnacle of the temple is the one the messianic drift of which is least certain. It obviously refers in general to the fanatical faith which scorns the use of means, but it probably also has reference to a contemporary expectation that the Messiah would make His appearance in a sudden and striking manner. He was supposed to be hidden till the hour of fulfillment should strike, and then He would appear suddenly, it was believed, in the midst of the nation assembled in the temple on some such public occasion as one of the annual festivals.[†] Probably if we know more completely than we do the details of contemporary messianic belief, we should be able to see the historical application of each

---

[*] See a remarkable series of papers on our Lord's temptation in *The Expositor*, 3rd series, vol. iii, p. 369 ff., by the Rev. W. W. Peyton.

[†] Schürer, II. ii, 16.

of the temptations still more clearly; but at all events Jesus left the wilderness steeled against the worldly and fantastic conception of the coming kingdom entertained by His fellow countrymen and determined to insist upon one which was moral and spiritual.

It is impossible, as one reads the Gospels, to help pitying the Jews, who expected a Messiah so different from Jesus, but we must remember three things. First, His conception was that of the Old Testament prophets, and, therefore, it might have been theirs too, since the writings of the prophets were in their hands. It was because they were unable to appreciate the depth and spirituality of their own sacred books that they failed to understand Him. Secondly, it was His part to teach and theirs to learn. He would have been no Messiah, not even a prophet of the Lord, if He had simply fallen in with popular opinions and expectations. Thirdly, the way prescribed by Him was the true path even to the objects desired by them. If they had consented to His leading and faced the lowly road of penitence and humiliation, can there be any doubt that He would have led them up to glory in the long run? What the history of Judea would have been, and what the history of the world, if they had accepted Him on His own terms, is, indeed, a question which defies human calculation, but we cannot hesitate to answer it at least so far as to say, that all the happiness and the glory predicted by the prophets would have been realized. These predictions, however, as well as the conduct of Jesus, were conditioned on the response of faith made by the people. This response was never forthcoming; and so the possibilities could never be fulfilled.

For a time, it looked as if Galilee were to respond to the appeal of Jesus, whose opening ministry was, therefore, full of hope and enthusiasm. But the response never came from a deep enough place; so that He could not commit Himself to the multitude, but had to fall back on the work of preparation. This is the explanation of the fact, that, while everywhere throughout His ministry speaking with perfect freedom of the kingdom of God, He was astonishingly reticent about the Messiah.[*]

---

[*] The question of the Reticence of Jesus is one on which the last word has not yet by any means been spoken. It does not concern His messiahship alone, as anyone can see for himself who will look up the following references in a single Gospel—Mark 1:44; 3:12; 5:43; 7:36; 8:26, 30; 9:9, 25, 30.

The Messiah was not, in every mind, an absolutely essential feature of the kingdom. This is seen even in the prophets of the Old Testament; for some of them, while predicting in glowing colors the messianic age, have no vision of the messianic King; and the same may be said of the postcanonical writers. From the reticence of Jesus on this point some scholars have been disposed to draw the inference that He Himself, at first at least, was not aware that He was the Messiah, but was only conscious, like the Baptist, of being a forerunner; and the intelligent reader of the Gospels may sometimes feel a doubt whether Jesus was not bound, if He knew Himself as the Messiah, to impart this knowledge more freely to those whose duty it was to acknowledge Him. But Jesus preferred to act as the Messiah rather than to bear witness to Himself; and He was not unduly reticent where any disposition was shown to look upon Him and His actions with an unprejudiced eye. But He could not entrust Himself to the multitude: their expectations were too impure. St. John mentions an occasion when they tried to take Him by force and make Him a king, but of such zealotic enthusiasm He could take no advantage: it only drove Him more and more in upon Himself.

At last, however, He did break through His reserve and cease to make any secret of His claims. His triumphal entry into Jerusalem was an offer of Himself to His countrymen as their Messiah, the *bona fides* of which it would be unreasonable to doubt. Yet it is an incident surrounded with tragic mystery. He Himself can have had little hope. In fact, He had so little that in the midst of His triumph He burst into tears; and, after entering the city, He allowed the crowd to disperse with nothing done. It was, indeed, only a crowd of Galileans, whose shouts of, "Blessed by the Son of David, who cometh in the name of the Lord!" awakened no echo in the cold and sullen heart of Jerusalem. Still Jesus had given to His hard-hearted and guilty countrymen their last chance, leaving no mistake as to the character in which He claimed their homage; and it was by them, not by Him, that the nation's charter of promise was torn up and nailed to a tree—an act to which, however, destiny affixed its seal, when, a few years afterwards, the Jewish state finally perished and Jerusalem was razed to the ground.

Such was the issue of laying the emphasis of the Kingdom of God on the first member of the phrase. Meantime, however, Jesus had been working out His own conception of it, laying the accent on the second member.

In the first place, He insisted on Repentance as a preparation for the kingdom. This was the very first word of His preaching; and it was a word which never disappeared. A great proportion of His recorded sayings consists of denunciations of sin. He denounced especially the sins of the upper and ruling classes; and, if He did not in an equal degree denounce the sins of the poor and the outcast, it was because it was unnecessary, as these came weeping to His feet, confessing their own sins.

To such penitents He conveyed the assurance of pardon, claiming that He had power on earth to forgive sins. And undoubtedly His meaning was that forgiveness was even more needed by the hard and haughty hearts of Pharisees and scribes. Indeed, He told such that, unless they came down from their arrogance and became as little children they could not enter the kingdom of God.

Inwardly the kingdom is one of Righteousness: this is its outstanding character. The greatest discourse of Jesus is wholly occupied with this theme, developing the conception of righteousness in contrast not only with current habits of living, but also with traditional maxims, and even the commandments of Moses.* Through the Sermon on the Mount, from first to last, there runs a strain of the most passionate moral earnestness. Never elsewhere in the world has there been taught so inward or difficult a morality, but it was to be the high prerogative of the kingdom of God to realize it.

The kingdom had, however, another side besides this stern one: it was Blessedness as well as righteousness. This side of it is developed

---

* Matthew 5:17 — "Except your righteousness shall exceed the righteousness of the scribes and Pharisees, ye shall also in no case enter the kingdom of heaven." The rest of the Sermon on the Mount is an exposition of this text, the righteousness required of Christians being contrasted first with that prescribed in the Mosaic law and the traditional exposition of the same (to the end of chapter 5), secondly with contemporary Pharisaic custom (6:1–18), and thirdly with the ordinary course of this world (from 6:19 to the end).

with a graciousness which charms the heart as well as an originality which excites the intellect in the Beatitudes. Each beatitude is a paradox because that in which blessedness is said to consist is a minus quantity. This defect, however, is only the empty place into which the positive blessing can rush; and the sum of the minus and the plus together is a divine overplus of blessedness. It is, indeed, happiness of a high order, consisting in such blessings as the vision of God and divine sonship (Matt. 5:8, 9), but it is only of such as are capable of these aspirations that the kingdom of God is to be composed.

Thus it is manifest that the good things of which the kingdom of God was the sum, as they presented themselves to the mind of Jesus, were totally different from those dreamed of by political and revolutionary zealots. And this fact was made still more evident when He summed them up, as He sometimes did, in such terms as "peace" and "rest." Again and again, where His ordinary usage would lead us to expect "the kingdom of God" in His sayings, there is substituted for it "life" or "eternal life."* And nothing could be a more significant indication of the intense religious preoccupation of His mind. To Him existence without God was not life, but death, but to live in God—thinking His thoughts, doing His will, enjoying His fellowship—was the sum of blessedness; and such was to be the blessedness of the kingdom of God.

In short, the thought of Jesus is prevailingly moral and religious. He began with the conceptions and the phraseology of the time, but He naturally and gradually drew away from them, out into the broad ocean. A glance at His parables makes this manifest. While some of them, like the Barren Fig Tree and the Wicked Husbandman, have a strongly Jewish flavor, others, like the Talents and the Rich Fool, belong to the realm of religion pure and simple; and many of the greatest, like the three of the fifteenth of Luke, while retaining marks of their Jewish original, have the most obvious application to the whole of humanity. So, when Jesus says that He has come to seek and to save that which is lost, we remember, indeed, that there is an allusion to the prodigal and abandoned classes of his own day, but the glory of the

---

* Luke 19:42; Matthew 11:28, 29; Mark 9:47; 10:30.

saying lies in its application to lost men everywhere. When He says, "Come unto me, all you that labor and are heavy laden, and I will give you rest," He has, no doubt, in view His contemporaries groaning under the traditions of the elders, but His words have, beneath this surface meaning, a universal application to all forms of spiritual unrest and anxiety. In short, as Jesus followed the guidance of His genius along this line, He passed from being the Messiah of the Jews to be the Savior of the world.

The entrance to the kingdom is, according to the mind of Jesus, a straight gate. Indeed, it admits only one at a time: everyone, be he Pharisee or publican, must go through the ordeal of repentance. Jesus was well aware how unattractive such a rule would be; and much of His teaching is occupied with the difficulties of those who, for one reason or another, found it hard to take His yoke upon them. This was undoubtedly the chief offense to the contemporary Jews, who expected to enter the kingdom in a body, without questions asked, and disdained to do so in the company of sinners. But this individualism of Jesus was at bottom identical with universalism because the conditions which He imposed might be accepted by anyone, whatever his previous history. They concerned man as man, not man as belonging to any race, caste or creed. The gate, though narrow excludes no child of Adam who is willing to repent. During His earthly career, indeed, Jesus felt Himself restricted to the lost sheep of the house of Israel, but the mission work of St. Paul and the other apostles was in the direct line of His principles; and it is entirely credible that He foresaw a time when many would come from the east and the west, to sit down with Abraham, Isaac and Jacob in the kingdom of heaven, while the children of the kingdom would, through their own impenitence, be doomed to outer darkness.

A point about which there has of late been hot discussion, and which is more important than it looks, is the question, whether or not Jesus thought and spoke about the kingdom as already come. It is allowed that, when He began to preach, He announced it as on the point of coming; and He often spoke of it as lying in the future—perhaps in heaven—but did He look upon it as already established on earth by means of His ministry?

In support of the position that He did, His saying may be quoted, "If I by the finger of God cast out devils, then is the kingdom of God come upon you" (Luke 11:20). Jesus regarded the coming of the kingdom of God as an invasion of the realm of evil, over which Satan rules; and, when the strong man armed was driven out in the cases of dispossession, the invading kingdom occupied the ground. In the same sense, when the Twelve returned and reported that they had cast out devils on a large scale, Jesus exclaimed, "I beheld Satan as lightning falling from heaven" (Luke 10:18). He meant that the frequent dispossessions were equivalent to the downfall of the prince of the empire of evil. It was the empire of sin, not the empire of Rome, that stirred the heart of Jesus—a striking proof of the spirituality of His aims, but also no doubt a cause of offense to those who thought that the first duty of every patriot was to get rid of that foreign yoke.

Another remarkable saying, "The kingdom of God is within you" (Luke17:21), would be more conclusive if it were certain that the preposition meant "within" and not "among." But probably it does mean "within"; for, apart from purely linguistic considerations, this meaning agrees well with the context: "When He was demanded of the Pharisees, when the kingdom of God should come, he answered them and said, The kingdom of God cometh not with observation; neither shall they say, Lo here, or Lo there; for, behold the kingdom of God is within you." They evidently expected it to come apocalyptically, at a certain moment and at a certain place, and in full-grown completeness, like a city let down to the earth out of heaven, but He taught that the methods of God are the very reverse—inward, unobserved, gradual. Very similar is His parable of the Seed Growing Secretly, "first the blade, then the ear, afterwards the full corn in the ear,"—one of the most characteristic of His sayings. And of kindred import are such parables as the Leaven and the Mustard Seed, both describing the growth of the kingdom from small beginnings to the perfect form.

In spite of such testimonies there are those who hold that Jesus' own view was apocalyptic. He believed, they contend, that the kingdom, being entirely a divine creation, was to appear in a moment, and He was waiting for it all the time. But this is simply an importation into modern scholarship of the view of the kingdom which deceived the Jews; and it converts Jesus Himself into a fantastic and disappointed dreamer, whom it would be impossible to accept as the Savior of mankind.*

Jesus Himself was there; and the kingdom had already come in His person, even if it had had no other embodiment. But round Him there sprang up a body, consisting first of the Twelve, then of larger numbers, in whom all the blessings which the kingdom comprised, such as repentance, righteousness, sonship, rest and life, were realized in growing measure.

In the Gospels nothing is more remarkable than the perseverance with which, in spite of the solicitation of other kinds of work, Jesus devoted Himself to the Twelve, evidently looking upon their training as one of the prime objects of His ministry.† But the organization of the wider circle of His disciples cannot but have also held a prominent place in His thoughts. The statements on this subject attributed to Him in the Gospels have been much called in question;** but it is more likely that He both thought and spoke more on the Church and the sacraments than He is represented to have done than that He spoke less. The history of religious movements proves that, with whatever energy and spirituality they may be initiated, they soon disappear, unless channels are provided in which their currents may be carried down to

---

* This applies to the work of Schmoller entitled *Das Reich Gottes* and to that of Johann Weiss entitled *Die Predigt Jesu vom Reiche Gottes*. In spite of the cleverness of Weiss' exegesis in detail, the picture of Jesus which he draws is an unintentional caricature. This fantastic figure is not the Savior and Lord of men, but only "a dreamer of the ghetto."

† "Inseparable from the image of his life is the fact that Jesus gathered disciples around himself. That in itself is not a peculiarity in that the same has been reported of several prophets and the Baptist. But what is indeed something new and peculiar is that fact that this side of the life of Jesus is standing out almost exclusively. Indeed, in this smaller, modest circle, in the closeness and quietness, the sum total of the effectiveness of Jesus took place. In this direct, immediate work from person to person He lived his life"—BOUSSET, *Jesu Predigt in ihrem Gegensatz zum Judenthum*, p. 55.

** That Jesus can never have spoken of the Church is denied by Holtzmann; but Ritschl, Beyschlag, Köstlin are on the opposite side. Cf. Holtzmann N. T. *Theologie*, p. 210, note.

subsequent times; and a religious genius of the first order must be an organizer as well as a thinker.* It is certain that Jesus did not work out the details of the creed, doctrine or discipline of the Church, but it is just as certain that the institution itself is His creation.

When Jesus was crucified, the Jews, no doubt, believed that His movement, which had seemed to them moonshine, was at an end, but, fifty years afterwards, when their political existence was blotted out, there had sprung up, all over the known world, countless communities, which, without any earthly center—without capital, court or army—yet acknowledged one heavenly King, obeyed the same code of laws, partook of the same blessings, pursued the same objects, and were united among themselves more closely than the subjects of any earthly sovereign. And from that day to this the kingdom of God has never ceased to grow.†

Robert Browning, in the opening pages of *The Ring and the Book*, compares the poet's art to that of the goldsmith, who, when he is working with the finest gold, has to make use of an alloy, in order to give the precious metal sufficient consistency to enable it to stand the action of his tools and assume the shapes which he desires. But, when the form is complete, he applies an acid, which evaporates the alloy and leaves nothing but the pure gold of the perfect ring. The poet's ingenious application of this image to his own art we need not follow at present, but the image seems to admit of being applied to the difficult subject which we have on hand. The popular conception of the kingdom of God was the alloy with which Jesus had to mix His teaching, in order to make it fit to mingle with the actual life of the world of His day. Without it His thought would have been too ethereal and too remote from the living hopes of men. He had to take men where He found them, and lead them step by step to the full appreciation of His sublime purpose for the world. He was not to be the king of the Jews, but King

---

* Contrast, as respects permanency, the influence of Whitfield, the orator, and Wesley, the organizer.

† Several chapters of *Ecce Homo* are occupied with showing in what sense Christ is a King and Christianity a Kingdom. What they offer is the speculation of a modern philosopher rather than a transcript from the mind of Christ; yet they are full of suggestiveness.

of an infinitely diviner realm, yet it was by aiming at the throne which He missed that He reached the throne which He now occupies.

And shall we say that in His case, when the ring was perfected, the alloy was blown away? Was it fated that the idea and the name of the kingdom of God should fade from the minds of men? It looks as if this had been the intention; for, whereas in the Synoptists we find the phrase everywhere, it is infrequent in the Gospel of St. John, and it does not appear at all in his Epistles; in all St. Paul's Epistles it does not occur as often as in the briefest of the Gospels; and in St. Peter's Epistles it is found but once. This is a remarkable phenomenon. Does it indicate that the apostles had forgotten the doctrine of their Master? or is it an instance of the freedom with which in that creative age the ideas of religion were grasped and its phraseology altered? The apostles were too thoroughly alive to repeat the words of others, even those of their Master, by rote. Each of them, according to his own genius and his own circumstances, expressed what the Holy Spirit had revealed to him in language of his own. After the fall of Jerusalem, Christianity had to go away among peoples to which a phrase like "the kingdom of God" would have been novel and confusing; and, therefore, the missionaries wisely avoided it, finding more appropriate phrases to take its place. Even Jesus, before the close of His life, outgrew it; and His teaching seems always striving to escape from it as from a fetter. It is impossible to subsume under it the very finest of His sayings. The phrase belongs, in short, to the "body of humiliation"* which for a time He had to bear, but from which He was destined to be liberated.

This is not, however, an opinion universally accepted. Far from it. Some of the most vigorous thinking of our century is associated with the proposal to revive the phrase as the supreme category of theology, as it was the title of the teaching of Jesus. In Germany it has long been a favorite expression. The Pietists spoke of their philanthropic and missionary endeavors as work for the kingdom of God; and the Ritschlians at the present day have given it as supreme a place in the realm of thought.† Among ourselves some are disposed to follow in the same

---

* Τὸ σῶμα τῆς ταπεινώσεως—Phil. 3:21.

† I sometimes wonder whether the force of this tendency has been due in any degree to the imperial ideas dominant in that country since the great victories of the Franco-Prussian War.

track for various reasons. Among English Nonconformists the phrase finds a welcome, as a rival to "the Church," on which, it seems to them, too much emphasis is laid by churchmen. But the strongest influence is the growth among us of social and patriotic sentiment in connection with religion. To be a Christian is not merely to save one's own soul, but to discharge one's duty to the world; it is to be part of an organism, with which we suffer and with which we triumph; it is to be an adherent of a great cause and to prove loyal to a divine Leader. It is evident that many such ideas and aspirations may be conveniently gathered together within such a phrase as the kingdom of God. Indeed, I have known those to whom this name has appeared to make everything new; and, when a watchword is capable of doing this, it cannot be looked upon with anything but respect. On the whole, however, the attempt to revive this term seems to be mistaken. We are very remote now from the world to which it belonged. To many Christians, living under republican forms of government, the very name of a king or a kingdom is something foreign and out of date. Whatever may be the case in Germany, to our ears the phrase as a name for Christianity has a sound of preciosity and make-believe; and there are far better names for the same thing. The attempt to revive it is due to a mistaken reverence for Christ, as if the repetition of His mere words were obligatory upon Christians it is a return from the spirit to the letter, an attempt to force thought back into a form which it has long outgrown.

Nevertheless, there are two words of our Lord which will always keep this phrase fresh and sweet in the mouth of Christendom: the one the second petition of the Lord's Prayer—"Thy kingdom come"—and the other the text, "Suffer the little children to come unto Me, and forbid them not; for of such is the kingdom of heaven."

PASSAGES IN WHICH JESUS REFERS TO HIS OWN DEATH:
Matthew 9:15; 16:21; 17:9, 12, 22, 23; 20:17–19, 22, 23, 28; 21:39, 42;
    26:2, 12, 18, 24, 26, 28, 31, 38, 39, 42, 45.
Mark 2:20; 8:31; 9:9, 12, 31; 10:32, 33, 34, 38, 39, 45; 12:8, 10; 14:8,
    21, 22–24, 36, 39, 41.
Luke 5:35; 9:22, 31, 44; 12:50; 13:32, 33; 17:25; 18:31–33; 20:9–18;
    22:14–22, 37; 24:7, 26, 46.

5

The Redeemer

IT is well known that, after the death of our Lord, the later scenes of His career took peculiar possession of the mind of the Church, and that in the apostolic writings His death and resurrection figure far more prominently than His miracles or His teaching. In fact, the apostolic theory of Christianity is built upon His death, resurrection and ascension. His death, especially, occupies a vast space in the apostolic field of vision: it is by His death that He is the Savior of the world. Now, it is sometimes contended that in this respect there is a striking discrepancy between the teaching of the apostles and that of Christ Himself because in the Synoptists there are not more than a couple of sayings of His about His death which are of capital importance; and He builds Christianity upon a totally different foundation. It is with the truth or falsehood of this contention that we have to occupy ourselves in the present lecture.

It must be confessed, that, at first sight, there does not seem to be much in common between the announcement of Jesus, that the object of His earthly mission was to set up the kingdom of God, and the statement of the apostles, that He came to die for the sin of the world. But in the last chapter we saw, that, while starting from the political hopes of His countrymen, Jesus, as soon as He began to speak what was distinctively His own language, employed "the kingdom of God" as a comprehensive term for the noblest blessings of life, such as repentance, forgiveness, the vision of God, communion with God and eternal life; and between this circle of ideas and the benefits associated by the apostles with the death of Christ the interval is not appreciable.

The impression that Jesus referred but little to His own death is due to a superficial reading of the Gospels. A closer acquaintance with them reveals the fact, that at no period of His ministry was the thought of His death foreign to Him, and that during the last year of His life it was an ever-present and absorbing preoccupation.*

In spite of the joy springing from His own enthusiasm and His early successes, His career was from the very commencement crossed by dark shadows. From the first the religious authorities were against Him, and it could not be long before He had forebodings of how far their malevolence might be carried. He reckoned Himself to be in the line of the prophets, and He knew too well what kind of fate they had encountered at the hands of Jerusalem. The premature end of His forerunner was a prophecy of what His own was likely to be. He never spared his would-be followers the knowledge, that their adherence to him would imply sacrifice—perhaps even the sacrifice of life itself—and He adopted as a kind of technical term for what they would have to endure for His sake the significant name of "the cross." But, if even the disciples were to excite to this extent the hostility of the world, what could the Master expect for Himself? He kept back as long as He could from the Twelve His anticipations of His own fate, but, when He did begin to speak, it was manifest that what He had to communicate had long been in His mind, craving for utterance.

It was not till they had confessed at Caesarea Philippi, that He was Christ, the Son of God, that He considered them mature and established enough to be able to bear the terrible secret, but "from that time forth began Jesus to show unto His disciples, how that He must go unto Jerusalem, and suffer many things of the elders and chief priests and scribes, and be killed, and be raised again the third day." Having once broken the ice, He returned again and again to the subject. Thus: "And Jesus, going up to Jerusalem, took the twelve disciples apart on the way, and said unto them, Behold, we go up to Jerusalem, and the Son of man shall be betrayed unto the chief priests and unto the scribes, and they shall condemn Him to death, and shall deliver Him

---

* I have not anywhere else seen the extent of space which this subject occupied in the consciousness of Jesus so finely brought out as in the articles by Principal Fairbairn referred to above.

to the Gentiles, to mock and to scourge and to crucify Him; and the third day He shall rise again." As occasion offered, He added trait after trait, to sharpen the outline of the tragic picture; and all the Synoptists mark with the utmost care the steps of this gradual unveiling of the future.*

But, although He pressed the subject home so deliberately on the attention of the apostles, they were totally unable to receive it. The first time He broached it St. Peter "took Him and began to rebuke Him" (Matt. 16:22), as if He were losing His mental balance, through melancholy, and allowing Himself to say things which would be injurious to the cause—a reply which appeared to Jesus such an immediate suggestion of the spirit of evil that He turned on St. Peter with "Get thee behind Me, Satan." Indeed, between all the disciples and their Master there sprang up at this time an alienation such as had never previously existed. They continued to dream of the thrones which they were about to ascend, and they disputed with one another which should be the greatest in the forthcoming kingdom, while clouds of disaster were accumulating on the horizon of his mind in darker and darker masses. Their minds were distracted with ominous suspicions, and He was tragically alone—"They were in the way going up to Jerusalem; and Jesus went before them; and they were amazed, and as they followed, they were afraid" (Mark 10:32). The misunderstanding on their side culminated in the treachery of Judas, and the loneliness on His side in Gethsemane.

That the subject which occupied His thoughts in these solitary musings was His death admits of no doubt. It grew upon Him from day to day and from month to month. He had to master the mystery and penetrate its secret. Sometimes it rose upon Him as an overwhelming horror, at other times He saw beyond it and could almost welcome it. This double point of view is expressed in a characteristic saying of the period: "I have a baptism to be baptized with, and how am I straitened till it be accomplished." Many features of the approaching catastrophe—as, for example, that it was to take place through the treachery

---

* See these series of texts in the different Gospels—Matthew 16:21; 17:22, 23; 20:17–19; 26:2, 21–24; Mark 8:31; 10:32–34; Luke 9:22, 44; 17:25; 18:31–33.

of an apostle, that it was to be at the hands of His own countrymen, that it was to interrupt His mission in the midst of happy labor, that it was to bring ruin to His native land—were revolting, and could not be contemplated without torture; yet, on the other hand, He knew that the dark providence must conceal a divine purpose—a purpose all the more charged with concentrated and complicated good to both Himself and others, the darker was the shape in which it was enveloped. His enemies might kill Him, but He could say to them, "Did you never read in the Scriptures, The stone which the builders rejected is become the headstone of the corner; this is the Lord's doing and it is marvelous in our eyes" (Luke 20:17)?

What was the prospect of ulterior good which enabled Jesus to triumph over the prospect of suffering? To discover this, we must scrutinize the sayings in which He most distinctly gives expression to His consciousness of what His death was to effect for mankind. Of these there are only two in the Synoptists, but they well deserve the most careful and exhaustive study we are able to bestow upon them. The one is the saying, "Even the Son of man came not to be ministered unto, but to minister, and to give His life a ransom for many"; and the other is the formula with which He instituted the last Supper, "This is the New Testament in My blood."

The first of these sayings sprang out of one of the most characteristic incidents of the tragic period just described. Two of the Twelve came to Him requesting through their mother, Salome, that they might sit the one on His right hand and the other on His left in His kingdom. Nothing could show more nakedly how far apart from His were the thoughts of His followers at that time than the fact that these two, belonging to the very innermost circle, should have made such a request; and the indignation aroused by their conduct in the rest of the Twelve betrayed too clearly that they had only given expression to ambitions with which all were palpitating. Jesus did not, in His reply, deny that there was to be any earthly kingdom, but He showed them how diametrically opposite to His was their estimate of what it was to be like. Their thoughts were frankly those of the world—that to be a king was to lord it over numerous subjects, and that to be great was to be served by many slaves—but His conception was precisely the re-

verse—"Whosoever will be great among you, let him be your minister; and whosoever will be chief among you, let him be your servant." Such was to be the rule in His kingdom, but the first to obey it
was Himself, and He was to obey it to the uttermost—"For even the
Son of man came not to be ministered unto, but to minister and to give
His life a ransom for many." Here was the key to His entire career: He
had always found His happiness and His honor in serving others and
doing them good, but the supreme illustration of the principle on
which he conducted His life was still to come—His final service was
to consist in giving His life a ransom for many.

This image of a ransom does not appeal to our minds as forcibly
as it would to those of the disciples, because the experience of being
ransomed, in the natural sense, is much rarer in modern than it was
in ancient times.* In the British Isles at present there do not probably
exist a hundred persons who have ever been ransomed, whereas in the
ancient world there would be such wherever two or three were met together. War was never a rare experience to the countrymen of Jesus,
and in war the process of ransoming was occurring continually, when
prisoners were exchanged for prisoners, or captives were released on
the payment by themselves or their relatives of a sum of money. Similarly, slavery was a universal institution, and in connection with it the
process of ransoming was common, when, for a price paid, slaves received their liberty. The Jews had, besides, numerous forms of ransoming peculiar to their own laws and customs. For example, the
firstborn male of every household was, in theory, liable to be a priest,
but was redeemed by a payment of so many shekels to the actual
priesthood, which belonged exclusively to a single tribe. A person
whose ox had gored a man to death was in theory guilty of murder, but
was released from the liability to expiate his guilt with his life by a payment to the relatives of the dead man (Num. 18:15; Ex. 21:30).

Such cases show clearly what ransoming was: it was the deliverance
of a person from some misery or liability through payment, either
by himself or by another on his behalf, of a sum of money or any other

---

* My friend Dr. John C. Gibson, of Swatow, has told me that it is very common
at the present day in China; he has himself ransomed a man.

equivalent which the person in whose power he was might be willing to accept as a condition of his release. It was a triangular transaction, involving three parties—first the person to be ransomed, secondly the giver, and thirdly the receiver of the ransom.

As regards the first of these parties, in the case of the ransom of Christ, the most important question is, what they are ransomed from. What is the nature of the misery or liability in which they are involved, and from which they require to be delivered?

Our Lord seems to have had in His mind a passage in the forty-ninth psalm.* This psalm is one of those, of which there are several in the Psalter, dealing with the mystery of life, especially as this is exhibited in the inequalities of the human lot. For the purpose of lightening the burden of this mystery, it sets forth, with rare poetic power, the things which wealth cannot do; and the chief of these is, that it cannot keep off the approach of death—

> None of them can by any means redeem his brother,
> Nor give to God a ransom for him:
> (For the redemption of their soul is costly,
> And must be let alone forever:)
> That he should still live alway,
> That he should not see corruption.

On account of this reference it has been argued that the evil from which Christ redeems us is death, or the fear of death. But, in point of fact, He does not redeem from physical death.

There is another saying of Jesus, also apparently occasioned by the same passage of the same psalm, by which we are led nearer to His meaning. It is the well-known question, "What shall a man give in exchange for his soul?" As "soul" is the same as "life," Jesus may seem in this saying simply to be supplementing the statement of the psalm, that none can redeem his brother's life from death, with the further reflection, that no man can redeem his own, but it is proved by the connection that He means more. Between the date of the psalm and the date of our Lord's utterance, the whole conception of death, and of what ensues after death, had deepened: and this deeper note enters

---

* Especially vv. 7, 8, 9, 15. I quote from the Revised Version.

into our Lord's words. The connection in which the verse occurs is this: "And when He had called the people unto Him, with His disciples also, He said unto them, Whosoever will come after Me, let him deny himself and take up his cross and follow Me; for whosoever will save his life shall lose it, but whosoever shall lose his life for My sake and the gospel's, the same shall save it; for what shall it profit a man, if he gain the whole world and lose his own soul? Or what shall a man give in exchange for his soul? Whosoever, therefore, shall be ashamed of Me and of My words in this adulterous and sinful generation, of him also shall the Son of man be shamed, when He cometh in the glory of His Father, with the holy angels." Here we are among a far more solemn order of ideas than that of the psalm. The death contemplated is not that of the body but of the soul, and the danger is that of an unfavorable verdict at the final judgment. That from which Christ ransoms may be called the fear of death, but, if so, it is the fear of death eternal; and the only method of taking this away is to take away sin, which lends to death its terror. From this no man can ransom himself, neither can any man ransom his brother, but the Son of man came to give His life a ransom for many.

Turning now to Him who pays the ransom, we observe that Jesus describes the payment of this ransom as the culminating purpose of his whole life—He "came" to minister and to give His life a ransom. In the circumstances in which this was spoken the reference could only be to a violent death—in fact, to the shedding of His blood. But it is to be observed that He does not here say, as He does elsewhere, that they would take His life, but that He would give it. His death was to be His own voluntary act. Service extorted by force is not greatness, but slavery. It was not as a slave that Jesus lived, and it was not as a slave that He died. No doubt wicked men took his life, as they had previously taken His ease, comfort and honor but He put so much magnanimity, at every crisis, into the surrender that the sacrifice was His own act, and He remained master of His fate. When He was nailed to the tree, He was not a mere martyr suffering what others inflicted on Him, but He was paying a ransom.

The dignity of the act is, however, chiefly brought out in the claim that He gave His life "for many." When prisoners were bartered at the conclusion of a war, the exchange was not always simply man for man. An officer was of more value than a common soldier, and several soldiers might be redeemed by the surrender of one officer. For a woman of high rank or extraordinary beauty a still greater number of prisoners might be exchanged; and by the giving up of a king's son many might be redeemed. So the sense of His own unique dignity and His peculiar relation to God is implied in the statement that His life would redeem the lives of many. St. Paul expresses the truth still more boldly when he says that Jesus gave His life a ransom "for all" (1 Tim. 2:6); but the two phrases come to the same thing, because the "many" spoken of by Jesus really include "all" who are willing to avail themselves of the opportunity.

The third party to the transaction is the one to whom the ransom is paid. It is obvious that in any transaction deserving the name of ransom this third party was in some respects the most important of all. He held the prisoner in custody, and, while others might offer a ransom, it was his to say whether or not he would accept of any, and whether he was satisfied with the terms proposed. In spite of these considerations, there are interpreters of this great saying of our Lord who ignore this aspect of the truth altogether, holding that only two things are essential in the case—namely, the misery of those who need to be redeemed and the price paid by the Redeemer. Everyone, however, can judge for himself whether or not this satisfies the conditions of the metaphor. For a situation in which only the two things just mentioned—misery and deliverance—require to be considered, there are many other metaphors which might have been employed, but this one, of a ransom, naturally suggests something more.

And that Jesus was thinking of something more seems to me to be especially implied in the words "for many." In whose eyes is it that Jesus believes His life will be regarded as an equivalent for the lives of many? Not His own merely—in that case His claim would be a vainglorious boast—but primarily God's. Unforgiven sinners may no doubt be said to condemn themselves to death and to descend to their doom with the force of natural law; yet they are in the hands of a just and holy God, and their doom is His sentence. It was to avert this and to turn it into a sentence of acquittal that Jesus gave His life.

It is true the death of Christ has a profound and manifold effect on the mind of man. The tranquility with which He met a death of unparalleled atrocity has set an example fitted to soothe the feelings of all who in the last agony remember Him, and to deliver them from the fear of death;[*] His faith, that death was not the end of existence but only a stage of transition to a higher form of life, breathes into our hearts also the assurance that death is the gateway of life;[†] and the sight of what sin inflicted on the Holiest and the Noblest is fitted to arouse in the mind a revulsion from sin and a passion of indignation against it. But by far the most important effect of the death of Christ was its effect on the mind of God.[**] To define precisely what this was may be impossible, and theologians may have made great mistakes in attempting to define it; yet we are safe in saying that it altered the relation of God to sinners. It did not make Him love them, for this He had always done; indeed, it was His immemorial love which gave Christ to His mission, but it removed an obstacle to the free outflow of the divine love. It effected this by annihilating sin; and this is what is implied in the idea of ransom.

I am very desirous not to put anything into this saying which does not belong to it, but I find it hard to believe that in the "many"

---

[*] This is Wendt's explanation.

[†] "This cannot mean that the same are exempt from death, the fate of all created beings, because submission to that fate is demanded by Jesus in certain cases as a test of loyalty to Him (8:35). Therefore, the opinion is that in this also the friends and fellows of the community of Jesus fall under death, his free-willed, guided-by-a-certain-purpose, yet guiltless death serves to their protection, that they in death may not experience full annihilation and purposelessness. Moreover to them, this work of Jesus serves the purpose that they are saved from the theretofore applicable divine sentence of the final destruction of life, that they shall gain a different judgment of death than was possible under the Old Testament and that they shall fear death nevermore"—Ritschl, *Rechtfertigung und Versöhnung*, II. 87, 88.

[**] Nine-tenths of the modern books on the Atonement are occupied with its effects on the mind of man, but nine-tenths of the Bible statements are concerned with its effects on the mind of God. All modern writers are aware that Jesus came to make good men better, but comparatively few have any idea that He came to make bad men good. Yet this is the Gospel.

here mentioned there is not an echo of the phrases of the last two verses of the fifty-third chapter of Isaiah, "He bare the sin of many," and "By His knowledge shall my righteous servant justify many." So, "to give His life a ransom" sounds uncommonly like a reminiscence of the words in the same chapter, "Thou shalt make His soul an offering for sin." If this be correct, Jesus must have thought of Himself as the Servant of the Lord, about whose substitution for sinners such wonderful things are said by Isaiah; and, in that case, we need not have any doubt what is intended when we are told that after His resurrection, He expounded unto the disciples in all the Scriptures "the things concerning Himself."* At all events the earliest Christian preaching applied Isaiah's picture of the Man of Sorrows to Jesus, and it did so expressly because the subject of the prophetic picture took away the sin of others by the sacrifice of Himself (Acts 8:32–35). It is beyond question that this was the faith of the Church immediately after our Lord's departure. St. Paul mentions as the very first article of the common tradition of Christianity, that "Christ died for our sins according to the Scriptures" (1 Cor. 15:3); so that the doctrine was no invention of his. He made it his own, indeed, by the intense conviction with which he grasped it and the thoroughness with which he expounded it, but it was equally the doctrine of St. Peter, St. John and the author of the Epistle to the Hebrews.

I am sticking rigidly, in this course of lectures, to the exposition of the words of Jesus Himself, without adding or subtracting; and yet there are points at which we cannot escape the question, whether the best guide to the meaning of His words be not the central beliefs of His first followers. When the first Christians knew that their Lord was risen and glorified, they knew also that their conception of His death, as the mere act of wicked men and as the termination of His career and His cause, was mistaken. They had still, however, to find an explanation of the mystery, and they found it in the belief that His death was a sacrifice by which He expiated the sin of the world. This was a conception of incomparable originality and grandeur, revolutionizing the whole doctrine of both man and God. Is it likely that it was an in-

---

* Luke 24:27. Even in His lifetime He applies Is. 53 to Himself, Luke 22:37.

vention of theirs?* Is it not far more likely, that this was the way which Jesus Himself found of solving the dark problem of His death and of seeing beyond it into regions of illimitable hope; and that He found it because it was true?

The other great saying of Jesus on this subject is the one emitted at the Last Supper. It is given by St. Paul, in the account of the scene which, he says, he "received of the Lord," in the following form, "This cup is the new testament in My blood"; St. Mark's form is "This is My blood of the new testament, which is shed for many"; and St. Matthew's, "This is My blood of the new testament, which is shed for many for the remission of sins." These different accounts have of late been not so much tested as tortured for the purpose of bringing out discrepancies and eliciting a meaning free from distinct theological coloring, but at least these three are substantially identical; that of St. Luke being less definite.† Whatever St. Paul may mean by saying that he "received" the account which he gives "from the Lord," he may at least be trusted to have satisfied himself that his report was accurate. It is contended that the theological coloring of the phrases is due to him, but

---

* This is powerfully put by Principal Fairbairn: "We have to consider both the apostles and the theory. It was a belief of stupendous orignality; they were persons of no intellectual attainments and of small inventive faculty. So far as the Gospels enable us to judge, they were curiously deficient in imagination and of timid understanding. They were remarkable for their inability to draw obvious conclusions, to transcend the commonplace, and comprehend the unfamiliar, or to find as rational reason for the extraordinary. Such men might dream dreams and see visions, but to invent an absolutely novel intellectual conception as to their Master's person and death—a conception that changed man's view of God, of sin, of humanity, of history, in a word, of all things human and divine—was surely a feat beyond them"—*Expositor*, 1896, p. 282.

† Since 1891 a controversy on the Lord's Supper, which has swelled to the extraordinary dimensions, has been going on in Germany. It was begun by Harnack, who published an essay on "Bread and Water the Eucharistic Elements according to Justin," in which he contended that the institution was originally so understood that its blessing was not legally confined to bread and wine, but only to eating and drinking, that is, a simple meal. This was opposed by Th. Zahn and Jülicher, the latter of whom, however, gave the controversy a new start by raising the question whether Jesus was really the Author of the institution, or whether He merely, in a moment of genial inspiration, conjured up the beautiful [*continued*]

may the influence not have acted in the opposite direction? The apostle quotes the words of his Master remarkably seldom, but there is no reason to suppose that he was either ignorant of them or indifferent to them; and a saying of Christ's like this, embodied in the most distinctive rite of His religion, was one likely to receive the keenest attention from such a mind. If the meaning of the death of Christ is a leading element of St. Paul's theology, it may very well be, that we are here at the fountain-head from which this element of his doctrine was derived.

It is nothing less than a calamity to the English-speaking world that this saying of our Lord, heard at every celebration of the communion, is marred by a serious mistranslation—Jesus being made to say, "This is the blood of the new testament," when what He did say was, "This is the blood of the new covenant."* It is the same mistake which makes us, to our loss, call the two halves of the Bible the Old and the New Testaments—names which have scarcely any meaning—instead of the Old and the New Covenants—names which are full of meaning.

A covenant is a transaction between two parties, each of which gives something to the other and receives something in return. This exchange is the essence of a covenant; and covenants are of all degrees of dignity according to the value of the objects exchanged. The most ordinary bargain, in which the buyer hands a coin across the counter and the seller an article of merchandise, is a covenant, but the word is generally reserved for transactions of greater moment, such as leagues or alliances between nations. The most solemn covenant between human beings is marriage; and the solemnity consists in this, that, whereas in other covenants the parties exchange things more or less valuable, in marriage they give themselves. This instance flashes

---

situation, without any ulterior design. The subsequent contributions to the controversy have come from Spitta, Haupt, Brandt, Grafe and many more; and every conceivable phase of the subject has been brought into view. An ample account of the whole will be found in the work of Schaefer cited at the head of this chapter, and brief accounts in *The Expositor* for July and August, 1898, by the Rev. G. W. Stewart, and in the second number of *Saint Andrew* by Professor Menzies.
* The Revised Version corrects this.

light on the religious use of the term; for, as in marriage man and woman, so in religion God and man give themselves to each other. This is the essence of religion, and the word "religion" itself, though of uncertain derivation, signifies in all probability nothing else. This, at all events, is the signification of the word "covenant" in Scripture, where it is often explained by the words of Jehovah, "I will be their God and they shall be My people." It is a remarkable fact that in the Old Testament the word "religion" never occurs. Its absence can only be due to the fact that other equivalents are employed in place of it: and of these the commonest is "covenant," which occurs about three hundred times. This shows how near to the very heart of Biblical thought Jesus was when He called the Last Supper a covenant, indicating that the essence of this ordinance is the same as that of all religion—God giving Himself to man and man giving himself to God.

Another unhappy result of the mistranslation above referred to is, that it obliterates the reference in this communion formula to one of the most remarkable predictions of the Old Testament—that in which Jeremiah says: "Behold the days come, saith the Lord, that I will make a new covenant with the house of Israel, and with the house of Judah: not according to the covenant which I made with their fathers in the day that I took them by the hand to bring them out of the land of Egypt; which My covenant they broke, although I was a husband unto them, saith the Lord: but this shall be the covenant that I will make with the house of Israel: After those days, saith the Lord, I will put My law in their inward parts, and write it in their hearts; and will be their God, and they shall be My people. And they shall teach no more every man his neighbor, and every man his brother, saying, Know the Lord: for they shall all know Me, from the least of them unto the greatest of them, saith the Lord: for I will forgive their iniquity, and I will remember their sin no more" (Jer. 31:31–34). When our Lord, lifting the cup in the upper room, said, "This is the new covenant," His meaning was, that this prediction of Jeremiah was fulfilled.

If it be remembered, that in the Old Testament the word "covenant" is equivalent to "religion," it will be felt how daring was the prediction of Jeremiah—nothing less than the abolition of the religion under which he himself lived and the substitution of a new one in its place—and the same reflection brings out the fundamental character of the statement of Jesus; for He was designating Himself as the founder of a new religion. Of course the new was not to be wholly new—neither Jeremiah nor Jesus intended this. The Deity was not to be changed; for Jehovah was the one living and true God; and there were to be innumerable other points of connection. Still the changes were to be great enough to justify the designation of the principal rite of Christianity as a new covenant.

The point of difference are indicated by Jeremiah with singular precision. First, the law was to be written on the heart. In the old religion the law was written on stone. It was external. It was the commandment of a distant Deity, imposed from without on the human will. Therefore, it was a yoke, harsh and hard to bear. But a law written on the heart is a light burden and an easy yoke. It is obedience to the will of One who is loved; and love makes duty easy. But how was love to be evoked more fully under the new covenant than the old? It could only be by a fuller revelation of the nature of God. This, therefore, is the next member of the promise—"They shall teach no more every man his neighbor and every man his brother, saying, Know the Lord; for they shall all know Me, from the least of them to the greatest of them." At first sight, this seems to refer to the universality of the knowledge of God; and it might be supposed to be a prediction of the extension of the knowledge of God to all men, Gentile as well as Jew, which was, indeed, to be one of the prominent features of the new religion. But it refers rather to the thoroughness of the new knowledge than to its universal diffusion. It is not a prediction that there will be no need of religious education, but that there will be no need of urgency in pressing it on the unresponsive, because God will appear in an aspect so attractive as to draw the hearts of small and great. In short, He will be revealed as the God of love. The love of God would, however, reveal itself specially in one way—in a much more thorough removal of sin than was possible through the sacrifices of the old covenant. And, therefore, the prophet gives this as the climax of the promise, "I will forgive their iniquity, and I will remember their sins no more."

This brings us to the most mysterious phrase in the our Lord's saying—"the blood of the covenant."

If our Lord's words about the new covenant carry us irresistibly back to Jeremiah, the words of Jeremiah carry us back as irresistibly far beyond his day; for, if there is to be a new covenant, there must have been an old one, and we naturally ask when and where the old one was made. As to this we are left in no doubt because in the very opening of his prediction, the prophet introduces Jehovah as saying, "I will make a new covenant with the house of Israel, and with the house of Judah: not according to the covenant that I made with their fathers, in the day that I took them by the hand to bring them out of the land of Egypt." So that it was at the era of the Exodus that the first covenant was made.

The scene is given in the twenty-fourth chapter of the Book of Exodus; and there is no more fundamental passage in the entire Old Testament; though, perhaps, its details are not stamped as distinctly as its importance would render natural on the memory of even careful students of the Bible.* What is popularly remembered about the Exodus is the deliverance at the Red Sea or the giving of the law at Sinai, but both of these were only preliminaries to the making of the covenant. The formation of this union between Jehovah and His people was the real purpose for which the enslaved nation was delivered from bondage; and the law was only the enumeration of the conditions laid down by Jehovah with a view to this transaction. In the passage quoted from Jeremiah, Jehovah says, "I was a husband unto them"; and this is looked upon as the occasion when this relationship, so fundamental and so familiar to all the prophets, was formed.

In examining more closely the details of the grand historical picture unfolded in Exodus, we must fix attention specially on the part

---

* "And He said unto Moses, Come up unto the Lord, thou, and Aaron, Nadab and Abihu, and seventy of the elders of Israel: and worship ye afar off: and Moses alone shall come near unto the Lord; but they shall not come near; neither shall the people go up with him. And Moses came and told the people all the words of the Lord, and all the judgments: and all the people answered with one voice, and said, All the words which the Lord hath spoken will we do.

"And Moses wrote all the words of the Lord, and rose up early in the morning, and built an altar under the mount, and twelve pillars, according to the twelve tribes of Israel. And he sent young men of the children of Israel, which offered burnt offerings, and sacrificed peace offerings of oxen unto the Lord. And [*continued*]

played in it by blood; for therein is to be found the key to the phrase of Jesus, "the blood of the new covenant."

As a preliminary observation it may be remarked, that blood has always played a prominent part in the formation of covenants.* When those who are remembered in our own history by the name of the Covenanters signed the solemn league, in the Greyfriars Church at Edinburgh, by which they were banded together, numbers of them opened a vein and subscribed the document with their own blood instead of with ink. What led them to do so was the natural conviction or instinct of man, that his blood is his life: they meant to say, that they would stand to what they had done with their life. This principle, which is at the root of all the solemn statements of Scripture about blood, is put into words in the Mosaic law: "The life of the flesh is in the blood; and I have given it to you upon the altar, to make an atonement for your souls; for it is the blood that makes an atonement for the soul" (Lev. 17:11). In Homer, at the making of an agreement between the rival armies beneath the walls of Troy, king Agamemnon recites the terms of the compact, and then the story proceeds as follows:

Moses took half of the blood, and put it in basins; and half of the blood he sprinkled on the altar. And he took the book of the covenant, and read in the audience of the people: and they said, All that the Lord hath spoken will we do, and be obedient. And Moses took the blood, and sprinkled it on the people, and said, Behold the blood of the covenant, which the Lord hath made with you concerning all these words.

"Then went up Moses and Aaron, Nadab and Abihu, and seventy of the elders of Israel: and they saw the God of Israel; and there was under His feet as it were a paved work of sapphire stone, and as it were the very heaven for clearness. And upon the nobles of the children of Israel He laid not His hand: and they beheld God, and did not eat and drink"—Exodus 24:1–11 (R.V.).

* "An absolute merging of two personalities into one, in this union of friendship, has been sought, among primitive peoples everywhere, by the intermingling of the blood of the two, through its mutual drinking or its inter-transfusion; with the thought that blended blood is blended life. Traces of this custom are found in the traditions and practices of the aborigines of different portions of Asia, Africa, Europe, North and South America, and the Islands of the Sea. Nor is there any quarter of the globe where traces of this rite, in one form or another, are not to be found today"—TRUMBULL: *Friendship*, p. 70.

> He said and pierced the victims; ebbing life
> Forsook them soon; they panted, gasped, and died.
> Then, pouring from the beaker to the cups,
> They filled them, worshiped the immortal gods
> In either host, and thus the people prayed:
> All glorious Jove, and, ye, the powers of heaven,
> Whoso shall violate this contract first,
> So be their blood, their children's and their own,
> Poured out, as this libation, on the ground.
> —*Iliad*, III. 292 ff.

Here the blood to be shed in case of unfaithfulness is compared to the wine which accompanied the offering, but in Livy, the Roman historian, we find the more original idea, that the shedding of the victim's blood was the symbol of what was to be done with the life of the violator of the compact. He mentions, that at the ratifying of a treaty the priest used to pray as follows:"Hear, O Jupiter, that the Roman people will not under any circumstances first swerve from this treaty; and, if they do, then strike them on that day as I here strike this animal" (I. 24). In terms extremely similar Jeremiah mentions that, when a treaty was formed, the sacrifices were divided into two halves, between which the contracting parties walked, offering, as they did so, the prayer that the same fate as had befallen the victims might be the lot of the one that broke the covenant first. The idea oat the root of all these customs is the same, but in the making of the covenant between Jehovah and Israel at Sinai it received a still more graphic and pointed application.

Early one morning, after the giving of the Law, the people were assembled, by the divine command, round a conspicuous plateau, on which was erected an altar, with twelve standing stones round about it. The altar suggested the divine presence, and, of course, the twelve stones stood for the twelve tribes; so that the objects before their eyes reminded the people that they were standing in the presence of Jehovah, with whom they were about to enter into covenant. The union did not, however, take place forthwith because the people were not yet fit to be united to the Most Holy. On this account victims were sacrificed; the work being done by the hands of chosen young men, because as yet there were no priests. The young men typified the fresh strength of the community; for the act in which they were engaged had to be performed with their whole soul. The blood, thus shed, was caught in basins and divided into two parts. The one half was thereupon sprinkled on the altar. That is to say, it was given to God, as an acknowledgment that their life had been forfeited to Him. This was a symbolical confession, that, as the blood of the victims had been shed, their own life might, in strict justice, have been taken. When, thus, by sacrifice and by the confession which it symbolized, they were purged from sin, they were fit for union with God; and, accordingly, at this point the law was recited, which Moses had written in a book, and the people, having heard it, responded, "All that Jehovah hath said will we do and be obedient." That is, they accepted and subscribed the conditions of union. Then, the other half of the blood, which had meantime been kept in readiness for the purpose was sprinkled upon the people—whether on their persons, or on the stones surrounding the altar, which represented them, is not made clear. In either case the meaning was, that the life which they had given away to God, as lost and forfeited on account of sin, was, now that sin had been removed, given back to them purified and reinvigorated, to serve as the force with which they should pursue a new career of obedience and fellowship.

Such, as nearly as we can make it out—though, in trying to reproduce experiences so ancient, it is easy to stumble—were the thoughts and emotions of this remarkable occasion; and they bring out the force and meaning of the blood of the new covenant. When, in the communion, we approach God, seeking union and alliance with Him, we have to pause; for we are not fit to come so close to the Most Holy. We have to turn our eyes to the cross of Christ and fix them on Him. And, as we do so, we feel, as they felt that day, when they saw the blood of the sacrificial victims poured on the altar, that, in strict justice, we ought to be in His place: we deserve to die, because we have forfeited our life through sin. The moment, however, we make this confession from the heart, we are freely and fully forgiven, and are ready for union with God. And, as the other half of the blood was sprinkled on the people, to signify that their lost life was restored, so is our life given back, potentiated with the virtue necessary for communion, holiness and usefulness.

Wendt, while admitting that the reference in our Lord's words, "in My blood" is to this scene at Sinai, denies that the sacrifice offered on that occasion had any reference to sin. But how does this harmonize with the description in Exodus of the sacrificial feast with which the making of the covenant wound up? Moses and Aaron, Nadab and Abihu, and seventy of the elders of Israel—that is, a large and dignified delegation representing the whole people—went up to the knoll where the altar stood, and there they did eat and drink. No doubt their food was the flesh of the sacrifices, the blood of which had been disposed of as we have seen, but the peculiarity of the feast was that it was a feast with God. Not that He partook of their food: no such crude idea is hinted at: but in some mysterious way they were made overwhelmingly certain of His nearness. It is said, "They saw the God of Israel, and there was under His feet as it were a paved work of sapphire stone, and as it were the very heaven for clearness." As they ate, the cloud opened above them, and the view upward became clear—up to the blue sky. But it was more than sky—a deeper, yet more pellucid blue than mortal eye had ever beheld—a pavement of sapphire, like the very heaven for clearness; and above it, using it as the footstool of His throne, a Presence ineffable made itself felt, not visible to the bodily eye, yet thrilling the soul with the consciousness of its proximity. "And," it is added, "on the nobles of Israel He laid not His hand." This is the word which shows the heart of the whole transaction.* That no man can see God and live, is a principle of the Old Testament throughout; yet here the divine presence was so shrouded in love and reconciliation that, instead of producing annihilating horror, it communicated only peace and delight. The picture is highly symbolical, but its intention is not difficult to trace. It describes the experience of consciences at peace with God through the blood of atonement, and of patriots rejoicing in the new career on which their

---

* "The sacrifice, being an offering to Jehovah, was piacular, atoning for and consecrating the people on their entering upon their new relation to Jehovah"— Professor A. B. Davidson, D.D., article "Covenant," in Hastings' *Dictionary of the Bible*, 1898.

nation had been launched through the reception of a new, purified and consecrated life.*

Thus I have endeavored to analyze the words of our Lord on this great subject; and, although they are fewer in number than might have been anticipated, yet, if we weigh instead of counting them, we cannot complain that He has said too little. He speaks like Himself—not in abstract terms and doctrinal propositions, but in metaphors and images borrowed from life and history. But His figures of speech are the imaginative equivalents of the doctrines of the apostles and the dogmas of the Church.† Perhaps, indeed, the Church might have remembered with advantage the proportion observed by her Master in the teaching of this side of the truth; for there has sometimes been a disposition to speak as if the death of Christ were the whole of Christianity, to the neglect of His life—His earthly life, which is our example, and His present mystic life in believers through His Spirit.

On the other hand we shall not estimate correctly the place which Jesus intended such subjects as sin, repentance and justification to hold in our thoughts, unless we bear in mind the place He has given in Christian worship to the sacraments of Baptism and the Lord's Supper, both of which are intended to keep these solemn facts continually before the consciousness of His people.

---

* The above exposition is the result of long pondering on a scene the importance of which I discovered for myself; but it agrees closely with that given by Kurtz in his *History of the Old Covenant* and his *Sacrificial Worship of the Old Testament*.

† Compare the weighty words of Kähler: *The So-Called Historical Jesus and the Spiritual, Biblical Christ*, p. 94: "We like to summarize our faith, the sum of the New Testament revelation, as 'God is love.' When did one learn to confess this? Not from the sermon which sounded from a mountain by a lake and was carried through the cities of Israel by messengers, through the sermon of the kingdom of God, however much of the subject may be contained in it. This dark picture should only gain its full meaning through Christ's work and life. 'Praise ye therefore God's love to us, that Christ has died for us,' Paul reminds us. John clearly says where he gained this insight: 'In this is love, not that we loved God, but that He loved us and sent His Son to be the propitiation for our sins. We know love by this, that He laid down His life for us; and we ought to lay down our lives for the brethren' (1 John 4:10; 3:16)."

THE PROPHECIES OF JESUS:
Matthew 7:21–23; 8:12, 13; 10:15, 23, 32–42; 11:20–24; 12:32, 36, 40–42; 13:30, 37–43; 49, 50; 16:18, 21, 27, 28; 17:9, 22, 23; 18:8, 9; 19:28–30; 20:19, 23; 21:43, 44; 22:1–14; 23:34–49; 24; 25; 26:12, 13, 29, 31, 32, 34, 64; 27:63; 28:10.
Mark 3:29; 6:2; 8:31, 38; 9:1, 9, 31, 41–49; 10:30, 31, 34, 40; 12:9; 13; 14:8, 9, 18, 27, 28, 30, 62.
Luke 6:22, 23; 9:26, 27; 10:12–15; 11:29–32, 49–51; 12:8–12, 35–59; 13:23–35; 14:15–24; 17:22–37; 18:8, 29, 30, 33; 19:11–27, 41–44; 20:9–18; 21:5–36; 22:18, 21, 29, 30, 34, 69; 23:43; 24:49.

6

The Judge

Up to this point I have said nothing of a possible development in the mind of Jesus. Did His views alter as His life went on? The declaration about His childhood, that He increased in wisdom and stature and in favor with God and man, justified us in looking out for the signs of such a development. Time and circumstances acted on Him as they do on all men, widening the horizon of knowledge and making clear the path of duty. Even His comprehension of Himself had its human limitations.

I do not, indeed, believe that it is possible to fix definite points in His life and to say, that up to these junctures He had never thought or spoken about certain aspects of His person or work, and that everything which the Evangelists represent Him as saying on these topics before the assumed dates must be treated as misplaced. By such arbitrary assumptions not only have the records been cruelly distorted, but an image of Jesus has been constructed as untrue to psychology as it is unjust to the testimony of those who knew Him best. All we can do is to note the great turning points of His experience and the predominant characteristics of the sections of His life thereby marked out. We can say for certain that at such-and-such a period His mind was possessed with this or that aspect of His mission, but to affirm that anything essential was at any stage altogether absent from His consciousness is to abandon the *terra firma* of evidence and let ourselves go adrift on a sea of mere speculation.

There are five conspicuous summits of His experience, with which we may connect the different epochs of His internal history — His First Visit to Jerusalem, His Baptism, the Great Confession of the

Twelve at Caesarea Philippi, the Transfiguration, and the Agony of Gethsemane.

1. The first epoch is that of His first thirty years. It lies beneath a thick covering of silence, but it must have contained everything. Like musical genius, the religious faculty matures early. "Heaven lies about us in our infancy," it has been said, but it lies far more about us in boyhood and youth. The intuition of God in the opening dawn of intelligence is extraordinarily clear, as is also the intuition of right and wrong; there is no problem of religion which has not presented itself to the questioning mind of a sharp-witted lad; there is no criticism of the world's institutions and practices so keen as that of youth, before its own time for action has arrived; and every possibility of subsequent achievement is dreamed about by a man before he is thirty. "What is a great life? It is a thought conceived in the enthusiasm of youth and carried out with the strength of maturity."*

Only one incident of this period in the life of Jesus has been preserved, but it is sufficient to suggest all. It reveals a mind happy, on the one hand, in the consciousness of God and, on the other, reverently inquisitive at the oracles of human authority. Already Jesus called God "My Father"; and, although we must beware of reading too much into this primary confession, there lies in it the germ of all that was most original in His subsequent doctrine. On the other hand, His ardent attachment to the temple and His thirst for instruction from the custodians of the oracles of God were foreshadowings of the opposite quality of His mind—His reverence for the institutions and traditions of the past. Thus, in miniature, are the two outstanding features of His ministry already discernible—His incomparable originality and His adherence to all that was true and sacred in the history of His native land.

2. The second epoch is introduced by the threefold crisis of the preaching of John, the baptism of Jesus, and the temptation. It is generally assumed that at His baptism Jesus first became aware of His messiahship, but of this it is impossible to be sure. The only thing certain is, that He then received the signal that the time was fulfilled, along with the final qualification for His public work imparted

---

* Alfred de Vigny.

through the descent on Him of the Holy Spirit.* But He may long have been waiting for the striking of the hour of destiny. At all events, when it came, it produced a prolonged access of emotion and thought, as is indicted by His being driven by the Spirit into the wilderness. The struggle which there took place in His soul was a conflict between traditionalism and originality, but it ended in the clear and unalterable resolution to follow His own genius. This, He well knew, would arouse the opposition of the representatives of religious and political authority, but He was far too full of divine enthusiasm for His great task to stand in dread of obstacles. It was with a rush of joy and hope which carried all before it that His ministry began. His own state of mind at this period stands forever embodied in the Beatitudes, which are a description not only of the character which He desired to produce in others but first of all of His own. They betray a mind so full of a blessedness springing from inexhaustible sources that it longs to assemble round itself the whole world of weary and suffering humanity, in order to make it happy by the communication of its own secret. Such was the character of the opening months of His ministry: He was happy in proclaiming the message with which He was charged and in performing the works of mercy which the Father had given Him to do; and the images which floated before the eyes of His spirit were irradiated with the hues of hope.

3. This epoch was followed by one of a totally different character, when the opposition which He had to encounter assumed such dimensions that He was compelled to see, rising to block His pathway in the distance, the image of the cross. In the Evangelists this third epoch is dated from the great confession at Caesarea Philippi, although that event only brought to light a condition of the mind of Jesus which must already have been for some time in existence. The great confession was, indeed, much more an epoch in the development of the disciples than in that of Christ Himself; and the failure to note this has led to much confusion of thought. It has even been contended that up to this point He was not fully conscious Himself of His messiahship; and it is assumed that at least He cannot have mentioned it before this, even to

---

* It is astonishing how the best results of modern inquiry into this crisis in the experience of Jesus are anticipated in Owen's great work on *The Holy Spirit*.

the extent of calling Himself the Son of man. Much more is it held to be evident that the disciples can never previously have acknowledged His messiahship in any shape or form. To support these assumptions the most violent measures have to be taken with the evangelic records; and the true nature of the great confession is mistaken.

It was, in the first place, in the fullest sense the testimony of the Twelve themselves. Herein lay its value. It was not something which others had suggested to them and which they accepted on external authority, whether from the Baptist, or from the demoniacs, or even from Jesus Himself, but the spontaneous expression of their own conviction, matured by long association with Him and by daily observation of His life. The suggestion, that He was the Messiah, had long been in the air; they had heard it from several quarters, but to every such witness they could have said at Caesarea Philippi, as the Samaritans did to their countrywoman, "Now we believe, not because of thy saying; for we have heard Him ourselves, and know that this is indeed the Christ, the Savior of the world." Secondly, it was a great religious act. It was not the cold drawing of a logical conclusion, but an uprising of conviction and devotion, in which they avowed that they would stand by the truth in face of contradiction, whatever might happen; and, therefore, Jesus traced it back to immediate inspiration from above. Such an act is a totally different thing from a mere expression of opinion, and does not of itself determine whether or not the same persons may have previously held the opinion now transmuted into an act of witness-bearing. Jesus had not imposed His belief on the disciples: He waited patiently till the conviction should arise in themselves of its own accord; and it was because this stage of maturity had been reached that He considered it judicious to communicate to them the conclusion at which He had arrived as to His own fate — "From that time forth began Jesus to show unto His disciples, how that He must go unto Jerusalem and suffer many things" (Matt. 16:21).

4. I have said that the great confession was more an epoch in the experience of the disciples than of their Master; yet to Him also it must have been an event full of satisfaction and joy; and it paved the way for the next epoch of His development, which consisted in the victory of His mind over the awful prospect of death. The maturity of the faith

of the disciples, which expressed itself in their confession, caused Him to feel that He had something solid beneath His feet, which would not give way, whatever might be the changes or chances of the future, because it was the work of God in the hearts of the disciples. An early death seemed, indeed, to be the end of everything for one who professed to be the Messiah because the Messiah was not to die but reign forevermore. It seemed the complete falsification of His faith in Himself. Certainly it appeared so to every Israelite, even to the most instructed of the Twelve. But Jesus saw over and beyond the awful terror; and the event which discloses the definite surmounting of this stage of development is the Transfiguration. On the Holy Mount joy and insight had obviously overcome all obscuration and eclipse; in the brightness in which His person was enveloped His glorification was anticipated; and again the voice for heaven, which had sounded at His baptism, ratified His consciousness of Himself. We now know the solution of the enigma: His death was to be the atonement for the sin of the world; and, as a reward for His uttermost humiliation, God was to raise Him to the throne which He now occupies. And that this was the solution presented to Himself is indicated by the representation that Moses and Elias talked with Him about the decease which He was to accomplish at Jerusalem. These were the representatives of law and prophecy; and the death of Christ was to be the glorious end of the law, as His exaltation was to be the fulfillment of all prophecy.*

5. The victory of the Transfiguration was not, however, a final and conclusive one. It astonishes us to come, so long afterwards, upon the scene of Gethsemane, with which we connect the fifth and last stage of His development. Gethsemane looks like a lapse back into the darkness of the third stage, out of which in the Transfiguration He had emerged. It may be taken to indicate that during the later months of His life there had been alternations in His soul between the terror of death and the sense of victory; and many things indicate that this supposition is not mistaken. Especially as death itself drew near and

---

* The presence of these two may also be intended to suggest the means by which His mind attained to the position of mastery over His fate; as, after His resurrection, in His intercourse with the disciples, "beginning at Moses and the prophets, He expounded to them in all the Scriptures the things concerning Himself."

the horrors of desertion and betrayal, injustice and hatred, with which it was to be accompanied, began to accumulate before His eyes; as human sin, directed against Himself, disclosed its uttermost malignity and hideousness; and as the iron of his position, in the character of representative before God of this guilty humanity, entered into His soul, the darkness enveloping His mind intensified, till the sense of it grew to be an agony. But it must not be forgotten that Gethsemane was a victory and not a defeat. He overcame the horror and despair, and emerged clam and confident, ready to face the very worst. Once again, indeed, as He hung on the cross, the refluent wave swept over His soul, till He cried out, "My God, My God, why hast Thou forsaken Me?" But again the access of troubled feeling was transitory; and it was with a strong voice and in perfect peace that at last He gave up the ghost. He knew that He was not dying in vain; nor were wicked men merely taking His life from Him: but, with prophetic eye, He already saw of the travail of His soul and was satisfied.

Both the interest and the difficulty of the development of the thoughts of Jesus about Himself concentrate themselves in His utterances about the portion of His destiny which was to come after His death. Those of His contemporaries who waited for the kingdom of God never thought of more than one appearing of the Messiah. The conceptions of the immediate followers of Jesus were similar; and during the first period of His ministry it seemed as if His destiny were to consist in a continuous and culminating series of successes. But gradually there disclosed itself, lying across His path, a dark gulf of misfortune, defeat and death, into which He and His fortunes were to be precipitated. To all others this disappointment was final; even His disciples could not understand that it was possible for His cause to disappear at this point and ever emerge again. But His eye saw farther, and He was able to accept death as the will of God, and yet look forward to a new career on the opposite side of it.

He foresaw and foretold especially three events—His Resurrection, His Coming-again, and the Judgment.

That He foretold His rising from the dead the third day is one of the fact most distinctly and unanimously testified by the Evangelists. They connect His announcement of this event with the first announcement of His death, and on every occasion when the latter occurs the former occurs likewise. Nor is there any chance in this: it belongs to the reason of the case; for what a dismal and meaningless prediction would His death have been, unless He had been able to accompany it with the assurance that He was to rise again.

In the whole field of the modern interpretation of the past I do not remember anything less creditable than the manner in which this prediction is dealt with by large sections of contemporary scholarship. Fixing on a prophecy of Hosea in the mere sound of which there is a superficial resemblance to the words of Jesus—"After two days will He revive us; in the third day He will raise us up; and we shall live in His sight"—they assume that Jesus had this passage in His mind, and that, as Hosea meant by "the third day" a brief but indeterminate period, therefore Jesus intended no more than to intimate that after a vague but brief interval of eclipse His cause would revive. The supposed reference to Hosea is so dubious, and the ignoring of the actual place which this prediction holds in the history of Christianity is so complete, that it is difficult to treat such an interpretation seriously.

The "third day" may be objected to because it is a specific prediction. Prophecy, it is contended, is not of events or dates, but of general principles, the view of prophecy being antiquated and exploded which found in the prophetic writings history written beforehand. This is very true; and it applies specially to the prophecies of Jesus, beneath which there lie always deep and broad religious principles; even this prophecy of His own resurrection is founded, as we have just seen, in the nature of the case. Yet there is another aspect of prophecy which ought not to be forgotten, and which is, indeed, at the present moment successfully challenging the attention of Old Testament students:[*] wherever there is prophecy of the more general kind, there is, though in much smaller quantity, prediction of the specific kind. This can easily be proved in the books of the Old Testament; and it is conspicuous in the words of Christ. Towards the close of His life es-

---

[*] See Giesebrecht, *Die Berufsbegabung der Propheten*, 1898, where the author, who was an adherent of the more extreme school of Old Testament criticism, gives a most interesting account of the process by which he was convinced of the presence, in considerable quantities, in the Prophets of specific predictions which were filled.

pecially we find such specific predictions as the treachery of Judas and the fall of Peter; and the day of His own resurrection is a prophecy of the same kind.

The real objection, however, to the third day is the disbelief that any such event as the bodily resurrection of our Lord actually happened. The spread of skepticism on this point in the theological schools of the Continent is by far the most serious feature of the history of religious opinion during the last decade of the nineteenth century; and, as it has become the fashion, it may spread much farther. Its fruits have still to be seen in the practical life of the Church. My own belief is, that, were it to become general, Christianity would wither at its very root.

What is maintained is, that Jesus only foretold in a vague and general way that His cause would revive in a short time. And this, it is held, was what happened. After the first stupefaction was over, the disciples awoke to realize that their Master, though His body was in the grave, still existed in another state of being; and so by degrees they got over their depression and resumed the work which He had dropped. Of course this is in open and violent contradiction to the story which the apostles told and which from their day to this has been at the heart of the creed of Christendom. Though their story is beset with many difficulties, yet it has a wonderful verisimilitude. It is supernatural, and yet most natural. Could anything bear the print of nature more legibly than the interview between Mary and Jesus at the sepulcher, or the twin scenes in which St. Thomas appears first as a violent doubter and then as a believer crying, "My Lord and my God"? Yet it is not by its contradiction to the evangelic record that the theory is condemned, so much as by its failure, from the psychological and historical point of view, to give an adequate explanation of the origin of Christianity. By those who deny the facts of the resurrection it is constantly taken for granted that the apostolic circle was in tremulous expectation of something extraordinary happening, and that the miracle was believed to have taken place because it answered to this expectation. Nothing, however, could be more completely the reverse of the truth, if any credit whatever is to be given to the records; for, according to them, the faith of the disciples had been stricken dead. The two travelers to Emmaus spoke of their hope as something which the death of their Master had utterly destroyed. The tale of the holy women seemed "idle" to those who heard it, "and they believed them not." Even of the five hundred who saw Jesus on the mountain of Galilee "some doubted."* To all appearance, in short, the movement of Jesus was completely at an end; His pretensions had been falsified by death—the last of all arguments—and nothing was left to His followers but to return to Galilee and hide their heads in shame and sorrow as mistaken and disappointed men. Such was the condition of the disciples when their Master died; yet within six weeks they were completely transformed: their faith in Christ and Christianity had revived; they were united and resolute, overflowing with enthusiasm and eager for action; and they were ready to lay down their lives for the testimony which they bore to Jesus. Between the death of Jesus and the day of Pentecost some event must have happened sufficient to account for such a transformation; they say themselves that it was the bodily resurrection and the ascension of their Master, and this would account for it, but the wit of man will never be able to devise another explanation which has even the appearance of likelihood. If Jesus had not risen, there would never have been a resurrection of Christianity.

The second event predicted by Jesus was His coming again; and it is in connection with this that we meet with the most perplexing of His sayings. These are seized upon with avidity by unbelievers as affording conclusive disproof of His authority; and many who love Him have felt with pain how difficult it is to reconcile them with absolute faith in His wisdom. The latest commentator on them, indeed, Dr. Erich Haupt, of Halle, concludes a detailed and careful examination with the assertion, that "we do not require to excuse Christ for his eschatology: in this region also He stands above His age, and what He has said fully participates in the authority of his words as well as of His person"; but he reaches this result only by the use of critical processes of elimination to which in this country we are not accustomed; and most of his readers will probably feel that he carries a figurative method of interpretation somewhat to excess.

---

* Luke 24:21, 11; Matthew 28:17.

There is one saying of Jesus on this subject to which we cannot be wrong in attributing cardinal importance. It is that in which He says that He is Himself ignorant of the day and the hour (Matt. 24:36). So utterly unlike is this to anything which a dogmatic Christianity would have been likely to attribute to Him, if He had not said it, that it may not only be reckoned among the most certain of His utterances, but allowed a regulative authority in the interpretation of others.

The chief difficulty is, that in other passages He does seem to fix the day and the hour. In His address to the Twelve as He sends them forth on their mission, He says, that they will not have gone over the cities of Israel before the Son of man be come; on another occasion He says, "There be some standing here which shall not taste of death, till they see the Son of man coming in His kingdom"; and—most important of all—in the great eschatological discourse of the twenty-fourth of St. Matthew, after describing what appears to be the end of the world, He adds, "Verily, I say unto you, This generation shall not pass till all these things be fulfilled."* Such passages appear to stand in direct contradiction to the one already quoted as cardinal and regulative, but, unless we are to suppose either that Jesus contradicted Himself or that He has been misreported by the Evangelists, a meaning must be found which does not involve the fixing of the day and the hour.

Haupt contends that the "coming" of which Jesus speaks is not always to be understood as the final one. Any conspicuous event in the history of Christianity may be spoken of under this designation; which might, for example, be applied to His own resurrection, or to Pentecost, or to the destruction of Jerusalem. The destruction of Jerusalem, especially, bulked largely in Christ's view of the future; there is not reason to doubt that He foretold it; and there were very good reasons why He should even predict its date. To one or the other, therefore, of these events His references to the immediate future must belong.† The most difficult passage to reconcile with this view is the one already mentioned in the twenty-fourth chapter of St. Matthew,

---

* Matthew 10:23; 16:28; 24:34.

† Russell, in *The Parousia*, argues ably that all the prophecies of Jesus were fulfilled in a single generation.

but it is worth noting that this verse is almost identical with one in the preceding chapter (Matt. 23:36), where the reference manifestly is to the destruction of Jerusalem; and it is possible that there may have occurred an accidental reduplication.

It cannot be denied that in the twenty-fourth of St. Matthew, and the corresponding passages in the second and third Gospels, there is a strange mixing up of what looks like the prediction of the destruction of Jerusalem with what looks like the description of the end of the world; and the one is represented as ensuing immediately upon the other. Beyschlag proposes here to apply the law of what is known in the interpretation of prophecy as Timelessness, the meaning of which is, that in the Prophets the sheet of the future is not outspread in such a way that the distance from point to point can be measured upon it, but is folded up in such a way that only a few successive outstanding events appear, while the spaces of time that are to intervene between them disappear.[*] Weiss applies the still more important principle, that prophecy is always conditional. God never says, through the lips of any prophet, what is to happen, whether in the form of weal or woe, without a reference either expressed or understood to human conduct. On the contrary, He even runs the risk of appearing to contradict Himself by leaving prophecies of good unfulfilled, when men sin, and of evil unfulfilled, when they repent. The great purpose of Jesus in all He says about the future is not to satisfy curiosity but to direct conduct, the sum of His teaching being an urgent admonition to watchfulness. Whether or not He represented the end as near, He certainly never intended it to be thought of as distant; and He does not intend it to be ever thus thought of. Christians can hasten it by their activity or postpone it by their negligence; and, however long He may delay His coming, the proper attitude of the Church will always be to be ready to receive Him every moment.

There are, besides, many other sayings of Jesus about the future which seem to reveal His deeper mind, and in which He appears to contemplate for Christianity a prolonged earthly history. Such is the passage in which He says that, before the end comes, the Gospel shall be preached through all the world as a witness unto all nations;

---

[*] Compare Salmond, *The Christian Doctrine of Immortality*, p. 304.

and side by side with it may be placed the saying about the woman who anointed His feet, that wheresoever the Gospel was preached in the whole world, her act would be repeated as a memorial of her love.* There is a whole series of parables in which He speaks of His kingdom as passing through a gradual development; and there are others in which He speaks about it as being taken from the Jews and given to a nation bringing forth the fruits thereof. Those who were first invited to the banquet of the Gospel refused the King's invitation with scorn, and on their heads had to descend the retribution they deserved, but still the wedding was to be furnished with guests: the servants of the king were to be sent into the streets and lanes of the city, and, when, after that, there still was room, they were to be sent farther off, to the highways and hedges. These parables reveal the most profound consciousness both of the real nature of the Gospel and of the actual course of human history, as time has revealed it; and it is not fair to the record either to leave them out of account or to attenuate their importance.†

The method of interpreting the consciousness of Jesus which has of late secured most favor among the younger theologians of Germany is that which accords a predominant influence in the formation of His ideas to the environment in which He grew up; and the account given by this school of the development of His thoughts about Himself is determined by this point of view. The knowledge that He was the Messiah came to Him, it is supposed, suddenly at His baptism; and, as His conception of what the destiny of the Messiah was to be agreed in general outline with that entertained by His contemporaries, He expected the will of God to be fulfilled for Himself in the catastrophic forms of the Jewish apocalyptic literature, one grand event succeeding another as in the popular program. The city of God would descend from heaven in a visible shape; all opposition would be swept out of the way by omnipotent force; and the end of the world would ensue. As the miracles of Jesus are not estimated highly by this school, being

---

* Matthew 24:14; 26:13.

† Titius draws attention to the fact that Jesus' views of married life, riches and poverty, and similar matters, are not influenced by reference to the nearness of the end of the world—*Die N. T. Lehre von der Seligkeit*, I. 72, 75, 80.

supposed to have consisted in a few simple cures, it is held that they cannot have answered to the expectations entertained by Him of what the Father was to do for His chosen agent. All the time, accordingly, He was waiting for a manifestation of omnipotent power which never came. At length His popularity declined, opposition grew irresistible, and death stared Him in the face. How was the mystery of delay to be interpreted? At this point occurred to Him the solution offered by a division of the messianic program into two parts: die He must, but after death He would return again, when all the glory would be given Him which He had waited for in vain; and this second coming He believed would take place within a generation.

Fascinating as this reading of the history is, especially when set forth with the literary skill of a writer like Baldensperger, it does not present an image of Christ which can satisfy those who seriously accept Him as the final Revealer of truth and the Savior of the world; for it is the picture of One who lived in an atmosphere of illusion and bequeathed to His followers something very like a delusion. It is not so intended, but it really revives the situation in which Jesus was placed by His enemies when they applied to Him the standard of their own messianic program and rejected Him because He did not fulfill it. So, this modern theory imputes to Him a program which was not fulfilled, and the inevitable inference against Him will not fail to be drawn by the general mind, however scholars may attempt to ignore the logic of their own position.

No doubt all the thoughts of Jesus were colored by the atmosphere in which He grew up, but it was not by apocryphal literature but by the Law and the Prophets that the substance of them was determined; and His whole life, from the temptation in the wilderness to the death on the cross, was a polemic against contemporary Jewish thought. Rejecting the popular Messianic ideals, He remained true, at the risk of His life, to His own deep and spiritual conception of His vocation. And, since in life He so severely adhered to His own vision, is it credible that in His hopes for the future He abandoned Himself to the fantastic and deceptive imagery of Jewish apocalyptic? This would lower Him to the level of His contemporaries, and would be a fatal flaw in His character.

There is one circumstance the bearing of which on this question is of great importance, though it has been little adverted to. It is not denied that Jesus had in His mind a somewhat extended program of what was to happen to Himself after his death. Not only was He to rise again, but a number of other events were to follow one another, to the extent of at least a single generation. Now, if the catastrophic conception of His second coming was the one which He entertained, it is not easy to see any reason for thus lengthening out the program of the future. The natural thing would have been that the resurrection and all the other items should be compressed into a single event. Why should there be any delay? He had been tried by delay too long already. Had His thoughts of the future been shaped by His own disappointment, the stupendous hope of His resurrection would have been identified with the complete realization of all His hopes. But the fact that in His prophecies of the future His resurrection is to be followed by the ascension, and that His second coming is to take place from heaven, points strongly to the conclusion, that His expectations of the future were of the same sober and spiritual order as His thoughts about the present.

The third and final prophecy of Jesus, as far as His doctrine concerning Himself is concerned, is that of the last judgment.

Although the catastrophic ideas of the Jewish Messianic program were alien to the mind of Christ, He looked forward to one catastrophe: in all His teaching about the future the terminus is a final judgment, by which men are to be separated according to character and assigned their respective destinies. Thus in the parable of the Tares and the Wheat, after the long period of uncertainty during which they grow together, there comes a day when the field is reaped and the tares are bound in bundles to be burnt; and in the parable of the Dragnet after the long labor of enclosing the fishes, there comes the moment when they are separated into good and bad. The most grandiose tableau of the judgment is the scene in the twenty-fifth of St. Matthew, in which the nations of men are represented as sheep and goats, which are to be separated into two vast flocks. So marked a feature in the teaching of Jesus is this final day of decision that He refers to it as "that day," without considering it necessary to specify the purpose to which it is devoted.

Now, in this scene of sublime and universal judgment Jesus is Himself the Judge. There is no thought in His teaching more frequent than this. Across the dim and conflicting images evoked by His other teaching about the future this one point shines with a steady and unchanging light. The writers of the New Testament repeat the fact, but it has its original seat in His own words. Even in the Sermon on the Mount, from which, it is supposed by the ignorant, all reference to the dogmas of Christianity is excluded, He says, "Many will say to Me in that day, Lord, Lord, have we not prophesied in Thy name? And in Thy name have cast out devils; and in Thy name done many wonderful works? And then will I profess unto them, I never knew you: depart from Me, ye that work iniquity." In the parable of the Tares it is the Son of man who sends forth "His angels to gather out of His kingdom all things which offend, and them which do iniquity." On another occasion He says, "The Son of man shall come in the glory of His Father with His angels; and then shall He reward every man according to his works"; and in yet another, "Whosoever shall be ashamed of Me and of My words, in this adulterous and sinful generation, of him also shall the Son of man be shamed, when He cometh in the glory of His Father with the holy angels."* Nowhere, however, is His position in this great scene so imposingly set forth as in the passage of the twenty-fifth of St. Matthew already alluded to—"When the Son of man shall come in His glory, and all the holy angels with Him, then shall He sit upon the throne of His glory: and before Him shall be gathered all nations; and He shall separate them one from another, as a shepherd divideth his sheep from the goats: and He shall set the sheep on His right hand, but the goats on the left." The next words of this description are "Then shall the King say"; and this description of Jesus as "King"—which is unique among His utterances, though the designation is closely akin to "Messiah"—rises spontaneously out of the situation; for the royal glory of the Savior is nowhere else so impressively revealed. The presence of the angels is especially deserving of notice. They attend Him as a king is surrounded by his courtiers, and they are obviously subordinate; in fact, as they are called in another passage just cited, they are "His" angels.

---

* Matthew 7:21–23; 13:41; 16:27; Mark 8:38.

An important question is, the relation which, in the position of Judge, Jesus is conscious of holding to the Father. The doctrine of the whole Bible is that God is Judge; and certainly it would be in accordance with the general body of Christ's teaching to assume that He thought of Himself in this character as the Vicegerent of God; for in all His works it was His pride to perform what the Father had given Him to do. This point of view, however, retreats into the background in these descriptions of the judgment, and no pains are taken to cause it to be remembered. Much more prominence is given to the fact that it is through Him that God judges the world than to the fact that it is God who judges the world through Him. In short, Jesus as Judge occupies a position of relative independence; and the spirit of the synoptic representations corresponds exactly with the statement in St. John, that "the Father judgeth no man, but hath committed all judgment unto the Son" (v. 22).

Dr. Wendt, following his usual habit of reducing the grander utterances of Jesus to the lowest possible terms, attempts to destroy the force of these statements by referring to the fact, that the apostles are also said to judge: "In the regeneration, when the Son of man shall sit in the throne of His glory, ye also shall sit upon twelve thrones, judging the twelve tribes of Israel" (Matt. 19:28). Manifestly, however, no relative independence is ascribed to them; their presence is entirely subordinate and ministerial. What is said about them has its counterpart in a statement like that of St. James, "Brethren, if any of you do err from the truth and one convert him, let him know, that he which converteth the sinner from the error of his way shall save a soul from death, and shall hide a multitude of sins" (v. 19, 20)—where the ordinary Christian is spoken of as if he could convert and save the soul, although the Scripture is unanimous in ascribing salvation to God alone. It may even be questioned whether in what is said about the apostles there is any reference to the last judgment at all. In ancient times to judge was one of the recognized functions of the king, and in the Old Testament it is frequently used as equivalent to kingship, the part being put for the whole. When, therefore, it is said that in the regeneration the apostles will sit on thrones and judge, this may only mean that they will be the rulers of the future; as we say of other great figures of the past, that they now rule the world from their thrones.

The place assigned in the last judgment to Himself in the words of Jesus is recognized by all interpreters to imply that the ultimate fate of man is to be determined by their relation to Him. He is the standard by which all shall be measured; and it is to Him as the Savior that all who enter into eternal life will owe their felicity.* But the description of Himself as Judge implies much more than this: it implies the consciousness of ability to estimate the deeds of men so exactly as to determine with unerring justice their everlasting state. How far beyond the reach of mere human nature such a claim is, it is easy to see. No human being knows another to the bottom; the most ordinary man is a mystery to the most penetrating of his fellow creatures; the greatest of men would acknowledge that even in a child there are heights which he cannot reach and depths which he cannot fathom. Who would venture to pronounce a final verdict on the character of a brother man, or to measure out his deserts for a single day? But Jesus ascribed to Himself the ability to determine for eternity the value of the whole life, as made up not only of its obvious acts but of its most secret experiences and its most subtle motives. The sublime consciousness of Himself which this involves is not to be mistaken. Yet it is no more than is implied in the daily necessities of the Christian life. If anything is Christian, it is the habit of praying to the Son of God. As soon as the Church began to live, it began to pray to its ascended Lord. St. Paul speaks of the whole body of believers as those who call upon the name of the Lord Jesus Christ; and in the Book of Revelation glory and dominion are ascribed by all saints to Him who hath loved them and washed them from their sins in His own blood. Even the heathen identified the early Christians by this mark, that they met to sing hymns to Jesus as God; and, in every century since, Christians have been the more distinguished by the same practice the more they have been Christian. Everyone remembers how the heart of Samuel Rutherford pours itself out to the "sweet Lord Jesus"; but a cavalier like

---

* This is most remarkably emphasized in the twenty-fifth of St. Matthew, where even the deeds by which the fate of the heathen is determined are reckoned as done to Him.

Jeremy Taylor prays directly to Christ with not a whit more of reserve. The finest hymns of Christendom are nothing but prayers to Christ clothed in the forms of poetry; and in these, every day, tens of thousands confide the secrets of their hearts to what they believe to be a comprehending and sympathetic ear. Does He hear these prayers? Does He know His worshipers? Is He acquainted with the griefs they lay before Him and with the raptures occasioned by His love? The very existence of Christianity depends on the answer given to this question; and nowhere is it answered more convincingly than in those sayings in which, by calling Himself the Judge of men, Jesus claims to have a perfect acquaintance with the secrets of every human heart.

Appendix A
Wendt's Untranslated Volume
on the Teaching of Christ

WENDT'S well-known book is at present our most detailed and handy account of the teaching of Jesus. But, in true German fashion, the author began with a thorough investigation of the record of our Lord's teaching in the Gospels, proceeding on the maxim that you cannot be sure what ideas are to be attributed to anyone till you have ascertained the amount of credit due to the documents in which these are contained. This preliminary volume has not been translated—the publishers apparently believing, perhaps with wisdom, that it would not be acceptable to the British public. But it is a book of three hundred and fifty closely printed pages, and a sketch of its contents will show, perhaps more clearly than anything else, where advanced scholarship stands at present in relation to this question.

Wendt begins with a description of what he obviously believes to have been the course of the life of Jesus. He says it forms the framework of St. Mark, the oldest of our Gospels.

It is as follows: Jesus at first was neither recognized by others as the Messiah nor expressly known to be such by Himself. He deliberately held back the public proclamation of His messianic title, and only at a comparatively late period of His career received from His disciples an acknowledgment of His dignity. Not till the very end was at hand did He permit the open acknowledgment of the fact or come forward with a claim to it Himself. St. Mark gives no hint that the Baptist knew or pointed out Jesus as the Messiah. According to his account, John indeed made known that the Messiah was about to appear, but not that Jesus was the Messiah; and at the Baptism the vision of the dove was seen by Jesus alone, as He alone heard the voice by which he was designated the Son of God. St. Mark then describes how, on commencing His public work, Jesus was recognized as the Son of God—that is, the Messiah—only by the demoniacs, whom, however, He sternly forbade to make Him known. The rest of the people, on the contrary, when they beheld His extraordinary works, at first inquired in bewilderment what was the significance of His activity and His person; and then, when they had had time to think, formed and uttered their opinions about Him—these, however, being such as involved a complete denial of His messianic dignity or, while acknowledging that He was sent of God, yet withheld the full acknowledgment. St. Mark gives prominence to the scene in which, in contrast with this behavior of the multitude, the apostles, through the mouth of St. Peter, gave expression to their conviction that He was the Messiah; and he sets in the fullest light his sense of the importance of this epoch-making incident by making Jesus, from this point onwards, introduce a new element into His teaching—the prediction, namely, of His own sufferings and the sufferings of those who confessed Him. Meantime, however, he sternly forbade the Twelve to make known the conclusion at which they had arrived; and, in accordance with this, the first outside the circle of the Twelve who publicly named Jesus the Son of David—the blind beggar, Bartimaeus, at Jericho—was commanded by the apostles to hold his peace. At this point, however, Jesus withdrew the seal of silence and immediately thereafter accepted the messianic homage of the pilgrims as He entered Jerusalem. This decided His fate with the hierarchy; and at last, in presence of the high priest, Jesus solemnly claimed the messianic dignity. St. Mark closes his account of the life of Christ with the story of how the heathen centurion, seeing His behavior on the cross, exclaimed, "Truly this was the Son of God."

This, according to St. Mark—and Wendt enthusiastically adopts it—was the outline of Christ's life, but, strange to say, the evangelist does not adhere to it himself. It is only by piecing certain parts together from his Gospel that you ascertain that this was the real course of events. These pieces, we can yet see, were originally joined; for the ending of one runs into the opening of the next when what comes between in the actual St. Mark is removed. The evangelist has allowed the historical outline to be crossed and blurred by a series of accounts of conflicts between Jesus and the hierarchy. This section also is cut up into fragments, which are scattered over the Gospel, but in the same way we can see, from the endings and beginnings of the different parts, that they originally formed a single whole. There is a third series, treated in the same way, which consists of passages setting forth the necessity and the value of suffering. And there are two other smaller series, which need not be further particularized.

Wendt does not hold that these different series of passages were different documents, which St. Mark incorporated in his narrative: the stamp of the same authorship is too unmistakably on them all for this. He falls back on the old statement of Papias, that St. Mark derived his information from St. Peter: and he believes that these series represent different discourses of St. Peter, or different groups of reminiscences, which the apostle was in the habit of delivering together in St. Mark's hearing. Thus there was one discourse in which St. Peter used to give the historical framework of Christ's life; then there was another in which he used to give a collection of anecdotes illustrative of the witty and pithy replies wherewith Jesus confounded opponents; and there was a series of sayings, enclosed within an outline of incident, in which were predicted the sufferings certain to follow the confession of Christ; and so on. St. Mark had these separately in his mind, but he had to combine them into a book; and not being a man of letters, he did it clumsily; and criticism has to take the patchwork asunder and restore the pieces to the places which they occupied as they came from the lips of St. Peter.

Observe this, however: these Petrine reminiscences do not make up the whole of St. Mark's Gospel. The evangelist incorporated other materials, derived from sources to us unknown but scarcely likely to be of the same dignity. And it is noteworthy that among the additions Wendt reckons some of the greatest miracles of our Lord—such as the Stilling of the Storm and the Feeding of the Five Thousand.

Wendt's treatment of the Gospel of St. John is of a startling character, but it is carried through with great boldness and ability. He discerns in this Gospel two totally distinct hands, not to speak of a third, to which the last chapter is due.

One of the writers is St. John himself. Wendt believes that the apostle was persuaded in his old age to collect his reminiscences, and these form the substance of the present Gospel. They consisted chiefly of sayings and discourses, perhaps bound together by a few slight threads of narrative, but no attempt was made by the apostle to give a connected life of Christ. This attempt was, however, made and carried through by a disciple of St. John, who incorporated the reminiscences of his master with his own ideas and fitted the whole within a historical framework.

In proof that the bulk of the Fourth Gospel is due to St. John, Wendt adduces the words of the Prologue—which, by the way, is not the work of the editor, but the apostle—"And the Word was made flesh, and dwelt among us (and we beheld His glory, the glory as of the only begotten of the Father) full of grace and truth." Further, the language throughout is that of a Hebrew, who had been brought up on the Septuagint. Especially by the sovereign way in which he makes Jesus handle the Old Testament the writer shows that he must have been in the closest touch with the Lord. It is true, there is a wide discrepancy between the language in which he makes his Master speak and that in which Jesus is made to speak in the Synoptists, but this is sufficiently accounted for by the powerfully developed spiritual individuality of the apostle; and the difference is confined to the form of Christ's words: it does not extend to the substance, which is identical with that found in the Synoptists. Of this Wendt has given detailed proof in the second—that is, the translated—part of his work. St. John has a peculiar vocabulary, but its leading catchwords are simply equivalents for the leading catchworks of the Synoptists, and the circle of Christ's teaching in St. John, when laid above the circle found in the Synoptists, corresponds with it point by point, although, of course, at some points St. John is more expansive and goes deeper.

Wendt's account of the other writer whose hand is discernible in the Fourth Gospel is a severe one. He expressly exonerates him, indeed, from deliberate falsification, but short of this there is nothing of which the bungler is not capable.

He has entirely obliterated the historicity of the career of Jesus, as criticism is able to exhibit it by judicious excerpts from St. Mark.

This career began in obscurity; for a long time Christ performed His acts of healing in secret and suppressed every allusion to His messiahship; the confession of the Twelve that He was the Messiah was the great crisis; thereafter, only, did Jesus venture to speak of His sufferings and death; and only towards or at the very end did He permit the messianic dignity to be ascribed to Him or to claim it Himself. The author, however, of the Fourth Gospel in its present form introduces allusions to Christ's sufferings and death from the very first, and takes every opportunity of asseverating that Jesus knew from the beginning that He was to be betrayed by one of the Twelve. In like manner he makes the Baptist recognize Jesus as the Messiah, clean against the representation of St. Mark; and as early as the fourth chapter he makes Jesus Himself say in so many words, "I am the Messiah," to a Samaritan woman. Many, indeed, are represented as denying that He is the Messiah, but allusions to the fact that this is His destiny are numerous from the very commencement of His career.

Even this total oblivion of the true course of the history of Jesus is, however, not the worst. This editor's very conception of Christianity is widely different from that of Christ, which is faithfully reproduced in his own peculiar dialect by St. John. The latter is deep, inward, mystical; the editor's is external and mechanical. For example, in the portions of the Gospel due to the apostle "eternal life" is a present possession of everyone who believes on the Son of God, but to the editor it is a possession which is to begin in the next world. And, in the same way, "judgment" is in St. John's mouth or Christ's process which is proceeding now—everyone who comes into contact with Christ is *ipso facto* judged—but to the editor judgment is a public scene, which will take place at the end of time. The same habit of mind is displayed in the way in which the editor relies on external proofs of the divine origin of Christianity. Jesus Himself rebuked the desire of the Jews for signs and refused to give them, but to the editor the miracles are the commanding evidence, and he has a kind of craze for emphasizing the importance of the testimony of the Baptist.

Unfortunately the editor has mixed up his own additions with the material derived from the apostle so closely that it is no easy task to separate the gold from the alloy. He has even intruded into the Prologue, interrupting its glorious march with two or three irrelevant remarks on his favorite topic of the testimony of John. But Wendt is not discouraged. He goes resolutely through chapter after chapter, excising now a long paragraph, then a verse or two, here a line and there a word; and he seldom has any hesitation. In the first chapter, for example, he cuts away the whole passage in which the Baptist bears testimony to the Lamb of God which takes away the sin of the world, together with the passages thereon ensuing in which St. John and others have their first interview with Jesus amid circumstances which have been supposed to bear marks, tender and unmistakable, of personal recollection. A curious specimen of the results of Wendt's method is found in the eleventh chapter—the account of the raising of Lazarus. Something proceeding from St. John is here the substratum, but verse by verse it has to be disentangled from the editor's additions. Lazarus had died, and Jesus came a long distance to console the sisters. He naturally talked with them of the certainty that their brother would rise again in the resurrection at the last day; and out of these remarks a story gradually spun itself of a resurrection effected by Jesus on the spot, but no such thing really took place.

Wendt is by no means unaware of the reluctance which will be felt by all who are acquainted with the spell of St. John, which appears to pervade every page of the Gospel and lends it a character so unique, to accept the theory of a twofold authorship, but he maintains that only on these terms is it possible to retain the apostolicity of the Gospel as a whole; for the historical framework is such as could have been constructed by no one acquainted at first hand with the course of Christ's career.

Perhaps Wendt's discussion of the First and Third Gospels is the most valuable part of his book.

He holds that both St. Matthew and St. Luke made use of St. Mark as we now have it—the last few verses of the last chapter of course excepted—and on this framework constructed their own narratives. Neither, however, had the discernment to excerpt, as criticism is now able to do, the real course of the history; and, therefore, they also, like the editor of the Fourth Gospel, let the Baptist recognize Jesus as the Messiah; they make Jesus perform miracles from the first in great publicity; and, while retaining the scene in which the Twelve acknowledged the messianic dignity of their Master, and other scenes in which He forbade them and others to make Him known, they do not recognize the true place and import of these incidents.

St. Matthew and St. Luke, however, display an agreement in incident and expression in the portions of their narratives not derived from St. Mark which requires explanation, and this is not to be found in the supposition that the one borrowed from the other, because St. Luke, the later of the two, is particularly shy and suspicious of St. Matthew. The explanation then must be that, besides the Gospel of St. Mark, they made use of another common source; and, going back on the old tradition of Papias, Wendt supposes this to have been the Logia of the apostle Matthew; for the author of our First Gospel is not this apostle, though it bears his name. Just as St. John made a collection of the sayings of the Master, his brother apostle had done the same before him; and, as St. John's editor transformed his reminiscences into a history of Christ, the authors of the First and Third Gospels did the like with the Logia of St. Matthew. Only, while the editor of St. John derived his framework from the tradition of the life of Christ current in the neighborhood of Ephesus at the close of the first century, the other two evangelists derived theirs from St. Mark.

The first and third evangelist made their excerpts from the Logia somewhat differently. The writer of the First Gospel, following his plan of grouping miracles, parables, etc., together, attached as many of them as he could, on this principle, to the materials which he borrowed from St. Mark. St. Luke, on the contrary, interpolated them in the form of two long connected narratives into St. Mark's framework. The reproduction was further modified in each case by the point of view and purpose of the writer; and from the fact that the Logia were not written, but handed down orally, it will be understood that both evangelists exercised considerable freedom. Although, therefore, there is a great deal of agreement between them, yet there are differences smaller and greater; and, by comparing them closely, it is possible to judge with a good deal of confidence in every case which reproduction is the more exact.

Wendt undertakes the task of reproducing the Logia word for word out of St. Matthew and St. Luke; and he prints the entire document in

Greek, thus giving us what even the apostolic Church did not possess. It is a bold undertaking, and, however much we may differ from him, hearty gratitude is due to him for it. He thinks he is able in many cases to make one of the evangelists correct the other; sometimes both are wrong, but, having got the exact words and restored them to their right places, we can correct them both. He makes far too little allowance, however, for modifications in the sayings of Jesus which may have been due to His making the same statements or using the same illustrations on different occasions. An itinerant preacher necessarily repeats himself, but, if he has any genius, he does not do so slavishly: he gives his illustrations different applications and points the same truths in different directions; and there is no irreverence in attributing to Jesus a thing so natural. Scholars constantly forget how brief the Gospels are, and how meager are the fragments preserved to us of what our Lord must have done and said.

Although both the First and Third Gospels are thus mainly derived from St. Mark and the Logia combined, yet both writers have added a good deal, derived from other sources to us unknown. This is especially the case at the beginning and at the end. The narratives of the birth, infancy and youth of Jesus are found in the First and Third Gospels, but Wendt does not believe that they were in the Logia, and evidently he attaches to them little importance. The same is true of many details of the death and resurrection. On the resurrection the author expresses himself with extreme caution. All the length he is prepared to go may be gathered form these words: "That the disciples had the conviction not only that they had seen the Risen Savior, but that by means of these appearances they had obtained distinct knowledge of His messianic person and their own apostolic vocation, appears to me, on account of the entirely analogous belief of St. Paul, to admit of no question."

To sum up, Wendt's aim, it will be seen, is to get behind the Gospels, which are secondary or subapostolic formations, to the apostolic materials out of which they were constructed with additions. St. Mark is nearest to an original document, but even it contains secondary additions, and its scheme of Christ's life is confused by the lack of literary skill. Out of St. Matthew and St. Luke another apostolic document can be reconstructed, but to the apostolic materials less trustworthy information has been added, and already the actual development of Christ's life has been forgotten. In St. John, also, we have an apostolic document of unique value, but it is hidden in another document, which breathes an entirely different spirit and has no sense whatever for the historicity of Christ's career. Among the secondary additions Wendt would reckon a great many of the outstanding miracles attributed to Jesus—such as the Changing of Water into Wine, the Stilling of the Storm, St. Peter's Walking on the Sea, the Resurrection of the daughter of Jairus, of the Widow's Son at Nain and of Lazarus, and, I suppose, also the bodily Resurrection of Christ Himself.

In the German preface to the second volume of his work Dr. Wendt complains of the slight attention bestowed on his first volume, but this misfortune has probably been a blessing in disguise because had the contents of the critical volume been well known in this country, the fact would probably have modified the welcome with which the translated volume has been received.

There are those, indeed, to whom such a presentation of the life of Christ may be a godsend. If a man has lost faith in the credibility of the Gospels and thus had his belief in the Son of God shattered altogether, the notion may be a highly welcome one that it is possible to get behind the actual Gospels and find a story, exiguous indeed and lacking in color, yet apostolic and true; for this may seem to give him Jesus back again and to relight the lamp of religion. Accordingly, this critical procedure is lauded in certain quarters as being not the destruction but the restoration of belief. The meaning, however, of such a claim requires strict definition. To anyone who has a full-bodied faith in Christ and confidence in the Gospels such a scheme of the life of Christ as is supplied by Wendt is pure loss. To the common man it is disastrous in the highest degree, because it means that, when the Gospels are opened and the most affecting words of Christ read, there cannot be the slightest certainty whether or not these sayings actually emanated from Him or were secondary formations due to minds which only partially comprehended His spirit; this cannot be decided before the termination of a critical process, in which no two of the learned entirely agree. The question is not one of whether or not perfect accuracy is to be found in every detail of an incident, or whether the precise force of every saying of our Lord has been comprehended by the reporter: it is whether the greatest of the miracles attributed to Him were actually performed, and whether a considerable proportion of the words put into His mouth ever came from His lips at all.

It may be that there lies before us a period in which the whole question will be thrashed out among ourselves on the lines on which it has been discussed in Germany. The impression, indeed, prevails in this country, even among the educated, that, the Tübingen theory being exploded, the credibility of the Gospels has been settled forever. This, however, is an over-sanguine view, and does not at all correspond with the state of opinion abroad. Wendt, on the contrary, is a moderate representative of a large and extremely able set of German critics. The growing familiarity of the public mind in this country with the theories of Old Testament criticism may pave the way for a similar treatment of the Gospels; and the theories, backed by great accumulations of learning, are ready to the hand of anyone who may wish to distinguish himself by giving a shock to orthodoxy. The process, once begun, would not be easily brought to a termination; for there is no end to the combinations which are possible when once it is taken for granted that the representations of the Gospels are not the actual facts, but creations of the imagination which have grown out of them.

Still there are aspects of Wendt's performance which are reassuring, even in view of such contingencies. Although to our insular notions his position appears extreme, he would be reckoned in the circle to which he belongs is a high degree conservative. He stands as the last term of a gigantic course of investigation, and, when his results are compared with the wilder ideas of the Tübingen school, the contrast is great. Even as they stand, the Gospels all belong, according to this author, to the first century, and in every one of them there is a large kernel proceeding directly from the apostolic circle. Wendt's detailed comparison, in his translated volume, of the teaching of Christ as reported by St. John with the same teaching as reported by the Synoptists, in order to prove their identity, is one of the most striking things in recent theology. The attempt to bring the Gospels far down and away from immediate connection with Christ has apparently failed. To use an illustration of Principal Rainy, the Gospel narrative, like a living creature, after being forcibly stretched away down into the second century, has drawn itself together again right back into the heart of the first century. The question is thus very much narrowed. Was it possible in so short a time, within the memory of men who had lived with Jesus, for the history to be so transformed? Could the course of Christ's career be so speedily forgotten? Could so many wonders, adorned with minute and lifelike details, be attributed to Him which He never performed?

It cannot be denied that there are some great difficulties in the Gospels, and we are indebted to Wendt for showing so clearly what these are. One thing, however, which makes one distrust his mode of approaching them is the stupidity which he is constantly attributing to the Evangelists. They have misunderstood Christ, according to him, where His drift is perfectly obvious; they have overlooked the connection of this and that, when it might have been seen with half an eye. This reaches a height in the case of the Fourth Evangelist, who simply peppers the noble narrative of St. John with wrong-headed remarks and disquisitions. Leaving the reverence aside which may be due to holy men who spoke as they were moved by the Holy Ghost, I am always suspicious of any theory which makes the writers of Scripture talk downright nonsense.

The truth is, Wendt's work is dominated from first to last by a theory. He makes no secret of it: on the contrary, he states it in the very first pages of the volume under review, and he makes it the standard for judging every statement in the Gospels. This theory is, that the life of our Lord pursued the course, already described, which he finds indicated in St. Mark—although even St. Mark is not true to it, St. Matthew and St. Luke are unaware of it, and the Fourth Gospel clean contradicts it.

The outline of the life of Christ, which Wendt thus makes the standard for testing the Evangelists, contains, indeed, a great deal to which no objection need be taken, but the denial that the Baptist acknowledged Jesus as the Messiah has very little to rest on. St. Mark, indeed, says that at His baptism Jesus saw the heavens rent asunder and the Spirit descending, but he says not a word to indicate that

He alone saw this vision and herd the voice which acknowledged Him as the Son of God. The whole scene has the appearance of being intended for others rather than for Him—the consciousness of Jesus did not require such external demonstrations to assist its operations.

But, asks Wendt, if the Baptist thus acknowledged the messiahship of Jesus, and if other testimonies to it arose here and there from the first, what importance was there in the great confession of the Twelve through the lips of St. Peter? This seems a formidable difficulty, but, when this question is asked, are we not overlooking the religious character of the confession of the Twelve? Their confession was not a dry inference from the observation of facts: it was an outburst of religious conviction, and a solemn vow by which they were prepared to stand. And truth, when it is realized and acknowledged in this way, has all the force of novelty, although it may have been heard long before by the hearing of the ear.

I have never been able to feel any force in the assertion, which Wendt repeats, that, if at the Baptism John had acknowledged the messiahship of Jesus, he could not afterwards have sent his message from the prison. The most elementary acquaintance with the psychology of religion ought to enable us to understand how a man who was in the Baptist's circumstances and had passed through all that he had undergone might come to doubt what he had once firmly believed.

Christ's practice of requesting those whom He healed not to make Him known, and of enjoining His apostles not to reveal His messiahship, is a perplexing trait, but I am not satisfied that Wendt's explanation is the correct one. St. Matthew quotes in explanation of it an ancient prophecy to the effect that the Messiah would not strive or cry or cause His voice to be heard in the streets; and this may be the true explanation—that it was due not to policy and deliberation, but to a subtle and delicate peculiarity of the temperament of Jesus. When it is recorded that Jesus enjoined one whom He had cured to tell no man, but that, in the ecstasy of restored health, the man blazed abroad the matter, are we quite certain that Jesus was displeased? We ourselves read the statement with an amused gratification, and I am by no means certain that this was not the effect on Jesus likewise.

If Jesus had kept Himself as obscure as Wendt represents Him to have done, and held back so long any hint of His messiahship, it is a question how far the public and the authorities would have been responsible for at last refusing to acknowledge His claim.

But the final question is, whether this figure presented by Wendt, and presented confidently by an increasing school in Germany, can be the veritable picture of Christ—the figure of One who had no pre-existence, but was the son of Joseph and Mary; who know some secrets of the medical art and by means of these healed the sick, but did not raise Jairus' daughter, or the widow's son, or the brother of the sisters of Bethany; who taught the words of eternal life, but was not Himself rescued from the power of the grave? Is this the authentic portrait of Jesus Christ? It is totally unlike the image presented by the Gospel of St. Mark as a whole. But, even if St. Mark did offer it—or any skillfully excerpted section of St. Mark—would it be credible? In my opinion it would be utterly incredible. We do not know for certain the dates of the Gospels, but we do know, almost to a year, the dates of the great, universally recognized epistles of St. Paul. This apostle was of almost the same age as Jesus, and he was at the full height of his powers when he applied his mind to the scrutiny of the life of Jesus. Now, what is the image of Christ presented in St. Paul's writings? Christ is the Judge of men, and, therefore, He must have a supernatural knowledge of their hearts; He is the Savior of the world, on whom the burdened conscience can lay the whole weight of its sin and the immortal spirit the whole weight of its destiny; He was before all things, and He now lives as the ascended Lord at the right hand of God; His name is above every name, and to Him every knee shall bow. This was not the faith of St. Paul alone: it was notoriously the faith of the whole Church within a single generation of Christ's death; for on this subject there was no difference of opinion among the first witnesses of Christianity. Now, is there any resemblance between this image and that which Wendt proposes to put in its place? It is true that, with the great exception of the resurrection, St. Paul does not mention the miracles of our Lord, but the entire image of the Savior presented in the Pauline writings—and the same is true of all the writings in the New Testament—is congruent and harmonious with a birth, a life and a death such as the actual Gospels depict, and it is utterly incongruous with such a history as Wendt puts together from the gospel within the Gospels. If Christianity from the very start was founded on a huge falsification, to however innocent causes the distortion of facts may have been due, it is vain at this time of day to attempt to begin it over again. Besides, if Christ was not the glorious Son of God whom the evangelists and apostles represented Him to be, but only this figure to which those who agree with Wendt would reduce Him, then it is far more evident that it is hopeless to repair the Christian religion upon these terms; for this is not the kind of Savior that the world requires.

Appendix B
The Book of Enoch

OF late this ancient document has again been attracting attention to itself. A lengthy fragment of it in Greek, comprising about a third of the entire book, and forming part of an important find of manuscripts made a few years ago at Akhmim, has been published by M. Bouriant; and a monograph on this discovery, from the pen of Dillmann, the great authority on the Book of Enoch, has appeared in the shape of a communication made by the late professor to the Academy of Sciences at Berlin. An annotated French version of the Greek fragment has come from M. Lods; and, most important of all for us, Mr. R. H. Charles has published a new translation of the whole book in English, with introduction, notes, appendices and indices, from which everything can be learned which is known on the subject up to date.

Perhaps it may be well to begin with briefly recalling its history.

In early Christian writings reference is made to a book bearing the name of Enoch, which is seriously accepted as the work of the patriarch and referred to as Scripture. These references are not, however, numerous; and soon the Fathers began to express themselves doubtfully, till at length Augustine gave the finishing stroke by rejecting it altogether. Thenceforward it disappeared, although one writer, Syncellus about A.D. 800, makes a long quotation from it. In the year 1773 Bruce, the traveler, brought from Abyssinia three copes of an Ethiopic manuscript, which proved to be the lost book. Of this an English translation by Lawrence, which is now quite obsolete, appeared in 1821. Other copies from Abyssinia dropped into European libraries from time to time; and in 1851 Dillmann published the Ethiopic text from five manuscripts, supplementing this service in 1853 with a

German translation, which has ever since been the basis of all scholarly investigations. At the conclusion of the British war with King Theodore of Abyssinia, a number of additional manuscripts found their way into the libraries of Europe, especially into the British Museum. These Mr. Charles has made use of in compiling his new edition. He has also, of course, incorporated the results of the splendid labors of Dillmann. His work is an able performance, and highly creditable to English scholarship; he expresses is own views with conciseness and decision; and, although the problems of the book are far from being settled, the materials are now accessible, and everyone can judge for himself what is the value of this relic of the past. It is, however, to be remembered that, in the English or German, we have it only at fourth hand; for the Ethiopic is a translation from a Greek version of a Hebrew original. There are ample indications in the book itself that it was originally written in Hebrew, and also that it originated in Palestine, probably in Galilee. It is about as large in bulk as the Book of Genesis, and is filled with a strange variety of material.

The entire books rests on a peculiar interpretation of the verse in Genesis which says that "Enoch walked with God, and was not, because God took him." The final clause is understood in the ordinary sense of a translation of Enoch similar to that of Elijah, but the first clause—that he "walked with God"—is taken to imply that he was favored with excursions, in the company of God, or rather of the angels, into remote regions of the universe, where wonders and mysteries of all kinds were revealed to him, along with copious disclosures as to the future course of the world.

Such a conception, it will easily be perceived, opened immense imaginative opportunities; for on such a journey, under such guidance, what corner of the universe might not be visited, and what secret might not be explored? From such a standpoint, near the very commencement of human history, a bird's eye view might be given of the whole course of the ways of God with men. Such a task would, however, have required the greatest powers. A Dante or a Milton would have been needed to sustain the toilsome journey and make the vast survey, and then to shape the whole into one continuous and consistent picture. The author of the Book of Enoch has, indeed, been called the Hebrew Dante, and his undertaking has been compared to that of Milton. But one is reminded of someone who was spoken of as a Carlyle with a wooden leg stumping down through the Puritan period. On the shoulders of Enoch there are, unfortunately, no "mighty pens" like those which bore up Dante or Milton on his divine path; if he may be said to possess wings at all, they are at most the leathern wings of a bat, capable only of brief and intermittent flights.

He never proceeds far on his way in one direction before he stops, and then he begins again at a totally different point. The book is not a whole in any artistic sense, but a series of fragments, glued together in anything but artistic fashion. When Dillmann issued his translation forty years ago; he persuaded himself that it was a continuous whole, the work of a single author, with only a few interpolations, which could easily be removed. But he subsequently reversed this opinion. And Mr. Charles, following Ewald, looks upon Enoch as being not so much an actual book as a collection of the fragments of an Enoch literature. At one period in the history of Hebrew literature, it seems, Enoch was a name round which literary activity revolved, as at an earlier period it revolved round David; and, as the surviving fragments of lyric poetry collected themselves under the name of David, so the apocalyptic fragments which survived were gathered under the name of Enoch.

According to Mr. Charles, there are half-a-dozen or more authors, but unfortunately, their works are far from being in the condition in which they left them. Nearly everywhere there are signs of alteration and mutilation. Worst of all, the final editor seems to have had in his hands a Noah apocalypse, purporting to give revelations made to Noah of a kind similar to those made to Enoch; and he thought fit to combine the two into a single book. Instead, however, of doing so in a rational manner, he simply chopped the Noah production into a mass of fragments, and sprinkled them promiscuously all over the original work. They turn up in every other page without rhyme or reason, rendering it exceedingly difficult to get any continuous sense, and sorely trying the editorial temper.

Whether or not this may have been the way in which the book came into existence, it is certainly true that there are several separate masses in it easily distinguishable; and it will be well to indicate briefly what these are.

The book opens thus: "The words of the blessing of Enoch, wherewith he blessed the elect and righteous, who will be living in the day of tribulation, when all the wicked and godless are to be removed. And Enoch answered and spake, [Enoch] a righteous man, whose eyes were opened by God, that he might see a vision of the Holy One in the heavens, which the angels showed me; and from them I heard everything, and I understood what I saw, but not for this generation, but for the remote generations which are to come." There follows a theophany, in which God comes forth to judge the world, ending with the verse which appears in St. Jude, "Lo, He comes with ten thousand of His holy ones to execute judgment upon them, and He will destroy the ungodly, and will convict all flesh of all that the sinners and ungodly have wrought and ungodly committed against Him." Then suddenly the writer wanders off into a description of physical phenomena, such as the regularity of the seasons and the like, the slender thread of connection being the contrast between the order of nature and the disorder of the life of sinners. This feeble transition is characteristic; and very often there is not even as much connection as here.

After this introduction, we come to the first long section of the book, which is a comment on the paragraph in Genesis 6 on the mixing of the sons of God with the daughters of men. Not only is this theme here handled at great length, but it recurs again and again throughout the subsequent book, forming one of the leading topics. The interpretation given is that the sons of God were angels; and this occurrence was both the fall of the angels and the origin of evil on earth, though these points of view are not always consistently maintained. The author knows the fallen angels so well that he gives the names of a score or more of them; and, indeed, his acquaintance with angels, both good and bad, is everywhere most intimate, and he displays great inventiveness in supplying them with names. The fallen angels corrupted the inhabitants of the earth by communicating to them evil secrets, such as witchcraft, the use of arms, the painting of the eyebrows, the use of pen and ink, and many other nefarious practices. Their offspring consisted of a race of giants a thousand ells high. Of course, the poor inhabitants of the earth could not long stand the proceedings of such Brobdingnagian neighbors; and a great cry rose to heaven, in answer to which the archangels were dispatched to slay the monsters. The fallen angels were bound down beneath the mountains, to await a more condign punishment at the consummation of all things. The spirits, however, of the giants escaped into the atmosphere, and these are the demons who now roam at large over the earth, plaguing the lot of man, but their time will also come.

Enoch, to whom the entire invisible world is as open and familiar as a man's own garden to himself, is thrown into contact with the imprisoned angels, who send him as their intercessor to beg for them the pity of Heaven. He draws up their petition in a regular document; for, though he enumerates the use of pen and ink among the evil arts taught by the fallen angels, he has great faith in his own powers of composition. In describing his journey to the palace of heaven, as the bearer of this document, the author unfolds all his rhetorical resources:

"And the vision appeared to me thus: behold, in the vision, clouds invited me and a mist invited me; the course of the stars and the lightnings drove and impelled me: and the winds, in the vision, gave me wings and drove me. And they lifted me up into heaven, and I came till I drew nigh to a wall which is built of crystals and surrounded by a fiery flame; and it began to affright me. And I went into the fiery flame and drew near to a large house which was built of crystals; and the walls of that house were like a mosaic crystal floor, and its groundwork was of crystal. Its ceiling was like the path of the stars and lightnings, with fiery cherubim between, in a transparent heaven. A flaming fire surrounded the wall of the house, and its portal blazed with fire. And I entered into that house, and it was hot as fire and cold as ice; there were no delights of life therein; fear covered men and trembling gat hold upon me. And, as I quaked and trembled, I fell upon my face and beheld in a vision. And lo! there was a second house, greater than the former, all the portals of which stood open before me, and it was built of flames of fire. And in every respect it so excelled in splendor and magnificence and extent, that I cannot describe to you its splendor and its extent. And its floor was fire, and above it were lightnings and the path of the stars, and its ceiling also was flaming fire. And I looked and saw therein a lofty throne; its appearance was as hoarfrost; it circuit was as a shining sun amid the voices of cherubim. And from underneath the great throne came streams of flaming fire, so that it was impossible to look thereon. And the Great Glory sat thereon, and His raiment shone more brightly than the sun, and was brighter than any snow. None of the angels could enter and behold the face of the honored and glorious One, and no flesh could behold Him. A flaming fire was round about Him, and a great fire stood before Him, and none of those who were around Him could draw nigh Him. Ten thousand times ten thousand were before Him, but He stood in no need of counsel. And the holiness of the holy ones, who were nigh to Him, did not leave by night nor depart from Him. And until then I had had a veil on my face, and I was trembling. Then He called me with His own voice, and spoke to me, 'Come hither, Enoch, and hear My holy word.' "

I have made this lengthy quotation in order to convey a notion of the writer at his best. The intercessory embassy, however, undertaken at so much peril, was in vain; and Enoch had to return and make known to those who had constituted him their patron that their case was hopeless.

Now follows another lengthy section, the character of which seems to be partly determined by what has just been described. Once having set out on his celestial travels, Enoch makes a peregrination of the universe; and its different localities are described, with the wonders and secrets which they contain. Here is unfolded a kind of universal panorama, in which such places and objects are described as Chaos, Hades, Gehenna, the stream out of which the heavenly bodies daily renew their fires, the tree of life, the windows of the winds, and so forth. All through the book this affectation of revealing physical and metaphysical secrets is an ever-recurring feature. It is especially characteristic of the fragments of the Noah book, which, as has already been indicated, are scattered, as if from a pepper-castor, over the Enoch composition. The principal effort of the kind is found in the latter half of the book, where there occurs a section entitled by Mr. Charles the

Book of Celestial Physics. It is a long-winded but clear and compact piece, which ought to be interesting to scientific antiquarians, as giving a fair idea of the astronomical notions of the period. It embodies a complete theory of the sun and moon, of the year, day and night, the seasons, and the winds. The winds drive the heavenly bodies, which issue from different doors in the firmament at different seasons. The sun is of the same size as the moon, but contains seven times the amount of fire. The year consists of three hundred and sixty-four days, neither more nor less. On this the writer is most peremptory, and appears to be conducting a polemic against a profane and innovating notion that it contains three hundred and sixty-five.

After this comes a section consisting of two visions—the one a brief but vivid vision of the Noachic Deluge, seen by Enoch; the other a symbolic history of the world. The latter is an astonishing performance. It opens in this way: "Behold, a bull came forth from the earth, and that bull was white; and after it came forth a heifer; and along with this came forth two bulls, one of them black and the other red. And that black young bull gored the red one and pursued him over the earth, and thereupon I could no longer see that red young bull." This white bull is Adam, the heifer Eve, the black and red bulls Cain and Abel. And so the history goes on remorselessly from century to century, men and nations being represented by different animals. The Egyptians are wolves; the Midianites wild asses; and so on; and of course the Hebrews are sheep or lambs. Difficulties, however, occur. Noah is a sheep, but how can a sheep build an ark? He has to be transformed into a man for the nonce. And the same metamorphosis happens to Moses when he goes up to the mount to receive the Law. The execution is, however, carried through with courage; and, though it is tedious, yet, when the eagles, vultures, kites and ravens swoop down on the sheep and pick out their eyes, it is not without picturesqueness.

The next section is again an attempt to set forth the history of the world. It may be called the Apocalypse of Weeks, because in it the entire history of man appears, from the standpoint of Enoch, as a series of ten weeks, each of which is characterized by some striking feature, such as the appearance of Noah or Abraham or Moses. But the section soon loses itself in eschatological declamation, especially concerning the woes which are to overtake the wicked in the latter days.

One or two fragments are tagged on to the end of the book which would hardly be worth mentioning but for a pretty description which one of them contains of the birth of Noah. At his birth "his body was white as snow and red as a blooming rose, and the hair of his head and his long locks were white as wool, and his eyes beautiful. And, when he opened his eyes, he lighted up the whole house like the sun, and the whole house was very full of light." Then it wanders off into grotesquery.

Thus I have as briefly as possible characterized the different sections, with the exception of one, which is the most important of all, because in it occur most of the passages which are supposed to have influenced the New Testament. This section appears near the center; it is long, and it may be called the Book of Similitudes, because it consists of three pieces which call themselves by this name. They are all of eschatological import: the first being a picture of heaven; the second an account of the events which will befall the earth when God visits it in the latter days, to clear out of it the sinners and inaugurate the millennium; and the third treating the same theme in a more hortatory style. As, however, we shall have to come back on this section, it need not at this point be further characterized.

A few words now about the date. Unfortunately this is exceedingly obscure. Mr. Charles arranges the different compositions, with great confidence, in chronological order, and his various dates cover about a hundred years—from B.C. 170 to 64. But the criticism passed on Mr. Charles' book by Dillman[*] touches this point with telling effect, and has, besides, a wide application to other scholars at the present time: "The practice of arranging the varying ideas or representations of anything in a straight line of chronological and genetic development, and thereby constructing a history of the subject, is very popular with certain recent schools, but he who has observed how old and new, even when, strictly considered, they are mutually exclusive, may yet coex-

---

[*] *Theologische Literaturzeitung*, 2nd Sept., 1893.

ist in one and the same brain, will always regard such constructions with suspicion."

There are several passages which, at first sight, appear hopeful in determining the date. There is the division of the world's history into ten weeks, each of which is characterized by some outstanding event. The outstanding event of the seventh week appears to be the publication of the Book of Enoch itself: "And after that, in the seventh week, will a generation arise, and many will be its deeds, and all its deeds will be apostate. And at its close will the elect of righteousness of the eternal plant of righteousness be elected to receive sevenfold instruction concerning the whole creation." Here "the plant of righteousness" is the Jewish people, as we learn also from other passages; "the elect of righteousness" are the Pharisaic party, to which the writer belonged; and the sevenfold instruction "concerning God's whole creation" is a name for his own invaluable lucubrations. Unfortunately, however, the weeks are very indefinite periods; and all we really learn is that the author lived after Elijah, who is the outstanding figure of the sixth week. The events of the three weeks after the seventh are, of course, purely conjectural, and do not help us at all.

In the other program of the world's history—that in which men and nations are represented by different kinds of animals—we seem to be certainly on the track, because the characterization is both copious and minute, but just at the critical point, although growing more minute than ever, it becomes unintelligible, as it is impossible to identify with their counterparts the different animals which are brought upon the stage.

Unfortunately, it is about the date of the Book of Similitudes, which, as I have already said, is the most important part, that the greatest doubt exists. Here there is a reference to an attack on the Holy Land by the Medes and Parthians, which seems a hopeful chronological datum, but it turns out to be capable of all sorts of interpretations; and, besides, according to Mr. Charles, the passage in which it occurs is an interpolation. Most hopeful of all, perhaps, appears at first sight a reference to the visits of "the kings and the mighty and the exalted" to certain sulphur springs "in the west, among the mountains of gold, and silver, and iron, and soft metal, and tin"; but, while

Hilgenfeld understands this of the congregating of the Roman nobility in the neighborhood of Vesuvius, Mr. Charles is positive that these springs must be sought in Palestine. And besides, according to him, the words occur in a passage inserted by an interpolator so stupid that what he says does not, perhaps, mean anything at all. Mr. Charles does not believe that there is in the book any reference whatever to the Romans, and therefore his lowest date is B.C. 64—the year in which Rome laid its grasp on Palestine. Baldensperger, on the contrary, feels the atmosphere of the irresistible, illimitable Roman rule everywhere in at least the Book of Similitudes—an opinion in which I agree with him, because Mr. Charles' explanation of the constantly recurring phrase, "the kings and the mighty," against whom the woes of the Book of Similitudes are launched, as a designation of the Asmonean kings and their backers, the Sadducees, goes to pieces on the fact that they are characterized as worshipers of idols. The mode in which he explains this away is really an illustration of a style of interpretation by which anything can be made to mean anything.

We turn now to the most important aspect of the subject—the influence of the Book of Enoch on the New Testament.

Mr. Charles gives in parallel columns a long list of coincidences of expression, amounting in all to about a hundred; and, besides, he enumerates several New Testament doctrines which may be supposed to have been modified by the teaching of Enoch. The quotations will strike different persons differently. Of the twenty, for example, found in the writings of St. Paul I should not consider a single one to be indubitable, while some are very far-fetched indeed.* Besides, it is to be noted that about a third of all the supposed quotations are from the Book of Similitudes, about which it is doubtful whether it does not quote the New Testament. But I wish to look at the subject from a viewpoint of my own, and investigate rather the influence of the book as a whole, and of its several masses, than enter minutely into the criticism of detached verses and phrases, about nearly every one of which opinions will differ.

---

* The most striking, perhaps, is "King of kings and Lord of lords"; but see Deuteronomy 10:17 and Psalm 136:3, to which Mr. Charles gives no reference.

When Enoch is spoken of as one of the books which may have influenced our Lord and His apostles,* we naturally inquire first of all what its spirit is—whether it is an inspiring production, which could have communicated to our Lord and to the writers of the New Testament something of the power with which they spoke and wrote. I have quoted already the characterization of the author as the Hebrew Dante or the Hebrew Milton. In my opinion, Baldensperger is far nearer the mark when he calls him "the patron of the scribes." Again and again in the book itself the hero is called "Enoch the writer"; and we saw how he edited the petition of the fallen angels. He is an idealized scribe; and his writing is precisely on the level of the hagadoth of the rabbinical schools. Though the book is as long as the larger books of the Bible, there is hardly a verse in it, from beginning to end, on which one would linger with pleasure or which one would delight to recall. Once, indeed, it says beautifully of the stars that they give thanks and praise, and rest not; "and to them their thanksgiving is rest." And not far from this there is a striking little paragraph, standing quite alone, without any connection with what goes before or what comes after, which reminds one of a famous passage in a Latin poet: "Wisdom came to make her dwelling among the children of men and found no dwelling place; then Wisdom returned to her place, and took her seat among the angels. And Unrighteousness came forth from her chambers; and she found those whom she sought not, and dwelt with them, being welcome to them as rain in the desert and dew on the thirsty land." But with these exceptions, and one or two passages already quoted, there is hardly a touch of originality or tenderness or power, while page follows page of the most barren and tedious commonplace or even nonsense. If the prevailing characteristic of the New Testament be the spirit of power and of love and of a sound mind, I should say that the spirit of this book is exactly the reverse.

The entire production is a glorification of Enoch. Around this hero of the schools not only these writings gathered, but others which are not included in this book but heard of in ancient literature. In the New

---

* This is the title of a book by Mr. Thompson on the pseudoepigraphic writings.

Testament, however, there is not a trace of hero worship bestowed on Enoch. Except in its place in the genealogy of Christ in St. Luke, even his name is not once mentioned in the Gospels or the writings of St. Paul. There is one remarkable passage in the Book of Enoch where the hero seems to be identified with the Messiah; and Baldensperger mentions that in the rabbinical writings there are passages where he is placed side by side with the Metatron, a hypostasis of the Divine similar to the Messiah. Had such notions had any place in the circle about Christ, Enoch would have been one of the first names suggested when the minds of men were occupied with the question who Jesus was, and they were making every kind of guess. Elijah was the favorite conjecture, and he would at once have suggested Enoch, as both were taken to heaven without tasting death, but never once was the suggestion breathed that Jesus might be Enoch.

No element in the Book of Enoch is more pervasive than the story of the sons of God and the daughters of men, interpreted in the sense already indicated. It is a disagreeable story, and it stains the book through and through. In one or two outlying parts of the New Testament there may be references to certain elements of this conception. There is the reference in Jude to the angels who kept not their first estate, and are reserved in chains, under darkness, against the judgment of the great day; and there is the similar statement in 2 Peter;[*] but the myth in its great features is not only avoided in the New Testament, but, consciously or unconsciously, opposed. The New Testament writers, and especially St. Paul, have to deal with the origin of the corruption and misery of mankind, but they go back, not to the sixth chapter of Genesis, but to the third.

In connection with this, reference may be made to the enormous development of demonology and angelology in the Book of Enoch, which displays the utmost familiarity with the orders, functions and names of the angels fallen and unfallen. The New Testament also has a copious angelology, but it is based on the Old Testament, and not on Enoch, whose extravagances it avoids. Mr. Charles points out two

---

[*] Possibly the much-discussed passage about Christ's preaching to the spirits in prison may refer to this.

New Testament notions about angels which appear to be borrowed from Enoch. The one occurs in our Lord's debate with the Sadducees about marriage, when He says that in the resurrection they neither marry nor are given in marriage, but are as the angels of God. Incidentally, in addressing the fallen angels, in Enoch, God speaks of marriage as something unnatural to them, though natural to men. The other case is the cry of the evil spirits in the Gospels not to torment them before the time. In Enoch the demons have permission to range at large till the final judgment. In both these cases we perceive, I should think, the influence of Enoch, but it is less likely that they are direct quotations from Enoch than references to popular conceptions which may at first have owed their origin to this book.

Another enormous element in Enoch consists of descriptions and explanations of physical phenomena, such as the sun, moon and stars, winds, thunder, mists, dews and the like. This part of his task is taken by the author very seriously, and he attaches to his explanations a sacred value. But, happily, this entire domain is ignored by the New Testament.

Nor does it indulge in programs of the course of the world, like the animal history to which reference has been made. The only thing possessing any resemblance to this of which I can think is the division of mankind into sheep and goats in our Lord's parable of the Last Judgment, but it is with contrast rather than similarity that in this case we have to deal. In the Book of Revelation there are passages resembling the Ten Weeks of the world's history, but this resemblance is due to the fact that Enoch and Revelation are both founded on the Book of Daniel.

This estimate of the extent of the influence of the book as a whole, and of its great masses, on the New Testament is, in my opinion, of importance, not only in itself, but on the question, to which we now turn, of the relation of the Book of Similitudes to the New Testament.

Here there is not only undoubted, but extensive, dependence either on the one side or the other. The more striking passages have been already quoted on pages 61, 62 of the text, and one more may be added:

"And in that place mine eyes saw the Elect One of righteousness and of faith, and how righteousness shall prevail in his days, and the righteous and elect shall be without number before him forever. And I saw his dwelling place under the wings of the Lord of spirits, and all the righteous and elect before him are beautifully resplendent as lights of fire, and their mouth is full of blessing and their lips extol the Name of the Lord of spirits, and righteousness before Him never faileth, and uprightness never faileth before Him." Several of the titles applied in the New Testament to Christ are given to his being, as the Anointed, the Elect One, the Righteous One, and very frequently, the Son of man. He has existed, "under the wings of the Lord of spirits," from before the creation of the world; and He is to be the Judge of men and angels at the consummation of all things.*

These are remarkable statements, and, if we could be sure that they are of pre-Christian origin, they would raise questions about the originality of the New Testament writers, and even of our Lord Himself. They would show at least that, in the period between the Old Testament and the New, the religious mind, working upon the messianic elements in the Old Testament, had in several important respects come marvelously near to the actual image of the Messiah as it was to be revealed by our Lord.

Mr. Charles almost takes the pre-Christian origin of the Book of Similitudes for granted; and this has of late been the prevailing tone of German criticism, but I have seen no arguments advanced in favor of this view which appear to me nearly as strong as those of Drummond† and others on the opposite side, while the impressions made on my own mind by the study of the book are not favorable to its originality.

Everyone, even at the first reading, must be sensible of the strongly Christian flavor of the quotations just made; and the pervasive character of this element in the Similitudes is in the strongest contrast to the microscopical similarities between the rest of the book and the New Testament.

---

* Mr. Deane's statement (*Pseudoepigraphia*, p. 92), that this idea does not occur in the Book of Enoch, is unintelligible.

† In *The Jewish Messiah*.

Drummond has shown, in detail, that the passages which refer to the Messiah in terms strikingly recalling the New Testament might be excised from the text, not only without mutilating it, but with the result of improving it. Moreover, the introductory words of the second Similitude, in which the argument is announced, are not in the least consistent with the contents of the subsequent pages as they now stand; and it is in these pages that the most important messianic passages occur. *The Book of Jubilees*, a Jewish production, dating from about the middle of the first century B.C., quotes the Book of Enoch eighteen times, but it contains only two doubtful quotations from the Book of Similitudes, and neither of these is messianic, the inference being that the Book of Similitudes, or at least the messianic paragraphs in it, must have come into existence at a later date.

The argument, however, which, in my mind, carries most weight, is that the Book of Similitudes is, obviously and confessedly, a perfect patchwork of interpolations. It is sprinkled all over with fragments from the Book of Noah; and it exhibits also additions from other quarters. Indeed, it is of such a nature that it must always have invited interpolation. I have already said that it is apocalyptic, and have tried to define the subjects of the various Similitudes. But the truth is, the Book of Similitudes belongs to that species of religious literature, unhappily not extinct even in modern times, which, properly speaking, is about nothing. It is a mere haze and welter of words, surging uneasily round dim images of the future and the commonplace contrast of the righteous and the wicked. Legitimate doubt might be entertained as to whether the messianic passages belong originally to the places where they are found, merely on account of the fact that, in idea and language, they have a certain amount of consistency and dignity.

The strongest argument on the opposite side is that, if these had been Christian interpolations, there would have been more Christianity in them—more definite references especially to the facts of Christ's life and death. This would be a good argument if it were contended that the interpolations were deliberately made for apologetic ends. It was common enough in the earliest Christian ages to make interpolations of this sort, as may be seen in other apocalyptic books of the period, like, for example, *The Testaments of the Twelve Patriarchs*.

But the argument loses its force if it is supposed that the insertions were made, not deliberately, but naively, the editor working up the substance of a Christian apocalypse along with his other materials. A Christian apocalypse of an eschatological nature need not have contained any more direct references to the history of Christ than are found in the Book of Similitudes.

The conclusion, therefore, to which we seem to be led is that it is hopeless to build any structure of history or speculation on a foundation of this kind. While the possibility of these being anticipations of Christian ideas cannot be denied, the probability lies on the opposite side; and at all events the literary condition in which they have come to us makes anything like certainty impossible.

If in any respect the Book of Enoch may be said to form a milestone in the course of development of religious ideas between the Old Testament and the New, I should say it is in its teaching about the state and the fate of the dead. With this subject we know that the human mind was at that period intensely occupied; and the Book of Enoch shows that, working on the hints supplied by the Old Testament, it had arrived at conceptions on which He who brought life and immortality to light by the gospel subsequently set His seal. The views of the book are by no means consistent throughout, but, on the whole, its conception of the present state of the dead, as well as of the proceedings in the great crisis of the last judgment and the issues which will follow, are far nearer than those of the Old Testament to the representations of the New Testament; and, indeed, there is hardly a feature of the New Testament teaching on these subjects, with the exception, of course, of the part played by Christ, which cannot be matched in the Book of Enoch.

For this and other reasons, the Book of Enoch and the other apocalyptic writings derived from the same period are well worthy of study; although it must be confessed that among all the products of the human mind they are the most unreadable. It is even well, for the sake of science, that nature produces men so constituted that they are able to cast themselves upon such relics of the past with enthusiasm and exaggeration, under the belief that they have discovered a new explanation of the secret of the gospel. Their labors will not be in vain;

for the investigation of authentic memorials of human experience is never wholly without reward. The rest of us, however, will probably do well, in the present case, not to pitch our expectations very high. Indeed, on looking closely into the matter, we perceive that the mystery of Christ is deepened rather than explained, because it is more difficult than ever to understand how a plant of such perfect beauty and perennial fruitfulness as Christianity could have sprung out of such a dry ground.

Bibliography

Chapter 2: The Son of Man
Weiss: *Neutestamentliche Theologie*, 1880, §16.
Beyschlag: *Neutestamentliche Theologie*, 1891, I. pp. 54 ff.
Holtzmann: *Neutestamentliche Theologie*, 1897, pp. 246–264.
Stevens: *The Theology of the New Testament*, 1899, cap. IX.
Nösgen: *Christus der Menschen-und Gottessohn*, 1869.
Bruce: *The Kingdom of God*, 1889, cap. VII.
Wendt: *Die Lehre Jesu*, 1890, II. pp. 440 ff.
Baldensperger: *Das Selbstbewusstsein Jesu*, 1892, c. VII.
Grau: *Das Selbstbezeichnung Jesu: Der Menschensohn*, 1896.
Boehmer: *Reich Gottes und Menschensohn im Buche Daniel*, 1899.
Abbott: *The Son of Man*, 1910.
Hertlein: *Die Menschensohnfrage*, 1911.
Krop: appendix on *La Question du Fils de l'Homme* in his book on *La Pensée de Jésus sur le Royaume de Dieu*, pp. 118 ff. 1897.
Dalman: *Die Worte Jesu*, 1898, cap. IX.

Chapter 3: The Son of God
Weiss: *Neutestamentliche Theologie*, §17.
Beyschlag: *Neutestamentliche Theologie*, I. 54 ff.
Holtzmann: *Neutestamentliche Theologie*, I. 265 ff.
Stevens: *The Theology of the New Testament*, Chapter V.
Bovon: *Théologie du Nouveau Testament*, pp. 412 ff.
Nösgen: *Christus der Menschen-und Gottessohn.*
Nösgen: *Geschichte Jesu Christi*, pp. 290 ff., 470 ff.
Grau: *Das Selbstbewusstsein Jesu*, cap. VIII.
Beyschlag: *Die Christologie des Neuen Testaments*, pp. 40 ff.
Dalman: *Die Worte Jesu*, cap. X.

Gore: *Bampton Lectures,* 1891.
Gore: *Dissertations.*
Wendt. *Die Lehre Jesu,* II. 428, ff.

Chapter 4: The Messiah

Weiss: *Lehrbuch der Biblischen Theologie des Neuen Testaments,* cap. I. etc.
Beyschlag: *Neutestamentliche Theologie,* I. pp. 39 ff.
Holtzmann: *Neutestamentliche Theologie,* I. pp. 188 ff.
Stevens: *The Theology of the New Testament,* Chapter III.
Baldensperger: *Das Selbstbewusstsein Jesu,* cap. V
Grau: *Das Selbstbewusstsein Jesu,* cap. V.
Wendt: *Die Lehre Jesu,* II.
Dalman: *Die Worte Jesu,* capp. I., XI.
Candlish: *The Kingdom of God.*
Bruce: *The Kingdom of God.*
Stanton: *The Jewish and the Christian Messiah,* 1886.
Issel: *Die Lehre vom Reiche Gottes im Neuen Testament,* 1891.
Schmoller: *Die Lehre vom Reiche Gottes in den Schriften des Neuen Testaments,* 1891.
Johannes Weiss: *Die Predigt Jesu vom Reiche Gottes,* 1892.
Bousset: *Jesu Predigt in ihrem Gegensatz zum Judenthum,* 1892.
Paul: *Die Vorstellungen vom Messias und vom Gottesreich bei den Synoptikern,* 1895.
Wrede: *Das Messiasgeheimniss,* 1901.
Holtzmann: *Das messianische Bewusstsein Jesu,* 1907.
Titius: *Die neutestamentliche Lehre von der Seligkeit. Erster Theil: Jesu Lehre vom Reiche Gottes,* 1895.
Schnedermann: *Die Israelitische Vorstellung vom Königreiche Gottes als Voraussetzung der Verkündigung und Lehre Jesu,* 1896.
Schnedermann: *Jesu Verkündigung und Lehre in ihrer geschichtlichen Bedeutung. 1. Hälfte: Die Verkündigung Jesu vom Kommen des Königreiches Gottes,* 1893. 2. *Hälfte: Die Lehre Jesu von den Geheimnissen des Königreiches Gottes,* 1895.
Krop: *La Pensée de Jésus sur La Royaume de Dieu d'après les Evangiles Synoptiques,* 1897. The author prefixes to his work a very full bibliography of the subject.

Chapter 5: The Redeemer

Weiss: *Lehrbuch der Biblischen Theologie des Neuen Testaments*, §22.

Beyschlag: *Neutestamentliche Theologie*, I. pp. 126 ff.

Holtzmann: *Neutestamentliche Theologie*, I. pp. 284 ff.

Stevens: *The Theology of the New Testament*, Chapter X.

Bruce: *The Kingdom of God*, Chapter X.

Wendt: *Die Lehre Jesu*, II. 504 ff.

Baldensperger: *Das Selbstbewusstsein Jesu*, c. VI.

Smeaton: *Our Lord's Doctrine of the Atonement.*

Ritschl: *Die Christliche Lehre von der Rechtfertigung und Versöhnung*, 1882, especially vol. II. cap. II.

Kähler: *Zur Lehre von der Versöhnung*, 1899.

Dale: *The Atonement*, 1881, especially Lecture III.

Denney: *The Death of Christ*, 1902.

Fairbairn: *Christ's Attitude to His own Death*, a series of articles in *The Expositor*, beginning October, 1896.

Schaefer: *Das Herrenmahl nach Ursprung und Bedeutung*, 1897.

Babut: *La Pensée de Jésus sur Sa Mort*, 1897.

Hollmann: *Die Bedeutung des Todes Jesu*, 1901.

Chapter 6: The Judge

Weiss: *Lehrbuch der Biblischen Theologie des Neuen Testaments*, §33.

Beyschlag: *Neutestamentliche Theologie*, I. 183 ff.

Holtzmann: *Neutestamentliche Theologie*, I. pp. 305 ff.

Stevens: *The Theology of the New Testament*, Chapter XII.

Bruce: *The Kingdom of God*, cc. XII. and XIII.

Wendt: *Die Lehre Jesu*, II. 542 ff.

Baldensperger: *Das Selbstbewusstsein Jesu*, cc. VIII. and IX.

Weiffenbach: *Der Wiederkunftsgedanke Jesu*, 1873.

Russell: *The Parousia*, 1887, pt. I.

Haupt: *Die eschatologischen Aussagen Jesu in den synoptischen Evangelien*, 1895.

Schwartzkopff: *Die Weissagungen Jesu Christi von seinem Tode, seiner Auferstehung und Wiederkunft*, 1895.

Muirhead: *The Eschatology of Jesus*, 1906.

Salmond: *The Christian Doctrine of Immortality*, 1898.

Mackintosh: *Essays towards a New Theology*, 1889.

Schweitzer: *Von Reimarus zu Wrede*, 1906.